CONFUCIAN VALUES
AND POPULAR ZEN

CONFUCIAN VALUES AND POPULAR ZEN

SEKIMON SHINGAKU IN EIGHTEENTH-CENTURY JAPAN

Janine Anderson Sawada

University of Hawaii Press
Honolulu

Library of Congress Cataloging-in-Publication Data

Sawada, Janine Anderson, 1953–
Confucian values and popular Zen : Sekimon shingaku in eighteenth
century Japan / Janine Anderson Sawada.
p.   cm.
ISBN 13: 978-0-8248-1414-4
1. Shingaku.   I. Title.
BJ971.S5S29   1992
299'.56—dc20   92–45047
CIP

Illustrations are from the 1917 woodblock reproduction of
Teshima Toan's "Jijo: Nemurizamashi" (For Boys and Girls: Waking
Up from Sleep), Meirinsha collection, Kyoto.

Publication of this book has been assisted by a grant from the Japan Foundation.

Designed by Kenneth Miyamoto

For Rina and John Anderson

CONTENTS

ACKNOWLEDGMENTS

MANY PEOPLE have helped me write this book. Wm. Theodore de Bary has been a constant source of encouragement and counsel throughout my studies, at Columbia University and beyond. Paul B. Watt first inspired me to research Shingaku; he patiently read through various drafts of this work and has offered both penetrating advice and continual support. Philip B. Yampolsky generously assisted me with reference problems and made numerous suggestions for improving the text. My understanding of Shingaku writings would be far less accurate if Yokoyama Toshio had not spent long hours answering my questions about passages in the original texts. I wish to thank him here for his generous hospitality and assistance during my stay in Kyoto from 1986 to 1987. Shibata Minoru, in spite of failing health, gave me access to his rich store of knowledge about Shingaku, as well as to the Shingaku writings held in his home, Meirinsha. I am especially indebted to Koyama Shikei, the current director of Sanzensha in Tokyo, for educating me about Shingaku and supplying me with materials from the Sanzensha collection.

Many others assisted me at various points during my research and writing. Peter Nosco gave the entire manuscript a close reading and made several comments that helped me refine it for publication. Richard Rubinger guided my work on the history of Japanese education. Umihara Tōru led me to significant writings about Shingaku and the history of Japanese education. Kinami Takuichi welcomed me to his home near Osaka and shared his own understanding of Shingaku texts. Ishikawa Matsutarō of Tokyo allowed me to use the collection of his father, Ishikawa Ken. Antonino Forte offered me both his friendship and a place to work in the Institute of Italian Culture in Kyoto. Thomas Selover and Mary Evelyn Tucker helpfully criticized portions of an earlier draft. Minamoto Ryōen, Michel Mohr, Ian James McMullen, Rodney Taylor,

Okada Takehiko, Elizabeth Harrison, Herman Ooms, and Henry D. Smith II each gave me useful suggestions and references. I am also grateful to Patricia Crosby, Susan Stone, and Sally Serafim for their help in bringing the manuscript through the publication process.

I appreciated having the opportunity to present portions of the research for this book at the Columbia University Seminar in Neo-Confucian Studies, the Society for the Study of Japanese Religion, the Conference on God: The Contemporary Discussion VII, and the East-West Center Conference on Japanese Spirituality. The participants of all these gatherings made remarks that assisted my thinking process and helped improve the book; I am particularly indebted to Harry Harootunian for his stimulating response to my paper at the East-West Conference.

The research and writing of this book were made possible by generous grants from the Japan Foundation, the Mrs. Giles Whiting Foundation, and Columbia University. I am also grateful to David S. C. Kim for his support over the years, and to my colleagues at Grinnell College, who were unstinting with their logistical help. I wish to thank the editors of *The Eastern Buddhist* for allowing me to use material in this book that appeared in an earlier form in their journal (vol. 24, no. 2: 99–104).

I am profoundly indebted to all members of the Sawada and Anderson families for their encouragement and help. The writing of this book coincided with the gestation and earliest years of my two children, Emilia and Xavier, and I am grateful for their presence during this long and productive process. I owe a special word of thanks to Teruko Sawada for caring for my children while I completed the last revisions of the manuscript in Japan in 1992. Throughout the years, Ryoichiro Sawada has not only assisted me with translation questions but has supported and sustained our family in countless ways.

EXPLANATORY NOTES

In the following pages, Japanese, Chinese, and Korean names are given in the customary order with the surname first. Romanized terms are Japanese, except where the term applies primarily to the Chinese context, in which case the Chinese romanization is given. Common placenames like Tokyo, Kyoto, and Osaka and well-known terms like Shinto are written without macrons. Age is given according to traditional Japanese reckoning, which is usually one year more than the Western count. Translations are by the author, except where noted otherwise.

INTRODUCTION

UNDERSTANDING the mind was a religious quest in early modern Japan. From the earliest stages of the Tokugawa period (1600–1868), thinkers in diverse social and intellectual contexts regarded the pursuit of the "true" mind as a distinct discipline, a path to human perfection. One of the terms used to designate this discipline was *shingaku*—literally, learning of the mind (or heart).[1] Sekimon Shingaku was a system for cultivating the mind that became popular in the less-educated sectors of Tokugawa society. It was founded in Kyoto by a dry goods clerk, Ishida Baigan (1685–1744), and was organized into a nationwide religious movement by his disciple, Teshima Toan (1718–1786). Modern scholars have studied Baigan and his ideas in considerable detail, but the later history of Shingaku has been neglected.[2] This book treats the development of Sekimon Shingaku from the founder's death until the end of the eighteenth century.

Baigan did not himself use the phrase "learning of the mind" to refer to his teaching. The rubric was introduced during the second half of the eighteenth century in association with Teshima Toan's peculiar emphasis on the idea of the "original mind" *(honshin)*. By the time Toan adopted the term *shingaku,* however, it had had a long history of usage in East Asia. The "learning of the mind" (Chinese *hsin-hsüeh*) originated in the Neo-Confucian revival of Sung China (960–1280). The Sung masters were inspired by the classical Mencian conception of the innate goodness of human nature and proposed that the discipline of the mind be the basis for moral living. They regarded this discipline as an alternative to the current Ch'an (Zen) teachings of the mind.

The great Neo-Confucian teacher Chu Hsi (1130–1200) articulates the quintessence of the learning of the mind in the preface to his commentary on the *Doctrine of the Mean*. He stresses the distinction between the "human mind," which is the arena of conflict between the legitimate and

1

illegitimate desires of the individual, and the "mind of the Way," which is endowed with universal moral principles.[3] The aim of the learning of the mind is to differentiate between the two aspects of the mind and to discipline the human mind, or one's selfish desires. To achieve this aim requires conscientious self-examination and the cultivation of a serious, reverent attitude. Through introspection, one gradually becomes sensitive to self-centered impulses, grows more aware of the needs of others, and corrects one's errors. The process of internal purification thus leads to fulfillment of moral obligations in the wider social context.

Wm. Theodore de Bary has elucidated the development of the "learning of the mind-and-heart" from its incipient phase in the Sung through numerous reformulations in the Yüan, Ming, and Ch'ing periods.[4] The forms of this learning that reached Japan in the sixteenth and seventeenth centuries had already been considerably modified by Chinese and Korean Neo-Confucians. In particular, the emphasis on conscientious discipline of the mind had become more pronounced through a lineage of thought that extended from the late Sung scholar-official Chen Te-hsiu (1178–1235) to the great Korean thinker Yi T'oegye (1501–1570) and his admirers in Japan, such as Yamazaki Ansai (1618–1682).

Several Tokugawa thinkers accordingly understood *shingaku* to refer to this introspective variety of the cultivation taught by Chu Hsi and his predecessors, Ch'eng Hao (1032–1085) and Ch'eng I (1033–1107).[5] Kaibara Ekken (1630–1714), who admired Chu Hsi even though he eventually expressed doubts about some of Chu's theories, regarded mind-learning as the orthodox tradition, rooted in the Confucian classics. He denied the claim of a later Neo-Confucian school to the title "learning of the mind":

> All the teachings established by the sages of old, without exception, were the learning of the mind. Yao and Shun transmitted the distinction between "the human mind" and "the mind of the Way." . . . However, ever since the rise of the learning of Wang Shou-jen [Yang-ming] of the Ming, people have been constantly setting up special theories of mind-learning. They explicate the writings of Confucius and Mencius while harboring the aims of Zen Buddhism. . . . They mistake the perception of the mind for the principle of Heaven and do not realize that there is a distinction between the mind of the Way and the human mind. . . . They give this the name "learning of the mind," but how can this be spoken of in the same breath with the learning of the mind that was transmitted by Yao, Shun, Confucius, and Mencius?[6]

As Ekken implies, in Ming China (1368–1644) the phrase "learning of the mind" came to be associated with the teaching of Wang Yang-ming (1472–1529). In Japan, the Neo-Confucian scholar Nakae Tōju (1608–1648) also developed a position that favored moral intuition and religious feeling over the formal, rationalistic aspects of the Ch'eng-Chu system. When Tōju was exposed to Ming writings, particularly those of Wang Yang-ming's disciple Wang Chi (1498–1583), his emphasis on the mind was reinforced.[7] By the middle of the Tokugawa period, *shingaku* was thus commonly identified with the teachings of Tōju and his student Kumazawa Banzan (1619–1691).[8]

The religious movement founded by Ishida Baigan was a popular Japanese outgrowth of the Ch'eng-Chu tradition of mind cultivation. Both Baigan and Toan drew heavily on the ideas of the Sung masters; in their talks and writings they do not refer to the ideas of Wang Yang-ming. Toan's Neo-Confucian reading was mostly limited to the works of Chu Hsi and his important predecessors.[9] However, when he applied the name *shingaku* to his teaching, Toan was not deliberately affiliating himself in a formal sense with a particular school of mind-learning—whether Ch'eng-Chu or Yang-ming.[10] Nor did he have any sustained contact with scholarly representatives of these schools in Japan.

In Tokugawa times, the word *shingaku* did not denote only the formal teachings of Neo-Confucian scholars. Currents of popular thought called "learning of the mind" had been in circulation at least since the first decades of the period. The earliest example of this trend is the anonymous work *Shingaku gorinsho* (The Learning of the Mind and the Five Moral Relationships), which was published in 1650 but circulated earlier in manuscript form.[11] The author discusses moral cultivation from a Neo-Confucian perspective, taking inspiration from the same classical tradition that Ekken and other Confucian scholars used to define *shingaku:* " 'The human mind is insecure, the mind of the Way is barely perceptible. Have utmost refinement and singleness of mind. Hold fast the Mean!'[12] . . . These sixteen words are the transmission of the learning of the mind of the immortal sages."[13] Other *shingaku* works followed in the 1660s and 1670s: *The Moral Precepts of the Learning of the Mind (Shingaku kyōkunsho), Questions and Answers about the Learning of the Mind (Shingaku mondō)*, and *The Learning of the Mind: A Mirror for Men and Women (Shingaku danjo kagami)*.[14]

These popular Japanese formulations of mind cultivation frequently include non-Confucian ideas. As Herman Ooms notes, "Most of these works were themselves collages, put together with elements from various traditions and from each other. No rigid lines separated Shinto from Neo-Confucianism."[15] The author of *Shingaku gorinsho* employs not only Shinto, but Buddhist and possibly Christian ideas. In the popular discourse of Tokugawa society, *shingaku* did not necessarily designate a specific form of Confucian learning; it could mean almost any type of moral or religious cultivation based on inner discipline. By the mid-seventeenth century the phrase appears in the title of a vernacular Buddhist work—*The Diagram of the Ten Realms of Mind-Learning (Shingaku jikkai no zu)*.[16] As the period wore on, Buddhist writers continued to use

shingaku to refer to their own version of mind cultivation. A work called
*The Learning of the Mind and the Seat of the Buddha (Shingaku hotoke
no za)* was published in 1730, and Muin Dōhi (1688–1756) of the Sōtō
school of Zen wrote a formal treatise titled *Discourse on the Learning of
the Mind (Shingaku tenron).*[17] An undated popular work, *Song of the
Path of Mind-Learning (Shingaku dōka)*, has also been attributed to the
great Rinzai master Hakuin Ekaku (1686–1769).

When Teshima Toan began to call his own teaching *shingaku* late in
the eighteenth century, several "learnings of the mind" were already circulating—both in scholarly circles and in the popular imagination. In
order to distinguish Toan's teaching from these other phenomena,
"Shingaku" was prefixed with "Sekimon"—the "school of Ishida." However, judging from the continuing appeal of *Shingaku gorinsho* and
related vernacular literature, a broad undercurrent of interest in the mind
remained alive throughout the Tokugawa period.[18] Sekimon Shingaku
was one particular systemization of this popular quest of the mind.

The present study explains how Shingaku members created a practicable system of self-improvement from the existing matrix of ideas about
the mind. Like many earlier *shingaku* works, the sermons and writings of
Baigan, Toan and their followers reflect diverse religious influences, even
while purporting to transmit the Ch'eng-Chu interpretation of the Confucian classics. Beginning with Baigan, Shingaku members culled ideas
from the major East Asian teachings—Confucian, Buddhist, Shinto, and
Taoist—and openly affirmed the fundamental unity of all these traditions.[19] Their teaching is thus often identified as a form of "syncretism."[20] This appellation is convenient, insofar as it indicates that
Shingaku was inspired by more than one religious tradition. But the
word "syncretism" is notoriously imprecise.[21] Robert Baird has concluded that "the only meaningful use of the term syncretism is to describe
a situation in which conflicting ideas or practices are brought together
into a new complex which is devoid of coherence."[22]

To the extent that "syncretism" carries such connotations, its application to Shingaku obscures an essential feature of the religion: the "felt
unity" or sense of coherence that the Shingaku members experienced. In
the context of its time, the Shingaku teaching was persuasive enough to
invite a serious commitment from numerous Tokugawa citizens. Even
though its philosophical ramifications were not fully worked out by
Teshima Toan and his disciples, the teaching as a whole is far from inco-
herent. The Shingaku openness to different religious elements was
shaped by a fundamental premise: human beings can reach moral perfection by experiencing the true nature of the mind. Religious doctrines and
practices function in the Shingaku system according to their compatibil-
ity with this credo. Although the teaching was not intellectually refined
in comparison with other Tokugawa schools of thought, we cannot dis-

miss it as "mere broadmindedness without any consistency of principle," as does Maruyama Masao.[23]

The doctrines and activities of this movement are best understood as part of a religious "synthesis"—a coherent, workable system that has evolved through a series of interactions among diverse religious traditions.[24] In this book I point out episodes of assimilation, identification, and reinterpretation that contributed to the Shingaku synthesis in the late eighteenth century. I concentrate on the interaction of Neo-Confucian and Zen traditions, for these were the dominant sources of the Shingaku teaching under Baigan's successor, Toan. Toan and his followers also drew upon Shinto, philosophical Taoism, and other forms of Buddhism, but an examination of these connections must await a future study.

Japanese and Western scholars have already given significant attention to Ishida Baigan and his ideas.[25] Since the publication of Robert N. Bellah's *Tokugawa Religion* in 1957, Shingaku has been associated with the debate over the role of religion in the rise of modern Japan.[26] Taking his cue from Max Weber's view of the contribution of Protestant "inner-worldly asceticism" to the development of the modern Western economy, Bellah set out to explore whether some aspect of Japanese religion contributed in a similar manner to the rapid growth of modern industrial Japan.[27] After surveying the various religious and economic ideas of the period, he concluded that religion did indeed play an important role in economic rationalization in the Tokugawa period. In his book, Bellah suggests that all the major sectors of the population—samurai, city dwellers, and peasants—shared an economic ethic characterized by inner-worldly asceticism.[28] He cites the emphasis on diligence and frugality in such religious groups as True Pure Land Buddhism and the Hōtoku movement of Ninomiya Sontoku (1787–1856). Ishida Baigan and his teaching are treated in greater detail to illustrate the way in which religion reinforced the economic ethic in the Tokugawa period. In closing, Bellah remarks:

> Japanese religion never tires of stressing the importance of diligence and frugality and of attributing religious significance to them, both in terms of carrying out one's obligations to the sacred and in terms of purifying the self of evil impulses and desires. That such an ethic is profoundly favorable to economic rationalization was the major point of Weber's study of Protestantism and we must say that it seems similarly favorable in Japan.[29]

This thesis generated a good deal of comment and criticism in the scholarly world. Bellah was taken to task for analyzing the Shingaku movement in terms of its social function only at the time of its emergence, ignoring the transformation it later underwent. Modern Japanese scholars had long interpreted Baigan's defense of the merchant class as evidence of his independent, critical attitude toward the hierarchical social system of the time.[30] After Baigan's death, they believed, Shingaku lost its original reformist ethos and degenerated into a common morality movement. Because later Shingaku preachers were sometimes employed by the Tokugawa shogunate and even based their talks on the contents of its ethical edicts, in this view they were nothing more than tools of the government—"robots of the ruling class."[31] Bellah's critics thus wondered how Shingaku, whose leaders consistently encouraged their constituents to uphold the established Tokugawa social system, could possibly have contributed to the new ways of thinking required by the modernizing process. The decline of the movement at the time of the Meiji Restoration was cited as evidence for this argument.[32]

Bellah, however, had correctly pointed out that Baigan never opposed the samurai-centered value system of his age; rather, he advocated that merchants be considered worthy of enacting it. The ethical teaching of the later Shingaku movement, with its implicit support of the class structure, did not differ significantly from that of Baigan.[33] The weakness of *Tokugawa Religion*, in fact, is not the author's historical understanding of Shingaku, but his theoretical framework. Maruyama Masao pinpointed the issue when he questioned Bellah's assumption that economic development is the central criterion for modernization as a whole. Rationalizing tendencies in the economic sphere do not necessarily lead to structural changes in the polity or the value system.[34] Shingaku and other groups fostered values that accelerated industrial development, but those same values may have worked against the transition to democracy or a more universalistic ethic—dimensions that some consider intrinsic to "modernization."[35]

Bellah has acknowledged the problematic nature of his original assumptions about the nature and effects of modernization.[36] *Tokugawa Religion* does establish, however, that the dissemination of ethical principles such as loyalty, filial piety, diligence, and frugality by religious groups was an important part of the development of modern Japanese culture. My research shows why Shingaku in particular became an effective force in that dissemination. Furthermore, although this book is not directly concerned with the issue of Japanese modernization, it elucidates aspects of the movement, particularly its educational activism, that may have helped prepare the Japanese people for the transformation of the Meiji era.

Japanese scholars have long appreciated Shingaku's significance as an educational force in Tokugawa society, but this feature of the group has received limited attention in the West.[37] In this volume I do not assay the difficult task of measuring Shingaku's educational impact in early modern Japan. I simply characterize the ideas and activities through which

Teshima Toan's educational concern played itself out and indicate the contributions he made to methods of popular instruction. Shingaku embodied a dimension of education that is not accounted for in standard institutional histories. "Education" in its broadest sense means the transmission of knowledge—an activity that takes place beyond as well as within the boundaries of academic structures. The approaches used by Shingaku teachers to convey their knowledge (primarily religious and moral knowledge) illustrate some of the ways in which the world of learning became accessible to the general public in the Tokugawa period. In order to provide a context for understanding Shingaku's role in the popularization of learning, I discuss in Chapter 1 the increasing demand for widespread dissemination of ideas in eighteenth-century Japan and various channels of knowledge that developed in response to this demand.

Shingaku after Baigan is notable more for the scope and effectiveness of its educational campaign than for the intellectual originality of its members. Nevertheless, Teshima Toan's version of his teacher's ideas is not without interest; it determined the content of Shingaku sermons for the rest of the movement's history. Indeed, the teaching became so closely associated with Toan that it was frequently called "Teshimagaku" ("the learning of Teshima"). Accordingly, I focus here on the ideas and accomplishments of Teshima Toan; at the same time I emphasize that Shingaku was a community, an order of individuals who shared a commitment to certain beliefs and practices. In Chapter 2, I examine this community— the lives of Toan and three of his immediate disciples as well as the organizing principles of the group during Toan's tenure.

It will become clear in the ensuing chapters that Shingaku was not simply a system of merchant ethics. It was a spiritual discipline regarded by its practitioners as the foundation for a universal ethic. As Bellah stresses, Ishida Baigan's ethics were intimately related to the mystical dimensions of his teaching.

> If we looked only at the ethical teaching, we could say that it was an interesting sort of exhortation but we could understand little of the intense motivation to fulfill these exhortations which the religious teaching aroused. . . . It is the linking of such motivation as this—of the weary for succor, of the troubled for repose, of the guilty for absolution—to the fulfillment of certain practical, ethical duties in the world which gives that ethic a dynamism which it could never have if it were mere exhortation.[38]

During the last years of the Tokugawa period, when Shingaku teachers concentrated almost entirely on propagating ethical values, the movement became associated precisely with "mere exhortation." My research on the development of Shingaku confirms, however, that the community retained strong religious underpinnings through the turn of the nineteenth century. In the following pages I intend to illuminate the "other side" of Shingaku—the mystical core that gave "dynamism" to its moral teaching. Ishida Baigan's emphasis on inner cultivation became more conspicuous in his successor's rendition of the teaching. Teshima Toan never tired of repeating that the beginning of all learning was the knowledge of one's own true nature or "original mind." In Chapter 3, I explain this concept and locate its intellectual and religious sources. The religious life that emanated from the Shingaku teaching forms the subject of Chapter 4: Toan's system for training adepts, the experience of the original mind, and the ethical implications of this experience. Chapter 5 follows up with a survey of the discursive and contemplative practices that Shingaku members employed to nurture their understanding of the original mind.

The religious aspect of Shingaku—the faith of its adherents in the power of the original mind and their expression of this faith through ideas and practices—helps explain the growth of the movement in the second half of the eighteenth century.[39] Teshima Toan and his disciples dedicated their lives to preaching the Shingaku message. In their view, knowledge of the true mind entailed concern for others, and this concern was best expressed by showing people how to reach spiritual perfection. Shingaku members felt impelled to help others improve themselves. Their mission to edify took several forms. The most distinctive was Toan's program for children, discussed in Chapter 6. However, the Shingaku "talk on the Way," tailored to large, public audiences, contributed most directly to the movement's popularity. Chapter 7 treats the development of this speaking form and Shingaku leaders' attempts to regulate the movement as its membership increased.

This book does not cover the history of Shingaku during the last decades of the Tokugawa period. However, the foundation for these late activities was laid in the second half of the eighteenth century. The true role of Shingaku in the formation of modern Japanese culture cannot be clarified without investigating the movement during its "golden age," when its methods and institutions were fully established and its ideas carried throughout Japan.

1

POPULAR LEARNING
IN TOKUGAWA JAPAN

IN ORDER TO understand the development of Shingaku after Baigan's death, it is useful first to explore the educational context and popular sources of inspiration that nurtured the movement during the eighteenth century. Only a limited amount of formal schooling was available to nonsamurai students at this time, but the pressure for greater public access to knowledge increased as the century came to a close. A growing number of informal channels of education helped shape Shingaku and allowed it to make its own contribution to popular learning.

I use the term "popular" to mean associated with the masses of people, which in Tokugawa society were mostly the "common" or nonsamurai classes: merchants, artisans, and peasants. One cannot safely generalize about Tokugawa period "commoners," for there was considerable differentiation and overlapping between and within these conventional groupings. Baigan, for example, is usually taken to represent merchant concerns, but he had strong ties with the peasant milieu in which he originated. Particularly in the development of education, factors such as the proliferation of printed literature and the surge in performing arts affected town dwellers more than the agrarian population. Shingaku originated in the merchant sector of Kyoto, and even as the movement expanded, its prominent members tended to be traders and artisans from large urban centers. However, the group penetrated the countryside to a significant degree: there is evidence of Shingaku schools in sixty-two rural villages, compared to about eighty-seven in urban centers during the late eighteenth and early nineteenth centuries.[1] In this book, therefore, "commoners" or "ordinary people" refers in a broad sense to both urban and rural nonsamurai groups.[2]

Most Japanese peasants, merchants, and artisans had little access to formal schooling during the eighteenth century. The Hayashi school, endowed by the shogunate, is representative of official school policies. It was originally established for samurai, although it later admitted a few commoners for special professional training.[3] Beginning in 1717, common people could attend lectures on Chinese learning (kangaku) at the school every other day; the alternate days were reserved for higher-ranking students. The lectures focused on the Neo-Confucian canon: the Four Books, the *Classic of Filial Piety*, the *Elementary Learning*, and *Reflections on Things at Hand*. But attendance was poor, whether from lack of time or interest, or because of competition from private schools. The school was closed to merchants, artisans, monks, and performers in 1793, and its exclusion of nonsamurai was reinforced in 1797, when the facility became the official shogunal college.

The domain schools (hankō) followed a similar pattern: most focused on classical Chinese studies and catered primarily to samurai children. Some instructed samurai separately according to rank.[4] A few domain schools were open to commoners early in the period, such as the Okayama school, which admitted nonsamurai, especially peasants, since its founding in 1666. (This policy was apparently discontinued in the eighteenth century.)[5] Other instances of commoners attending domain schools are mostly from later in the period. Even these students were relatively privileged, often the sons of village headmen or wealthy merchants. In general, as Ronald P. Dore remarks, "there is . . . no evidence that any fief admitted commoner students to the main fief school in large numbers or on a footing of equality with samurai students."[6]

The local school (gōgaku) played a more significant part in schooling the lower classes, particularly in the late Tokugawa period. A number of local schools were set up by domain or local authorities, or with their support, expressly for the purpose of instructing commoners. Some of these schools were designed for children, but many offered moral instruction to nonsamurai adults. Several introduced Chinese studies; others concentrated on teaching practical skills—writing, reading, and abacus calculation.[7] The local schools for adults are sometimes called kyōyusho, "places of moral instruction." In some domains, the authorities invited lecturers to speak at the schools regularly each month or to tour the rural areas. Occasionally, the moral instruction school itself developed from circuit lecturing arrangements. In the 1790s the shogunal intendant of the Okayama region arranged for Confucian scholars to speak at certain temples and to tour remote areas periodically.[8] With the cooperation of local peasants, this system led to the founding of a moral instruction school, where the lectures could be held regularly. In Yonezawa the Confucian scholar Hosoi Heishū (1728–1801) also arranged for school teachers to conduct rural lecture tours, and in both Yonezawa and Nagoya advocated that official schools double as facilities for commoner learning. The schools held open lectures and discussions, and stressed "reading off" Chinese characters in Japanese *(sodoku)*—modifications that rendered the material more accessible to busy peasants and townsfolk.[9]

Interest in nonsamurai education was not limited to government authorities and their Confucian employees. Several local schools were founded or maintained through private initiatives (some received official support later). Early examples are Gansuidō in Sesshu (1717), Kaihodō in Edo (1723), and Kaitokudō in Osaka (1724).[10] Schools that were completely independent of the authorities often had less restrictive admissions policies than official and semiofficial institutions. Most "private academies" *(shijuku)* aimed at providing higher education for samurai youth but did not stress rank and class as much as the official schools; many admitted commoners.[11] The majority of these schools concentrated on Chinese classical studies, although several specialized in medicine, Western learning, or National Learning (Kokugaku).

Another type of private facility, the *terakoya* or so-called temple school, educated children of commoners at the elementary level.[12] The *terakoya* was usually a flexible arrangement in which a person of some learning in the community offered instruction in writing (and, in some cases, reading and arithmetic) to the local children. The school had its origins in medieval times, when Buddhist priests taught boys who had been sent to the temples as novices. The instruction was gradually extended to include samurai children and finally all neighborhood children. By the Edo period, *terakoya* teachers themselves were mostly townspeople or farmers; some were of samurai background and less than a fifth were Buddhist priests.[13] The typical *terakoya* was fairly small, with twenty or thirty youngsters ranging in age from six or seven to twelve or thirteen years old. Both girls and boys were admitted to most schools, though measures were taken to keep them segregated. The children were not required to attend daily, for they were often needed at home to help with the family business. The *terakoya* often had some communal function in its own right; it could be located in the precincts of a Buddhist temple or Shinto shrine. Sometimes it was simply the home of the instructor, who in rural communities frequently taught more from a sense of social responsiblity than as a means of livelihood. The *terakoya* teacher usually received seasonal gifts from the children's parents rather than fixed payments.

Both official and private schools grew in number in the late eighteenth century. During the Tanuma era (1767–1786), the period in which Teshima Toan brought Shingaku to full institutional development, the shogunate was beset by administrative inefficiency and political corruption.[14] In addition, an unending series of droughts, floods, diseases, and famines during the 1770s and 1780s reduced the peasants and urban poor to desperation, causing frequent rebellions.[15] Ruling authorities began to see moral instruction as one way of restoring the social order. Herman Ooms notes that "the ruling elite in the country felt an urgency to develop learning and to reorder the world by redressing men's hearts and minds through cultivating the correct values."[16] The new concern for education became even more prominent in the Tenmei and Kansei eras (1781–1788, 1789–1800). Both domain and shogunal officials increased their support of popular education. Local governments issued numerous ethical tracts for the edification of their constituents and established more special schools and classes for nonsamurai. After 1786, the political scene was dominated by the reformist policies of Matsudaira Sadanobu (1758–1829), a close advisor to shogun Ienari.[17] Sadanobu was not unaware of the effects of natural disasters on the populace. He encouraged instruction of the common people by traveling preachers, including Shingaku members, in the belief that their ethical teachings would help decrease infanticide, which was reportedly rampant in famine areas.[18] Sadanobu also sponsored Nakazawa Dōni's lectures for day laborers in Edo. Several shogunal intendants employed Shingaku preachers for comparable purposes.[19]

Private initiation of educational facilities for lower-class students also increased conspicuously during the late eighteenth century.[20] Especially among merchants and landholders of some economic capacity, this trend reflected a growing appetite for knowledge—not only for practical skills that might enhance the family profession, but for more abstract forms of learning. With the cultural expansion that had been taking place in Japan throughout the eighteenth century, citizens of all classes now lived in a world that was increasingly complex, both socially and intellectually. Given the socioeconomic disorder that especially characterized the last decades of the century, life for many was more unpredictable than ever before. People were seeking knowledge that could enhance and give order to their lives in the changing society of the time. The demand for learning stimulated forms of education that often took place outside the spatial boundaries of moral instruction schools or *terakoya*. In addition to the cultural traditions that were impressed on young people at home and the practical training apprentices gained on the job, people were educated by artistic performances, public talks, government proclamations, travel experiences, and popular literature. Between work hours an enterprising merchant with a thirst for knowledge might take in a play one day, visit the domain school for a public lecture the next, slip out the following evening to hear a Buddhist sermon, and top off the week with a Shingaku "talk on the Way"—all the while with a book in hand for browsing in spare moments.

Ordinary people could therefore continue learning long after their *terakoya* years. Moral education, in particular, was far from inaccessible to the unlettered. The shogunal and domain authorities often issued proclamations intended for the edification of their subjects. These notices listed ethical injunctions and ideals, usually in formal language (mostly Chinese characters); local leaders with a modicum of literacy were responsible for reading the notices out to the public on regular occasions. The Shingaku preacher Nakazawa Dōni took on the role of itinerant "village reader" when he based his sermons on the items contained in the shogunal edicts. Other texts were "translated" in public as well, such as *The Essence of the Expanded Meaning of the Six Precepts (Rikuyu engi tai i)*.[21] The same method was applied to the prefaces of the "five-household association" *(gonin-gumi)* registers, which contained regulations regarding proper behavior for members of the group.[22] The prefaces were reread to the villagers periodically throughout the year. A more casual source of knowledge, especially for the city classes, was the world of entertainment and the performing arts. Although they did not systematically argue particular moral or philosophical viewpoints, dramas, comic plays, and poetry effectively conveyed powerful ideas. Among Shingaku teachers, Dōni in particular realized the potential of such sources; he frequently alludes to them in his talks.

The explosion of travel and interchange between urban and rural areas of Japan that began in the early Edo period also accelerated the spread of knowledge among the lower classes. Some formal restrictions on travel still existed, but these became less effective as the period wore on.[23] Numerous travelers of all classes used the Tokugawa highway network for trade journeys, pilgrimages, and commuting to and from Edo (as required by the alternate residence system for domain lords). These trips and the travel literature they generated intensified the rising demand for knowledge of the world.[24] The expansion of travel was a key factor in the growing activism of perhaps the most influential popular educators of all—preachers and storytellers, two groups whose identities sometimes overlapped. These figures frequently journeyed through towns and villages to exhort, recite, or perform in public. Itinerant speaking was generally the reserve of those imbued with a religious vision: Buddhist preachers, Shinto popularizers, and, in the latter half of the Edo, Shingaku teachers.

Wandering speakers had been active in Japan since long before the Edo period. The telling of battle tales such as *Heike monogatari* or *Taiheiki* by blind *biwa* (Japanese lute) players and storytelling monks had become an art in medieval times and gained renewed popularity in the Tokugawa era. The development of the popular talk, *kōshaku* or *kōdan,* had roots in the activities of these entertaining raconteurs *(kōsha-*

kushi or *kōdanshi).*[25] Professional storytellers invariably charged a fee, a custom that presumably distinguished them from preachers who simply wished to convey a religious message. The storytellers worked in designated public places (such as Shijō Kawaramachi in Kyoto) and in Buddhist temples, Shinto shrines, neighborhood schools, or even private homes.[26]

During the Edo period the preaching activities of Shinto teachers underwent considerable development. Partly in reaction to the attempts of earlier theorists to synthesize Shinto and Neo-Confucian ideas, by the early eighteenth century Shinto figures arose who sought both to popularize Shinto and to purify it of extraneous, overly speculative elements. This "purification" was accompanied by the gradual liberation of Shinto from the longstanding tradition of "secret transmission," which restricted public access to the teachings. The most famous of the new Shinto preachers was Masuho Zankō (1655–1742).[27] His activities were a natural development of the storytelling or "street-corner talks" *(tsuji dangi)* conducted outdoors by Buddhist monks, masterless samurai, or other literate persons. His teaching was neither systematic nor scholarly; he drew freely from many sources, including Buddhist and Confucian traditions, even though he anathematized these teachings for having defiled the purity of true Shinto. Zankō spoke directly to people's concerns, emphasizing virtues such as honesty *(shōjiki)*, harmony, and the fulfillment of one's allotted role in society. As Peter Nosco points out, his talks were tailored to the needs of people with limited education: "His doctrines were concise and easy to understand, and his ability to communicate his message with such mnemonic devices as enumeration or puns probably made it more palatable to a broad audience of townsmen."[28]

Shinto popularizers like Zankō helped shape the sociorhetorical context in which Shingaku preaching emerged. Ishida Baigan himself was part of the new "street Shinto" trend—in his early years he was so determined to proclaim the way of the *kami* (Shinto gods) that he roamed the streets, ringing a bell to attract listeners.[29] Numerous other figures enlivened the world of public speaking in the Tokugawa period. One skillful raconteur, Baba Bunkō (1718–1758), reportedly pretended to be a Shingaku preacher; he was eventually executed for speaking on topics sensitive to the shogunal authorities.[30] Another storyteller, Shibata Kyūō (1783–1839), ultimately joined the Shingaku movement and used his speaking skills to become the most popular Shingaku preacher of the nineteenth century.

Both Shinto preachers and professional storytellers were indebted to long-established Buddhist teaching traditions. Sekiyama Kazuo has documented the historical association between Buddhism and the oratorical arts in Japan.[31] During the Muromachi period (1392–1573), the *otogishū,* or "conversation partners," who entertained domain lords often dressed as monks. Buddhist garb continued to signify the role of teacher in early Tokugawa times; as counselor to the shogun, the Neo-Confucian scholar Hayashi Razan was compelled to keep the appearance of a monk. Popular Buddhist preaching increased in the Edo era, especially in the Pure Land communities.[32] Even storytellers and preachers who did not advocate Buddhism often had some Buddhist background. Masuho Zankō was allegedly a Nichiren priest for many years before turning to Shinto.[33] Baba Bunkō had been a monk for a time as well. The storyteller Shidōken (1683–1765) returned to lay life after training under a Shingon priest, but even later he told stories under the guise of a monk, probably for practical reasons. As Sekiyama points out, clerical dress was desirable if one wanted to make a good living from public reciting and storytelling during this time.[34]

The association between the wandering bonze and the art of popular preaching remained alive in the public mind until near the end of the Tokugawa era. At the same time, other kinds of speaking forms developed in early modern Japan, independently of Buddhism or Shinto. Through teaching experience, some Neo-Confucian scholars broadened their oratorical skills. The presentations given by Neo-Confucian teachers, also called *kōshaku,* were usually academic lectures intended for regular students. Such expositions covered a range of styles, from line-by-line exegeses to homilies on the meaning of a particular passage. The art of expounding Confucian texts was popularized by the fifth shogun, Tsunayoshi (r. 1680–1709), who frequently lectured to domain lords, members of the nobility, government officials, and doctors. The shogun's personal habit did not signal the beginning of an institution, but it did serve to promote the practice of public lecturing by Neo-Confucian scholars.[35] During the Genroku period (1688–1703) the Hayashi scholars occasionally lectured at their school or to the shogun, though their speaking style is said to have been rather poor.

Yamazaki Ansai was the first to emphasize lecturing as the principal method of teaching in a Neo-Confucian academy. He believed firmly in the authority of the teacher, and his students were encouraged to concentrate on the content of his lectures rather than on their own ideas or interpretations. Ansai's disciple Satō Naokata (1650–1719) became a successful lecturer in his own right. His talks, punctuated by humor and analogy, were evidently more engaging than most Confucian presentations; his services were in great demand among domain lords, and he continued to attract listeners well into his late years. Naokata's speaking style is lauded by various writers of the time.[36]

The pedagogy of Ansai's Kimon school laid the foundation for Neo-Confucian lecturing throughout the Edo period. The practice of lecturing was not without its critics, however. Both Itō Jinsai (1627–1705) and Ogyū Sorai (1666–1728) disapproved of the exegetical lecture and advocated study methods that allowed for more attention to the individual needs of students. Sorai regarded lectures as stultifying, degenerative, and slick—in his view, they were akin to Buddhist sermons.[37]

> The meaning of individual words, the sense of the phrase, the purport of the chapter, the construction of the book, the ostensible meaning, the implied meaning, the varying interpretations of the commentators, even down to historical snippets and anecdotes and the etymology of characters; everything, in fact, which has any connection with the text is lumped together, laid out in order like goods in a shop, strung out like pearls on a necklace. . . . The lecturer cultivates a well-modulated voice to charm the ears of his listeners. The worst of them mix in a few funny stories to wake up sleepers in the audience, and some mercenary ones stop not far short of suggesting an increase in their fees. It is a practice which degrades the teacher's character and corrupts the student's intellect.[38]

Despite such criticisms, the expository lecture was adopted by Neo-Confucian educators and became an accepted teaching method at domain and other schools. However, these lectures were directed primarily at regular, full-time students—mostly samurai. There was no legacy of "Confucian preaching" in Japan comparable to the long tradition of Buddhist oratory. Neo-Confucian scholars did not commonly address large, popular audiences, particularly during the first half of the Edo period.[39] Even when domain or local schools arranged for their teachers to give presentations to commoners, the lectures were not always successful; Dore cites instances of inattentive listeners and lack of interest.[40]

A few Neo-Confucian scholars did develop popularizing skills. Hosoi Heishū, the son of a wealthy Owari farmer, was educated by private tutors in Nagoya and studied Japanese poetry composition in Kyoto.[41] Because of his education, Heishū could identify with the status and manners of a samurai, despite his peasant background.[42] His writings include essays about the edification of samurai, domain lords, and their children; he served as tutor to the lord of Yonezawa. But Heishū was exceptionally active in popular education as well. In addition to organizing the teaching tours and classes for commoners mentioned earlier, Heishū himself gave eloquent sermons. One of his talks in Nagoya in late 1783 was reportedly attended by several thousand people. The sermon (of which a record survives) incorporates a considerable amount of narrative—tales of people who embodied filial piety in the face of extreme difficulty—and does not adhere to a specific classical text.[43] By telling stories, Heishū could maintain the attention of his listeners while imbuing them with such ideals as sincerity *(makoto)*. His speaking style resembled that of the professional storytellers and traveling preachers discussed above. One early modern source renders the following judgment: "Someone like Hosoi Heishū . . . was eloquent and spoke well to ordinary women and men; but insofar as he departed from the [precise] meaning of the terms when lecturing, it was just like hearing the exposition of a preaching monk."[44] The same style, with its storytelling interludes aimed at imparting basic moral values, characterizes the sermons of Shingaku preachers Nakazawa Dōni and Shibata Kyūō. In fact, Heishū often used phrases characteristic of Shingaku, such as "original mind" or "true mind."[45] However, Heishū's activities, like those of many other Neo-Confucian scholars, were confined to the domains in which he was employed. He had neither the mandate nor the infrastructure to bring his teachings to people all over the country. Thus, despite his considerable speaking and organizing skills, Heishū could not disseminate his ethical ideals on a large scale. In contrast, less-educated Shingaku teachers pushed their message into rural and urban areas throughout Japan in less than half a century.

The Transmission of Confucian Values through Vernacular Literature

Besides the increasing influence of preaching, reciting, and other oral media during the period, informal education in the Edo era was greatly enhanced by the dissemination of vernacular writings, especially in urban areas. The new wealth and leisure of the city classes, the spread of literacy, and the development of printing technology earlier in the period all led to the production of large numbers of books at a relatively reasonable cost. Texts that once had been the domain of an educated elite—mainly Buddhist monks and the nobility—now circulated widely. As many works were printed in the Japanese vernacular scripts *(kana)*, knowledge of the more difficult Chinese characters was no longer requisite for access to written culture.[46] The high culture contained in the Chinese works was mediated to the less educated by an amorphous group of popular writers; in the first half of the Tokugawa period, these "cultural translators" were mostly low-ranked or masterless samurai, courtiers, Buddhist priests, and scholars. According to Richard Lane, "Much of the prose literature of this early [pre-Genroku] period is didactic in nature: it represents a person of education—often himself in reduced circumstances—attempting to explain both to the townsmen and to the new generation of *samurai,* the tradition of knowledge and morality that constituted his own world."[47]

Popular writers throughout the Tokugawa period were not generally an intellectual elite, but they were more educated than their readers. Because of this midway position, the authors could fulfill the important role of simplifying and spreading knowledge. Their vernacular writings, *kanazōshi,* provided a good portion of the townsperson's ongoing education.[48] Such writers also made use of the block-print illustration techniques that had developed earlier in the period. The publication of illustrated didactic works peaked in the eighteenth and early nineteenth centuries.[49] Engaging pictures were frequently inserted in popular ethical tracts, *iroha* books, and children's textbooks in order to maintain the reader's interest.[50] In contrast, illustrations were not a common feature of the standard Neo-Confucian texts used to teach samurai at domain schools.[51]

Without access to these popular reformulations, Ishida Baigan and Teshima Toan would have had far greater difficulty creating their own brand of learning. The core texts of the Neo-Confucian program could not readily be consumed in their original form by those who lacked training in Chinese. Most Shingaku leaders could read Chinese to some extent, but, being busy townspeople, they relied heavily on vernacular renditions of the classics. These and other Confucian-inspired popular works, especially *kyōkunsho,* played an important part in the development of Shingaku. Some *kyōkunsho,* or "moral learning books," were written predominantly in Chinese characters (such as the *kakun* or "house codes"), but the most widely used didactic writings were chiefly in *kana.*[52] Shingaku preachers were familiar with various types of morality books—merchant literature, stories of virtuous people, tracts for women and girls, and Japanese renditions of Chinese works, among others. Some of these categories overlap.

By "merchant literature" I mean vernacular works that specifically addressed the concerns of the merchant or town dweller. The best-known example of this genre is *Townsfolk's Grab-bag (Chōnin bukuro)* by Nishikawa Joken (1648–1724), a Neo-Confucian scholar who was influenced by Kaibara Ekken. The book is a collection of ethical and practical advice for merchants, written in popular style. *Matters That Townsfolk Ought to Consider (Chōnin kōken roku),* by Mitsui Takafusa (1684–1748), lists the vices that merchants should avoid in order to make and keep their fortunes.[53] These works circulated widely by the middle of the Edo period; along with other merchant-oriented books, they transmitted such values as frugality, diligence, loyalty, and honesty. The genre was expanded by Shingaku authors, who in the first stages of the movement were generally merchants themselves. Teshima Toan's father, Muneyoshi, wrote a tract called *Night Talks for Merchants (Akindo yawasō).* Ishida Baigan contributed *Frugality: a Discussion of Household Management (Kenyaku: Seikaron),* and Toan himself wrote *For Townsfolk: Building the Foundation of One's Fortune (Chōnin: Shindai hashiradate)* and *Maintaining One's Fortune as a Townsperson*

(*Chōnin shindai naoshi*).⁵⁴ Because of their emphasis on the mind, the Shingaku writings tend to adopt a more internal perspective on the merchant ethic than is found in the earlier works. Toan's *Building the Foundation of One's Fortune* thus reflects on the moral and spiritual aspects of a set of financial guidelines contained in an older merchant tract.

Stories of virtuous persons, especially individuals who displayed an unusual depth of filial piety, were also a rich source for Shingaku teachers. Such tales were ostensibly based on fact; they are sometimes called *jitsuwa* or *jitsuroku*, "true stories," or *kōshiden*, "tales of filial children." Although some stories are simply translations of Chinese accounts, a great number were written about Japanese paragons of virtue. The tales were widely in print during the seventeenth and eighteenth centuries. The catalogue of a late-eighteenth-century book dealer who catered to Shingaku followers includes an entire section titled "Vernacular Books on Loyalty and Filial Piety." A quick survey of the eighteen works listed reveals that many were written or compiled by persons trained in Neo-Confucian studies. Three were authored by Shingaku members.⁵⁵ Three other works included in the book list, *Stories of Filial Children of Our Country* (*Honchō kōshiden*, 1684), *The Evergreen Tree* (*Tokiwagi*, the story of a loyal wife; n.d.), and *Record of Good Deeds in Japan* (*Yamato izenroku*, 1689), were written by the seventeenth-century writer Fujii Ransai, a pious Confucian who studied under Yamazaki Ansai.⁵⁶ Ransai's tales of virtue typify the kind of literature that Shingaku teachers used to inspire their audiences to the possibility of moral perfection.

Neo-Confucian scholars also produced Japanese versions of Chinese works; these were often entirely new works written in the spirit of the original. Yamazaki Ansai's *Japanese Elementary Learning* (*Yamato shōgaku*), for example, is not an exact translation of Chu Hsi's *Elementary Learning*, but aims at conveying the gist of the Chinese text.⁵⁷ Discourses addressed to women and girls formed another popular genre during this period. These works usually detailed the proper conduct of women; some were collections of anecdotes about female paragons of virtue, such as *Stories of Chaste Women, in Kana* (*Kana retsujo den*), which is also included in the Shingaku book dealer's list.⁵⁸ This type of literature was undoubtedly familiar to Shingaku preachers; it functioned as a model for Toan's own contributions to the genre.⁵⁹ Some tracts for women were patterned after Neo-Confucian texts: *The Elementary Learning for Women* (*Onna shōgaku*), *The Doctrine of the Mean for Women* (*Onna chūyō*), and *The Analects for Women* (*Onna rongo*).⁶⁰ The most famous book in this class is *The Great Learning for Women* (*Onna daigaku*), attributed to Kaibara Ekken, which circulated extensively, particularly in combined publication with other material considered beneficial for girls and women.⁶¹ Ekken produced a number of vernacular discourses that were widely read and probably had a substantial impact on popular moral values in the Tokugawa era.[62]

In his survey of moral education during the early modern period, Furukawa Tetsushi emphasizes the educational impact of the various morality books. A 1753 source advises that people of common status read Kaibara Ekken's *Precepts for Daily Life in Japan (Yamato zokkun)* and *Precepts for Family Life (Kadōkun)*, Nishikawa Joken's *Townsfolk's Grab-bag*, Fujii Ransai's *Record of Good Deeds in Japan*, and Teshima Muneyoshi's *Night Talks for Merchants*.[63] In his *Night Talks*, Muneyoshi in turn informs his readers that Ekken's and Joken's works are appropriate for people whose reading abilities are limited.[64] Another 1753 work, *Miscellany of Long-lasting Moral Teachings (Kyōkun zatsu nagamochi)*, also recommends Ekken's and Joken's writings (among others) as books that can be read without difficulty. Works considered appropriate for female readers include Ekken's *Great Learning for Women* and Ansai's *Japanese Elementary Learning*.[65]

These are only a few of the most prominent works that transmitted Confucian values and ideas of self-cultivation to ordinary people in the Edo period. Books of this kind became popular just as the Shingaku community was taking shape in the mid-Edo period, and their number continued to multiply during the second half of the period. Furukawa attributes the later proliferation partly to the influence of Shingaku itself.[66] Indeed, Shingaku writers became experts at mediating the ideas that they gleaned from Neo-Confucian compilations and other sources. By means of stories, popular idioms, and pictures, they advanced the process of cultural translation begun by earlier vernacular writers, generating not only merchant literature, stories of filial piety, and tracts for women, but also booklets for children and other discourses on self-cultivation. Toan and his disciples accelerated the transmission of moral and religious ideas in Tokugawa society mainly through oral sermons and lectures. But like earlier Neo-Confucian popularizers, such as Ekken, Joken, and Ransai, they also made written contributions to the spread of learning.

Popular Sources of Zen

The followers of Baigan drew heavily on Buddhist as well as Neo-Confucian writings. Like the *kyōkunsho*, or morality books, Buddhist sermon texts were published in great numbers during the Edo period, particularly in the Pure Land and Nichiren sects.[67] The *kana hōgo* was one of the most popular types of homiletic literature. *Hōgo*, or "Dharma talk," is a Buddhist discourse meant for the general public; *kana hōgo* is a Dharma talk written in the Japanese vernacular—ordinarily *kana* combined with Chinese characters.[68] In practice, when confronted with the task of presenting scriptural material to large, popular audiences, Buddhist preachers read the passages off in Japanese rather than according to the Chinese *(on)* pronunciation and syntax. Often they simply presented the gist of the Chinese text in their own words, reformulating or translating technical Buddhist terms into the native idiom. The writing of *kana hōgo,* or vernacular Dharma talks, involved a similar process of adaptation to popular needs.

During the Edo era, Dharma talks reached all sectors of society—farmers and townsfolk as well as samurai—a far broader range of people than were exposed to written sermons in the medieval period. Writers of the earlier discourses had been inclined to stress the value of the monastic life; they depicted worldly occupations as an interim phase on the path to a higher religious state. In the early modern period, Buddhist preacher-writers were more aware of the exigencies of daily life; they frequently used people's immediate concerns as a vehicle for conveying Buddhist doctrines and popular moral values. Their Dharma talks now became more widely read than the Buddhist scriptures themselves; the latter, written in Chinese, were still relatively inaccessible to most common people.

Teshima Toan and his followers were well acquainted with vernacular Dharma talks and other popular Buddhist literature; ideas from these writings often surface in Shingaku sermons. Several of the Buddhist works used by Toan date back to the Kamakura (1192–1333) and Muromachi periods. Along with such classics as Kamo no Chōmei's *Awakening of Faith (Hosshin shū)* and *My Ten-Foot-Square Hut (Hōjōki),* and Musō Soseki's *Dialogue in a Dream (Muchū mondō),* Toan probably read such works as *Mud and Water from Enzan (Enzan wadei gassui [shū]).* The latter is a popular work by the Rinzai monk Bassui Tokushō (1327–1387), who taught a practical, simplified form of Zen.[69] But Toan cites the words of two other pre-Tokugawa writers, Mujū Ichien (1226–1312) and Ikkyū Sōjun (1394–1481), even more frequently. Mujū was a disciple of the early Rinzai teacher Enni Ben'en (1202–1280), but he was well acquainted with the ideas of several Buddhist sects. His *Sand and Pebbles (Shasekishū)* was one of the few Zen-oriented works suited to less-educated readers in the early Tokugawa period, and its parables circulated widely throughout the era.[70] Mujū's skillful use of humor as a didactic tool in his writings was a model for later preachers and provided homiletic material for diverse religious contexts long after his death.[71] Teshima Toan drew on *Sand and Pebbles* from time to time to embellish his own talks.[72] Mujū Ichien preaches tolerance in his writings, warning against the error of doctrinal exclusivism, an attitude that resonates with Toan's perspective.[73]

Zen master Ikkyū Sōjun is another prominent Buddhist voice in

Shingaku discourse. His popular image was well embedded in Japanese culture by the mid-Edo period. Ikkyū was a complex, unconventional figure who criticized the corrupt Zen establishment of his day. His Chinese poetry reveals a keen sensitivity to the paradoxes and conflicts of the religious life.[74] However, as James Sanford points out, many "Ikkyūs" live in the Japanese public mind; some were fabricated from pseudohagiographic and folkloristic traditions that have little relation to the historical Ikkyū.[75]

The Ikkyū most pertinent to "Teshima Shingaku" is the Zen master who conveyed his teaching to ordinary people through vernacular prose and poetry. Several popular tracts and verses have been attributed to Ikkyū; whether or not these works are authentic, they implanted the image of a serious, creative Zen teacher in the minds of many readers in the Edo period. The role played by the vernacular writings in Shingaku three hundred years after Ikkyū's death testify to the continuing power of that image. Toan based one of his own works, *No Eye: A Word to the Wise (Me nashi yōjin shō)*, on an annotated version of *Water Mirror (Mizu kagami)*, a popular discourse attributed to Ikkyū.[76] The Shingaku leader probably read other Japanese prose works associated with Ikkyū, especially *The Naked Truth about Amida (Amida hadaka monogatari)*; he was also familiar with Ikkyū's Japanese poems and some of the secondhand literature about him.[77] The popular anecdotes about Ikkyū that burgeoned in the Tokugawa period (collected in *Tales of Ikkyū [Ikkyū banashi]*) present an image of the Zen master that is less prominent in Teshima Shingaku. Sanford notes that these quasimythological stories, which depict Ikkyū as an outrageous, comical individualist, represent "the next step beyond *kana hōgo:*"

> If vernacular sermons made the assimilation of difficult Buddhological propositions more palatable to the masses, these lively tales make the messages of the *kana hōgo* slide down as easily and tastily as a bowl of sweet, fried eel. Like the Tokugawa Pure Land School's exemplary *Myōkōnin-den* stories of eccentric and noble "fools of Amida" or the at times quite comic *"dōwa"* ("moral stories") of the emergent Shingaku school, the Ikkyū tales show much closer psychological affinities with *kyōgen* (crazy-word) farces, *kyōka* and *kyōshi* "crazy-poems", and the vulgar *senryū* side of the *haiku* tradition than with the Ashikaga *Nō* plays or the classical poetry of the Gozan schools.[78]

The "comic *dōwa*," however, is not characteristic of the Shingaku school in its early and intermediate phases. Shingaku speakers were always open to the use of humor and narrative as didactic devices, but both Baigan's and Toan's talks are more sober and purposeful in tone than *Tales of*

Ikkyū. The humorous "talk on the Way" typifies Shingaku in a relatively late phase of its history.[79]

Along with Mujū, Musō Soseki, and other medieval popularizers, through his writings "Ikkyū" continued to transmit a simplified, accessible form of Zen throughout the Tokugawa period. However, Shingaku teachers derived even more inspiration, both intellectual and stylistic, from Zen masters of their own era. Until the Edo period, Zen learning had been the domain of the clergy and upper classes: "popular Zen sermon" was virtually a contradiction in terms.[80] But the efflorescence of Japanese Zen into a preaching tradition gained momentum in the seventeenth century. In Peter Haskel's estimation, this was a period of creative debate, experimentation, and development in the Zen school. It was also a time of reaction against late Muromachi Zen, which had been greatly weakened by monastic corruption and formalized practices. A number of Zen teachers arose in the early Edo period who, in different ways, sought to restore authentic Zen and teach it directly to the people.[81] Several of them influenced Teshima Toan's ideas and teaching approach.

The Shingaku leader's works contain references to Suzuki Shōsan, Shidō Munan, Baiten Mumyō, and Bankei Yōtaku. Toan may have been familiar with the popular works of Takuan Sōhō as well. There are significant differences between the personalities and teachings of these Zen figures; in terms of scholarship or style of expression, one may hardly mention Takuan and Shōsan in the same breath. Nevertheless, all of these teachers furthered the popularization of Zen that had begun in medieval times. The new "popularization" did not necessarily involve accretions from esoteric Buddhism, devotionalist practices, or folk beliefs. Haskel enunciates the difference clearly:

> During the late Middle Ages, popular Zen signified a vulgarized, syncretic teaching designed to attract the support of the rural populace and the new military, mercantile and artistic classes emerging in the provinces. By contrast, popular early Tokugawa Zen teachers such as Bankei sought to simplify and disseminate Zen not by forsaking or diluting its teachings in favor of more traditional forms of Buddhism, but by clarifying them, reducing them to their essentials and presenting these in a manner that was at once familiar and direct.[82]

The new Zen popularizers either preached to lay audiences or wrote vernacular discourses that were read by later generations; often they did both. Like other preachers of the time, they dispensed with Chinese expressions and difficult terminology in both their writings and their sermons.

Takuan Sōhō (1573–1645), a Rinzai monk, became the head of

Daitoku-ji temple in 1669, but resigned soon after to pursue a life of study and monastic retirement. Takuan was advisor to the shogun and a distinguished scholar but also an active disseminator of Zen. Although his writings were mostly intended for samurai or nobility, many are in the vernacular, and by the eighteenth century these works were widely read.[83] Takuan's Dharma talks circulated under various titles throughout the rest of the period, in both manuscript and block-print editions. Takuan also stands out as a Buddhist thinker who squarely faced the rising intellectual challenge of Neo-Confucianism in the early Tokugawa period.[84] He was well acquainted with Neo-Confucian texts, as can be seen from the frequent references in his writings to the Ch'eng brothers, Chang Tsai (1020–1077), and Chu Hsi.[85] Takuan used his knowledge of Neo-Confucian discourse to interpret the issues raised by the Sung masters from a Mahayana Buddhist perspective.

Two disciples of the Rinzai master Gudō Tōshoku (1577–1661) also wrote Dharma talks that were familiar to Toan. Baiten Mumyō (1607–1676), who took the tonsure at the relatively late age of fifty, wrote *The Dharma Talks of Zen Master Baiten (Baiten Zenji hōgo)* in 1672. The talk was reprinted in 1773 with a preface by Hakuin. Baiten's fellow disciple Shidō Munan (1603–1676) also became a monk rather late, when he was fifty-two. His Dharma talks, *Record of This Very Mind (Sokushinki)* and *Record of the Innate Nature (Jishōki)*, were published in 1671 and 1672.[86] Munan was especially sensitive to the needs of lay people, perhaps because of his own lengthy period of study in that status. His style of writing reflects this popular orientation:

> His works, predominantly in the *kana* syllabary with few Chinese characters, are direct and colloquial in the extreme. He makes no pretense of fine literary style or erudition, though we can be in no doubt of his keen native intelligence and gather from his allusions that he was familiar with certain basic texts of Buddhism and Confucianism.[87]

Like other Buddhist preachers of his day, Munan used Neo-Confucian language to teach his ideas. This tendency is particularly evident in *Record of the Innate Nature,* where Munan comments on passages from the *Analects,* the *Great Learning,* the *Mean,* and the writings of the Ch'eng brothers.[88]

Suzuki Shōsan (1579–1655) is said to have studied under Gudō as well, but he also had connections with the Sōtō school of Zen. Shōsan was a shogunal retainer who fought in the battles of Sekigahara and Osaka; he did not become a monk until he was forty-two years old. He worked independently of the Zen establishment, traveling and preaching extensively. Shōsan advocated practices that were not strictly orthodox in the Zen sects, such as the recitation of the *nenbutsu* ("I name Amida

Buddha"), and he deemphasized koan study. He produced several works that reached a wide audience in the Edo period, including *kanazōshi*, or didactic tales. Before Shōsan took the tonsure, he wrote *A Safe Staff for the Blind (Mōanjō)*, a vernacular tract that aims to reconcile Confucian objections to Buddhism. In his later years he wrote a number of other popular Buddhist discourses, the most important of which is *Right Action for All (Banmin tokuyō,* 1661).[89]

In the latter work Shōsan argues that the ordinary work of lay people can be the locus of enlightenment. In fact, the unity of Buddhist truth with one's occupation in daily life was Shōsan's principal emphasis. He repeatedly impresses on his readers that the Dharma and the "law of the world" are one and the same.[90] He advises farmers, for example, that there is no Buddhist practice outside of farming itself. The key, he implies, is internal attitude; when this is correct, all trades are the means of spiritual emancipation. Shōsan was not just mouthing an ideal; he even refused to ordain samurai who came to him for the tonsure.[91] He believed that the proper work of the samurai was simply to serve his lord, just as the merchant's task was to make profits for the sake of society and the artisan's to excel in his craft. Although he vigorously proclaimed the superiority of Buddhism, Shōsan was dominated by such concerns as serving one's lord and fulfilling one's allotted occupation; his writings rely heavily on Confucian-style ethical exhortation.[92]

Shōsan did not leave behind a school that propagated his brand of popular, Confucianized Zen. But his ideas did not fade away; they blended with various other influences and lived on in the popular mind. Ooms argues that Shōsan's teaching helped generate ways of thinking that persisted throughout the Edo period.[93] In this general sense, Shōsan is significant for the understanding of Sekimon Shingaku. Toan wrote a brief preface (and minimal notes) for the 1778 reprint of *A Safe Staff for the Blind*, but he rarely refers to Shōsan in his own works.[94] However, both Shōsan and Toan emphasized Confucian ethics, the importance of one's allotted trade, and the ordinary person's potential for finding "enlightenment" within the everyday working context. Moreover, true to his samurai background, Shōsan was deeply concerned with preparation for death. He often stressed the importance of realizing the foulness of the body and destroying it by means of the selfless mind. Teshima Toan also advocated the idea of destroying or "forgetting" the body.[95]

Bankei Yōtaku (1622–1693) is another seventeenth-century source of "Shingaku Zen."[96] Bankei received his training in the Rinzai tradition under Unpo Zenshō (1568–1653) and the Ming teacher Tao-che Ch'ao-yüan (J. Dōsha Chōgen, d. 1662), but he gradually developed his own teaching of *fushō no busshin*, "the unborn Buddha-mind." He favored a simplified, practical approach to teaching Zen and rejected traditional koan study. Bankei sought to impart the experience of the unborn to people directly, without relying on words or theoretical explanation. Like the Zen figures discussed above, he used the everyday details of people's lives as a vehicle for conveying his teaching; he saw no need to quote from the sutras or records of the patriarchs. In fact, he refused to identify his message with any particular teaching, even Buddhism or Zen. Furthermore, like others of his time, Bankei received some Neo-Confucian schooling in his youth; his quest for enlightenment was spurred by a desire to know the meaning of the term "bright virtue" in the *Great Learning*. Bankei demonstrated some familiarity with Confucian works later in life as well.[97]

Like Shōsan, Bankei did not leave behind a school that furthered his teaching of the unborn Buddha-mind. However, during his lifetime Bankei gave public sermons to large audiences and conducted sizable *kessei,* three-month training periods held at Zen temples in winter and summer. His most famous training session, held in 1690, involved nearly 1700 monks, but the audience included lay people of various classes as well.[98] Apparently, only a few of Bankei's sermons were recorded, but when they were published later in the Tokugawa period, they did not fail to have an impact, at least in Shingaku circles.[99] Bankei's sermons were the single most important source of Teshima Toan's Zen learning.[100]

In Chapter 3 I discuss specific connections between Toan's ideas and the teachings of Bankei and other Zen figures mentioned above. To varying degrees, Takuan, Munan, Shōsan, and Bankei all had some background in Neo-Confucian studies; Munan and Shōsan used Neo-Confucian language in their preaching. Moreover, Baiten, Munan, and Shōsan spent a good portion of their lives as lay Buddhists and, along with Bankei, tailored their teachings to the daily concerns of lay people. Toan, a busy merchant, found the vernacular works of these teachers both accessible and pertinent to his interest in self-cultivation. The Shingaku leader employed the themes he picked up from earlier Buddhist writings as well as the ideas of these Zen preachers to create a Zen-oriented, popular version of the Neo-Confucian learning of the mind. He saw the Zen masters' use of Neo-Confucian language as a confirmation of his own belief in the underlying unity of both teachings. Moreover, the Zen teachers' outreach to common people provided a model for Shingaku educational activities.[101]

Like other religious popularizers of the Edo period, Toan and his disciples specialized in simplifying and adapting canonical truths to popular needs. In doing so, they helped satisfy a growing demand in the late eighteenth century for widespread communication of religious and moral knowledge. Following in the footsteps of traveling preachers and storytellers, Shingaku teachers transcended the limitations of the Confucian school lecture by carrying their version of self-cultivation directly to people throughout Japan. Their reformulation of the high culture, taught to samurai students in more formal settings, was facilitated by the proliferation of vernacular literature, both Confucian-style ethical tracts and popular Buddhist discourses. In the following chapters, I look more closely at Shingaku itself—the lives, ideas, and practices of Toan and his disciples—in order to define more precisely the movement's contribution to religious learning in Tokugawa Japan.

2

TESHIMA TOAN AND
THE SHINGAKU
COMMUNITY

THE SURVIVAL and expansion of the Shingaku movement after Ishida Baigan's demise is largely due to the teaching and organizing efforts of his successor, Teshima Toan.

Most of what is known about the life and personality of Teshima Toan is recorded in the anecdotal biography compiled by his disciples, *The Memoir of Master Teshima Toan (Teshima Toan sensei jiseki)*.[1] He was born in Kyoto in 1718 to a daughter of the Uekawa, a prosperous merchant family in the business of dry goods. Toan's father, Teshima Muneyoshi, also called Gaigaku, was a lover of learning in his own right. He wrote several works on the proper behavior of merchants, most notably the aforementioned *Night Talks for Merchants (Akindo yawasō)*.[2] Muneyoshi was adopted by his wife's family but ultimately retained his own name; his son Toan in turn received the name Uekawa for a time, along with the responsibility for continuing the Uekawa lineage.[3]

We have little information about Toan's childhood. In the *Memoir* he is said to have been bright and inquisitive, frugal, and considerate of others. If he happened to see any discarded food, he would put it in a place where sparrows and mice could eat it. He would even dry out old tissue paper, use it repeatedly, and finally use it as toilet paper. Like Baigan, Toan is depicted as a model of thrift and modesty.[4] Apparently, he was a determined idealist from his youth, resolving at an early age to exemplify the moral Way of the ancient sages. He promised himself that he would refrain from three errors: neglect of the family business, mistakes in sexual matters, and disharmony with his relatives. He believed that for a person of his station in life, this simple program of self-improvement was the best foundation for fulfilling the Way.

Toan lost his father when he was thirteen years old and his mother when he was eighteen, after which he was placed under the care of his paternal grandmother. Perhaps because of these early losses, Toan was particularly sensitive to the needs and traditions of his extended family. He is said to have helped his relatives whenever they were in difficulty and meticulously to have carried out commemoration rites for his ancestors, late parents, and friends. His attachment to his parents exemplified the Confucian ideal of filial piety; after they died, he tried to maintain things just as they were, reportedly even refusing to change their wastebasket.

Toan's ritual life reveals a similar reverence for his predecessors. In middle age he began to visit the image of Kannon at the Kiyomizu temple; his parents had done the same when he was a baby, to pray for his health, and he did not want to forget their love for him. He paid obeisance to the Hase Kannon and the Sumiyoshi *kami* (a Shinto deity), just as his father had, and visited the grave of Jimon, a Buddhist priest whom his grandmother had revered. In short, Toan had great respect for family tradition: "he never changed anything his ancestors had done, unless it was unavoidable."[5]

Teshima Toan married in 1744. His wife was a member of the Sugie family; she receives little or no mention in his works.[6] In the same year, Toan's grandmother died; he had been particularly attached to her and was apparently overcome with grief. It is said that when a tree his grandmother had planted withered twenty-five years later, it upset him deeply; he had the trunk carved into a walking stick, gave it a name, and even wrote an essay in honor of the occasion.

In Toan's nineteenth year he met Baigan and began to study under him. After two years of spiritual training, he had an "enlightenment" experience, which Baigan officially acknowledged. The young Toan had only seven more years with his teacher. When Baigan died in 1744, he left behind a handful of committed disciples.[7] They were deeply saddened by his passing and wrote farewell notes to him in which they pledged to apply and spread his teaching even more conscientiously than they had while he was alive.[8] The followers assembled soon after the funeral and agreed to support each other in carrying forward Baigan's mission. They established regular meeting dates and a schedule for lectures *(kōshaku)* and study circles *(rinkō)*.[9]

Aside from the lecture system that Sugiura Shisai set up in Osaka and Jion-ni's teaching activities in Edo (both of which began in 1747), in the years after Baigan's death, lectures and discussions remained confined to the Kyoto area and continued to attract chiefly members of the merchant class.[10] Until 1761, a period of seventeen years, Saitō Zenmon, also known as Hokuzan, took charge of the group's affairs. Zenmon was born in Kyoto in 1700; his family, like Toan's, was in the business of dry goods. He entered Baigan's school in his thirties and eventually became the leading disciple. Baigan's biographers tell us that Zenmon was the first disciple to "know his nature" *(sei o shiru)*:

> Though our teacher [Ishida Baigan] always said to the pupils that they should know their own nature, there were only two or three who believed this. Among these Saitō Zenmon deeply believed it, and day and night concentrated on meditation *(kufū)* as much as possible. One night, unexpectedly hearing the sound of a drum, he knew the nature. Hereupon, more and more, conviction arose, was daily nourished and finally became complete. Thereupon, Zenmon from the depth of his conviction helped his friends, but still their aspiration was weak.[11]

Another source adds that Zenmon's "discovery" *(hatsumei)* became even clearer when he happened to hear a cat cry on a roof during a fire. Nevertheless, "he did not tell Master Baigan about these [experiences]. Nor did Master Baigan ever teach him how to see into the nature."[12] If this rather cryptic testimony is to be given credence, Zenmon reached "enlightenment" without receiving either counsel or explicit approval from Baigan. Yet Baigan relied heavily on his senior disciple for assistance; Zenmon sometimes substituted for his master in teaching.

From these few details it appears that Baigan allowed his closest follower considerable leeway in the cultivation and interpretation of his insight into the nature. Baigan's own mystical experience had been informed by both Neo-Confucian and Zen traditions, but Zenmon's was apparently weak in Confucian elements.[13] Judging from the little we know, Zenmon was more disposed than Baigan to emphasize the role of sudden, Zen-like intuition in the understanding of the nature or original mind. This difference may have some significance in the development of Shingaku religious life, for after Baigan's death, Toan regarded Zenmon as both teacher and friend. Zenmon was not only the new leader of the entire group; he had also been a bosom friend of Toan's late father and thus exerted a special influence over the younger man. Perhaps Zenmon had facilitated Toan's entry into Baigan's school in the first place; if so, Toan and Zenmon's relationship lasted from before 1735 to the latter's death in 1761, a period of at least twenty-six years. In fact, when Toan received his own first insight into the original mind, he initially reported it to Zenmon and only later went to Baigan for official approval.

Baigan had regarded Toan as a promising student, reportedly predicting that Toan would become his "Mencius" (Confucius' successor). During Toan's nine years with Baigan, however, his position was actually that of a young adept among several older disciples. He received the influence of the other followers, especially Zenmon, along with Baigan's own instruction. Toan's father's Confucian ethics and devotion to Buddhist and Shinto deities, as well as his grandmother's Buddhist piety undoubtedly combined with these later influences to shape Toan's inter-religious spirituality.

Teshima Toan's public duties as a Shingaku member began in 1760, when he gave his first lecture and led the memorial rites for Baigan on the seventeenth anniversary of the founder's death. Early the next year he began a morning lecture course on the *Doctrine of the Mean* at Baigan's "Schoolhouse," while Zenmon continued to lecture in the evenings on the *Great Learning*. Komori Baifu and Sugiura Shisai passed away in 1760, and Zenmon himself died in the eighth month of the following year. Lecture programs had been established at several locations in Kyoto,[14] but aside from Tomioka Ichoku, Toan was the only direct disciple of Baigan still alive. A month later, he transferred the management of the Uekawa household to his son Wa'an and retired from the family business to concentrate his energies on teaching. He was forty-three years old.

Toan was diffident about his status as a teacher; he felt that he had attained the position virtually by default. We are told that he began his lectures with the following disclaimer:

> I am not qualified to teach, but my elders have already passed away; I have no choice but to lecture while I am still learning. Of course, I am unlettered, but my teacher's doctrine was simply to have people know the innate nature. When one knows it, the way to embody it is extremely easy; that is why I will try to introduce it to you.[15]

Judging from his writings, Toan was familiar with a considerable number of books, but many were probably annotated or written in the Japanese vernacular; he himself wrote mostly in Japanese. He considered himself "unlettered" in the sense that he was not well versed in Chinese. Rather than as a teacher in his own right, he preferred to think of himself simply as a transmitter of Baigan's teaching, a companion along the path with others who sought goodness. This modest style was reflected in Toan's habit of referring to members of the movement as "friends" or "companions" *(hōyū)*. He would say, "I am not one who can become the teacher of others," or "I do not become a teacher of others by choice."[16] His biographers depict Toan as open and humble; he listened carefully to others' opinions, regardless of their status. His concern was simply to have people understand the teaching he had inherited from Baigan.

Beginning in 1764 Toan began to lecture nightly on the *Mean* and *Essays in Idleness (Tsurezuregusa)*. Many people in his audience reportedly "knew their original minds." This evening program was "the start of Master [Toan] giving lectures on a large scale."[17] He began a course of talks on the *Explanation of the Diagram of the Great Ultimate* (Ch. *T'ai-*

chi t'u-shuo) in the fourth month of that year and, from the fifth month, set up a schedule of afternoon lectures on the Four Books. About this time he also began to travel to outlying areas to give talks. The Shingaku membership gradually increased, and Toan initiated biweekly meetings for the regular disciples. He cared deeply that they preserve certain standards of conduct and wrote several admonitory works with this aim in mind. Toan felt responsible to his teacher Baigan for the success of the movement:

> He wrote a booklet, titling it *Lineage of the Disciples of Master Ishida.*
> When someone came to know the innate nature, he recorded it therein,
> and each time he went to Toribe Field and reported it [in front of the
> grave of Master Ishida]. Furthermore, fearing there might be disciples
> who would abandon their studies, he recorded a warning about it in
> the margin of the *Lineage of the Disciples* and read it out.[18]

Toan's sense of decorum and his conscientious compliance with the etiquette appropriate to his social status is vividly depicted in his biography. He showed his respect for the ruling authorities in various ways and tried to ensure that there be no friction between Shingaku members and local governments. This etiquette was not simply a matter of expedience: Toan's reverence for those above was an integral part of his world-view. "Whenever he passed in front of a government proclamation notice, he would always take down his umbrella, bow deeply, and refrain from using his walking stick."[19] He also handled official documents with respect. The same courteous attitude was evidently extended to people in general. If visitors arrived, Toan would interrupt whatever he was doing and greet them immediately; he read letters the moment he received them. The Shingaku leader's simple dignity was expressed in his dress as well. Until he was fifty years old, he is said to have worn "a hemp cloth garment with a 'withered tree' print in the summer and a light blue wadded cotton garment in the winter."[20]

Toan was also imbued with a sense of religious awe. He consistently bowed when passing in front of Shinto shrines and Buddhist temples. Moreover, every morning and night, even on his deathbed, it is said, he bowed to the gods, buddhas, and sages, and to the spirits of his ancestors, his late parents, and Baigan. He strictly followed Baigan's precedent in carrying out certain annual rituals: he offered up rice cakes in front of a copy of the *Analects* at the New Year and burned incense in front of an image of Confucius at the winter solstice.

The Shingaku leader changed his residence and lecture place several times within Kyoto. In late 1765 he moved to Chōsō-machi, where he established a regular lecture hall called Gorakusha (House of Five Joys), the first of a series of Shingaku "meetinghouses" *(kōsha).* In 1768 Toan was asked to lead the rites at the twenty-fifth annual memorial service for Ishida Baigan, indicating the preeminent position that he had come to occupy in the Shingaku community.

Toan's accomplishments during the next twenty years are reflected in his writings, which began to appear with increasing frequency in the 1770s. Two early works are the *Admonition (Dansho)*, printed in 1764, and the final version of Baigan's *Memoir*, published in 1769.[21] *Notes of a Conversation (Zadan zuihitsu)*, which treats the relationship between Toan's teaching and the ideas of Zen master Bankei, was printed in 1771. By 1773, Toan had begun teaching children; he published *Early Lessons (Zenkun)* and *For Boys and Girls: Waking Up from Sleep (Jijo: Nemurizamashi)*. *Clearing Up Doubts about Knowing the Original Mind (Chishin bengi)* and a regulatory work, *Principles for the Assembly of Companions (Kaiyū taishi)*, were issued the same year. Several other codes of conduct followed throughout the 1770s and 1780s, known collectively as the *Group Rules (Shayaku)*.

The year 1776 was pivotal for the Shingaku leader. He led a thousand and some hundred disciples in a memorial service for Baigan at a temple in the Kyōgoku district of Kyoto. In honor of the occasion, he presented two talks: "Lecture on the Writings Left Behind [by Master Baigan]" *(Isho kōgi)*, which takes its cue from the first passage of Baigan's *City and Country Dialogues (Tohi mondō)*, and "An Explanation of Spiritual Protection for Women" *(Onna myōga kai)*, which was distributed in leaflets *(se-in)*. Soon after, Toan dispensed with formal dress and began to wear *kin'i*, a hooded outfit that symbolized his withdrawal from the public world: he was approaching the traditional retirement age of sixty.[22] It was at this time that he adopted the name Toan.

During the last ten years of his life, Toan continued his energetic efforts to spread the Way. He published *An Explanation of No Calculation (Shian nashi no setsu*, 1777), *New Talks from Chōsō (Chōsō shinwa*, 1780), the children's reader *New Teaching of Words of Truth (Shinjitsugokyō*, 1781), and, shortly before his death in 1786, *No Eye: A Word to the Wise (Me nashi yōjin shō)*. He also oversaw the establishment of numerous meetinghouses. In Kyoto alone, following Shūseisha in 1773, he set up Jishūsha (1779), Meirinsha (1782), and Kyōkeisha (1784). One of Toan's most important acts was to send his disciple Nakazawa Dōni to preach Shingaku in Edo in 1779. Two years later he sent another steadfast Shingaku member, Fuse Shōō (1725–1784), to Osaka for the same purpose. Meiseisha, the principal Osaka meetinghouse, was founded in 1785.

Toan's two sons succeeded him as leaders of the group. A few details about the life and character of Toan's first son, Teshima Wa'an, are contained in a short biography attributed to Uekawa Kisui (Toan's second son).[23] Wa'an came into the world, as his father had, in the Uekawa residence; it was the fifteenth day of the second month of 1747.[24] An anecdote about Wa'an's childhood illustrates his deep sense of filial piety. One night, when he was about thirteen years old, Wa'an was conversing with others by the light of an *andon* lamp.[25] His father passed by and reproved his son for being wasteful; he asked Wa'an to turn down the lamp. The boy dutifully obeyed. His mother appeared shortly afterwards and observed that the light was too dim; she asked Wa'an to turn up the *andon*. He complied without a word. Toan soon passed through the room again and reiterated his previous order. The same scenario was repeated a number of times, but young Wa'an continued to yield to each of his parents, never complaining about the contradictory demands placed upon him.

Wa'an's purported equanimity and good nature were enduring traits. He grew up to be a deferential man who maintained congenial relations with others. Like his father, he reportedly was frugal in his personal habits and respected the customs of those who preceded him. He meticulously carried out household duties, we are told, but always consulted his parents about the details and never insisted on his own opinion. Wa'an was exposed to his father's teaching activities from an early age and soon came to feel responsible for carrying forward the Shingaku mission. He determined to conquer his shortcomings and immersed himself in a life of self-cultivation. After Toan moved to Gorakusha in 1765, his son is said to have visited him there morning and evening, and to have accompanied his father regularly on his lecture tours. He also studied under Tomioka Ichoku (1717–1787), another of Baigan's direct disciples.

Wa'an is said to have engaged in "quiet sitting" *(seiza)* or contemplation whenever he had free time—he did not neglect it even when the weather was extremely hot or cold. One night, when the youth was nineteen years old, he experienced a spiritual breakthrough during a session of quiet sitting. He used other methods of self-cultivation as well. When he first began studying Shingaku, Wa'an started a diary, which he called "A Record of Timely Practice" ("Jishūroku"). It is identified in his *Memoir* as an account of his progress in the discipline of "maintaining reverence" *(jikei)*. In addition to quiet sitting and self-reflective writing, every day Wa'an worked on one of the "problems" *(sakumon)* that Baigan and Toan used to train their students. After formulating his own answer to the problem, Wa'an would correct himself by opening and reading the teachers' solutions. Wa'an allegedly recorded and reflected on all his father's words, even brief remarks.

In 1778 Wa'an adopted a son, Muneyasu, a descendant of Toan's uncle on the Teshima side. Four years later Muneyasu was given responsibility for the affairs of the Uekawa household, and Wa'an changed his own name to Teshima Ka'uemon.[26] At this time he also took the literary name Wa'an and retired to Gorakusha, as his father had done before him. He was thirty-seven years old. Wa'an took over many of Toan's teaching responsibilities and began to develop his own following of students. Judging from excerpts of the talks included in Wa'an's *Memoir,* the thrust of his teaching was identical to his father's: "The path of learning is just to know the original mind and not violate it."[27]

Wa'an became ill in the early part of 1791 and passed away the same year, on the twenty-fourth day of the tenth month; he was only about forty-five years old. When he felt he was about to die, he performed his ablutions (with some assistance) and put on better clothing. We are informed that he bowed in the direction of his ancestors' shrine and called his family and friends to him. One by one, he offered them parting words of counsel and comfort, and then he wrote a death poem expressing his debt to his father. At the dying man's request, Ariyama Gentō (d. 1796) read aloud from a book that Wa'an had recently received. It is said that Wa'an passed away peacefully while sitting upright with his hands together. He is buried near the rest of his family in the Toribeyama cemetery in Kyoto.

Toan's second and adopted son had far more impact on the history of Shingaku than his older brother Wa'an, if for no other reason than his comparative longevity. Kisui was born in 1748 and died in 1817, when he was seventy years old. In contrast to Wa'an, who led the movement for only five years, Toan's second son was in charge for a period of about twenty-six years.[28] Uekawa Kisui is thought to have been the fourth son of a man called Shiga Mohyōe Morinobu and a woman of the Fukushima family.[29] As a boy, he loved to study. He became adept at reading and writing Chinese characters and may have been one of the most learned Shingaku leaders. There is some evidence that Kisui's original family had samurai origins, which might account for his relatively advanced education.[30] Although Kisui apparently became interested in Shingaku in his teens, he was not formally adopted by Toan until 1768, when he was already twenty-one. Thus, he may have had more literary training in his youth than Toan's natural son Wa'an.

Following an unspecified period of study under Toan, Kisui had an "enlightenment" experience in 1767, when he was twenty years old. After his adoption the following year, Kisui began to accompany his father and Wa'an on lecture tours and to record Toan's talks, which he invariably discussed with his brother. We are told that Kisui took pleasure in improving himself and in advancing along the Way. He is depicted by his biographers as a sober man:

His gravity was like that of a mountain, unmoving. His calmness was like that of water resting in a deep pool. He had such dignity that it was difficult to venture to approach him, but his gentleness was like the tranquillity of a spring day. In his self-discipline, he resembled one who was fasting. Ordinarily he never displayed joy or anger in his countenance. He did not speak indiscriminately of people's good or evil [points], and he did not quarrel with others. He was "straightforward and loved rightness."[31]

Kisui was also an orderly person: he kept his study tidy, with his books, writing materials, and even wastepaper neatly arranged.

Although references to Confucian works dominate his writings, Kisui was familiar with certain Shinto and Buddhist texts as well. He followed the established Shingaku custom of speaking on Shinto works from time to time. In 1809, for example, he lectured on the "Age of the Gods" ("Kami no yō") chapter of the *Chronicles of Japan (Nihongi)* at the residence of Lord Mizuno, the chief retainer of the domain lord of Bizen. He spoke for a number of days, and more than one hundred people are said to have attended. Typically, however, Kisui used Confucian language. He emphasized such Confucian virtues as wisdom and propriety: one had to polish one's internal knowledge, he would say, in order to exhibit proper behavior. Once that inner wisdom is gained, he affirmed, it is much easier to act correctly; that is why Shingaku places priority on knowing the original mind.

There is little doubt that Neo-Confucian learning as developed in the Sung period by the Ch'engs and Chu Hsi was Kisui's chief source of intellectual inspiration. His *Diagram of the Transmission of the Learning of the Mind (Shingaku shōden no zu)* is clear evidence of this preference.[32] The chart depicts the transmission of mind-learning all the way from Fu Hsi and the ancient sage kings of China, the Duke of Chou, Confucius, and his disciples, Mencius, Chou Tun-i (1017–1073), the Ch'eng brothers, their followers, and Chu Hsi directly to Ishida Baigan and his school. There are no continental or Japanese mediators involved in the transmission between Chu Hsi and Baigan. The Ch'eng-Chu schools that were active in the seventeeth and eighteenth centuries in Japan (such as the Kimon and Hayashi schools, or the Bokumon school of Kinoshita Jun'an, 1621–1698) are completely ignored. Even Baigan's teacher Oguri Ryōun (d. 1729) receives only cursory mention in a biographical note on Baigan.

Because the diagram was created in 1792, it is tempting to attribute the motivation for this interpretation of Shingaku ideas to a desire to conform to the intellectual climate of the time.[33] The Kansei edict against heterodox learning, which proclaimed the superiority of Chu Hsi's teaching, had been issued shortly before. Kisui was undoubtedly aware of past suspicions of Shingaku teaching, such as those of the Kyoto city magistrate in the 1760s. Perhaps he felt he could gain official favor by depicting the "Learning of the Mind" strictly in terms of its Sung heritage. He could not claim formal association with any of the Japanese Ch'eng-Chu schools, for there was none. Indeed, Sekimon Shingaku was criticized by Confucian scholars as often as not.

However, fear of appearing heterodox was not Kisui's conscious or primary motive.[34] His own disposition led him from an early age to see Shingaku as a legacy of the Sung masters reformulated by Baigan—a teaching that had little substantial connection with Shinto, philosophical Taoism, or Zen. Kisui felt compelled to clarify the Shingaku transmission because he suspected that casual observers and perhaps some members themselves were confused about the sources of Baigan's teaching. In his preface to an explanatory essay attached to the lineage chart, Kisui remarks:

> Those who have not yet ascended the hall or entered the room [of the learning of the mind] do not realize its significance and say, "The two masters, Ishida and Teshima, base their learning on Buddhism" or "their teaching follows Lao-tzu and Chuang-tzu." This is only because they find it difficult to peep into an enclosure that is several fathoms high. Accordingly, recently I created the "Diagram of the Transmission of Shingaku."[35]

Kisui sought to strengthen Shingaku's Neo-Confucian image in other ways, especially through his prolific writing of prefaces, postfaces, and headnotes for works by Shingaku members under his supervision.[36] Though a more subtle means than his chart, these commentaries helped set the ideological boundaries of Shingaku. Kisui's postface to a work by Ariyama Gentō, "Rules of Quiet Sitting" ("Seizagi"), for example, makes no reference to Buddhism in spite of the conspicuous role played by Sōtō Zen traditions in the text itself. Kisui also instituted organizational changes during his tenure in order to help centralize the Shingaku movement (as described in Chapter 7). By the early nineteenth century, problems associated with the growing number of members seemed to threaten the integrity of his father Toan's teaching.

Kisui's purifying and centralizing efforts did not go unchallenged within the movement. When he attempted to advertise the Ch'eng-Chu lineage of Shingaku by requesting that his chart be displayed as a hanging scroll in the Shingaku meetinghouses, the Edo members were opposed.[37] It seems they were not reluctant to limit Shingaku to Confucian sources so much as fearful that Kisui's neglect of the Hayashi school, officially sanctioned as a transmitter of Chu Hsi's teachings in Japan, would cause trouble for the Edo group in its dealings with the shogunal authorities.

There may even have been some opposition to the chart in Kyoto, since it could be taken to imply that Baigan's unique teaching was merely a recapitulation of Sung learning. Kisui's attempt to control the conferral of Shingaku teaching certificates also elicited reactions.[38] But Kisui apparently had little tolerance for those who did not abide by his policies, such as the disciples of Nakazawa Dōni, Hōjō Gen'yō (fl. 1787–1814), and Ōshima Urin (1755–1836). He stubbornly maintained a longstanding rupture with Wakizaka Gidō (d. 1818), who had been expelled from the movement by Toan in earlier years but was later rehabilitated for work in the Edo area by Dōni.[39]

In spite of these internal tensions in the Shingaku community under his leadership, Kisui carried his father's teaching far and wide. According to his biographers, at least ten thousand new disciples joined the movement and more than a hundred new meetinghouses were founded under his direction. His efforts to depict Shingaku as a form of orthodox Neo-Confucian learning and to regulate members' teaching activities are Kisui's most distinctive contributions to Shingaku history. He died in 1817 and is buried near his adopted family in Toribeyama.

Teshima Toan had, in addition to his sons, several close disciples such as Ariyama Gentō, but his most influential follower was Nakazawa Dōni.[40] Although Dōni was a close friend of Fuse Shōō and was very likely influenced by him to join the Shingaku community, he is traditionally considered Toan's disciple. He was born on the fifteenth day of the eighth month of 1725 into an old Kyoto family of weavers that had settled in the Nishijin district. Like many merchant and artisan families of the time, the Nakazawa were devout members of the Nichiren sect of Buddhism. Their faith was strict and exclusivistic; it is said that whenever Dōni's parents received offerings dedicated to buddhas of other sects (such as Amida), they gave the goods to strangers and would not allow even the servants to enjoy them. The employer chosen for Dōni when he reached the age of apprenticeship was also a firm Nichiren believer.

Immersed in this atmosphere of strong faith, Dōni became religiously inquisitive from a young age. As a boy he enjoyed asking questions about both Confucianism and Buddhism. He especially wondered why his parents believed so strongly in the "Wondrous Dharma" *(Myōhō)* of the Nichiren teaching.[41] During his years of apprenticeship, Dōni began to struggle seriously with issues of faith and doubt. It occurred to him that the chant of the Nichiren believers could simply be empty words and that Buddhist images of deities like Kishibojin were just wooden structures.[42] As the years passed, we are told, Dōni gradually realized that the meaningfulness of Buddhist chants and images depended on the state of his own mind.

Dōni's biographers emphasize that as a youth Dōni had little time to study because of the exigencies of his family's business. He gained only a modicum of reading and writing ability. But religious knowledge was accessible in other forms during the Tokugawa period; whenever Dōni could take time off from work, he attended lectures and Buddhist sermons. As he grew into manhood, he continued to question the meaning of "Wondrous Dharma" but reportedly received no satisfactory answer, not even from priests of the Nichiren sect. It was not until Dōni was in his forties that he found the solution to his question.

One winter day Dōni made his way to a lecture series given by Zen master Tōrei (Enji, 1721–1792), a leading disciple of the Rinzai master Hakuin. At one point in the sermon (which was open to both clergy and laity), Tōrei admonished his listeners: "Fish live in water without being aware of the water, and human beings live in the Wondrous Dharma without being aware of the Wondrous Dharma. First seek your own dwelling place."[43] These words provided the key Dōni had been seeking. We are told that he rushed home and began meditating every night.[44] His enlightenment is described as follows:

> On the dawn of the seventh day [of meditation] his mind became clear and open: he felt as if he were looking at the clear sun in the blue sky. At that moment, he discovered the principle of the one word "Wondrous" and also comprehended that "this very body is the golden Amida."[45] He always used to say that the joy [that he felt on that occasion] was indescribable. This took place on the eleventh day of the eleventh month.[46]
>
> About the fourth month of the following year, when he went to the toilet, he discovered the principle of "Dharma" as well. For example, even though food has one flavor, it comes out divided into two kinds of excrement: this is the Wondrous process of nature. The ears have a Wondrous Dharma; the eyes have a Wondrous Dharma. The Wondrousness depends on the form. Hearing sounds is Wondrous; the ears are the Dharma. The eyes seeing various objects is Wondrous. Even the fingers, all five of them, are each endowed with Wondrous Dharmas. Because the body and the mind together are the Wondrous Dharma, one can even call this "all dharmas are true form."[47]
>
> The joy [that the master felt] when he experienced discovery again like this was incomparable. When he came out of the toilet, he heard a crow cry "kaa! kaa!" and he comprehended how "everything under Heaven and within the four seas takes part in the Wondrous Dharma."[48]

Dōni's enlightenment experiences are described in the language of Nichiren, Zen, and even Pure Land Buddhism. Confucian and Shinto ideas apparently did not play a prominent part in these pivotal events. Although we are informed that Dōni believed in the unity of the three teachings (Confucianism, Shinto, and Buddhism) from his childhood, here the non-Buddhist teachings recede into the background.

Tōrei's reference to "Wondrous Dharma" in his Zen sermon had the effect of directing Dōni's quest inwards. The sermon and Dōni's subsequent Zen-style meditation accelerated his personal realization of the significance of the Wondrous Dharma. According to Dōni's biographers, Zen continued to play an important role in his religious development even after his encounter with Tōrei. Hoping to have the validity of his discovery confirmed, he arranged an audience with Zen master Reigen (Etō, 1722–1785), another Hakuin disciple. During the meeting, Reigen tested the depth of Dōni's understanding by means of Hakuin's famous koan, the sound of one hand clapping. Dōni passed the test, we are told, and received the master's full approval.

Thereafter, Nakazawa Dōni reportedly deepened his understanding further under the auspices of various monks and distinguished Confucian teachers. Eventually, he chose the "Learning of the Mind" taught by Teshima Toan as the most appropriate vehicle for his faith. His Shingaku biographers, perhaps concerned to indicate that Dōni's faith was inspired not only by Buddhist traditions, conclude that "in the end, [Master Dōni] penetrated the ultimate meaning of the principle of nature and fully clarified the principle of the unity of the three teachings."[49]

Dōni taught a truth that he believed was common to the Buddhist, Confucian, and Shinto traditions. His popular talks do not impose Nichiren or Zen on his audience to the exclusion of other ideas. Like Baigan and Toan, he explicitly advocated openness to all these teachings. Dōni was sensitive to the human potential for intolerance, perhaps in reaction to the strict Nichiren atmosphere in which he grew up. In one talk, he warns Shingaku members that to accuse Buddhist teachings of *itan* (heresy) before comprehending them deeply is an act deserving of punishment.[50] Dōni never fully relinquished his Buddhist perspective, even though his talks on the Way *(dōwa)* were typically centered on Confucian moral ideals. Indeed, the multireligious tone of Dōni's talks gave the Confucian-oriented Kisui misgivings, as he indicates in his preface to *Old Man Dōni's Talks on the Way (Dōni-ō dōwa)*:

> I have carefully examined this book and it has profound significance. However, originally the Old Man [Dōni] was born in Kyoto and grew up in the middle of the busy marketplace of the merchant families; he had little time off from working at his livelihood. Therefore, [his wisdom] does not come from reading and studying books. It is simply that he has penetrated the innermost meaning of human nature and the principle. In the style of speaking that he ordinarily uses for instruction, he draws analogies or borrows odds and ends recollected from his experience—the words of Shinto, Confucianism, Buddhism, and Taoism, as well as the skills of all kinds of masters, foolish talk and daz-

zling rhetoric,[51] and the songs of village children. He uses [this style] in order to elucidate the innermost meaning of the teaching of the sages—the living, direct truth.

I only fear that those people who hear his talks or read his books will be carried away by the profundity and mystery of the meaning and fail to act with respectful gentleness and kind sincerity, or that they will become attached to such phrases as "transmitted separately outside the teachings and not dependent on words"[52] and "books are the dregs of the sages."[53] Even if they have any "energy to spare after carrying out [their obligations],"[54] they may simply abandon reading the books of the sages and worthies in favor of this. Or else when they grasp the great principle of the "Unity of the Three Sages,"[55] they may jumble up the conduct of Buddhist clergy and lay people, or they may insist on the theory of seeking for the deep and clarifying the subtle and look down on renowned Confucians and distinguished monks. Or yet, they may entertain themselves with foolish talk and dazzling rhetoric, and fail to know the teaching of "conquering the self and returning to propriety."[56] Or perhaps they may put this book in their bosoms and teach others indiscriminately, failing to discern the way of learning for the sake of oneself. None of these are the true intention of the Old Man.[57]

Kisui attempts to present Dōni's colorful discourse as grounded in the Neo-Confucian learning of "human nature and principle"; in fact, Dōni's critical religious experiences were shaped by Buddhism. In his public talks, Dōni depicted the fundamental aims of the Buddhist and Confucian teachings as identical, but in his own life of faith he drew inspiration mostly from Nichiren and Zen traditions. But Kisui's fears that Dōni's teachings might be misconstrued were not entirely groundless. In 1794, a few years after the Kansei edict against heterodoxy was issued, the head of the Hayashi college issued a statement to the effect that Dōni's Shingaku was not orthodox Chu Hsi learning.[58]

Dōni's importance in the history of Shingaku does not derive from his religious openness, a trait that all Shingaku believers shared to varying degrees, but from the stylistic innovations that he introduced into Shingaku preaching. Since he had already sought and found his own kind of enlightenment, Dōni already possessed a certain maturity and confidence when he joined the community. We are not told that he underwent a "discovery of the original mind" or that he received a formal acknowledgment from his Shingaku elders (in addition to the Zen master's approval he had earned earlier). Evidently Dōni's appreciation of the "Wondrous Dharma" was considered equivalent to the Shingaku version of enlightenment.

Because of Dōni's religious maturity, and undoubtedly also because of his speaking skill, in 1779 Toan sent Dōni off to Edo to substitute for himself in a teaching commitment. Thereafter, Dōni perfected his colorful approach to Shingaku preaching, and his listeners steadily multiplied.

Before long he established a regular schedule for talks on the Way and children's lessons *(zenkun)*. Two years after his arrival in Edo, he built a meetinghouse that provided greater seating capacity than had hitherto been available. The house, called Sanzensha, became the headquarters of the Shingaku movement in the Kantō area (eastern Japan).[59] Around the same time, Dōni began to lecture upon request to various domain lords and their families who stayed in Edo. He reportedly had speaking engagements of this kind daily, in addition to his Sanzensha schedule.

Dōni made further inroads in teaching members of the samurai class than any of his predecessors. Shibata Minoru tells us that the lords of about ten domains (along with their families, household staff, and retainers) heard Dōni's talks on the Way and underwent Shingaku training.[60] I noted in Chapter 1 that Dōni was employed for several years by the shogun's councillor Matsudaira Sadanobu to teach day laborers at their gathering place in Tsukudajima in Edo, and that he based some of his sermons on the government proclamation (issued in 1711) designed for the moral edification of commoners. By the time Dōni was at the height of his preaching career, the shogunate and the Shingaku movement shared, each for their own reasons, the goal of teaching ethics to common people in both urban and rural areas. However, Shingaku advocacy of officially approved ethics predated Dōni's and his disciples' employment by the authorities. As early as 1773, Toan had unobtrusively inserted a summary of the 1711 proclamation into his *Principles for the Assembly of Companions (Kaiyū taishi)*.[61] The edict emphasizes the same points that Toan taught: the importance of the Five Moral Relations,[62] working hard, and not lying or gambling. Modern critics often charge that Shingaku lent itself out to serve the needs of the shogunate, but what has been taken for expedience was at least initially a matter of conviction. Toan and his followers spread conventional moral ideals long before shogunal officials asked them to do so.

As Dōni's preaching reputation grew, he traveled extensively, teaching not only in the eastern part of Japan, but very often in his home area of Kyoto. His lecture itinerary for 1796 is probably typical of the pace he kept during the height of his popularity:

second month Sanzensha (Edo)

fourth month Kōshinsha (Edo)

seventh month Kamifusa Kisarazu (midwestern Chiba)

eighth month Kōfu (central Yamanashi), Nagoya, Mino-Ōgaki (Gifu), Kyoto

tenth month   Izushi, Sekinomiya, Toyooka, Yujima, Wadayama, Ikuno, Fukuchiyama, Tanba no Kashiwahara, Sasayama, Hachi-jōshin and Kameyama (mostly today's Hyōgo prefecture)

This particular circuit was followed by a teaching stint in five Osaka meetinghouses during the early part of the next year; Dōni apparently did not return to Edo until the seventh month of 1797.[63] Dōni's teaching journeys ultimately extended to twenty-seven domains and led to the establishment of twenty-one meetinghouses under his supervision.[64] His and his followers' activism supposedly also helped bring about a decrease in the rate of infanticide in some of the impoverished rural areas in which they taught. Shibata suggests that this improvement was not simply the result of the preachers' moral exhortations; they also employed concrete relief methods, such as passing around collection boxes to gather funds for the children of the destitute.[65]

Nakazawa Dōni died in 1803. We are told that his passing was mourned by people of all classes, from domain lords to common folk. He left few writings behind, but several of his sermons were recorded by followers. A series of talks that he gave in Osaka was printed under the title *Old Man Dōni's Talks on the Way (Dōni-ō dōwa)* in 1791. It was followed by sequels in later years, along with Dōni's version of *Early Lessons (Zenkun)*.[66] A number of unpublished records of Dōni's dialogues with his disciples are also extant.[67]

The Shingaku Community

Toan's effort to organize the Shingaku group was an important factor in the development of the movement in the latter half of the eighteenth century. An early step in this direction was his creation in 1773 of *Principles for the Assembly of Companions (Kaiyū taishi)*, a set of guidelines for members, which remained in effect even after Toan's death.[68] In the guidelines Toan discusses qualifications for three leadership positions: director *(tokō)*, deputy *(hojinshi)*, and assistant *(kaiyūshi)*. He uses the language of the *Analects* to indicate the proper attitude of a leader:

> "The gentleman is broad and impartial,"[69] "conciliatory but not accommodating,"[70] and "gathers together with others but does not create factions."[71] You should look up to this teaching of the Sage [Confucius] and regard harmony in the Five Relations as your principle.[72]

Toan elaborates on these themes by means of Chu Hsi's commentary:

> The commentary says: " 'Broad' means universal. 'Partial' means biased. Both mean being affectionate and generous with others. However, 'broad' is public-minded whereas 'partial' is self-centered.[73] . . . 'Conciliatory' is not having a contrary attitude. Being 'accommodating' is having the intention of being fawning and partial.[74] . . . To dwell with many people in harmony is called 'gathering together with others.' However, [the gentleman] does not have the intention of being fawning and partial, so he 'does not create factions.' "

> You should reflect on these three phrases. In a group gathering there is no self. . . . The teaching of the Sage is simply to remove the self. [These phrases] mean that you should be careful not to violate the teaching of the Sage.[75]

In short, one of the essential qualities of the Shingaku director was the ability to promote harmony in the group. Moreover, although Toan organized his members in a fairly hierarchical manner, he did not believe there should be any fundamental differentiation between leaders and followers. Together they made up a community of "friends" striving for a selfless way of life. As he puts it, they were not to compare themselves with others, thinking "I am valuable," "I am senior," "I am wealthy," or "I am knowledgeable." The choice of a director was thus determined not by merit but by practical considerations: "Appointment of the director is not a selection based on virtue or learning. . . . You should assign this job to a person who has few obstacles [to fulfilling the task]." In the same vein, Toan viewed as unqualified candidates the following:

> Persons who do not have permission from their master, father or mother.
> Persons who are busy with their family occupations.
> Persons who have few [people to act as] substitutes for them.
> Persons who have few friends and intimate acquaintances.
> Persons who are not suited.

Toan goes on to admonish that the deputy and the assistant be chosen according to the same criteria. All three leaders were ostensibly coordinators and facilitators rather than spiritual authorities: "The persons in these ranks are not what is known in the world as 'senior scholars.' Their purpose is simply to assist the advance of learning and to facilitate good communication."[76]

Toan's view of the Shingaku movement was essentially communalistic. He frequently stressed the importance of cooperation among "friends" or "companions." In 1782 he directed that "the elder companions, [who have been in the group] until now, cordially take care of and lead [the other members]" and that all followers "become truly gentle and harmonious, and more and more affectionate and kind [with each other]."[77] Two years later he requested that "on occasions of leisure, members from city and country, from far and near should endeavor to visit each other and to have friendly relations."[78]

The lecturers *(kōshi)* were most instrumental in the actual spread of Shingaku. They were responsible for moderating discussions, presenting lectures and talks on the Way, and teaching children—both at the meetinghouses in their own regions and at large. Beginning in Toan's time, the lecturers were formally required to have had the experience of "knowing the original mind"; they would be officially certified by a Shingaku master. The "elder companions" *(rōyū)*, however, may have been the most influential members of the Shingaku community. They helped out with lecturing and other teaching tasks, and also served as role models and counselors. Along with the directors and lecturers, the elder companions decided who was qualified to teach, which books were appropriate for study, and whether proposed lecture tours were suitable. In the *Group Rules (Shayaku)*, Toan regularly advises members to proceed with a course of action only after consultation with the directors and elder companions. On one occasion, he implies that his own decisions about rules for the Shingaku community were reached in consultation with the elder companions.[79] To be sure, Toan had final authority, but the tone of his guidelines indicates that some decisions in the Shingaku community were reached by consensus, at least among the senior members.

Becoming a student of Shingaku required not only commitment to its teaching, but commitment to the group itself. The members were undoubtedly aware of belonging to a unique group and many felt pride in upholding its standards. Sharing a particular code of conduct encouraged the members to identify with the group.[80] Consultation with the elder companions, fellowship with peers, and responsibility for younger members were all ways of furthering this communal spirit. Commitment was also reinforced by reverence for Shingaku leaders, both past and present. This attitude was cultivated through master-disciple relations and regular ritual events honoring the deceased. According to his *Memoir,* Toan and other disciples commemorated Baigan's death every year through acts of purification, ceremonial offerings, and inspirational talks. The same practice was adopted in memory of Toan after his death, and the members of each meetinghouse also paid their respects to the deceased founder of that house in a yearly ceremony. Similar memorial ceremonies are carried out to this day by Shingaku associates.

The rites performed on these occasions were not elaborate.[81] On the day in question, all the leaders and members associated with a particular area would gather at the meetinghouse early in the morning to begin preparations for the ceremony. An image of the deceased was displayed on the main wall, candles and incense sticks were set up, and a sample of the deceased's calligraphy was displayed. Food was ceremonially offered: soup made with tofu, *chameshi* (rice boiled in tea), persimmons, and numerous other dishes. Once the master of ceremonies had completed the offerings, members of all ages and both sexes passed through the room to bow and pay their respects. After the ceremony, the "housemaster" *(shashu)* or lecturer would give an appropriate homily; there might also be group contemplation or interchange between teachers and disciples. In conclusion, the members would sit together on a *tatami* mat and express their feelings of appreciation for the deceased.

Traditionally, clothing for these occasions was made entirely out of hemp, and the food, consumed after the rites were concluded, was simple and sparse. Visits to the grave of the deceased were included in the day's activities where feasible. Toan himself visited Baigan's grave throughout the year and conscientiously "reported" the condition of the community to his late teacher.[82] It is likely that his own successors, beginning with his children Wa'an and Kisui, adopted similar practices. The Shingaku "community" thus included not only the living, but also the spirits of its founder and late leaders.

The meetinghouse was usually occupied by a housemaster. Some housemasters were simply members who offered the use of their private homes for local meetings. Ishida Baigan had set a precedent by using his own home in Kyoto as a place to lecture and to meet with disciples. This house had been called the "Schoolhouse," or *Kōsha* 黌舎, by his immediate disciples, who continued teaching there after the founder's death. Evidently taking his inspiration from Baigan's system, Toan institutionalized the meetinghouse, or *kōsha* 講舎; the term now added the connotation of *kō,* "association," to that of "school." *Kōsha* was a common term in Tokugawa period discourse. As Tetsuo Najita points out, it implied a community of faith and trust, an "inner space" where members of a group could meet and discuss among themselves:

> The compound kōsha refers to a community with a shared spiritual purpose—*kō*—gathering at a prescribed place—*sha*. . . . The beginnings of this tradition can be traced as far back as the seventh and eighth centuries when Buddhist holy men gathered in small groups to study scriptures and hold prayer meetings. In time, however, the kō came also to be used as a proselytizing vehicle . . . that permitted ordinary individuals to summon other faithfuls to gather in a communal setting to recite, for example, holy words from a sacred text—*nenbutsu kō*.[83]

The idea of a group of people who share the same religious vision is encompassed in the Shingaku understanding of *kōsha* as well. Najita goes on to remark that the "Shingaku kō" expanded into a network of "moral confraternities of like-minded faithfuls" whose principle of trust was centered on the charisma of the founder, Ishida Baigan.[84] Another important factor involved in the shaping of the Shingaku "communal space," however, was the Shingaku teaching itself. Baigan's idea of "knowing the nature," reformulated by Toan as "knowing the original mind," provided an ongoing focus of faith for his followers. The group activities of the Shingaku "faithfuls" consisted mostly of study, discussion, and cultivation of this ideal.

It is worth noting that the ideograph for *kōsha* includes the same character, *kō* (Ch. *chiang*), that is found in the term *chiang-hsüeh,* the Chinese custom of "learning through discussion" that was revived in the Sung by Chu Hsi. In this tradition, small groups of students gathered together to discuss ideas and learn with their teacher.[85] Such methods were also used in private academies in Tokugawa Japan. Toan and his colleagues were probably not aware of the history of the term *chiang* in Chinese Neo-Confucianism. But they shared the same spirit of group learning and discussion that imbued the Neo-Confucian vision—a vision that they saw themselves as representing in a later age and on a simpler level. The Shingaku understanding of its enterprise included both the idea of commitment to a religious group, which is the thrust of the term *kō* in Japanese, and the sense of academic activity, especially group discussion.

The Shingaku *kōsha,* then, was a community of faith and an association of learners, but it was also a physical structure with spatial boundaries. Each house was given a name, usually based on a classical allusion, that was formally acknowledged by the movement's leaders in Kyoto. Beginning with Gorakusha in 1765, Toan initiated a network that would eventually include over 180 schools.[86] He himself founded the three Kyoto meetinghouses that would become the administrative centers of the movement: Shūseisha (House of Cultivation and Improvement), Jishūsha (House of Timely Practice), and the headquarters, Meirinsha (House of Clarifying Moral Principles).[87] The structure of the Shingaku meetinghouse is described by Bellah:

> The *kōsha* was usually a rather simple building 25 to 30 mats in width. A large part of it was taken up by the lecture hall. In the center of this was a *tokonoma* [alcove] usually containing some auspicious motto. Above and to the right of this was a small shrine to Amaterasu, and above and to the left the likeness of the master of the *kōsha,* the *shashu.*[88]

Drawings of Meirinsha published in 1790, however, indicate that it was divided into several small rooms. At the entrance to each hung a plaque on which was written, purportedly by Toan himself, the purpose of the room: "Counsel," "Polishing," "Beginners," "Good Guidance," "Training," and "Women."[89] It is likely that for lectures the sliding screens were opened up, as they are on occasion in many Japanese houses, so that the smaller rooms could be made into a large hall.

The founder, Ishida Baigan, had not distinguished between lectures for the public and guidance for his close disciples; the Schoolhouse had been used for relatively small gatherings of committed people. But as Shingaku approached the peak of its popularity at the end of the eighteenth century, its talks and lectures were often attended by large numbers of people. In such cases the presentations were not necessarily held in the meetinghouses, but at prearranged places with greater seating capacity.

The meetinghouses functioned to some extent as small, private schools, though not as routinely as the private academies and *terakoya* (the so-called temple schools) of the time.[90] Shingaku schools had no ranking or merit system, and no fees were required in exchange for the instruction that was provided. The basic purpose of the institution was to provide a meeting place for members; Toan frequently calls the houses "support meeting places" *(kaihojō)* in his writings. In rural areas, the meetinghouses also served as stopping-over points for itinerant lecturers. Instruction of the public, both children and adults, took place in the meetinghouses, but in contrast to the instruction in many *terakoya*, the content of the teaching was invariably moral rather than practical in nature. Later in the period, some meetinghouses received the support of local authorities and, in this sense, may be compared to moral instruction schools *(kyōyusho)*.

Toan set standards regarding the physical structure of the meetinghouse building, the activities for which it could be used, and its daily schedule. Meirinsha and the other important houses provided models for those in more remote areas. Some of Toan's concerns about the establishment of meetinghouses are contained in an undated memorandum that he addressed to followers who proposed to set up houses. One of his primary concerns was financial; he insisted that funds for the support of the meetinghouses should be collected only from people who were already part of the community of faith: "It is all right to establish a meetinghouse if you are able to come up with the expense money for it by making agreements only with people who are deeply committed [to Shingaku]. It is absolutely forbidden to solicit people who have no special commitment."[91] Toan was attentive to the ethics of money in general, perhaps partly because of his merchant background. In a set of guidelines dated 1781, he implies that members should avoid borrowing from each other but urges them, in the event that they do borrow, to be precise in repaying such loans; the admonition was repeated in a circular sent out three years later.[92] More important, members were not to engage in transactions outside the community. Toan repeatedly forbade receiving either loans or gifts, or lending money to others.[93]

The policy of refusing fees for teaching, which originated with Baigan, appears to have been strictly maintained, at least during the eighteenth century. Shiraishi Masakuni claims (perhaps in reference to later Shingaku practice) that gifts or offerings from the public were accepted on special occasions, namely the five seasonal festivals *(sekku)*, as was common in other educational institutions.[94] However, Toan's instructions could be interpreted as proscribing precisely such practices. In fact, Shingaku meetinghouses and activities in urban centers were generally financed during this period by members themselves (a few houses received assistance from interested individuals in the neighborhood). Many Shingaku members worked full-time at their various occupations and the more successful evidently had at least modest sums at their disposal. Even in rural areas, core members had sufficient income to maintain the movement's local activities; meetinghouses in country villages were often financed by village headmen or other prominent private citizens, or else by two or three members who pooled their funds.[95] The meetinghouse itself was not infrequently the residence of a committed follower.

From Toan's perspective, in any case, money received from the uncommitted was unacceptable. The memorandum quoted above expressly forbids soliciting resources for the building of meetinghouses from nonbelievers. In another undated notice, which was probably posted in the meetinghouses, Toan explains the rationale for his policy of not receiving anything in exchange for teaching: "Because I give these lectures by way of learning, I strictly refuse to accept any admission charge or thanks offering. My intention is to discuss as much as possible, even if just with one person. My hope is that those who so desire will participate without the slightest hesitation."[96] It is said that when people pressed Toan to receive a gift for his services, he stubbornly refused, claiming that he was simply transmitting Baigan's teaching and was not a professional *jusha* (Confucian scholar). He would reiterate the implications of the above remarks, namely that poor people who desired to study would be effectively excluded if he accepted admission fees. It would seem that Toan's general audiences, in contrast to the regular Shingaku activists who supported the meetinghouses, included a significant number of people who had little or no income.

The question of fees was not an idle issue; when Toan was just establishing himself as leader of the Shingaku movement in the 1760s, his unusual practice of not accepting fees or gifts aroused the suspicions of the Kyoto town magistrate. Toan defended himself by saying that he had sufficient money for his living expenses, since he was retired and had no other financial responsibilities. "I am provided with clothing and food by my son Gen'uemon [Wa'an], so I have no other needs."[97] There is no reason to doubt Toan's claim; the Uekawa ran a prosperous business and probably generated enough profit to help support the movement as well.

The number of times Toan defended this policy and cautioned the members about it indicates that it was a matter of grave concern to him. The no-fee tradition was integral to his faith insofar as it had been established by the founder Baigan. But Toan's sensitivity about this matter also suggests that the practice of refusing fees was the exception rather than the rule for teachers in the mid-Edo period. The refusal to accept money signaled the peculiar social status of Shingaku preachers. Without the support of an ecclesiastic establishment like that enjoyed by Buddhist or Shinto teachers, or the educational qualifications to present themselves as authentic Confucian scholars, Toan and his followers carved out their own unique position as ostensibly disinterested mediators of learning. Toan was well aware of his ambiguous social identity. On one occasion he was asked why he wished to be cremated rather than receive a "generous burial" as might be accorded a Confucian scholar. Given the cremation tradition followed by his own family as well as the need to conserve land, Toan replied, it would be inappropriate to receive a full burial as if he were a "real" Confucian scholar: "A person who has virtue and sets himself up in the position of a Confucian scholar is a special matter. I am not in that position."[98] He felt that only persons who have "from childhood done nothing other than study the [Confucian] Way and establish the teaching" and who thereby serve as models for other people may be considered Confucian scholars. From Toan's perspective, it was acceptable for these *jusha* to insist on the Confucian view and allow themselves a full burial.[99] However, he added,

> I am not in that position. I have quit my livelihood and am infirm, so I happen to be free; together with persons who have the same commitment, I speak about the Way at the same time as I study it. Since I cannot just exist, I read Japanese [*kana*] books and gather people together; people believe I, too, am an ordinary Confucian scholar, so they have doubts [as to why I practice cremation]. [Yet] I am an average retired person.[100]

Here Toan hints at the confusion with which he and other Shingaku speakers were sometimes regarded; he was often at pains to prove that he was not a paid teacher or a professional *jusha*. Underlying Toan's modest disclaimers of scholarly status, however, was also a critical attitude toward the world of professional learning. In the same discussion of burial practices, Toan goes on to fault Confucians who insist on correct ritual for the dead while neglecting filial piety and deference in their relations with living family members.[101] Both Baigan and Toan disapproved of Confucians who were versed in the classical texts but lacked the inner wisdom of the "true" scholar.[102] The ensuing chapters will show that the conception of learning as an internal endeavor was a central premise of the Shingaku teaching.

3

TESHIMA TOAN'S
TEACHING

THE IDEA that Teshima Toan sought to convey to his listeners through the entire range of his educational activities was the importance of "knowing the original mind" *(honshin o shiru)*. This concept has its locus classicus in *Mencius* (6A:10): when one ignores the good impulses that arise naturally in one's own mind and violates universal values such as humaneness and rightness, one "loses" the true mind. The idea of the innate goodness of human nature as formulated in the phrase "original mind" continued to play a prominent role in later East Asian thought. Chinese Buddhists adopted the term to describe their own understanding of the enlightened mind; it became especially common in Ch'an discourse. But it was through the work of the Neo-Confucian thinkers of the Sung period that the idea of the original mind as conceived by Mencius was more fully developed and related to the task of self-cultivation. This tradition of mind-learning influenced Japanese Neo-Confucian spirituality in turn. In reality, Sung scholars such as the Ch'eng brothers used the term "human nature" (Ch. *hsing*) more frequently than "original mind," and Ishida Baigan followed suit. It was not until Toan's time that "mind" rather than "nature" became the trademark of the developing Shingaku community.[1]

Teshima Toan's reverence for past tradition and the ways of his predecessors is reflected in his conservative approach to Ishida Baigan's teaching. His emphasis on knowing the original mind was essentially a reformulation of Baigan's own teaching and Baigan's lifelong religious goal, "knowing the nature." In *City and Country Dialogues (Tohi mondō)*, Baigan uses the word "mind" or "heart" *(shin, kokoro)* almost interchangeably with "nature."[2] Toan's wholehearted adoption of "mind" along with the qualifier "original" was merely intended to clarify Baigan's message, since "mind" in its wider sense could be taken to include self-

51

centered levels of consciousness. Toan also felt that his unlearned listeners could grasp "original mind" *(honshin)* more easily than the less familiar term "nature" *(sei)*.[3]

The reason for Baigan's and Toan's concern with the nature or original mind was fairly straightforward: "Unless one knows the nature, one cannot follow the nature."[4] According to the *Doctrine of the Mean* (chapter 1), "to follow one's nature is called the Way." The ultimate goal of Baigan's teaching was the "Way" *(dō, michi)*, the moral tradition handed down by the ancient sages and Confucius. This goal is often defined as harmony in the Five Relations—the relations between ruler and subject, parent and child, husband and wife, old and young, and the relations between friends. The implications of knowing the nature or original mind were therefore practical and concrete. The internal religious experience of "knowing" was inextricably linked with moral living.

In Toan's works, knowing the original mind means finding a level of consciousness that is free of subjective conceptualizing tendencies and the "self" that they assume. The original mind is an awareness that is spontaneous and unselfconscious, beyond egocentric ways of thinking and feeling. Toan particularly emphasizes that the original mind is "empty and mysterious" *(kyorei)* or "mysteriously clear" *(reimyō)*. The phrase "empty and mysterious" (Ch. *hsü-ling*) was originally used by Chu Hsi to describe "clear virtue" (Ch. *ming-te*, J. *meitoku*) in his commentary on the *Great Learning*.[5] As de Bary points out, the use of the word "empty" or "vacuous" *(hsü)* in Sung Neo-Confucian texts is ambiguous; it can have either negative or positive connotations.[6] In Chu Hsi's comment on clear virtue, it takes on the positive sense of an "openness" unimpeded by selfish desires; because of the innate clear virtue, one's perception of universal moral truth can be unclouded and impartial.

It is partly in this sense that Toan uses words like "empty" to characterize the original mind. He repeatedly stresses that to say the original mind is empty does not imply that nothing is there.[7] Words like "clear (virtue)" and "empty" also symbolize that the original mind is beyond verbal description, it is "both there and not there."[8] In this sense, the terms are essentially what Wayne Proudfoot calls "placeholders": their primary function is not to give a precise description of the ideal realm, but to signify that it is intrinsically beyond any description at all.[9] In *Notes of a Conversation*, Toan says that "a person's original mind is an empty, mysterious thing; as there is no way to describe it, it is said to be 'clear' and given the name 'clear virtue.' "[10] In another dialogue he reiterates: "The virtue of a person's mind cannot be represented [by any form], nor does it manifest any sound or smell; there is nothing by which to indicate it, so it is called 'empty.' Calling it empty does not mean there is nothing there."[11]

The use of negatives to "name" rather than describe the realm of the original mind is a common feature of Shingaku discourse. Terms such as "no mind," "no self," "no thought," "no body," and "no eye" as well as the somewhat more descriptive phrases "no calculation" and "no discrimination" abound in the writings of Toan and Nakazawa Dōni. The phrase "no mind" (*mushin*, Ch. *wu hsin*) has a long history of usage in East Asian religion. It originated in philosophical Taoism and was adopted by Chinese Buddhists to refer not to the absence of a mind, but to the "true mind" that is free from all illusions or wrong views. In the Sung period, the term was reinterpreted by Neo-Confucian thinkers to mean an unself-centered state in which one has "no mind of one's own."

Toan appears to follow this tradition in his understanding of no mind: it is a moral self-transcendence whereby one identifies the entire creation as one's self and acts accordingly with love for all. As Baigan had before him, Toan re-evokes Ch'eng Hao's doctrine of "having no mind" and forming "one body with Heaven and earth and all things."[12] When speaking about the original mind, Toan often refers to this sense of unity between one's self and the cosmos. It seems to be an ethical communion with mystical overtones, based on traditional substance metaphysics.[13] Speaking of the joy of knowing that one has found the Way, Toan holds forth on this mystical union between the self and the universe:

> One is so vast that one extends to the limits of heaven, one is so free that one enters even into the tiniest particle; whether making the flowers bloom, the birds fly, or the fish swim, even the flowing of the four seasons, the pealing of thunder or the vibration [of the earth], there is nothing that "I" do not do. Life has no end, the causes of death are destroyed, and even if [the true self] is placed in cremation, "fire cannot burn it, nor can it drown in water."[14]

Underlying this feeling of union with all things is the message of liberation from selfishness: no mind means no selfish mind. In the same way, when Toan uses the term "no self" (*muga, ware nashi*), he is not necessarily alluding to the Mahayana Buddhist doctrine whereby all beings literally have no abiding self-nature of their own. He may be referring simply to the attitude of centering on others rather than oneself.

The other negative terms in Toan's talks (many of which, unlike "no mind," are not common in Ch'eng-Chu Neo-Confucian texts) also "name" the ideal rather than describe it. "No thought" (*munen*), for example, is a Buddhist term denoting freedom from illusory thoughts or subjective conceptions of reality; as Toan points out, "no thought" is the same as "right thought" (*shōnen*), which is one of the disciplines of the Eightfold Path in Buddhism.[15] " 'No thought,' he reminds us, "does not mean having no thoughts."[16] The term "no body" (*mushin, mi nashi*) had a peculiar appeal for Toan. In his view, once one knew the true nature of the mind, the nonexistence of the body was a matter of course. He did not mean by this that the physical body would literally cease to be. The Japanese word *shin* or *mi* has connotations of "self" or "person" as well as "body." Toan's understanding of "body" resembles that of some of the Zen popularizers to whom he turned for inspiration. "Mind," namely, the enlightened Buddha-nature, and "body" are key terms in Shidō Munan's writings. "Body" denotes not simply the physical body, but also the internal impurities that hinder enlightenment and cause suffering, in other words, "the egotistic, unillumined mind-body of an individual in his unenlightened state."[17] For Toan as for Munan, "destroying" or forgetting the body ensures the realization of the original mind, or "enlightenment." Toan believed that when one has "no body," evil (the domination of the person by self-centered needs) becomes impossible. "When the body obscures the original mind, that is evil. If one has no body, how can one do evil?"[18] Suzuki Shōsan also provided Toan with some ammunition for preaching about "no body." In his preface to the 1778 reprint of Shōsan's early work *A Safe Staff for the Blind (Mōanjō)*, Toan remarks: "Suffering is close at hand in the attachments of the body. However, it is not difficult to forget the body. If one so wishes, one can definitely forget the body. It is not difficult to give up one's own evil."[19] In reply to a disciple who inquired about the meaning of a poem in the same text, Toan states that, although it is not something he can easily put into words, "when one knows the original mind, one has no body."[20]

The Shingaku leader used another Zen term, "no eye" *(me nashi)*, in much the same way as "no mind," "no self," and "no body." The image of the eye represents the "I," the self-centered ego that sees itself as subject in a dualistic relationship. In *No Eye: A Word to the Wise*, a commentary on Ikkyū's *Water Mirror (Mizu kagami)*, Toan simply redefines "no eye" as the original mind that is free of self-centered calculations.[21] His vocabulary contrasts subtly with that of an earlier Buddhist commentator on *Water Mirror* who identifies "no eye" with "innate nature" *(jishō)*—the original Buddha-nature of sentient beings, which is free of deluded passions.[22]

More than any of these terms, however, Toan relied on a phrase of his own coinage to characterize the original mind: *shian nashi,* "no calculation" or "no premeditation." "Calculation" (Ch. *ssu-an*) was not a common category in Chinese Neo-Confucian discourse, but the Japanese word *shian* was in general use in the Edo period. Satō Naokata, a fervent advocate of the learning of the mind transmitted by Chu Hsi and Yi T'oegye, uses the word *shian* in his discussion of "mastering quietude": "In settling important matters, one should carefully premeditate *(shian)* and then act. That 'premeditation' is quietude."[23] This usage of *shian* has connotations of pondering, deliberating, reflecting carefully, or planning. The word itself apparently had no negative connotations; indeed, Naokata uses *shian* in a positive way, insofar as he identifies it with the ideal of quietude.

From the perspective of a Zen master, however, "premeditation" or "calculation" could have very different implications. The act of pondering or premeditating could be seen as blocking one from the ideal state, rather than being directly conducive to it. In the opening passage of *The Mysterious Record of Immovable Wisdom (Fudōchi shinmyōroku)*, Takuan uses the word *shian* in his discussion of the proper attitude for successful sword-fighting:

> Although you see the sword that is coming to strike you, if you do not rest your mind on it, but keep the rhythm of the sword that is about to strike, without thinking about striking back or harboring any calculations or discriminations *(shian bunbetsu)*—if the moment you see the swinging sword, you do not rest your mind on it in the least, but take the advantage just like that, seizing hold of your opponent's sword, you will wrest toward yourself the sword that is about to pierce you, and it will become, contrarily, the sword that cuts down your opponent.[24]

In response to a query regarding where one should "place" one's mind, Takuan implies that it is best not to concentrate it in any particular spot, but rather to let it pervade the whole body and respond to things freely as they arise.[25]

> If by some chance you decide to concentrate it in one place, it will be taken up by that one place and its function will be deficient. If you calculate [where you are going to place it], you will be taken up by the calculation, so without harboring any calculations or discriminations, you should throw your mind into your entire body and, without your fixing it here or there, it will totally fulfill its function in those various places.[26]

More than a century before Toan, Takuan characterized the original mind—the mind of "no mind"—as free of calculations:

> When one thinks something in one's mind, insofar as discrimination and calculation arise, we call it the mind of the "existent mind." What we call the mind of "no mind" is the same as the aforementioned original mind: it does not harden or become fixed, it is the mind in which there is neither discrimination nor calculation nor anything at all.[27]

Toan and Dōni not infrequently combined the word *shian* with *bunbetsu*, "discrimination," as does Takuan. In *No Eye: A Word to the Wise* Toan uses such expressions as "calculation and deluded discrimination" and "the deluded thinking of calculation."[28] "Calculation and discrimination" also appears several times as a set phrase in Toan's *Essentials of*

Good Guidance (Zendō shuchi) and *Master Teshima's Oral Instruction: Talks for Beginners (Teshima sensei kuju banashi [shonyū banashi]).*[29] Nakazawa Dōni uses the same expression in his *Talks on the Way.*[30] Both teachers also employed the similar expression, "consideration and discrimination" *(shiryo bunbetsu).*[31]

Although Takuan's Dharma talks are listed in the Shingaku book dealer's catalogue, Toan does not refer to them extensively in his own writings. Takuan contributed along with other seventeenth-century Zen popularizers to the pool of religious ideas from which Shingaku drew, and his language about the original mind free of calculation clearly previews the sense of Toan's later teaching. With Toan, however, "no calculation" becomes a set phrase, a distinct category of religious experience. In fact, Toan claimed to be the first to teach no calculation as an ideal in itself.[32] Of course, no calculation may also be seen as an elaboration of Baigan's teaching. In *City and Country Dialogues,* Baigan uses such terms as *shichi,* "self-centered knowledge," and *shiryo,* "(self-centered) consideration." He warns that the nature cannot be understood through one's private thinking; attempting to do so is like using a lamp behind closed doors instead of the natural sunlight.[33]

For Toan, *shian* meant unnecessary mental activity centered on one's own needs. Occasionally he used the word in a neutral sense to denote a kind of planning or pondering preliminary to action in general. Thus, one of Toan's questioners wonders whether acting without *shian,* without premeditation, might in fact lead to wrongdoing.[34] Sometimes Toan employs another word, *hakarai,* which has nuances of "arranging," "contriving," "discussing," in the same way he uses *shian:* "If there is anything at all toward which [the mind] is directed, that is human arranging [*hito no hakarai*]. When the arranging ceases, one grasps [the original mind] for oneself."[35]

At other times, *shian* is depicted as a temptation or self-justification that leads to wrongdoing, as in the case of a thief who decides to loot at the scene of a fire or a person who devises excuses for not getting out of bed in the morning.[36] *Shian* also connotes anxiety or preoccupation with regard to one's actions. The idea of over-anxiety as a form of self-centeredness is a Confucian theme that goes back to Mencius' story of the man of Sung who destroyed his corn crop out of an excess of zeal (2A:2). In *Reflections on Things at Hand* (Ch. *Chin-ssu lu*), a well-known Neo-Confucian compilation included in the official Shingaku curriculum, Ch'eng I says: "If one seeks anxiously, that is merely selfishness."[37] The following interchange between Toan and one of his followers illustrates the same theme in terms of calculation:

Someone asked, "I was greatly dejected to part with my old mother who was over eighty years old. However, when I thought about it again, I felt very happy, as if I had been relieved of a burden, that she had not met with any disaster, and that I, too, for my part, was well and [therefore] could see her off. So, although it appeared as though I had deep consideration for my mother, it seems that my attitude was 'It would be nice if she would depart early, while I am still well!' In spite of myself, I find it difficult to distinguish: was this an excess of deep regard, or was it, to some extent, the feeling that she was a bother?"

[Toan] answered, "This was not thinking, how nice if she would die, but just worrying too much. For that reason, you could have the feeling after she died that you were relieved of a burden. These are all attitudes of the ordinary person [*bonpu*]. The reason for this is that you worried too much and calculated in various ways—'If I die before she does, she may grieve, or she may be in distress.' You were constantly calculating about various things that had yet to happen. That is the realm of the ordinary person."[38]

Calculating is thinking too much. In *Notes of a Conversation*, Toan cites a passage from the *Analects* about a certain Chi Wen-tzu, an overly cautious man who is criticized by Confucius for thinking too many times before deciding on a course of action. The extra thinking constitutes calculation; it is no longer the natural thinking of the original mind.[39] Elsewhere Toan illustrates the same point with an anecdote about one of the Ch'eng brothers, who made a rough count of the pillars of a building, then counted them a second time more carefully and arrived at a different number. When a disciple counted the same pillars, he came up with the same number as the original rough count. "If we consider it this way," concludes Toan, "errors are always [made] after putting forth calculations."[40] Toan also identifies *shian* with cunning *(takumi)*, a defect that Ch'eng Hao mentions in *Reflections on Things at Hand:* "Being selfish, one cannot take purposive action to respond to things, and being cunning, one cannot be at home with enlightenment."[41]

The classic illustration of the ideal of spontaneous moral action is Mencius' example of the instinctive human response to a child about to fall into a well (2A:6). One's natural goodness may be hindered by considerations of self-interest. Fung Yu-lan's comment on this passage offers a workable definition of *shian:*

> Let us suppose . . . that, instead of immediately acting, the person concerned pauses to think about the matter. There may then arise in him such thoughts as "gaining the favor of the child's parents" or "the praise of neighbors and friends." These thoughts, being no longer straightforward reactions, are therefore selfish.[42]

However, the boundary between thinking in a spontaneous, natural way and calculating in a selfish manner is not necessarily clear-cut. According to Toan, the shift from spontaneous thinking to self-centered calculating is a gradual process, a kind of progressive stagnation. *Omoi,* the thought of the original mind, and *shian,* calculation, are the same in origin; when the original mind becomes caught up in things, its thought process is distorted and produces self-centered calculations.[43] It is only at this point that calculation and spontaneous thought can be distinguished. Toan describes the process of distinction:

> When the initial part of the arising thought is distorted,[44] that is called both "self" and "selfish calculation." For example, when your parents say "do this," the thought "no" does not arise from the beginning. At first the thought "yes, I will" arises. But just at that point, "no" emerges; it distorts [the thought of the original mind] and does not let you move. That is called selfish calculation. However, the original mind's thought is straightforward, so it tries to advance, [insisting that] it is wrong to say "no." But the calculation once again suppresses this; it rationalizes the wrong in various ways and distorts the thought of the original mind. Even so, the thought of the original mind is averse to forced reasoning and tries with all its might to advance.[45]

Toan conceived of calculation as stagnant and sluggish in comparison with intuitive thinking *(omoi)*—like ice in relation to freely flowing water. The thought of the original mind, as Toan expresses it, is "one step behind," slower than the original mind itself; self-oriented calculations, being "congealed" distortions of thought, are still farther removed from the original mind.[46] The original mind, spontaneous thinking, and self-centered mental activity constitute a progressive ossification of consciousness. Because of the subtlety of this conception, Toan was repeatedly asked to elaborate on the difference between calculating and thinking. On one occasion he responded,

> If one has to go somewhere on an errand and thinks, "I'll go," that is not calculation. But if one becomes lazy and thinks, "I just don't want to go today," that is calculation. . . . After you know your original mind, you can discern that the thinking that I mentioned first is like flowing water, and calculation is like frozen water. Then, it is a question of preventing that water from freezing. Unless you know the original mind, you cannot possibly prevent the water from freezing.[47]

Calculation is not only self-centered but self-conscious. If one is aware of good as "good" or of joy as "joy," one is not experiencing the awareness of the original mind but consciously intellectualizing—a state of mind that an innocent child would be incapable of.[48] If one knows that one is not intellectualizing, that knowledge itself is intellectualization. Natural thinking is an unselfconscious activity, whereas calculation is a stagnated, rigidified form of thought, so "one inevitably becomes aware of it in one's mind."[49] Self-conscious cogitation appears to be directed by an inner subject or ego, whereas the original mind cannot be experienced within a subject-object framework. The Shingaku founder Baigan learned this point when he presented his understanding of the nature to his own teacher, Oguri Ryōun: he was advised to abandon the "eye," or viewpoint *(me)*, which was still engaged in observing that nature.[50] Toan gave similar advice to those of his disciples who presumed to know their original minds:

> You all constantly claim that now you see without calculating or you hear without calculating. [You may believe that] . . . you alone are free of calculations, but in that case you retain the viewpoint from which you regard yourself as free of calculations. While you are still a beginner, just as you are, earnestly penetrate the fact that you have no self. Here, too, at first you will have the viewpoint from which you regard yourself as being free of calculations, but if you do not enter [the realm of no self] at that point, you will never be able to abandon the viewpoint of no calculation.[51]

There are parallels between Toan's ideas and those of Munan, Shōsan, and Takuan, but in his discussions of no calculation Toan turns most directly to Zen master Bankei for inspiration. Toan shared with Bankei the attitude that one should teach religious truth in accordance with the needs of ordinary people, and like Bankei, who reduced his message to one key idea—the mysteriously clear, unborn Buddha-mind, Toan also concentrated his teaching on a single theme—the uncalculating original mind. Toan's remarks in *Notes of a Conversation* and *An Explanation of No Calculation (Shian nashi no setsu)* along with scattered references in other texts demonstrate the special regard that he had for Bankei. *Notes of a Conversation* is conspicuous in this respect. The questioner has just been reading Bankei's vernacular Dharma talks and is struck by the similarity between Bankei's ideas and those of Toan. When he requests an explanation of the exact relationship between the two teachings, Toan simply equates no calculation with Bankei's "unborn" *(fushō)*—the pure Buddha-mind that is innate in every human being and beyond dualistic conceptualization.[52] According to Toan, "unborn" is another name for the original mind, for as Bankei said, it "transcends thought, clearly distinguishing all things."[53] Toan also identifies the unborn with the Neo-Confucian notion of "clear virtue," the innate goodness with which each human being is endowed by Heaven. One of the premises of this equation is that Bankei's spiritual journey had begun as a search for the meaning of clear virtue and ended with the discovery of the unborn.[54]

In *An Explanation of No Calculation* again Toan relies directly on Bankei to explain the original mind of no calculation:

> The world is all of the same nature; Buddhists call this "Three Worlds, One Mind."[55] Thus the two teachings, Confucianism and Buddhism, differ greatly in their respective methods of teaching and guiding [people], but the point at which they ultimately arrive is a single principle.

Consequently, the realm of no calculation and the unborn Buddha-mind are the same. . . . The original mind with which one is endowed at birth by one's parents is empty and mysteriously clear. Bankei called this emptiness "unborn." "Unborn" means "not a single thought is born"[56]—it is the place where everything is thoroughly understood and judged before thought arises. Therefore he also called it "mysteriously clear."[57]

In his sermons, Bankei frequently uses the term "mysteriously clear" (*reimyō*) to describe the unborn.[58] The operation of the Buddha-mind is mysterious: it has the power to know, to be "clear" about things without becoming involved in intellectual discrimination. One of Bankei's favorite ways of explaining this wonderful power (*tokuyō*) of the unborn Buddha-mind was adopted wholesale by Toan to illustrate his own concept of the nondiscriminative realm. When one is in the realm of no calculation, all things can be distinguished without effort: "When each of you remains without thinking anything at all, you do not take the sound of a crow cawing out back to be the chirp of a sparrow, nor mistake the bark of a dog for the meow of a cat."[59]

Toan's teaching of no calculation thus closely resembles the idea of transcending discriminative thought that Bankei and other Zen masters taught. To be sure, Toan believed that freedom from calculations and discriminations is integrally related to moral selflessness: for Toan, no calculation essentially meant no self-centered thoughts. But in the Mahayana Buddhist world-view that gave rise to Zen, the transcendence of dualistic discrimination is also a prerequisite of true moral activity. The selfless work of the Bodhisattva is mandated by the realization that conventional thinking is based on illusory categories of subject and object. Once these categories are transcended, one inevitably acts in accordance with the empty nature or intrinsic interdependence of all beings.[60] True compassion is therefore the direct result of a transformation in one's epistemological framework.

Nevertheless, there is little evidence that Toan advocated the full implications of the Buddhist concepts of nondiscriminative thinking and "no self." Despite his identification with Bankei and other Zen thinkers, Toan's world-view appears to be based on substantialist metaphysical premises; in other words, he believed that reality is, or includes, substances of enduring self-identity.[61] Although Toan expounds on the transcendence of discriminative thinking in his talks, he says less about the empty or transient nature of the phenomenal world. The thrust of his "original mind" and "no calculation" may simply be the notion of unselfishness, couched at times in mystical terms. These ideas resonate strongly with Mencian and Neo-Confucian traditions of mind-cultivation.

Although Toan uses the language of Bankei and other Zen masters to characterize the original mind that is free of calculations, his own teaching was not necessarily an accurate version of Zen. Bankei himself has little to say on the subject of "emptiness" or "dependent origination" in his sermons, so it is not surprising that Toan shows no awareness of these ideas in his own appraisal of the Zen message. The Shingaku leader took Bankei's words at face value, on a level where there is indeed common ground between the "unborn Buddha-mind" and Chu Hsi's "unobstructed clear virtue." Both are imparted to all human beings at birth, and both involve a pure, spontaneous awareness that manifests itself in moral living. As Toan says; "Bankei's [teaching] was merely to have people return to the state in which they were born. Since our teaching is also like this, I say it is the same."[62] Furthermore, although Bankei himself may not have understood his final discovery of the unborn in terms of "clear virtue," some of his language regarding the unborn reflects the very text he was loath to recite as a boy—the *Great Learning*, probably accompanied by Chu Hsi's commentary. Just as the unborn Buddha-mind is pure and clear, yet able to distinguish and manage all things, the clear virtue of the original mind is pure and unimpeded, yet able to respond to all things.[63] This terminological similarity facilitated Toan's identification of his own ostensibly Neo-Confucian teaching, "knowing the original mind," and Bankei's idea of abiding in the unborn Buddha-mind.

Bankei's role in shaping Teshima Toan's thought, along with the contributions of Munan, Shōsan, and Takuan, confirms Shingaku's debt to the popular Zen developments of the early Tokugawa period. Conflation with native Zen was a marked feature of the process by which Neo-Confucian mind-learning was indigenized in Japan. Indeed, the same process is illustrated by Zen influence on Shingaku praxis.

4

KNOWING THE ORIGINAL MIND

TESHIMA TOAN urged all his followers to experience the realm of the original mind for themselves. But the Shingaku master was especially concerned with guiding his most committed disciples to attain this internal knowledge. The popular image of Shingaku as a group of morality preachers traveling the countryside to share their message publicly with anyone on request is belied by the instructions Toan gave to his followers both in the *Group Rules* and informally on a number of occasions. In regulatory documents sent out in 1781 and 1784, Toan stressed that introductory talks for those who have just joined Shingaku are "not to be given as regular talks." Introductory talks are intended only for people who have seriously committed themselves to the learning of the mind; such people should be taken aside as a group to hear the talks. Toan hastens to add that the talks are not a secret teaching, but they might be misunderstood by the uninitiated.[1] Toan further forbids his new members from sharing his guidance with even their next of kin; only those who are dedicated to the Way can benefit from his words. Toan was concerned to preserve the image of Shingaku as a serious discipline: "When people who are not committed hear this, they reduce it with one sweeping judgment, saying this thing called Shingaku teaches matters of no importance. Therefore, as a rule, you are forbidden to speak of this outside [the group]."[2] Toan may have feared that if the special teaching that he introduced in the internal sessions were made public, it would be misunderstood, much as it had been in the 1760s, when his activities were investigated by the Kyoto city magistrate. He wished to ensure the acceptance of his growing movement by government authorities and by society in general.

The instruction reserved for committed members of the Shingaku community is recorded in several extant texts (that were not designed for public circulation). The teaching contained in these texts was generally known as *zendō*, "good guidance" or, simply, "guidance." The guidance talks deal with a narrower range of concerns than the other "discussions" *(zadan)* or the more free-wheeling "talks on the Way" *(dōwa)*. Their principal topic is the contemplative practice that members used to stimulate and reinforce insight into the original mind. Toan's disciples recorded the guidance that he gave on five different occasions and drew up a compilation called *Essentials of Good Guidance (Zendō shuchi)*. This collection sheds much light on Toan's approach to advanced religious education—and on that of later Shingaku teachers, for the work was apparently intended as a kind of teaching manual for Toan's disciples.[3]

After Shingaku teachers gave a public lecture, listeners who showed serious interest in pursuing the Way were invited to receive additional instruction. Many, though not all, of the Shingaku guidance talks were aimed at people who had recently committed themselves to the quest of the original mind.[4] Toan usually opens his "talks for beginners" with some general remarks on the nature of mind-learning. He says that Shingaku training is a form of learning by which people come to know their minds. But it is not the only one: Shinto, Confucianism, and Buddhism are all ways to understand the mind. (He implies here that Shingaku is distinct from all three teachings.) All paths, however, teach that it is difficult to find one's true mind. All the more extraordinary, Toan reminds his listeners, that Ishida Baigan successfully worked out a way in which even uneducated people could find their true natures. The Shingaku teaching can be grasped quickly, as long as one has faith.

Shingaku life involved a commitment to join with others along the path of spiritual cultivation under the guidance of a teacher. Toan frequently refers to the initial commitment in his writings as "establishing one's resolve" or "setting one's heart [on the Way]" *(kokorozashi o tatsu,* Ch. *li-chih).* This common phrase in Neo-Confucian discourse denotes making up one's mind to pursue the learning of the ancient sages and to enact it in one's daily life.[5] For Toan, the act of setting one's heart on the Way is the first step of faith: "Today, if people set their hearts on learning, no matter who they are, it is difficult to say that they have no faith. To set one's heart is itself to have faith in the Way."[6]

Although Shingaku teachers routinely propagated the ethical values of trust and loyalty, usually in terms of relations between retainers and domain lords or apprentices and masters, faith or trust *(shin)* also signified a specific religious attitude adopted during the early stages of the Shingaku path. New members needed to believe in the possibility of knowing their original minds, and they had to dedicate themselves to actualizing that possibility. Their commitment was signaled by submission to a teacher.

In *Clearing Up Doubts about Knowing the Mind,* Toan compares the process through which beginners overcome their initial doubts and place themselves under the authority of a Shingaku master with the relationship between a doctor and a patient. Once one has surrendered oneself to the doctor's care, one is well on the way to "recovering" the original mind. The doctor's healing arts are the method by which a person can come to know the true mind: "The patient learns how to know the mind by following this system and, in the end, by means of the system goes beyond it."[7] The learning of the mind thus could not proceed until a relationship of trust was established between the disciple and the master. Keeping this faith is difficult, Toan warns, because teachers of perfect moral caliber, like Confucius, are no longer available; compared to the Sage's immediate disciples, people today have less confidence in their teachers and are therefore less likely to commit themselves firmly from the outset. Faith is something that develops gradually and cannot be forced. On one occasion a disciple asked:

> "It's not that I don't believe in the Way. But it is rather difficult to solidify my commitment to believe. What should I do in order to develop greater commitment?"
>
> [Toan] replied: "Your commitment does not develop because you do not see the Way thoroughly. However, you cannot reach the point of being thorough all of a sudden, either. . . .
>
> "Faith is not something that develops as you wish from the beginning. Each time you actually have an inkling, you should know that you are making progress."[8]

Ultimately, faith itself increases as one "sees" the Way (or the original mind) more clearly:

> In faith there is extreme shallowness as well as depth, and as Master Ch'eng says, this "shallowness" and "depth" depend on whether or not one sees the Way clearly. In accordance with how accurately one sees the principle, one can carry it out in one's person as well. This is the important point; one must first penetrate deeply the nature that one has perceived. . . . It seems to me that to actualize this point thoroughly is the art of advancing in faith.[9]

Toan compares the deepening of the Shingaku adept's faith to the different levels of illumination received from a lamp, the moon, and the sun. In the beginning, he says, "you simply feel the desire to know your original mind and, when your faith is aroused, you ask for guidance in seeing and hearing."[10] At this point, one's spiritual level is still immature; one has had no serious doubts. If a "slight wind" comes along, the light of one's relatively weak commitment will be blown out. As one begins to question things more deeply, one develops a greater capacity for faith. Toan believed that doubt and faith were integrally related: one could not gain enough faith to discover the original mind until one had experienced severe doubt. We are reminded here of Zen master Hakuin's "great ball of doubt": "At the bottom of great doubt lies great awakening. If you doubt fully, you will awaken fully."[11] In Shingaku, too, one develops and then confronts one's doubts. After undergoing the training of "seeing and hearing," one reaches the interim level of "moonlight"—a brighter, stronger understanding that cannot be extinguished. Occasional problems may dim that light, but one's faith will grow stronger as one trains further, and at a certain juncture the "sun" will emerge. At this point, one's doubts will be dispelled; all will suddenly become clear.

Toan stressed to new members the importance of abandoning their preconceptions. All concepts of the mind, even the "learning of the mind" itself (Shingaku), must be removed before one can train in earnest. Toan began one session by asking whether the adept had already engaged in any type of learning (gakumon); the follower was advised to set aside such knowledge, whether it be Neo-Confucian or Zen learning. The disciple had best become an infant, a tabula rasa, who would answer the master's questions simply "according to what one can see and hear."[12] At this fundamental stage of training, any form of learning, whether Confucian, Buddhist, or Shinto, would hinder one's progress.

A prominent theme in Toan's discourses for beginners is the idea that the universe consists of two basic aspects: form and formlessness. He affirms that, on the one hand, everything that has visible form, whether an ashtray or a human body, is a metamorphosis of the earth. Heaven, on the other hand, is the basis of everything that is empty or invisible. It is the sky and the space around one's body; it is also the mind. The mind is not part of the tangible realm.

> When most of you think, "this is the mind," or "that's the mind," you are probably imagining that the mind is a thing inside your chest that reflects: "I'll go, I'll come back; shall I do this? I'll do that." Those [thoughts] are all shadows of what is seen and heard; they are the mind of speculation, the "deluded mind."[13]

The source of these "shadows" is the "smaller mind" of calculation and discrimination; these mental habits develop because of poor education or other pernicious influences as one grows up. Only the true mind occupies the realm of "empty heaven."

At the same time, Toan claims that the earth and the forms created from it are also "empty."

> For even though one has form, if one is not aware of it, isn't that being empty? Thus, when you are quite asleep you are empty, but when you open your eyes, you don't feel that your body is gone—you instantly create this preconception (shian).[14]

Similarly, he argues that if one focuses on one's stomach, at that particular moment one completely forgets one's hands; and if one concentrates on one's face, both hands and stomach will vanish from one's consciousness. Since one is normally unaware of the individual parts of one's body, they are "empty." From Toan's perspective, we are creatures of forgetfulness: we "live by forgetting—this is the reason for emptiness."[15] Even when one deliberately tries, it is impossible to remain constantly aware of one's body. Furthermore, when one is totally engrossed in an activity, such as viewing cherry blossoms, one forgets the body naturally: one becomes lost in the object and, thus, "empty." From the perspective of this experience of no self *(ware nashi)*, the body is simply an "empty gourd."

Faced with the difficult problem of conveying an experience that, by his own estimate, was not entirely communicable through words or rational analysis, Toan devised a program of "experiential education" for his disciples. Its aim was to deepen the students' awareness, so that they would be able to identify an inner state of which they had never been fully conscious.[16] The trainees were told to ask themselves: How am I seeing and hearing, if "I" (my self, my body) am not here? This question epitomizes Toan's approach to knowing the original mind. In the guidance sessions, he conducted one-on-one dialogues with his followers in order to help them experience the point of the question for themselves. At first he would interrogate the disciple centering on the objects of two senses, sight and hearing. He would bring out an object, often a fan, and ask the disciple to identify it. After receiving the simple reply "it is a fan," Toan asked the disciple what saw the fan. The answer, "My eyes saw it," did not satisfy the Shingaku master. He would point out that one is not ordinarily conscious of seeing by means of one's eyes. To answer that one's eyes see the fan indicates that one has been through an intellectual process in which one recalls that one has eyes, the organs that are responsible for seeing.

The same exchange would be repeated centering on a sound, often produced by striking something. How does one hear the sound? Only a "small man," admonishes Toan, would answer that he hears with his ears. It is not the eyes and ears that see and hear: there is another "master" *(aruji)* who is responsible for these functions. A verse by Zen master Munan is quoted to emphasize the point: "The ears do not hear, the mind does not hear, the body does not hear. You should realize that That is hearing."[17] Thus, it is not one's ears, nor one's body, nor even the discriminative mind that controls the function of hearing. This may be demonstrated, says Toan, simply by ordering oneself not to hear: one discovers that the functions of the body are not really under one's control after all. Toan interpreted the involuntary nature of sense perception as evidence of a "larger" mind. Analysis of the operation of the senses served as a method for helping students grasp the existence of the original mind. "What sees is not in one's abdomen *(hara)*, so what hears isn't either. What hears is somewhere else."[18] Toan recommended that the beginner first understand these two "masters"—the agents of sight and hearing.

On one occasion, after Toan took out his fan and the disciple spontaneously identified it (without trying to calculate the "right" reply), the fan was brought forth again and the query repeated. When the student answered, "It's still a fan," Toan rejoined:

> No, that "still" is no good. There is something [in you], which is attached to the previous fan, that says, "He's taking out this thing that I already know," so the word "still" comes out. As an experiment, try asking a child of about three or four. No matter how many times you take the fan out, the child will say nothing but "fan." Therefore, the word "still" comes, after all, from calculating.[19]

The response that the mind knows the fan was also shown to be inadequate. The mind that appears to the disciple to "know" the fan is not the true mind but an illusory, temporary construct that has developed from years of distorted mental habits: "To be sure, the mind, too, undoubtedly knows, but what sort of thing is that mind? Is it round or is it square? Is it red or is it white? Is it inside the body or outside the body?"[20] Here Toan seems to draw on the same pool of discourse that informed Hakuin's response to the question of how to "awaken" one's mind: "Is it mind that asks this question? Is it nature? Do you call it spirit, or do you call it soul? Does it reside on the inside, on the outside, or in the middle? Is it blue or yellow, red or white?"[21]

For Toan, too, it was important to establish that the mind in the true sense could not be described or "located" inside the body. He often expounded on the misconception that the heart or mind is some sort of round thing ("ball of fire") inside the body, using a number of metaphors to demonstrate that neither animate nor inanimate beings contain such a spirit entity. If one cuts open a cherry tree, for example, one does not find anything in it that resembles a bud or a flower, even though it is the "nature" of cherry trees to produce buds and flowers. If one guts an eel, slicing it lengthwise down the middle, it continues to wriggle, but nothing like a "mind" pops out. The wriggling of the eel and the perennial blossoming of the cherry tree demonstrate the existence of an intrinsic, internal nature—a "mind"—but it is formless, not physically located inside those things. In the same way, there is no soul *(tamashii)* or spirit in the human body, despite legends (sometimes depicted in plays) concerning the emergence of fire-ghosts *(onibi)* from people's bodies when they die.[22]

Once he had established the formless nature of the mind, Toan would proceed to the next question: "In the moment you are looking at this fan, what is the mind? There can be only one answer."

"The fan is the mind," the member would finally reply. In other words, at the moment of encounter, everything that one ordinarily regards as an object in relation to oneself as subject is actually the mind itself. The object becomes the subject. "If one knows one's mind, all things of creation are one's mind," says Toan. The nature of the original mind is simply to reflect whatever comes into its purview. If Toan now repeated his original query, "What knows that this fan is a fan?" he would receive the correct reply: "The fan knows."[23]

The same approach was applied to all of the "Six Roots," that is, the five senses and consciousness. Step by step, Toan led his listener through the succeeding stages of training.

"What hears this sound?"
"The sound hears it."
"That's good. What knows that it is a sound?"
"The sound knows."
"Good. What is the mind in that moment?"
"The sound is the mind."
"Good."[24]

Similarly, when one smells the fragrance of burning aloeswood, it is not "I" but the fragrance itself that knows there is a fragrance. In one talk, Toan interprets this point in Neo-Confucian terms.

"When we are not burning anything is there a pleasant smell in the nose?"
"No, there is none at all."
"That place where there is no smell is what is called 'empty' *(kyo)*. When someone comes to clean, [one's capacity to] know the foul odor instantly is 'mysterious' *(rei)*. In the same way, discerning that a pleasant smell is a pleasant smell and that a foul odor is a foul odor is what is called 'unobscured' *(fumai)*.[25] The passage in *Reflections on Things at Hand,* 'Open and completely unbiased, responding to things as they come,' refers to this point as well."[26]

In short, the spontaneous, impartial act of perception, in this case centering on the olfactory sense, is evidence of the original mind at work.

Having successfully demonstrated to his disciple the selfless nature of the function of smell, Toan would move on to the remaining senses. If hot mustard is placed on the tongue, the hot substance itself knows that it is hot: in that moment, the mustard is the mind. If somebody pinches one's body, the pain itself is the mind. If one thinks, "I was pinched" or "a needle pricked me," one is already far along in the process of mental analysis and therefore removed from the experience. Or, when it is cold and one puts on warm clothes and draws near a fire, it is not one's self, but the cold that makes one do these things.

After covering sight, hearing, smell, taste, and touch in this way, Toan introduced the last level of training, "consciousness" *(ishiki)*. He would take out different objects, such as a pipe and a fan, and ask which is longer and which is shorter. "The fan is shorter and the pipe is longer," would come the reply. The answer was simple enough; it was based on a spontaneous cognition and was unlikely to be affected by selfish calculations. But consciousness, in Toan's view, was the crucial stage of the discipline, for it was related to all the other senses. It was the sphere in which "the manager disposes of affairs."[27] He also speaks of consciousness as "the critical realm in which one moves toward 'making the will sincere,'" and refers to the analysis of the operation of the senses as "investigating things and extending knowledge."[28] Toan thus uses the language of the *Great Learning* to characterize the sequence of religious training. However, the Shingaku understanding of the program of the *Great Learning* differed significantly from the orthodox Ch'eng-Chu view. A brief description of the Neo-Confucian hermeneutical tradition concerning the "investigation of things" will clarify the Shingaku reinterpretation.

The text of the *Great Learning* outlines a series of phases of learning, beginning at the most fundamental level of personal cultivation and culminating in the establishment of worldwide peace. The cultivation of one's personal life involves the "rectification" or "straightening" of the mind, which in turn depends on "making the will sincere." In order to make one's "will" or "intention" sincere, one must first "extend knowledge" (Ch. *chih-chih,* J. *chichi*) through the "investigation of things" (Ch. *ko-wu,* J. *kakubutsu*). The extension of knowledge through the investigation of things is therefore the beginning of the learning process.[29] Chu Hsi rearranged and supplemented the commentary of the *Great Learning* in order to emphasize the primary role of investigating things and extending knowledge in the learning sequence. For Chu, "investigating things" meant investigating the principles of things.[30] The same enterprise is indicated in Neo-Confucian texts by the phrase "investigating principles to the utmost" or "fathoming principles" (Ch. *ch'iung-li,* J. *kyūri*). "Investigating" means trying to determine why things are as they are and what they should be;[31] in the Ch'eng-Chu tradition, it involved reading books, discussing with others, and dealing with daily affairs.[32]

The premise underlying this concept of "investigating" is that everything, including the human mind, is endowed with universal moral principles. Chu Hsi therefore advocated a dual approach to learning: cultivation of the internal moral sense combined with examination of the workings of human society and the phenomenal world. The moral understanding inherent in one's own nature would be articulated and refined through scholarly study of the classics and experience in the world of affairs. Eventually one would arrive at a thorough comprehension of unchanging principles. "Investigating things" was thus a means of confirming or disproving the intuitive impulses of the mind, which in itself was susceptible to distortion or obfuscation by harmful influences. The balancing of inner and outer sources of knowledge in this way would prevent the subjectivization and consequent fragmentation of moral standards. Since Chu Hsi believed that investigating principles involved reading classical Confucian works and digesting their content through discussion and careful deliberation, book learning was an integral part of his program of education. Without personally confronting, grasping, and reflecting upon the words of the ancient sages, students would lack clear, public standards by which to counterbalance their private perceptions of moral truth.

Overreliance on the authority of the mind as a source of moral knowledge is precisely the charge that Chu Hsi's followers leveled at Wang Yang-ming's later interpretation of the *Great Learning*. In contrast to Chu, Wang interpreted the extension of knowledge to mean "extending one's innate knowledge of the good" *(chih liang-chih)*; it did not mean gaining knowledge in an intellectual or scholarly sense. For Wang, extending knowledge implied perfecting the sense of right and wrong that is innate in the human mind. The process by which this was to be achieved, "investigating things," involved correcting the evil thoughts or desires that arise in the mind when one comes into contact with "things" —events toward which one's will is directed.[33] From this perspective, to "investigate" means to correct what is wrong. As Wang says, "to rectify that which is not correct is to get rid of evil, and to return to correctness is to do good. This is what is meant by investigation."[34]

Wang Yang-ming's interpretation of "investigating things and extending knowledge" was founded on his belief that there are no principles outside of the mind; essentially, he identified mind and principle. In his view, to ascertain principles by examining everything that one encounters, as Chu Hsi had advocated, would result in the separation of the mind and principles.[35] Wang believed that such a procedure would distract students from personal cultivation by causing them to attend to the "fragmentary, isolated details" of the various things to which they were exposed.[36] Investigating things should involve not researching the particular principles of external affairs, but rather purifying one's own mind of evil tendencies; one will thus perceive its innate principles clearly and make the right moral decisions in all situations. The emphasis in Wang's program is therefore on cultivating the capacity for moral spontaneity;

reading and discussing the classics are no longer essential to the process of investigating things.

Neither Baigan nor Teshima Toan refer in their discourses to Wang Yang-ming; they regarded the Sung masters as their mentors.[37] Nevertheless, in Shingaku "extending knowledge" and "investigating things" did not imply scholarly activities. In fact, these expressions (J. *chichi kakubutsu*) are not common in Shingaku writings as a whole. Baigan was once asked why he did not discuss the topic in his major work, *City and Country Dialogues*. By way of responding, he explained his view of the extension of knowledge:

> When you grow morning glories, if you put a bamboo or wooden support stake next to the vine, it will coil around that stake and flourish. Otherwise it will not be able to climb up. It is the same with wisteria and other such plants. Even in these things, one can see the extension of knowledge. The plant does not consciously will to coil and climb up; it follows the direction of the stake naturally. The nature of the plant, through which it grows and flourishes, is no different [from human nature]. Thus, the extension of knowledge occurs through what I know inside myself.[38]

In other words, plants as well as human beings have internal natures that are naturally endowed with all the principles they need in order to live properly. The extension of knowledge is simply the application of these inner principles ("innate knowledge") in the external realm. In the above exchange, Baigan's questioner further objects that perfect knowledge inheres only in sages and that we can work our way up to their standard only by completely understanding the principle of each individual thing, one by one. Here we have the Ch'eng-Chu view of "investigating things," according to which the mind alone is not sufficient as a source of moral principles.

Dismissing such objections, Baigan and his successors continued to emphasize the internal aspect of the extension of knowledge. When Teshima Toan is asked in his *Recorded Sayings* to explicate a passage about the investigation of things attributed to Ch'eng I, he makes no mention of examining the principles of things themselves.[39] Instead, he stresses the disposition of the mind as it encounters things. For Toan, the point of "extending knowledge and investigating things" was the same as his teaching in general: one must become free of the self and respond to all situations spontaneously "just as they come." The intuitive response is naturally the correct one, for it reflects one's good original mind. Affairs and objects or their principles are not themselves the focus of study; they merely provide occasions for looking into one's own mind. In Shingaku, "investigating things" or "investigating principles to the utmost" was thus essentially an internal procedure. The mind can be restored to its pure and selfless state without detailed study of external things.

Toan was not a scholar of Confucian texts, and he did not overtly take issue with Chu Hsi's interpretation of the program of the *Great Learning.* He shared the basic Neo-Confucian faith that unchanging principles are imbued both in human nature and in the cosmos and taught that, when one's mind is purified of calculations, "one becomes one with the principles that are inherent in all the things that one encounters."[40] Toan fully accepted the existence of universal principles in things themselves. Nevertheless, he did not stress the need for balancing mind cultivation with externally oriented study. In his talks and writings, the Shingaku leader concentrates mainly on the process of purification—removing calculations in order to reveal the innate principles of the original mind. The Shingaku approach has much in common with that of Wang Yang-ming, for whom investigating things also meant removing selfish impulses from one's mind and following its innate principles. Like Wang, Toan insisted that the fundamental source of moral wisdom was one's own mind: his "knowledge of the original mind" parallels Wang's "innate knowledge of the good." Both concepts are derived from Mencius' philosophy of the innate goodness of human nature. Moreover, in both Wang's and Toan's "learning of the mind," book learning is reduced to an auxiliary role in the process of self-cultivation. In Shingaku, however, the deemphasis on books was partly a pragmatic adaptation to the needs of its unlettered constituents.[41] In his talks Toan displays no sense of having diverged from Chu Hsi's position. He simply does not consider the issues in a systematic, scholarly manner; his aims are practical. In *Good Guidance,* for example, the Shingaku master leads his students, step by step, through the actual experience of "investigating." For the members, the object of the investigation was the process of sensation and cognition itself.

Toan accordingly used the rubric "investigating things and extending knowledge" to refer to the analysis of this process introduced in the guidance sessions. "Investigating" simply meant making an effort to realize the selfless nature of the sensory-cognitive experience; it involved looking at a fan, for example, and realizing that one's self is not the agent of that particular visual perception. It was not "I" who saw the fan, but the fan itself. After completing this "investigation" of sensory experience, the Shingaku adept would next enter the phase of training centered on "consciousness," or "making the will sincere." Here the aim was to make moral choices in accordance with the understanding one had gained from the preceding analysis of basic sensory experience. Toan compared this part of the learning sequence to the trigger release on a gun. It was the pivotal point that determined whether one would "hit the target," that is, make the right moral decisions.[42]

Toan assumed that the universe had an order that could be understood intuitively, without calculating or conceptualizing. Just as one instantly knows that a pipe is longer than a fan, he suggested, one can naturally know the truth of all complementary relationships: heaven and earth, hot and cold, master and retainer, and so forth. The truth is clear enough in simple sensory perception; one does not mistake the color black for the color white or a bell for a drum. But when it comes to a deeper kind of knowing, one's "small mind" can interfere, producing erroneous views: "If one does not serve one's master as master, even while seeing that he is one's master, that is because one does not comprehend this [principle of] long and short."[43] The hierarchical relations of all things have concrete ethical implications. Short things follow long things; good is "long," whereas evil is "short." To choose the long over the short is the Way. One need only learn to "transfer this simple operation of differentiating long and short to all things."[44] The intuitions of the original mind, which transcend the intellectualizing tendencies of self-centered consciousness, naturally conform with the moral order of the universe. Shingaku training at the level of consciousness meant learning to choose these original intuitions over the calculations. Toan considered this stage of learning critical because it had direct implications for action. Ideally, the student would become sensitized to the innate principles of good and evil, and make correct choices on the basis of those principles.

Many of the themes that Toan presents in his *Oral Address* to Shingaku beginners are repeated in *Master Nakazawa Dōni's Talks for Beginners*. This similarity is not unexpected, since Toan's guidance talks were used as models by his disciples. Like his teacher, Dōni used physical objects and gestures to convey his message. In order to demonstrate the nature of sensory perception, he would hit the podium with his fan and ask the audience how many blows were struck. He would then point out that while his followers were listening to him strike the blows, nothing existed except the sounds themselves. Or Dōni would raise the lens of a pair of spectacles from behind an open fan in order to simulate the moon rising over a mountain (from the audience's viewpoint). "Now, while you were looking at this moon," he would inform his followers, "neither Jirō hyoe nor Tarōhyoe, neither Ogin nor Osayo existed."[45] In other words, perception occurs spontaneously, without premeditation; the participation of a subjective self is not required.

Dōni had slightly more propensity than Toan to allude to Buddhist scriptures, but he transmitted the same points that Toan had standardized for the talks.[46] In one interesting aside, Dōni cautions his followers not to think lightly of the fan used in the guidance sessions. He suggests that the fan has a special function in Shingaku, like the *hossu* (horsehair whisk) used by Zen masters. The fan is useful in conveying the Shingaku message because "there is no such thing as being deluded by a fan" (whereas one might be deluded, perhaps, by verbal discourse). The sight of the fan presents the disciple with an opportunity to transcend the dualism of seer and seen—to glimpse the realm of the original mind.

Both Toan and Dōni stressed to the novices that Shingaku training was a contemplative discipline that ultimately could not be explained in words. In Dōni's Zen parlance, Shingaku is "a special transmission outside the scriptures, not founded on words and letters"; it is "a transmission of mind by mind."[47] Toan urged the members to persevere, even if they could not understand "what hears sounds" or "what sees the fan." If necessary, they could speak with companions who were more advanced along the path and who could provide assistance in mastering the contemplative discipline.[48] Dōni also exhorted the new members to persist in their quest and to be honest and humble.

> And those among you who have an idea, stay afterwards and try asking the fellow [Dōni] who gives guidance. Come tell me, whatever it is. I don't like the type who says, "If I tell you, you'll laugh." You must not be unwilling to admit defeat. Abandon your false pride, tell me whatever it is, and go home.
>
> If you have no answer, it is best to say that you do not. Once you do that, for my part I will say, "That is thus and so," and each time [this happens] you will come closer.[49]

Discovery of the Original Mind

At some point during the process of contemplative effort, the Shingaku student's understanding would "burst open." The individual would suddenly experience the "nonexistence" of the self directly, not just intellectually. This event was usually called *honshin hatsumei,* or *honshin o hatsumei suru,* "discovering the original mind"—often abbreviated to *hatsumei,* which literally means "make clear" or "bring to light." Occasionally Toan used other terms; near the end of one talk for new members, he identifies the initial insight into the selfless nature of the original mind as *hotsugo,* "awakening," and calls it "the beginning of enlightenment" *(satori no hajimari).*[50] The Shingaku leader often stated that the original mind, innate in every human being from birth, gradually becomes covered up by self-centered mental dispositions as a result of poor education and bad habits. I have translated *hatsumei* as "discovery" in order to bring out this sense of revealing or uncovering what has always been there.[51] The use of "discovery" also serves to distinguish *hatsumei* from *satori,* the moment of self-knowledge in Zen, which is usually translated as "enlightenment." Toan himself rarely used the word *satori* to refer to Shingaku discovery.

The first insight into the original mind often occurred unexpectedly.

Dōni describes the culmination of the "seeing" phase of training as follows: "If you go without sleep for two or three nights, set up a stick of incense in the dark, and gaze at its burning end, the moment you forget the thought 'What sees? What sees?' it will burst upon you."[52] Or, if one is concentrating on the operation of hearing: "Face a Buddha [image] and strike the wooden fish;[53] just when you've forgotten the thought 'What hears? What hears?' the 'Haa!' [of insight] will emerge."[54] These remarks might be taken to imply that the first insight into the original mind takes place while one is practicing the contemplative exercises described in the previous section. In fact, the exercises would not necessarily bring on the experience of discovery directly. They were designed to increase the beginner's receptivity to a new level of consciousness so that the discovery might occur more quickly. It is said that Toan deliberately initiated the guidance sessions in order to reduce the time needed for his followers to reach the initial awakening. According to the testimony of a Shingaku master called Sugiura,

> This "knowing the original mind" is an extremely important matter. In the time of Master Ishida, for three years or even five years, everyone engaged in contemplative practice, suffered, and then at length came to know [the original mind]. Then, as there were few who joined this school, Master Teshima deplored [the situation]. . . . He proposed to explain it himself so that all of you could quickly grasp the contemplative discipline.[55]

Although the participants in the guidance sessions gained insights during their dialogues with the master, in most cases the actual experience of discovery came about randomly. The purpose of the training sessions was to lead people as close as possible to a state of "religious vulnerability"—to have them open their minds to the possibility of the event, but not necessarily to bring on the discovery itself. Toan describes the process in the following way:

> Our teaching strips away students' layers of wisdom one by one. . . . When there is only one layer left, when the mind of faith is developed to the utmost, the time comes. Either one hears the sound of a bell, or is startled by the noise of a drum or a dog's bark, or one looks at a bird, or views blossoms. At that moment, one suddenly forgets that one last layer of skin, and sees and hears directly—this is the emergence of the original mind.[56]

The progression from insights gained in the course of contemplation to the actual discovery of the original mind bears some resemblance to the Rinzai Zen learning process. Akizuki Ryōmin, in a discussion of the significance of Chao-chou's famous *Mu* (Ch. *Wu*) koan,[57] touches on a similar distinction between meditative insight and enlightenment. When working on this koan, the adept concentrates the entire body and mind on the one word "Mu": the individual *becomes* the word "Mu." This identification engenders the realization that it is not "I" who is puzzling over the "Mu," but the "Mu" itself that is puzzling over the "Mu."

> Everything outside of the "Mu" disappears; at that moment, if you move your legs and walk, step by step, it is the "Mu" that is walking. . . . [This] is the *samādhi* of the word "Mu"; it is the manifestation of "Cosmic Consciousness" right in front of you.
>
> However, this is not yet enlightenment. It is nothing more than one type of Zen meditation. This meditation . . . bursts open in response to some sensation. For example, in the middle of his Zen meditation, Śākyamuni by chance saw the morning star. At such a moment . . . one has a sort of flash of intuition. That is "enlightenment." . . . Zen [students] call this "seeing into one's nature" *(kenshō)*.[58]

In a similar sense, the testing of the "Six Roots" of sensation and cognition was merely a contemplative method used by Toan. It could prepare the student to be receptive to the experience of the selfless nature of the senses and consciousness; but the discovery of the original mind itself could not be programmed. The force of the discovery experience, which was invariably brought on by a chance sensory or cognitive stimulus, derived partly from its unexpected quality. This involuntary quality, the sense that an insight results from factors beyond one's control, is a common feature of mystical experience.[59] It is characteristic of Shingaku "enlightenment," beginning with the founder Baigan. In one episode, Baigan was struck by the unity of the cosmos, human nature, and the moral principles of filial piety and deference. Later, after another year of unrelenting contemplative effort, Baigan was lying in a state of exhaustion when he suddenly heard a sparrow cry. The abrupt sensation prompted him to shed his final "layer of skin," the self. On both occasions Baigan felt a sense of harmony and ecstatic peace.[60]

Baigan's successor discovered the truth after practicing the discipline of contemplation for a period of about two years. According to his *Memoir,* after taking a bath one evening, Toan suddenly realized, "I am not wearing my *yukata* [cotton kimono]; my *yukata* is not adhering to me!" He no longer perceived a subject, "I," Toan, relating to an object, *yukata.* The *yukata* and Toan were one. Toan's realization was not yet complete, however. When he reported the insight to his old friend Saitō Zenmon, instead of approbation he unexpectedly received a great blow to the face (his teeth are said to have been loose for the next three weeks). This sort of interchange in association with the enlightenment experience is strikingly reminiscent of the "blows and shouts" method of Rinzai Zen by which masters virtually startled their disciples into enlightenment. In

Toan's case the blow had the intended effect of completing his break-through, which Baigan duly acknowledged.[61]

Accounts of the discovery experiences of some of Toan's disciples are also extant. In fact, the meticulous inclusion of the circumstances and date of this event in Shingaku biographies confirms that the first insight into the original mind was regarded as a vital juncture in Shingaku religious life. Toan's natural son, Wa'an, is reported to have found his true mind as follows:

> In former times, [Wa'an] studied under Master Toan and Master Tomioka, and he was not remiss in the contemplation of "fully pene-trating one's mind" and "investigating principles to the utmost." One night in the winter of Meiwa 2 [1765], he engaged in quiet sitting until the middle of the night, when in a flash he comprehended. In his heart he understood the statements that our former teacher [Baigan] heard the cry of a sparrow, that in his chest it was like a great ocean, and that he abandoned the viewpoint from which he was conscious of his own nature. Master [Wa'an] was nineteen years old.[62]

We are told little about the actual import of Wa'an's realization, except that he identified strongly with Baigan's experience of the nature as described in the founder's *Memoir*. As a spiritual role model, Baigan was still a living force for later generations of followers. Moreover, at least during Toan's time and in his immediate family, quiet sitting was evidently very much a part of the regimen that was thought to lead to the experience of the original mind.

Uekawa Kisui, Toan's adopted son, experienced his true mind in the course of a dialogue with his father:

> In former times, [Master Kisui] studied under his father, Master Toan. Day and night he devoted himself to putting into practice the theory of "investigating principles to the utmost" and "fully penetrating one's nature." Whereupon, when Master [Kisui] was nineteen years old, on the twenty-sixth day of the twelfth month, in the winter of *hinoto i,* the fourth Meiwa year [1767], he heard the sound of a bell at the break of day and experienced some insight. Thus, he went right to Gorakusha, had an audience with Master Toan, and related what he had grasped. Then Master Toan smiled. He explained all about a dialogue that Kusunoki Masashige had had long ago with a Zen monk while on his way back from paying respects at the Kasuga shrine in the southern quarter.[63] Even as [Master Toan] spoke, [Master Kisui] suddenly opened up and was enlightened. At this point, Master Toan acknowl-edged [the discovery]. In addition, he instructed [Master Kisui] that he must not neglect "preserving and nourishing."[64]

Here again, there are few details about the exact nature of the insight gained by Kisui. We are informed that the initial breakthrough was stimulated by a random sensory experience and that there was a subsequent exchange with a master in the course of which the "enlightenment" was completed. Toan's closing counsel to Kisui is similar to that which he himself had received from Baigan: further cultivation must not be neglected.

In both of the above accounts a Neo-Confucian expression is used to denote the contemplative practice that led to the mystical experience: "fully penetrating one's mind and investigating principles to the utmost" *(jinshin kyūri)* or "investigating principles to the utmost and fully penetrating one's nature" *(kyūri jinsei)*.[65] Toan did not use these phrases frequently in his talks, perhaps because they would not have been easily understood by his less-educated listeners. In the biographies, the phrases are used almost in a formulaic manner, rather than in the way in which they were understood by the Sung masters. The thrust of the expressions here is related to Toan's interpretation of the contemplative exercises of the senses as the "investigation of things" (a phrase that, in Ch'eng-Chu parlance, is roughly equivalent to "investigating principles to the utmost"). Evidently, the Shingaku formula "investigating principles to the utmost and fully penetrating one's nature" refers specifically to the contemplative discipline that beginners used to prepare themselves for knowing the original mind. In fact, in his response to the Kyoto city magistrate's inquiry in the 1760s, Toan uses the equivalent phrase "extending knowledge and investigating things" to refer to the contemplative practice that he had inherited from Baigan.

Although the particular experiences of Shingaku followers differed, even this brief overview of discovery episodes indicates common features: strenuous contemplation, a sudden insight often occasioned by a random sensory stimulus, and a sense of resolution of all doubts. The experience also included testing by a master, leading to a fuller realization and, at length, a formal acknowledgment of the validity of the experience.[66] The claim to have known one's nature or original mind was not accepted without a challenge. The three principal leaders of the movement during the eighteenth century—Baigan, Toan, and Kisui—completed their experiences only after interaction with their elders. With the exception of Wa'an's *Memoir,* all the accounts of discovery cited above include some reference to a formal acknowledgment of the experience.[67] Indeed, in his talks Toan repeatedly asked his followers to present their insights to a master or elder for approval. One had to undergo the experience oneself, but proper acknowledgment was required to ensure that it was valid. To neglect this step might lead to a mistaken understanding— what Toan calls an "absent-minded awakening" *(ukkari hotsugo* or *hōshin hotsugo).*[68]

The experience of the original mind was central to Shingaku life in a social as well as a religious sense. This is demonstrated by Toan's institution of the *Dansho,* or Admonition, a document that was conferred on adepts after they discovered their original minds. The content of the Admonition is concise and straightforward. It declares in no uncertain terms that members who have known their original minds will be strictly held to standards of conduct worthy of the founder, Ishida Baigan. Evil of any kind, in thought or deed, is enjoined; contravention will lead to being "disowned by our former teacher," in other words, to being expelled from the school.[69] An addendum urges the member receiving the Admonition to appreciate the blessings endowed by heaven and the shogunal rulers. The document was conferred soon after the follower experienced the original mind, in a special ceremony conducted before an image of Baigan and a sample of his calligraphy. Initially, these ceremonies were conducted only at Meirinsha.[70] The ritual was followed by a visit by the disciples to Toribeyama, where they reiterated their commitment in front of the founder's grave.

Disciples who had not received the Admonition were not considered full-fledged members. The conferral of the Admonition was a de facto system of certification; it functioned in much the same way as the seal of approval *(inka)* given to Zen practitioners as evidence of their enlightenment or the document conferred upon graduates of certain performing and martial arts schools. The receipt of the Admonition represented a critical juncture in the life of the Shingaku disciple; the individual was now entitled to religious education at a different level from the instruction given to beginners or the general public. Furthermore, from Toan's time only recipients of the Admonition were allowed to teach Shingaku publicly.[71]

The discovery of the original mind was thus the beginning of the disciple's serious pursuit of the Way. The conferral of the Admonition, which invited public recognition of this new status, was a sort of commencement that marked the entry of individuals into the Shingaku religious community and signaled their acceptance of the rules and responsibilities stipulated by the elders. The standards of conduct applied to those who had experienced the original mind were stricter than the requirements for the beginner or occasional student. The bestowal of the document in a special ceremony enhanced its function as a rite of passage. The disciple was now a true disciple of Baigan and Toan. Pledging commitment in front of the founder's grave served to reconfirm the new identity and to implant the member ritually within the "community of friends." Later, Toan drew up other documents and circulars that impressed upon members their responsibility to the group and its ideals. But the employment of the Admonition as a "certificate of discovery" was a relatively early step in Toan's transformation of his teacher's study group into an organized religious community; he used it to maintain control over the quality of Shingaku as it spread throughout Japan.

Before concluding this discussion of the Shingaku discovery experience, it is instructive to compare it briefly with the Zen and Neo-Confucian conceptions of "enlightenment" that may have informed it. The experience of enlightenment in Zen is, of course, based on a long tradition that goes back to the spiritual awakening of Gautama Buddha himself; "enlightenment" or "seeing into one's nature" is the first aim of Zen students. As in Shingaku, the nature or mind itself is considered to be the source of enlightenment; Hakuin said, "When you awaken, it is your own mind that is Buddha."[72] Zen enlightenment is an experience that each person must undergo alone; one cannot depend entirely on either the Buddhist scriptures or the words of Zen masters for assistance. At the same time, these aids are not completely eschewed; various *upaya,* or "expedient means"—especially koans and meditation—are considered conducive to enlightenment. But Zen *satori* is considered extremely difficult to attain. Bankei, for example, found the truth only after years of austerities, which brought him close to death.[73]

"Enlightenment" also played a role in the Neo-Confucian tradition, although a far less central one than in Zen.[74] As a religious experience, it involved a mystical feeling of harmony with the entire universe and the moral principles believed to inhere in it. The event could also include a sense of intellectual revelation. After a long process of study and reflection, guided by the aim of moral development, the individual might gain insight into a particular principle, "a sudden release," which was sometimes accompanied by considerable emotional intensity.[75] Appreciation of natural beauty often served to enhance such experiences.[76]

Ishida Baigan probably absorbed some Zen ideas and practices from his teacher Oguri Ryōun, but as de Bary notes, the Shingaku founder's experience typifies Neo-Confucian mysticism as it developed in the Ming.[77] The moral and aesthetic aspects of this tradition of enlightenment are prominent in the *Memoir* account of Baigan's experience. Toan seems rather to have been struck especially by the truth of no self or nonduality. His discovery account, unlike Baigan's, does not refer to his apprehension of moral values or the oneness of human nature and the cosmos. These themes could be construed as implications of his nondualistic apprehension of the *yukata,* and we know from his talks and writings that Toan was sensitive to these dimensions generally. Nevertheless, the insight singled out for inclusion in his biography—the realization that presumably impressed Toan most strongly at the outset of his career—was the truth of nonduality. The "Neo-Confucian" overtones of his experience remain in the background—forgotten or perhaps regarded as unworthy of inclusion.[78]

In fact, the practical features of Toan's and his disciples' discoveries closely resemble the event of "seeing into one's nature" in Zen. In both Shingaku and Rinzai, master-disciple interchanges played a pivotal role in the religious training that led to enlightenment. The teasing or testing to which Shingaku members were subjected, whether in guidance sessions or in other contexts, is reminiscent of the legendary confrontations between Zen masters and their disciples (though the Shingaku exchanges tend to be more subdued). Moreover, Toan's institution of the Admonition as a means of acknowledging the Shingaku disciple's attainment is comparable to the Zen certification system. In contrast, although Neo-Confucian students undoubtedly sought confirmation of their insights from teachers or older colleagues, such "enlightenment" episodes were not generally recognized in a formal manner, nor were they regarded as qualifications for teaching the tradition.[79] The occasional mystical experiences of Neo-Confucian scholars were never institutionalized in these ways, not even in the schools that most emphasized spiritual introspection.

Furthermore, the Shingaku discovery of the original mind was understood as the "beginning of virtue," the first step in a long process of cultivation. Although Neo-Confucian enlightenment was also conceived as one stage in a gradual course of self-improvement rather than as a final spiritual goal, the overall Shingaku sequence seems more closely related to the Rinzai conception of enlightenment. From the conventional perspective of the Zen novice, "seeing into one's nature" might appear to be an end goal to be sought diligently. But, in fact, the first insight was not necessarily the only one—many Zen masters underwent several enlightenments of different degrees of intensity.[80] Toan's contemporary Hakuin, who had a series of experiences himself, was particularly concerned with the continuous aspect of Zen learning. Just as knowing the original mind was only the beginning of Shingaku cultivation, "seeing into one's nature" was merely the first step in Hakuin Zen. In the latter system, enlightenment was nourished through a graduated training program based on a sequence of koans, most of which were intended for use after seeing into the nature.[81] Shingaku cultivation of the original mind (including the use of "koans") also took place after the initial discovery episode.

Shingaku "enlightenment" praxis thus bears a striking resemblance to Rinzai, though it also reflects certain strains of Neo-Confucian spirituality. Nevertheless, as noted in Chapter 2, Toan's teaching of the original mind is not based on the same philosophical premises as the Buddhist concept of enlightenment. Perhaps more important, the practical implications of Shingaku discovery were quite different from those of Zen enlightenment. The lifestyle of a dedicated Zen adept was normally ordered by the Buddhist precepts; it encompassed celibacy and vegetarianism, neither of which were adopted in the Shingaku community.[82] The discovery of the original mind also seems to have been easier to attain than Zen enlightenment. Indeed, the brevity of the period required by some Shingaku members to find their original minds provoked criticism by Buddhist clergy, who might spend decades in their own quest.[83] Many Shingaku followers achieved discovery within a few years of committing themselves to the Way; Toan found his original mind after about two years of study. He admits in one talk that the apparent facility of the Shingaku teaching caused outsiders to doubt its value, but within the community rapid progress was understood rather as a sign of strong faith.[84] Shingaku members did engage in strenuous contemplation and group study, but many followers were busy working people; the time they could devote to formal training was limited by practical exigencies.

Preservation of the Original Mind

In the guidance sessions discussed above, Toan aimed to have the members perceive in a nonsubjective manner. The "seeing and hearing" exercises prepared the Shingaku practitioner for a spontaneous insight into the original mind. Once the experience occurred, it became the basis for a deeper level of education intended to bring the "germ" of the original mind to full realization. Postdiscovery training was, in effect, a continuation of the process introduced in the beginners' talks, but it placed additional emphasis on the implications of discovery for the members' conduct.

Counsel for those who had discovered their original minds is recorded in the fourth and fifth talks of *Essentials of Good Guidance. Oral Instruction Immediately after Discovery (Hatsumei sokuji no kuju)* is identified in a title note as the teaching to be given when the Admonition is conferred upon members. *Oral Instruction for Persons Who Have Discovered [the Original Mind] (Hatsumei no hito e no kuju)* summarizes themes that appear in previous parts of *Good Guidance.* Both talks serve to reinforce and elaborate the material introduced to new members; Shingaku training after discovery was not dissimilar to that which preceded it.

After a discovery was reported, the teacher first checked whether the disciple had indeed mastered the six stages of comprehension. Had the individual understood how to (1) see without eyes, (2) hear without ears, (3) taste without a tongue, (4) smell without a nose, (5) feel heat and cold without a body, and (6) differentiate (for example, the length of an object) without calculating? In sum, had the member personally experienced that "I" am not responsible for bodily movement or action? Toan opens one postdiscovery talk with a paradoxical demonstration of the implications of no self:

A student and I met, and I asked him, "Is there anything here or not?"
He replied, "The old man [Toan] is here." At that point, I explained: If
you had replied that nothing was here, it would not be true. If you had
taken the view in your mind that nothing was here, on the contrary, it
would be because you had the "one thing," calculation. Now, you said
the old man is here; that is called "not one thing."[85] The reason is that
right now you are not you—you are the old man named Toan. I am a
youth of about twenty named Ichihyōe. Neither Toan nor Ichihyōe has
a self. If one has no self, there is only heaven-and-earth and all things.[86]

Before one experiences the selfless nature of the original mind, one feels a
division between oneself and others; this division can lead to resentment
and conflict. After discovery, the division vanishes, because the whole
world ("heaven-and-earth and all things") becomes "I"—this is the meaning of enlightenment *(satori)*.[87] The sun, moon, seas, grass, dirt, and
trees—the entire world—are now perceived as "my body." Toan equates
this vision with Ch'eng Hao's idea that "the humane person takes heaven-
and-earth and all things to be one body."[88] He also points out that if there
is "no body called 'I,' " there is no death; that is why Ikkyū said on his
deathbed:

> I will not die. I will not go anywhere. I will stay
> here. Don't ask; I won't say anything.[89]

Toan warns his listeners not to misunderstand the implications of discovery. He feared that some immature members might conclude: "I am
nothing at all," "I am empty space." This was not the message he intended
to convey.[90] For Toan, "empty space" is the invisible vital energy *(ki)* that
makes up the universe. "Heaven" or "the principle of heaven" directs the
vital energy; it is the subject or master of all things, including the movement of one's body. In the guidance sessions, Toan gave small demonstra-
tions of this point; on one occasion he asked a certain "Ichihyōe" to
stretch out his hands: "If you raise and lower them as if you were striking
a drum, trying like this to strike a drum or pound some rice cakes
(mochi) . . . don't you forget your body? The master called heaven is
using your body and its form and vital energy, so even though the body is
there, it seems as though it is not."[91] Ichihyōe's body is still present, but
the subject of his actions is not a self "inside" his body; it is a larger Self or
master. Similarly, when Toan twists Ichihyōe's hand, the pain is felt not
by Ichihyōe, but by the invisible master who "dislikes it and tells it to
stop." The same metaphor applies to the mind. Toan challenges his listeners to plan on deceiving him in some way; he questions them a
moment later, and they admit that they "felt bad" while intriguing against
him. The conclusion is that immoral acts, such as deception, "twist" the
original mind: the inside of the mind hurts and one feels bad. Toan
quotes from Bankei to support his argument: "Our parents give us only

the unborn Buddha-mind at birth, but we turn it into a fighting demon, hungry ghost, or beast."[92] "This 'turning into,' " remarks Toan, "is the twisting of the original mind"; one must strive not to twist it.[93]

After ascertaining that the student had truly understood the nature of the original mind, Toan would introduce the main theme of postdiscovery guidance: preservation. The initial experience of the true mind was conceived simply as a first step, and a tenuous one at that: "The extent to which each of you has known the original mind is like barely peeping at it through the eye of a needle. If you blink even once, you lose sight of it. Thus, the true scholar is the person who, having found a single aspect of the original mind, cultivates and builds up that realm so as not to lose sight of it."[94] Toan tried in a number of ways to impress upon his followers the importance of preserving the original mind. In 1772, he issued a set of guidelines entitled *A Summary of Guidelines for Those Who Know the Original Mind (Honshin o shiru mono wa mamorubeki no tairyaku)*. Like the Admonition, this document was given to the members individually soon after they experienced discovery. It opens with the declaration that "to realize the original mind is truly the beginning of virtue." Now that the members knew the source of goodness was within themselves, they were responsible for maintaining consciousness of that potential. They had just commenced a lifelong endeavor to "preserve a state in which one never loses this selfless mind."[95]

The *Summary* makes two additional points of an admonitory nature. Knowledge of the original mind does not excuse arrogance on the part of the member: one must not "boast of oneself as number one and say whatever one likes." Overzealousness is another manifestation of spiritual pride; beginners should not take it upon themselves to teach the Way to others. Toan goes on to give succinct advice on this point: "It is extremely inappropriate to advocate the Way forcefully to someone who has no aspiration [to follow it]. It is also inappropriate if one fails to lead toward goodness a person who does have the aspiration. One must be able to discriminate in this way."[96] Debating with scholars or Buddhist clergy was expressly forbidden. Evidently some Shingaku adepts were so full of fervor that, despite their comparative lack of education, they confidently preached their message to established teachers and religious professionals.

Toan also warns newly enlightened disciples not to neglect reverence for the Shinto gods and the buddhas. Experience of the original mind did not exempt one from carrying out conventional religious obligations. Indeed, Toan believed that sincere respect for higher beings was the natural outcome of knowing the original mind, for the beings themselves were "the form of the original mind" and had "utmost value."[97] In Shingaku, the essence of human nature was conceived as transcendent and as such was represented by deities and other worthy beings.[98] The gods and buddhas were a particularly pure embodiment of the innate goodness of the mind. Like Confucian ethical behavior, the performance of Shinto and Buddhist devotions was thus a natural manifestation of one's original mind. This attitude was at the base of all Shingaku discourse about the unity of the three teachings. Toan's own conscientious treatment of Shinto deities, Buddha, Confucius, his ancestors, and his teacher Baigan illustrates the value he attributed to devotional activity.

Toan did not purport to advocate any particular method of cultivation, but he did suggest a general framework for mastering the Way. In order not to "fabricate" the body (and thereby lose the original mind), he advised that "when one moves one's body, one should operate it while looking into one's mind and closely investigating whether 'I' am moving it. Doing this is called 'straightening the internal through reverence and squaring the external through rightness.' "[99]

The quoted expressions derive from the commentary on the second hexagram *(k'un)* of the *Book of Changes:* "The superior man is reverent so as to straighten his internal life and righteous so as to square his external life. As his reverence and rightness are established, his virtue is no longer an isolated instance."[100] In the Sung Neo-Confucian texts, "reverence" or "seriousness" (Ch. *ching*, J. *kei*) and "rightness" (Ch. *i*, J. *gi*) represent two fundamental dimensions of religious life, inner piety and social morality.[101] The fulfillment of both aspects is identified with the all-encompassing virtue of humaneness (Ch. *jen*, J. *jin*), a state in which selfish desires are transcended. Ch'eng I defined reverence as "concentrating on one thing," which Chu Hsi interpreted to mean "doing one thing at a time."[102] But "reverence" also implied a serious, respectful attitude toward all things. The word is often used in Neo-Confucian discourse to indicate the contemplative aspect of self-improvement in general.[103]

Toan similarly believed that "straightening the internal through reverence" was the aspect of cultivation that one carried out when not directly "dealing with affairs." For the merchants, artisans, and other working people to whom he addressed his teaching, such "ordinary times" would have been their off hours, perhaps early in the morning and late at night. For Toan, the way to achieve reverence was twofold. First, one needed to appreciate the value of knowing the original mind. Even after the last layer of skin, the last remnant of the "human self," had given way to the true mind, one who had been long accustomed to it would easily "put the skin back on." Consequently, one should be grateful to know the true mind even for a moment; as Toan says, were it not for the efforts of "Master Ishida," even that brief glimpse would be impossible. Accordingly, members who found the original mind were advised to pay their respects and give thanks at Baigan's grave in Toribeyama.[104] The cultivation of a sense of gratitude was part of what Toan intended by "reverence."

Second, one should practice reverence by reminding oneself at all times that there is no "I" in one's body that directs its sensations and actions; it is not "I" who sees and hears and moves. Constantly renewing this perspective would eventually lead to the full concentration and attentiveness implied by the idea of reverence. Toan speaks of this process as "polishing one's innate virtue" or the "effort of daily renewal."[105] As one engaged in this introspection day after day, one would gradually become aware of the "dirt" of the human self and thereby wash it away, uncovering the original mind. But if one neglected this internal polishing and allowed the self free rein, it would dominate one's being through the five senses: "If the human self becomes inflated, the eyes will be selfish about forms, the ears will be selfish about sounds, the nose will be selfish about fragrances, the mouth will be selfish about flavors, and the body will be selfish about its own convenience. These selfishnesses will become obstinate and obscure the original mind."[106] The senses were therefore not only a vehicle for the first insight into the original mind; after discovery they continued to be the locus of the battle against the human self.

In Shingaku, the dynamics of selflessness as a basis for moral behavior were conceived in eminently concrete terms. Deep analysis of one's true relationship to things and people was the key to ethical conduct. This approach, characterized as "the mind that follows form" *(katachi ni yoru kokoro),* was transmitted to Toan, at least in germ, by Ishida Baigan.[107] Toan regarded the approach as an illustration of the Ch'eng brothers' idea of "responding to things as they come." But his colorful rendition of this idea probably brought its meaning home to his listeners more effectively than anything they might have read (if they could) in Neo-Confucian textbooks:

> People are creatures who simply respond. To begin with, if you wish to have a smoke, the pipe immediately says, "I'm here." Then, when you pick up the pipe, the tobacco pouch says, "I'm here." With that, the barrel of the pipe declares, "Fill me up here." There is not one thing that is not like this. We completely exclude everything else that calls [for our attention]: nothing else exists. In short, we simply respond to things as they present themselves, one after another. Please think about this carefully.[108]

Toan made the ethical thrust of this idea of total "responsiveness" explicit through engaging examples from everyday life:

> When you run into another person at a pool of water or on a narrow road, the approaching person moves over in the same direction in which you do, and you both do the same thing, saying "Hoi! Hoi! Hoi!" This is because, at the moment you run into each other, the idea

"I'll move over" is created in both of you at the same time, whereupon you both do the same thing at the same time. The matter is settled when one of you extinguishes the body. That is, when you abandon the idea "I'll move over" and, without moving, simply become the other person, [the situation] clears up at once.[109]

The ultimate implication of the contemplative aspect of cultivation (reverence) is that one's relationship with an "other," whether an object or another person, is not a dualistic experience. When one gives up the subjective point of view, only the needs of the other party remain for consideration. The abdication of the "I" automatically reveals the correct course of action. When one encounters one's parents, one *is* one's parents and consequently treats them just as they would wish. The identification of oneself with all things and all people thus leads to a justification of the morality of the Five Relations.

The second aspect of Toan's program of cultivation, "squaring the external through rightness," is essentially the correction of one's behavior according to these moral principles. Relying on the nondualistic consciousness of the original mind, one can decide whether or not a particular action is appropriate in a given situation and proceed accordingly. Toan taught that the original mind can differentiate right and wrong in the same way that it can discriminate between long and short. The interpretation of "rightness" as an act of decision probably derives from a comment by Chu Hsi: "Rightness means the mind's making a decision. As it makes the decision inside, the outside becomes regular and correct, and everything is in its right place."[110] Ideally, the conduct of the Shingaku member would be determined through this inner process: "When your mind moves, when you want to say something or are about to do this or that, whatever it may be, try to return to your original mind: you should say and do only those things that are not shameful either internally or externally. Not having anything of which one is ashamed is called rightness."[111]

In Toan's view, whatever bad habits people may have built up over the years, once they become aware of the inner source of goodness, they will not lightly violate its dictates. At the very least, they will no longer inadvertently do wrong. The original mind thus functions as a kind of conscience or inner sense that helps one choose the right conduct. As Toan's remarks indicate, the presence or absence of shame in the original mind signals whether one is about to "go wrong" or not. As long as one listens to one's own mind, the correct course of action will be clear. Calculations may try to interfere, but the intuitive goodness of the original mind can still make itself felt. Shingaku followers were taught to be particularly careful when "dealing with affairs" to discern whether or not their minds were being influenced by self-centered calculations.

Developing sensitivity to the "inner voice" of the original mind was a process of transformation that required sustained, dedicated effort. Toan considered preservation of the true mind to be more difficult than the initial discovery of its existence. In one talk he estimates that it might take five or ten years of constant and sincere effort for newly enlightened members to reach maturity in their conduct.[112] Indeed, Toan's repeated attempts to regulate his disciples' behavior suggest that some of them had trouble keeping in touch with their original minds after discovery. In *Clearing Up Doubts about Knowing the Mind* we hear of Shingaku members who behaved poorly even after their knowledge of the original mind was formally acknowledged.[113] When questioned about this apparent contradiction, Toan asserts that knowing the original mind is simply the basis for moving toward goodness; each person must take responsibility for preserving the right perspective and advancing along the path to perfection. Nurturing the original mind after discovery is as essential as caring for a child from birth until maturity. Nevertheless, Toan remarks: "People rarely accumulate this nurturing. Therefore it is indeed possible for you to say that you don't see its effect [in my disciples]. I couldn't avoid giving some answer [to your question], but it is a point about which I am deeply ashamed."[114] The wayward disciples had failed to nurture their original minds sufficiently. They had stopped renewing the experience of no self in their perceptions and actions; selfish calculations had come into play in their daily relations with others.

The conferral of the Admonition was a central ritual in the sequence of Shingaku religious life. It bears repeating here that the content of this tract is entirely admonitory in nature. However fleetingly or profoundly the disciple may have "known" the original mind, from that point onward, he or she was to give first priority to moral conduct. As a reminder of this point, Toan requested that a lecture on the Admonition be conducted on specified days twice a year at Meirinsha; the tract was to be read out twice a year at the other meetinghouses.[115] Over and over, Toan reiterated to his followers that a moral life is entailed by the experience of discovery; keeping harmony in the Five Relations and working hard at their allotted tasks was the path that lay before them.[116] A 1780 set of guidelines, *The Original Mind, As Each of You Has Discovered* (*Ono ono honshin wa on-hatsumei no tōri*), that was circulated in the movement as a whole (rather than given to individual members) implies that the original mind *is* the Way. It encompasses an entire framework of virtues founded on filial piety and loyalty:

> The original mind is simply revering those above and having compassion for those below, completely fulfilling loyalty and rightness in regard to one's lord and retainers, being filial and caring toward one's father and mother, getting along well between husband and wife, having good relations between elder and younger, considering one's ser-

vants as one's children and generously bestowing true love on them, and diligently working at one's heaven-allotted trade—nothing more than this.

When I state it in this manner, it may seem to be a great number of things. However, if one begins by being utterly devoted to one's master and carefully carrying out one's duties, and by cheerfully serving one's parents through filial deeds, in each case considering how to reassure their hearts, then one will naturally take good care of the family business.[117]

In short, all moral and civil obligations, including success in one's work, were based on the practice of two cardinal virtues, loyalty and filial piety. The original mind would naturally manifest in conduct that accorded with these values and their derivatives: chastity, deference, honesty, frugality, patience, charity, and diligence. Toan rarely discoursed on any topic without advocating these virtues. Even *Notes of a Conversation,* a dialogue concerned primarily with the ineffable realm of no calculation and the unborn Buddha-mind, concludes with a set of specific moral injunctions.[118]

True to his Neo-Confucian sources, Toan did not fail to stress to Shingaku members the importance of keeping a balance between the inner and outer dimensions of cultivation: neither reverence nor rightness should be neglected. Chu Hsi had pointed out the reason for maintaining this equilibrium: "If one has reverence but not rightness, what one does will be wrong. If one has only rightness but not reverence, there will be no foundation. How could one practice rightness?"[119]

Rightness is the standard by which to judge one's conduct. Reverence is the internal discipline through which one prepares to hold oneself to that standard. Toan's rationale for balancing the two aspects agrees with Chu Hsi's, but he expresses it in his own terms. He warns his students that even after they have an experience of no body or no self, since the habit of calculating and intellectualizing is deeply ingrained, the self may reemerge rather easily.

> Consequently, if you do not completely master no self by maintaining reverence in ordinary times, you will have difficulty discriminating when dealing with affairs. Moreover, even though you may master no self ordinarily, when dealing with affairs, if you do not carefully determine whether or not [your impulse] is a calculation and follow rightness, you will make a mistake.[120]

One needs to have a firm foundation in the contemplative discipline of "mastering no self," so that when one is faced with a moral decision, one will be able to distinguish right from wrong. Even with that foundation of reverence, however, one must be very attentive at the moment of the decision, because calculations are apt to interfere with one's judgment, simply out of force of habit. And once a mistake is committed, the emotional aftermath will further complicate the pursuit of selflessness. "When you feel remorse, it is impossible for your body not to come into being."[121]

Toan emphasized to followers who had already discovered the original mind, as he did to beginners, that the guidance he shared with them was confidential. He also forbade his listeners to discuss their own mystical experiences with the uncommitted. Comments by newly enlightened members about how it felt, for example, to "see without eyes" might hinder the spiritual progress of people who did not yet desire to know the original mind. The extraneous intellectual baggage that people had built up from birth had to be peeled away, layer by layer, in accordance with the sequence of Shingaku training.[122]

The phases of religious life discussed above under the rubrics of beginners' guidance, discovery, and preservation were not entirely distinct in the actual lives of Shingaku members. The "seeing and hearing" exercises were an important means of preparing the student for the discovery of the original mind. Postdiscovery cultivation was conceived in terms of reverence and rightness. However, insofar as "reverence" meant the awareness of no self, it was the same attitude that Toan advocated in his talks for beginners. The contemplative exercises were designed to help novices prepare for the first glimpse of their true nature, but they could also inspire more advanced disciples to renew and prolong their insights. The framework of inner attentiveness balanced with moral behavior pertained in a general sense to the entire Shingaku program both before and after discovery. This broader view of the sequence of Shingaku religious life should be kept in mind as specific methods of Shingaku cultivation are considered in the next chapter.

5

METHODS OF CULTIVATION

SHINGAKU MEMBERS cultivated their understanding of the original mind through group study and contemplation. Both of these approaches had been advocated by Ishida Baigan, but Teshima Toan took steps to systemize them.

Group Study

The main form of Shingaku group discussion was the "support meeting," or *kaiho* (literally, "meet and support" or "gather and encourage"), which originated in Baigan's regular monthly meetings. The latter had taken place three times a month and were attended chiefly by committed members of the group. Baigan's immediate disciples continued to hold the discussions after his death, but it was not until 1773 that Toan drew up guidelines for the support meetings. In *Principles for the Assembly of Companions,* he explains the meaning of *kaiho,* using the language of classical Confucianism:

> Tseng-tzu said: "[A gentleman] gathers *(kai)* friends by means of culture and through his friends supports *(ho)* humaneness" [*Analects* 12:24]. The ancients did this even more. All the more reason to ask how our comrades can remove the impurities with which they have long been imbued, if they fail to rely, even for a short time, on the support of the assembly of companions. One should be careful not to neglect [this].

In an annotation to the above, Toan adds that

> from olden times, unless one depended on one's friends, it was difficult to advance along the Way. For this reason, Tseng-tzu taught that when one takes the words that appear in the writings of the sages and worthies, gathers with friends to discuss their meaning together, and

91

polishes one's mind, the shameful aspects in one's mind lessen day by day, the virtue of humaneness in one's original mind is slowly illuminated, and one gradually advances along the Way.[1]

The meetings were thus intended to provide a forum in which the goodness in oneself and one's companions would be "supported" or reinforced through discussion of classical learning.

The sessions were originally designed for those who already had some insight into their natures;[2] participants were usually affiliated with the particular meetinghouse in which the meeting was held. These regular members received more advanced education than the occasional visitor or the general public. In 1784 Toan reminded his followers to make a clear distinction between public lectures and open discussions (*zadan*), on the one hand, and support meetings, on the other: casual listeners were excluded from the in-house study sessions.[3] During Baigan's lifetime and in the years immediately after his death, such distinctions between levels of teaching were not vital. But after Shingaku lectures and talks on the Way grew popular on a large scale, it became desirable to differentiate public activities from the more intimate sessions between the master and his core disciples. In these smaller meetings, the common aspirations of the participants allowed for a freer, deeper exploration of the issues than was possible in the public gatherings.

Toan generally promoted the idea of community among his members and reiterates this theme in his remarks on group study. He does not downplay individual cultivation; in fact, he echoes typical Neo-Confucian themes of self-reliance, such as "getting it for oneself" and "being watchful over oneself when alone."[4] But Toan is equally concerned with establishing a communal approach to the learning of the mind: "Unless one is extraordinarily gifted (one out of ten million people), it is difficult to learn on one's own. Constantly separating oneself from close communication with one's good friends is like abandoning the task of training (polishing) oneself."[5]

Given the difficulty of learning by oneself, it behooved the serious student to join with others on the same path. Toan viewed the group meetings as an opportunity for members to reinforce their religious faith as well as their commitment to each other. Spiritual growth in Shingaku was not an individual affair, but a group process that involved regular encounters between the followers, quite apart from their public activities. The leader of the support meeting was ordinarily a director, a lecturer, an elder companion, or a housemaster. Under the leader's direction, the participants reflected on ideas expressed in classical texts and tried to relate these notions to their own experiences of finding and preserving the original mind. The meetings did not purport to be intellectual debates or exegetical discussions of fine points in the texts. They were intended to strengthen the original mind of each participant: "The essential purpose of the support meeting is to remove selfish desire and to perfect the original mind's virtue of humaneness."[6]

Three methods of interchange were used in the support meetings: the "study circle" *(rinkō)*, the "reading group" *(kaidoku)*, and the posing of "problems" *(sakumon)*. The participants of a study circle would gather in a room, usually in the local Shingaku meetinghouse, and sit facing each other around a low table. The central seat was reserved for the leader of the session. After an exchange of bows, a member who had been appointed ahead of time would explicate a passage from a designated text and answer questions about it asked by the other participants. Following a certain amount of discussion and debate regarding the correctness of the speaker's understanding, the leader of the meeting would clarify the authoritative view and offer guidance related to the issues that had emerged.

The reading group was conducted in a similar manner. Members took turns reading aloud from a specific text, interrogated each other, and debated the meaning of the passages. The leader in attendance would give a homily on a related topic when the occasion demanded.[7] In *Principles for the Assembly,* Toan specifies the texts to be used in the study circle and reading group: the Four Books, *Reflections on Things at Hand,* the *Elementary Learning,* and Ishida Baigan's *City and Country Dialogues* and *Frugality: Discussion of Household Management.*[8] The use of texts as a basis for discussion may seem at odds with Toan's dismissal of book learning elsewhere. In fact, the Shingaku leader distinguished the role of book learning prior to the member's initial insight into the original mind from its function afterwards. Discursive learning and textual study could hinder the quest for the original mind, but after the experience of discovery, such methods helped reinforce the member's understanding.

The method of "problems" or "questions" characterized Shingaku religious education from its beginnings until late in its history. Originally, the word *sakumon* (Ch. *ts'e-wen*) denoted the questions posed to students who sat for civil service examinations in China. In early Tokugawa Japan, Itō Jinsai adopted the term to refer to the interrogative phase of group study in his school. Like the Shingaku members, Jinsai's students took turns explicating texts and answering questions asked by their peers. The organizational rules of Jinsai's group stipulated that

> after all lectures are over, the president proposes a problem (J. *sakumon*) . . . or topic of discussion . . . to test the students. Each presents his solution . . . which is paraphrased or criticised by the

president, but without giving ratings. If an immediate answer cannot
be given, the problem may then be answered at the next meeting. . . .
Questions asked and answers given shall also be recorded.[9]

Jinsai's informal study sessions were apparently discontinued as Kogidō increased its enrollment, but the method of posing problems for discussion was a lasting feature of the school. Since the students were
required to provide written answers to the questions, the *sakumon*
method also served to teach Chinese composition.[10] Ogyū Sorai later
used a similar approach in his own seminars *(kaidoku)*;[11] here, too, the
students spoke in turn on issues drawn from the classics. By the mid-eigh-
teenth century the *sakumon* method was an accepted pedagogical technique in private schools, including Shingaku meetinghouses.

The disciples of Baigan and Toan apparently included some solutions

Like Kogidō and other private academies, the Shingaku network had
originated in a small group of committed students centered on one
founder-teacher. Baigan, like other Confucian educators, had presented
a problem related to the day's topic and required written answers from
his disciples. After all the members offered their answers, Baigan gave the
conclusive interpretation, also in writing.[12] The questions came to be
called *sakumon* and the answers, *taisaku*. Under Toan these exchanges
remained a regular feature of Shingaku study, along with the study circle
and reading group.[13] Moreover, within the Shingaku community the
teachers' final answers, especially those of Baigan and Toan, were held in
high esteem and preserved for use in later support meetings to establish
the conclusive view of the issue at hand. These authoritative answers
were not intended for general circulation and were probably handed
down as a kind of secret transmission. Nevertheless, some Shingaku
members did note the answers, and in time various records came into
existence.[14]

The disciples of Baigan and Toan apparently included some solutions
to *sakumon* in their teachers' "recorded sayings" *(goroku)*; they appear
alongside the masters' responses to questions asked by the disciples themselves or by more casual visitors. In *Collected Dialogues Left Behind by
Master Teshima (Master Toan's Recorded Sayings) (Teshima sensei ikō
tōmon shū [Toan sensei goroku])*, Toan responds in his usual straightforward manner to queries about the daily cultivation of the original
mind, the virtues of patience and humaneness, and other such topics.
The question-and-answer form characterizes several other Shingaku
compilations as well; indeed, the bulk of Toan's writings seem to be
records of such dialogues. The Shingaku leader was frequently asked to
clarify textual ambiguities. In *Recorded Sayings* he is interrogated on a
wide range of sources, including the Four Books, the *Record of Lin-chi
(Rinzai roku)*, Munan's *Record of This Very Mind (Sokushinki)*, Essays

in Idleness (Tsurezuregusa), Japanese Analects (Warongo), Chuang-tzu,
the *Elementary Learning,* poems by Ikkyū and Saigyō (1118–1190), sayings of the Zen patriarchs, and the works of Chu Hsi and the Ch'eng
brothers.

In some cases, the exchanges between Toan and his disciples are not
simply questions and answers, however. Rather than reasoned discussions about morality, religious life, or classical passages, they resemble
Rinzai koan sessions. These Shingaku dialogues apparently represent
intuitive communications that cannot be understood through conventional rules of logic. Occasionally Toan used this enigmatic type of problem to test his pupils' understanding of the teaching. The following
examples are excerpted from his *Recorded Sayings:*

Q: What about the source of the mind?
A: I don't know.
Q: You answer "I don't know," but what is it that answers "I don't
know"?
A: Even though I don't know, when I touch it, I remember;
When it comes, I know, and when it departs, I forget.
That, too, I forget.[15]
Q: What about the single path of ascendance [to enlightenment]?
A: Silence.[16]
Q: Right in front of your eyes—what is it?
A: Right in front of my eyes.
Q: What is the form of the mind?
A: Formless.
Q: How about "formlessness is itself form, true form"?
A: I don't know.
Q: What do you think, is your voice your own thing or another thing?
A: Is your voice another thing or your own thing?
Q: What about when thoughts of the mind and thoughts of form are
extinguished?
A: I lower my head and sleep.
Q: How do you abandon your self and see the Buddha-nature?
A: Eyes do not see eyes.
Q: Is the mind inside the body, or is it outside?
A: You may seek it, but in the end it is unattainable *(fukatoku).*[17]

Judging from Toan's *Recorded Sayings,* the Shingaku master employed
this cryptic style of dialogue not infrequently, probably in small group
meetings or one-on-one encounters with his disciples. It is not always
clear in the text whether Toan himself is asking the questions. In general,
sakumon were generated by the teacher, not by a disciple seeking information or clarification; they were deliberately designed to transmit the
teaching of the original mind. However, sometimes the student seems to
initiate the exchange:

Q: How can I pass through the gateway?
A: What are you saying?
Q: How can I pass through?
A: What are you trying to pass through?
Q: If one knows the innate nature, of course there is neither coming nor going. Where is the barrier?
A: You have already finished making the barrier. Why do you try to pass through it?[18]

Occasionally, Toan was challenged by his disciples:

Question: When a certain person struck the *tatami* mat with a fan and said, "Make this sound," a friend replied by taking out a fan. That is how [the friend] responded.
Toan answered: Wrong. That is nothing but the transient speculation *(geryō)* of the world.
Someone asked: Old man, you try making the sound.
Toan answered: You come and ask without [relying on] words or deeds; then try making the sound yourself.[19]

In the preceding chapter we saw that Toan confronted his followers in the guidance sessions with paradoxical questions ("What sees the fan?"). The type of question used to train new members, who had yet to find their original minds, was not necessarily different in tone from the problems posed to older members to help reinforce their understanding. The Shingaku master was responsible both to stimulate and to strengthen the experience of no self in his disciples; he employed enigmatic questions to accomplish these goals at different stages of his training program.

Nakazawa Dōni also used *sakumon* to test his disciples. We do not have a published record of Dōni's conversations with his disciples, but several extant compilations of Shingaku question-and-answer sessions include Dōni's contributions. In one such collection, "Questions of the Ishida School, Classified" ("Sekimon sakumon ruiju"), Dōni's dialogues range from reasoned discussions of points of faith to puzzling Rinzai-style conversations.[20] Dōni's answers are usually concise, if not blunt. The following conversation exemplifies his down-to-earth style:

Question: I heard that Zen master Ikkyū urinated into the open eyes of the Jizō of Seki. Was [master Ikkyū's] wisdom authentic, even though he did such things?
Master Dōni replied: Every single day, we urinate in our parents' faces.[21]

Other exchanges highlight the concept of the original mind. In Shingaku the true mind was variously identified with the entire universe, with heaven, and with the absence of a body or subjective self:

Q: Does the original mind have a sound?

A: The sound of heaven-and-earth and all things—that is the sound of the original mind.

Q: What is the source of the mind?

A: Heaven.

Q: What is delusion? What is enlightenment?

A: When deluded, one uses the mind by means of the body. When enlightened, one uses the body by means of the mind.

Q: "Enter the heart of the person who faces you." What does this mean?

A: It means to become selfless, whether you are facing your master, your parents, your relatives, or a stranger.[22]

These conversations probably typify the *sakumon* that Shingaku masters used in the late eighteenth and early nineteenth centuries. But some of Dōni's dialogues are even more enigmatic:

Q: Do the plum blossoms in the painting produce fruit?

A: The plum tree in my garden produced about three *to* this year.[23]

The tone of certain Shingaku *sakumon* suggests that they may indeed be Zen koans adapted for use in a lay context. The compilers of the Shingaku "problem" collections certainly had an eye to the Zen inspiration of these dialogues, for they modeled the titles of their manuscripts after famous Zen collections. "Kenmon: shijū hassoku" (Seeing and Hearing: Forty-eight Cases) was probably inspired by *Mumonkan* (The Gateless Barrier), which also contains forty-eight "cases."[24] The forty-eight Shingaku *sakumon* are undated and unsigned, but they are traditionally attributed to Teshima Toan.[25] The collection was originally recorded in the vernacular and only later written up in Chinese characters.

In view of the kind of questions Toan uses in *Essentials of Good Guidance,* it seems possible that he did have a hand in creating if not the actual manuscript of the forty-eight cases, at least some of the problems included in it. One of the queries recorded in the "Cases" is the main question that Toan put to beginners in the guidance sessions: "What hears? What sees?" Other cases rephrase Toan's concern with "no mind," "no self," or the larger "Mind" that is not located in the physical body: "Take out your mind and show it to me!" The question "Is the mind inside or outside?"—also duplicated in Toan's guidance talks—echoes Hakuin's query about the location of the mind noted in Chapter 4.

One of the "Cases"—"What were you before you were born?"—recalls the famous question attributed to Hui-neng, the sixth Ch'an patriarch: "What was your original aspect before your father and mother were born?"²⁶ A similar *sakumon,* "What will you become after you die?" is virtually identical to the koan "Where will you go after death?"²⁷ And the case "What is unborn, undying, and cannot be burned by fire?" is equivalent to the Zen saying "It enters fire but is not burned, it enters water but is not drowned."²⁸ "The bridge flows, the river is still" is borrowed whole from Zen literature: it is originally attributed to the Chinese Buddhist layman Fu Ta-shih (497–569).²⁹ Other Shingaku *sakumon,* "How can you see with your eyes closed?" "Hand me the fan without using your hands," and "Try saying the *nenbutsu* with your mouth closed!" employ a common Zen locution.³⁰ According to one tradition, when Emperor Hanazono (1297–1348) offered a melon to the Zen monk Shūhō Myōchō (1282–1338), the emperor reportedly remarked, "Take this without using your hands," whereupon the monk replied, "Give it to me without using your hands."³¹

In Shingaku as in Zen, the struggle to understand these paradoxical commands was believed to help one transcend dualistic thinking. It is not one's eyes that see or one's hands that hold a fan or a melon; it is not one's mouth that says the *nenbutsu.* In his guidance talks Toan uses similar questions combined with discursive interludes to teach the same point: sensation and physical movement are not controlled by the particular organs of the body or by a self-conscious "I." One's perceptions and actions are the spontaneous response of the original mind to whatever circumstances arise; one simply "responds to things as they come."

The Zen origins and nuances of all the "Forty-eight Cases" and other Shingaku *sakumon* are beyond the scope of this study, but even the few examples cited above show that Shingaku in the late eighteenth century was significantly influenced by Zen koan practice. Although the *sakumon* method was a common teaching device in other schools of the time, in the Shingaku movement it was broadened to encompass Rinzai-style questions. To be sure, the above *sakumon* represent only one among several types of communication that took place in the Shingaku support meetings; passages from Confucian and Shingaku texts provided the main topics of discussion in the study circle and reading group. Moreover, Toan never officially recommended the use of Zen texts for group study. Nevertheless, on some occasions, all books were put aside as Toan used koanlike problems to test the depth of his disciples' understanding: to what degree did they truly know the original mind and comprehend its implications? Toan did not hesitate to use enigmatic questions and paradoxes to ensure that his followers fully grasped the truth of the mind.

Group study in Shingaku therefore encompassed rational, discursive learning centered on Confucian and Shingaku texts and intuitive, koanlike training inspired by the Rinzai tradition. For Toan there was no contradiction between these two kinds of "dialogues": each had its own function. The koan mode of discourse served to stimulate or reconfirm the students' experiences of their original minds; textual studies helped them to understand and articulate those experiences. Both methods contributed to the process of cultivation.

Contemplation

The Shingaku enthusiasm for discussion and dialogue was balanced by a quieter means of self-improvement. Meditation, mainly in the form of a practice called "quiet sitting," played a significant part in Shingaku training. Quiet sitting (Ch. *ching-tso*, J. *seiza*) had originally developed in the Sung period as part of the Neo-Confucian masters' emphasis on internal discipline. Taking inspiration from Chou Tun-i's doctrine of "regarding quietude as fundamental" *(chu-ching)*, Ch'eng Hao, Ch'eng I, and their successors began to engage in a type of seated contemplation.[32] The practice is frequently mentioned in Chu Hsi's works as well, even though Chu had reservations about quiet sitting.[33]

Chu Hsi did not entirely dismiss the practice, but like Ch'eng I, he preferred to think in terms of "reverence," a quality that, in his view, pertained to both quiet and active phases of cultivation. Chu was concerned that students might engage in quiet sitting excessively, at the expense of their daily affairs or book learning. He believed that over-emphasis on quietude was the error of Ch'an Buddhist meditation (Ch. *tso-ch'an*, J. *zazen*). Chu thus shifted away from the quietistic inclinations of Chou Tun-i and his own teacher, Li T'ung. For Chu the active aspect of learning, often expressed as "investigating principles to the utmost," required conscientious book learning and study. He counseled one student to engage in "a half-day of quiet sitting and a half-day of reading"; later Neo-Confucians used the same formula to refer to the necessary equilibrium of quietude and activity.

Chu Hsi regarded quiet sitting chiefly as a means of enhancing the learning process. The practice could help one become single-minded and attentive in preparation for the other phases of learning. The point was not to eliminate thought, but to prepare the mind to receive and apply knowledge. Some people, especially those with poor retentive powers or a short span of attention, might even benefit from engaging in quiet sitting exclusively for extended periods. But Chu felt that most students should combine quiet sitting with reading, assisting other people, or dealing with everyday business. He stressed the need for an overall "effort" or "practice" (Ch. *kung-fu*, J. *kufū*) of self-cultivation that encompassed both activity and contemplation. Chu also promoted quiet sitting as an aid to health; it could provide relief from overwork or act as a curative for illness. In one text he affirms that he practiced quiet sitting intermittently in order to gain the energy to continue his studies. In a let-

ter addressed to a sickly student, the Neo-Confucian thinker even pre-
scribes a few details of the physical technique for quiet sitting.[34] In general, however, he did not establish any fixed method, posture, or time
duration for quiet sitting. Such rules would regiment the practice and
make it into a system in itself, separate from the students' overall effort of
investigating principles through daily affairs and reading. In Chu Hsi's
view, as Rodney Taylor notes, "the very generality of the practice is a part
of its inner content."[35] Taylor believes that attention to the techniques of
meditation was not characteristic of Neo-Confucian quiet sitting:

> In terms of Chu Hsi's recommendation of technical meditative tech-
> niques . . . such techniques simply continue to be outside the normal
> practice of quiet-sitting. The only reference seems to be limited to dis-
> cussion of curing illness. Not only does this hold true for Chu Hsi's fre-
> quent discussion of the practice, but it also is upheld by the continuing
> tradition of Confucianism even in those periods where much emphasis
> was placed upon the practice of quiet-sitting, for example in the Tung-
> lin School at the end of the Ming period, and the Yamazaki Ansai
> School at the end of the Tokugawa. . . . Short of occasional references
> to such techniques for the curing of illness and restoration of health, I
> find no association of these techniques with quiet-sitting as it is usually
> discussed.[36]

The concern that quiet sitting might develop into a special system in
itself, separate from the more active stages of learning, was reiterated by
Japanese advocates of the practice, such as Satō Naokata of the Kimon
school. Naokata wrote several works concerning the quiet aspect of cultivation and the correct approach to quiet sitting.[37] Some of these writings are in vernacular Japanese and were therefore accessible to the less-
educated sectors of Tokugawa society, although they were probably
intended for members of the samurai class.[38]

Naokata covers the principal themes associated with quiet sitting in
the Ch'eng-Chu tradition: it is the discipline for cultivating the mind, the
basis for reverence, and a counterpart and preparation for book learning.
Quiet sitting is not a random moment of self-reflection, but a discipline
that requires serious commitment. Essentially, it is the effort to purify
one's mind of idle thoughts so that it will be focused and calm. Naokata
warns that one must practice this discipline in advance—in the ordinary,
tranquil periods of the day. If one simply waits until one is in the midst of
the "battle" of affairs, it is unlikely that one will be able to maintain control over the mind. It is important to work on the nature while it is still
in its "unmanifest" *(mihatsu)* phase, before one's feelings have been
"aroused" or stimulated by external events or objects.[39]

As one progresses in the exercise of quiet sitting, one becomes composed and serene; one understands the process of sensation more clearly.

"Until the cry of a bird or the sound of the wind reverberates in your mind, it is the realm of the unmanifest *(mihatsu no ba)*."[40] If one is conscious that it is a bird or the wind, one is already experiencing the realm of after-the-fact awareness, the "manifest realm" *(ihatsu no ba)*. The immediate sensory experience of seeing and hearing is "preconscious"; one is aware of seeing only after the moment of sight itself. The more one practices quiet sitting, the more sensitive one becomes to the original state of mind in which one is not yet thinking about or reacting to the stimulus.[41] For Naokata, the cultivation of this sensitivity through quiet sitting was an essential part of successful learning. Discussing the Way or reading the classics would have little meaning without the "reverence" gained through contemplation.[42] Without developing inner discipline through quiet sitting, one's mind would not be serene enough to absorb knowledge. True to the Chu Hsi tradition, Naokata believed that quiet sitting had a beneficial effect on study.[43] It could lead to a more personal experience of the principles contained in the classics, as opposed to superficial learning "for the sake of others."[44] He criticized Confucian scholars of his time for engaging in too much study and debate.[45] Naokata felt it was useless for scholars to read many books, write, or lecture without a foundation of contemplation. One's reading and writing were bound to involve errors and omissions if they were pursued in an agitated state of mind.[46] Thus, quietude was the requisite of a good teacher. "Worldly" or "vulgar" Confucians who failed to work on themselves through quiet sitting were not qualified to teach the real meaning of the Neo-Confucian texts.[47]

Yet, like his Neo-Confucian predecessors, Naokata faulted Buddhists with too much emphasis on quietude. He acknowledged the resemblance between quiet sitting and Zen meditation but declared that it was only superficial. Buddhist quietude was "a dead thing" that involved the rejection of human relations and moral duties. The Neo-Confucian practice, in contrast, was designed to unify quiet and active cultivation, leading to more effective enactment of moral laws and human government.[48] Naokata objected to what he interpreted as the static quality of Buddhist spiritual discipline:

> The Buddhists basically place priority on "seeing into the nature" and "the path of enlightenment"; this is the practice of becoming extinguished. They regard being empty and extinguished, like a dead thing, as essential. They simply quiet the mind and make it clear, but insofar as they destroy activity, they seek to become like withered trees and dead ashes.[49]

In contrast, he argues, Neo-Confucian quiet sitting is merely the effort to abandon idle speculation; it does not repress natural human activity.

Hence, one should not become lost in the experience of quiet sitting, but remain alert and responsive to whatever happens: a visitor may appear, one's family or business may demand attention. One should simply deal with the matter and return to the previous state of calmness. While dealing with these affairs, one must try to preserve the attitude of calm single-mindedness attained in quiet sitting, regardless of how agitated the external situation may become.[50] Naokata considered quiet sitting to be more spontaneous and less regimented than Zen meditation:

> Zen meditation is sitting in the lotus position, looking at the tip of one's nose, concentrating one's mind below the navel and extinguishing thought. Zen meditation is something that is done deliberately. It is something that is done not in one's spare moments, but at fixed times with exactly one or exactly two sticks of incense, or for one time period or two time periods. Consequently, one becomes constrained and one's mind congeals and does not circulate. One's body and mind become dead things. In quiet sitting, one does not establish the number of sticks or time periods in that way. It is something one does in the morning or evening, in the daytime or at night, after having been involved with affairs—either in the free time after concluding one's business or in the free time after reading books and writing notes—whenever one is not doing anything else.[51]

Naokata was aware that Chu Hsi himself had once described the correct posture to be used in contemplation in a letter to a disciple. He admits that Chu's description resembles the method for Zen meditation but argues that the Sung master prescribed the lotus position in this particular case only for the sake of the disciple's health. "The appearance resembles Zen meditation but the purpose differs greatly," he insists.[52] Naokata firmly upheld the view that quiet sitting should not be systemized or regulated in any way.

The practice of meditation in Shingaku had originated with Ishida Baigan, who came to know his nature after a period of contemplative effort under Oguri Ryōun's guidance. Baigan's *Memoir* mentions that his disciples practiced quiet sitting, and there are references to quiet sitting in the founder's own writings as well.[53] After the movement came under Toan's control, quiet sitting remained an important if not dominant part of what was meant by *kufū*, or "contemplative effort."[54] An illustration in Toan's work *For Boys and Girls: Waking Up from Sleep (Jijo: Nemuri-zamashi)* shows a man meditating in front of a stick of burning incense (see fig. 15, p. 134). Moreover, the Kyoto government's criticism of Toan's activities as "Zen-like" in the 1760s was probably instigated by reports that he was teaching some sort of sitting meditation.

In Shingaku discourse of this period, "quiet sitting" and "contemplative effort" are often coupled in one phrase: *seiza no kufū* referred to the process by which members found their original minds, often after grappling with problems posed to them by their masters.[55] In contrast to Satō Naokata, who considered quiet sitting a preparation for reading and other forms of academic activity, Teshima Toan discouraged book learning during the period leading up to the discovery of the original mind. In Toan's system, contemplative effort, including quiet sitting, is explicitly linked to the goal of knowing the original mind; it is the primary means of accelerating the experience of discovery. Toan's son Wa'an discovered his original mind while engaging in quiet sitting deep into the night.[56] Nakazawa Dōni reportedly found the truth after the proverbial seven days of quiet sitting (which in his case may as well be called Zen meditation).[57]

A remark in Toan's *New Talks from Chōsō (Chōsō shinwa)* indicates his own view of the role of quiet sitting in coming to know the original mind:

> When you do quiet sitting, unless you go on thinking "I want to know, I want to know" all the way through, you won't be able to know the original mind. But it is a mistake if you believe that as long as you continue thinking this, you can know [the original mind]. . . . In the end, you'll be able to know it only if you sincerely immerse yourself single-mindedly, day and night, in the thought "I want to know, I want to know." At that time, when you are doing quiet sitting, the point at which you do not seem to be thinking is nonetheless when you are thinking: "I want to know, I want to know [the original mind]." And the point at which you do seem to be thinking is calculation. As long as you sincerely immerse yourself, constantly thinking "I want to know, I want to know," you'll be able to know [the original mind] quickly; work on it from this perspective. Doing this is called contemplative practice.[58]

It is not conscious deliberation or intellectual reflection, but the spontaneous, unselfconscious desire to know the original mind that leads to discovery. The "contemplative effort of quiet sitting" allows this natural impulse to reach fulfillment. Naokata also distinguished between unselfconscious and self-conscious states of mind or between the "unmanifest" and "manifest" realms of experience. Like Toan, he explained the difference in terms of sensation and cognition: hearing a bird's cry and knowing that it is a bird's cry. But Toan saw the self-conscious or dualistic phase of this process in a more negative light than Naokata; he taught that one must transcend this realm, which he called *shian* or calculation. For Naokata *shian* was equivalent to quietude itself; in his writings the term simply means "pondering" or "premeditation" and has none of the undesirable connotations that it holds for Toan ("cunning," "temptation," "selfishness"). Naokata believed that all important decisions required a period of pondering or forethought. *Shian* was therefore the fundamental aim of quiet sitting, not a hindrance to it.[59] In contrast, Shingaku quiet sitting was not a preparation for discursive thought so much as a means of reducing its influence—at least until after the discovery of the original mind.

Given this fundamental difference in perspective, it is not surprising to find that Toan and his followers deviated from the Ch'eng-Chu tradition of quiet sitting in other ways. In particular, they were not as concerned as Chu Hsi's followers that quiet sitting might become a system in itself, separate from moral cultivation. This attitude is confirmed by Ariyama Gentō's "Rules for Quiet Sitting" ("Seizagi"), the first Shingaku text to deal specifically with quiet sitting.[60] Gentō was a close disciple of Teshima Toan who recorded some of his teacher's talks, most notably *Notes of a Conversation* and *New Talks from Chōsō*. According to Uekawa Kisui's postface to the "Rules," Gentō studied with Toan over twenty years (since the mid-1760s); he was one of Toan's oldest disciples. Gentō's preface to the "Rules" is dated 1785, the year before Toan died; it is unlikely that he wrote the work without Toan's knowledge. Judging from comments in the preface and the postface, Gentō had been conducting quiet sitting meetings for some time before he wrote the rules, probably with Toan's approval. However, Gentō says that he approached Teshima Wa'an for active support; by this time Toan had transferred his administrative and teaching responsibilities to his first son. In his postface to the work, Toan's second son, Uekawa Kisui, avows that he himself requested publication of the "Rules." (Publication was apparently delayed until three years after Toan's death, for the postface is dated 1789.) The text thus had the imprimatur of both of Toan's sons; quiet sitting was undoubtedly an important part of Shingaku practice during the late eighteenth century.

In his preface to "Rules for Quiet Sitting," Ariyama Gentō touches on two standard themes in the Neo-Confucian conception of quiet sitting. First, he stresses the idea that quiet sitting is the key to the cultivation of reverence—the way to develop one's innate goodness. It is a means by which, with effort, one can reach and maintain a pure state of mind. Second, quietude must be balanced by activity. Cultivation in quiet periods is the foundation for good action, and action that accords with moral principles will bring peace of mind. The goal of quiet sitting is thus not an "empty quietude" *(kyosei)* in which one rejects affairs.

Gentō fails to reinforce the latter point with a critical reference to Buddhist meditation; unlike Naokata, he does not carry on the longstanding Neo-Confucian tradition of characterizing quiet sitting by contrasting it with Zen practice. Since Gentō was acquainted with Chu Hsi's remarks on quiet sitting, possibly through the Kimon texts themselves, he had surely been exposed to the view that overemphasis on quietude is the characteristic error of Buddhists. Gentō's failure to reflect this view may have been a conscious decision rather than an oversight; in any case, he thereby reformulated the Ch'eng-Chu tradition of mind cultivation in such a way that it was more open to Buddhism. This shift in perspective is confirmed by his reliance on Buddhist sources in the main text of the "Rules."

The preface reveals the extent to which contemplative practices were affected by the practical needs of the Shingaku community. The reported conversation of the author, Teshima Wa'an, and a critic suggest that the Shingaku approach to contemplation was group-oriented, reflecting the communal nature of the Shingaku enterprise that Toan so often stressed. Quiet sitting is depicted not as an irregular recess from study enjoyed by individual scholars, but as an opportunity for bringing one's friends together and mutually reinforcing each other in the pursuit of the Way. In Gentō's view, quiet sitting by oneself was appropriate for those who were learned and talented but not for the "dull and stupid" (meaning the author and his companions). In Shingaku, group effort was esteemed for its role in encouraging even the contemplative experience, which is fundamentally personal and individual. This communal emphasis does not necessarily represent a break with Neo-Confucian contemplative traditions. Both continental and Japanese scholars may have practiced quiet sitting together occasionally. In general, however, sitting alone appears to have been the norm, even in those schools (such as the Kimon) that promoted quiet sitting most actively. Certainly the benefits or disadvantages of group sitting had not been a common subject of debate among Neo-Confucian scholars.

Gentō's position on the issue of systemization and technique also reflects his concern for the practical needs of the members. In the preface to the "Rules," the author is asked to justify the need for any regulation of contemplation at all: Chu Hsi had explicitly repudiated the institution of a particular method for quiet sitting. Gentō simply replies that Chu's stated position was not intended to apply to quiet sitting in a group setting. He ignores Chu's opposition to systemizing the schedule, posture, and breathing technique of quiet sitting in any context; for Chu and his followers, too much attention to these details would allow the sitting to become an end in itself.

The Shingaku preference for regulation and group orientation partly reflects the social circumstances of its members. Many Shingaku practitioners were unable, at least until they retired, to devote themselves full-time to educational activities. They participated in Shingaku programs in accordance with their work schedules, dropping in at the local meeting-house before or after their daily business. Perhaps some members dedicated certain days entirely to quiet sitting, support meetings, or lectures, but this could not have been a daily occurrence for the majority. It would have been a challenge for an ordinary merchant or artisan to take breaks in the work day in order to meditate in the same way that students at Neo-Confucian academies could take recesses from their reading. Gentō's use of the phrase "dull and stupid" was a conventional expression of modesty, but it may also signal his awareness of the members' less-privileged socioeducational background and their inability to pursue the contemplative path as intensively as full-time scholars. The Shingaku community was a refuge for busy townspeople and villagers; it provided a special social structure and space (the meetinghouse) in which they could commune with each other and engage in self-cultivation. Under these circumstances, Gentō's concept of "friends merging their resolve" and keeping each other "awake" during quiet sitting sessions was eminently sensible.

In his postface to the "Rules," Uekawa Kisui reiterates many of the themes contained in the preface. He argues strongly in favor of quiet sitting, saying it is the "essential art" of maintaining reverence and thus "the critical task of students." He does not omit the standard cautions that quietude is not a static, lifeless state and that one needs long practice in order to master it. Kisui was most concerned with preserving the Ch'eng-Chu basis of Shingaku thought; he evidently regarded quiet sitting as an important legacy of the Sung masters. Nevertheless, Kisui seems as oblivious as Gentō to the contradiction between Chu Hsi's position against systemization and Gentō's attempt to regulate the practice of contemplation.

A careful look at the sources of the "Rules for Quiet Sitting" reveals the peculiar configuration of traditions from which Gentō drew. Nearly all classical references in the preface are from *Mencius;* there is one allusion each to the *Doctrine of the Mean,* the *Book of Changes,* and *Chuang-tzu.* In addition, the Neo-Confucian masters Ch'eng Hao, Lo Tsung-yen, Li T'ung, and Chu Hsi are all named as teachers of quiet sitting, although Chu is the only Neo-Confucian master quoted (three times in the entire text).[61] Both the preface and postface of the "Rules" purportedly transmit the orthodox Neo-Confucian learning of the mind. In the rules themselves, however, Gentō's sources change significantly. Except for an opening line from Chu Hsi, there is no further reference to Confucian works.

Gentō's "Rules" show the direct influence of a genre of Buddhist literature that concerns the correct method and posture for meditation. Regulatory texts of this kind, which emerged in China partly under the influence of T'ien-t'ai discussions of meditation, were known as *zazengi* (Ch. *tso-ch'an i*), or "rules for sitting meditation."[62] By the thirteenth century several such texts were in circulation in China. The earliest extant example of a complete *zazengi* appeared in 1202 as part of a revised edition of Ch'ang-lu Tsung-tse's *Ch'an-yüan ch'ing-kuei* (Compendium of Zen Monastic Rules).[63] This work (or a later edition of it), supposedly inspired by the monastic rules of Po-chang Huai-hai (770–814), was the basic source for the principles of Zen meditation drawn up by the Japanese Sōtō master Dōgen (1200–1253).[64] There is little difference between Dōgen's work and the 1202 meditation rules in the treatment of posture and such practical issues, although Dōgen eliminates some passages and adds remarks about his own view of meditation.[65]

The Chinese Zen rules were intended to provide practical guidelines for Zen adepts and thus treat meditation in a more concrete fashion than other, more theoretical Zen works.[66] Gentō takes the same approach in his rules, which consist entirely of practical advice on how to sit, walk, bow, and so forth during the quiet sitting sessions. At the conclusion of the rules, the author even provides a diagram of the intended seating arrangement and the ritual instruments to be used. The name of Gentō's text, "Seizagi" (靜坐儀), also suggests that he took his inspiration from the *zazengi* (坐禪儀) tradition. Few, if any, available Neo-Confucian texts prescribed the practical details of meditation; Gentō, free of qualms about Buddhist influence, turned for material to the most accessible treatments of contemplation—Japanese Sōtō texts. His description of the full cross-legged position used in seated meditation is thus the same as that of Dōgen's *Fukan zazengi,* although the position of the hands is reversed from right to left. The language used in the two texts to describe the appropriate clothing and the position of the thumbs differs slightly, but the import is the same. The need for straight posture and the recommended arrangement of the tongue, lips, and teeth are described in identical terms. The closing statements of the two sets of rules are tellingly parallel. "This is the essential art of sitting meditation" becomes, in the Shingaku text, "This is the essential art of quiet sitting."

"Rules for Quiet Sitting" is more concise, however, than *Fukan zazengi;* several elaborations on bodily posture in the latter (for example, lining up the ears and shoulders) are omitted. Moreover, Chu Hsi's comment about focusing on the area below the navel and looking at the tip of the nose is inserted in the opening passage of Gentō's rules.[67] Most significantly, *Fukan zazengi* contains considerable material on the meaning of Zen meditation that does not appear in the Shingaku rules: Gentō does not discuss Sōtō teaching. The common ground shared by the two texts is strictly one of practical detail and overall regulatory purpose.

The Shingaku author relies on more than one source in his description of the correct method for contemplation. In his view, contemplation should involve fixed periods of walking as well as sitting. He seems to

have in mind the tradition of "walking Zen," or *kinhin,* although he pre-
fers the alternative term *kanpo,* literally, "slow walking." By the late
eighteenth century, Gentō could have drawn on a legacy of Sōtō literature regarding the practical details of walking during meditation sessions. The Sōtō monk Menzan Zuihō (1683–1769) had already written
Kinhinki (Rules for Walking Zen), which was printed along with his disciple's notes of an oral presentation of the rules.[68] (The content of
Zuihō's work pertinent to Gentō's own "Rules" is largely based on
Dōgen's writings, which in turn draw on earlier Ch'an sources.) In his
section on walking meditation, Gentō again confines himself to physical
details, leaving out any reference to the underlying philosophy. Like
Zuihō, the Shingaku writer advises his readers to bring their hands
together, to "look at the ground about one fathom ahead," and to "use
breathing as a measure; one breath is equal to half a pace." The Sōtō
rules are more detailed regarding the correct position of the torso, legs,
and shoulders during walking, and the two texts differ somewhat in their
definitions of the length of a pace. But, in general, Gentō simply repeats
the basic points. While walking, one must not "look around or up and
down" nor shuffle one's feet noisily. One should walk slowly and keep
silence. Most of the language used in this part of the "Rules" is identical
or similar to that of the Sōtō guidelines.[69]

The final section of Gentō's work, called "The Order of Quiet Sitting
Meetings," moves into yet another sphere of discourse. Here the author
suggests the specific order in which the meditators should bow, sit, and
walk; the details of the sequence are probably peculiar to Shingaku. The
use of incense sticks to mark time was a common practice at the time,
and Gentō's proposal that the leader strike an object called a *sūgu* at the
beginning and end of each phase of meditation is comparable to the use
of a bell in Zen sessions. The *sūgu* itself, however, is unique to Shingaku;
it is a sort of wooden clapper carved in the shape of a mythological
tigerlike animal of ancient Chinese lore (Ch. *tsou-yü*). The *sūgu* was used
to signal ritual order not only in quiet sitting, but in Shingaku ceremonies
in general.

Gentō meticulously fixes the sequence of events, the time of day, and
the duration of the periods for sitting and walking. This approach is
remarkable in the history of Neo-Confucian mind cultivation. Faithful
followers of Chu Hsi consistently eschewed such regimentation, fearing
that quiet sitting would become a system in itself, separate from active
moral cultivation and thus comparable to "lifeless" Zen.[70] But Gentō and
his sponsors had no such apprehensions. The author stresses the balance
of activity and quietude in his preface but remains confident that his own
regulation of contemplation will not lead to the separation of quiet sitting from more active forms of self-cultivation. Perhaps this attitude also

reflects the reality of the lives of Shingaku members, who could dedicate themselves to an activity such as quiet sitting only for limited periods. Self-improvement through daily affairs was a necessary part of their approach to learning; it did not require special emphasis.

Shingaku was now a full-fledged religious community. It was perhaps inevitable that attempts be made to organize even a personal experience like contemplation on a relatively large scale. Gentō believed that group sitting would be beneficial to his companions and that it could proceed smoothly only if the method, time, and sequence were regulated. Hence, even while professing to transmit the teaching of the Sung masters, he enlisted the help of Sōtō traditions to develop a practical system of quiet sitting for the Shingaku community.

Most of the Shingaku methods of cultivation discussed in this chapter were group-oriented. Toan and his disciples often stressed that only exceptionally talented people could improve themselves without the help of others. A communal approach was applied to all learning, whether in the context of textual study, discussion, or contemplation. In the support meetings, discussion of classical texts took the form of study circles and reading groups. The meetings also involved dialogues based on problems posed by the master. Although this method was originally used by Confucian teachers to test their students' knowledge of classical learning, in Shingaku the questions encompassed enigmatic exchanges inspired by Rinzai koans. The questions were designed to lead the student to a direct, nondualistic experience of the original mind. Within the support meetings, textual and discursive study coexisted with this more intuitive approach to learning. Contemplation in the form of quiet sitting was another important segment of Shingaku training in the late eighteenth century. It was closely associated with the experience and preservation of the original mind. For practical reasons, Toan's disciple Gentō advocated group quiet sitting according to specific rules and schedules. In doing so, he deviated from the orthodox Neo-Confucian tradition of mind cultivation and turned instead to Sōtō texts for detailed advice on how to meditate.

6

SHINGAKU
FOR CHILDREN

THE DISCURSIVE and contemplative methods used for training committed members were essential phases of the Shingaku educational program. Such disciplines were thought to reinforce the "enlightened" perspective of the original mind, which (as seen in Chapter 4) implied a reaffirmation of particular moral values. In Toan's view, when one experiences "no self," one's treatment of another person is determined by the needs of that person: one "becomes" that person, just as one "becomes" a fan. In mature Shingaku spirituality, the enactment of such virtues as filial piety and loyalty was therefore inspired by a radical reorientation of ordinary, dualistic consciousness. But Toan's program as a whole was developmentally structured; he sought to accommodate the needs of children as well as adults. Shingaku teaching for children consisted chiefly of practical etiquette and ethics. Toan believed that an early grounding in moral values was a necessary foundation for the mature understanding of the original mind.

It was not until Toan consolidated his position as leader of the Shingaku community that he created texts and activities for children. In the early 1770s he began publishing works written expressly for children or based on talks that he had given to groups of youngsters. Toan's concern for child education is best exemplified by his *Zenkun,* or *Early Lessons,* first published in 1773. It is a lesson series for children that Toan offered on set days of the month. The main part of the text is ostensibly for boys and the remainder for girls, but in reality all the talks were presented to audiences of both sexes. The seating for boys and girls was divided by a screen.[1] Male pupils ranged from seven to fifteen years old and females from seven to twelve. As with adult Shingaku programs, no formal introduction was required for admission; the classes were open to everyone. According to Toan's guidelines, the lessons were to begin at about two o'clock in the afternoon on the third, thirteenth, and twenty-third days of each month. The children could wear ordinary clothes, the same clothes they wore when helping out with family work (such as weaving) or practicing writing at the *terakoya*. During the sessions the youngsters were required to keep quiet, avoid blocking each other's line of vision, be careful about fire, and, in general, be considerate of others. Fees, gifts, or payments of any kind to the teachers were expressly forbidden, in keeping with Toan's general policy.[2] A printed page was distributed to each child who attended the class. These block-printed leaflets *(se-in)* contained brief summaries of the day's lesson in simple language. After the pupils had attended the whole series of talks, they could have the individual leaves bound together into a booklet.[3]

The text of *Early Lessons* consists of four parts, each of which contains five points. A fifth part and an appendix are designed especially for girls. Part 1 deals mostly with the theme of respect—respect for divine beings, for one's ancestors, and for one's parents. In the morning, when the children wake up, they should wash themselves, pay their respects to the Shinto god, and bow in front of the Buddhist altar. These rituals could take place at home, since Japanese houses often contained miniature Shinto shrines and Buddhist altars. Toan reminds the children that the Shinto deity is the source of all they have (food and clothing), whereas the Buddhist altar contains the spirits of their deceased great-grandparents and grandparents. It is also owing to the efforts of their ancestors and parents that they have food to eat.

Detailed instructions are given for the various circumstances in which children should show respect to their parents. Before each meal, they should bow to their parents and very politely ask permission to begin eating (by saying, "O-meshi o-agari asobasare soroe"). They may begin eating only after receiving approval. Chu Hsi's compilation the *Elementary Learning* makes a similar prescription: "Going to their mats to eat and drink, they were required to follow their elders: the teaching of yielding to others was now begun."[4] A comparable procedure was to be followed before retiring for the night. Toan further instructs his wards to bow and ask their parents' permission when they wish to go out. Once permission is received, they should bow again and say, "Maitte sanjimashō" (literally, "I am leaving and will return"). Upon returning, they should declare, "Tadaima kaerisorō" ("I have just returned"). The practice of announcing one's departure and arrival, still followed in Japan today, may also have roots in the classical passages of the *Elementary Learning:* "[A son,] when he is going abroad, must inform (his parents where he is going); when he returns, he must present himself before them."[5]

Generally, children are advised to do exactly as their parents wish, promptly and with a cheerful attitude, whether in regard to clothing, food, washing themselves, fixing their hair, or going to the *terakoya*. Furthermore, they should not cry without reason. This, says Toan, is the meaning of filial piety. In the second part of the text, the Shingaku leader cautions the children against lying. Shibata Minoru compares this point with another exhortation in the *Elementary Learning:* "A boy should never be allowed to see an instance of deceit."[6] Toan impressed on his young audiences that, even though others may not be aware of one's deceptive words or behavior, one's own original mind knows. Since the gods and buddhas are one with that mind, they also know. When one does something that makes one feel ashamed inside, even in private, the gods and buddhas dislike it. In Shingaku, the innate sense of morality was identified with the standards represented by Shinto and Buddhist deities; ethical conduct and devotional piety were seen as mutually reinforcing.

Toan duly enumerates other things that children should avoid: gambling, games (which can lead to fighting and resentment), clandestine amusements, and, in general, anything that attracts attention. Children should not kill living things needlessly; they must not tease animals for amusement, tie them up, hit dogs or make them run, catch birds and mice, or take the heads and wings off insects. The Shingaku master marshals a variety of arguments to convey this point. He warns that such behavior is totally contrary to the teachings of both Confucius and Buddha. Since all things are one's body, to hurt one of them is like hurting oneself. Furthermore, if one adopts the habit of killing living things as a child, one will become "skilled" at it and eventually face retribution for the wrongdoing one has committed. Toan also enjoins bragging and rudeness, and forbids boys and girls from playing together in the same place: mistakes between the sexes are grave offenses that both Confucius and Buddha deplored.[7]

Part 3 addresses further issues of human relations and etiquette. The children must avoid occasions of evil: if they keep good company, they will naturally grow up to be good people. This classic Confucian theme, encountered in Toan's *Principles for the Assembly of Companions,* is also articulated in the *Elementary Learning:* "To urge one another to what is good by reproofs is the way of friends."[8] Furthermore, the children should not make fun of people with deformities; in both China and Japan, Toan warns, many such people became angry enough to kill their tormentors. An anecdote serves to reinforce the point: "I knew someone recently whose nose fell off because of syphilis, so people made fun of him; he became extremely resentful and carries a deep grudge. It is truly a fearful thing."[9] The children should not laugh behind people's backs when they are entering or leaving (a room), for this can engender resentment as well. Likewise, it is important never to mistreat "girl-servants" and "young apprentices." One must not hit others; they, too, have parents who love them. Besides, Toan adds, one never knows what degree of injury one might inflict; ultimately, hitting someone risks both that person's life and one's own (because of the punishment of execution). Echoing the *Elementary Learning,* which states that "the desires should not be indulged,"[10] Toan also warns the children not to develop preferences for certain kinds of food and clothing. If they become accustomed to indulging themselves when young, it will lead to problems later in life—financial ruin or even death from starvation. Moreover, the children must never accept anything or give anything away, nor should they borrow or lend from others without the approval of their parents. According to the teaching of the sages, filial children never regard anything as their own: everything belongs to their parents.

The fourth part of *Early Lessons* is concerned with health and miscellaneous issues of self-improvement. Toan recommends that the children voluntarily undergo moxa cautery once a month. One should regard it as an act of filial piety, not just as a preventive health measure; otherwise one will tend to neglect it. It is easier to undergo moxa cautery if one's main motive is to reassure one's parents that one is not susceptible to epidemics or food poisoning. The children are also counseled not to injure their digestion by eating strange things or by eating too much; they should eat moderately. Shibata relates this counsel to *Analects* 1:14 (also cited in the *Elementary Learning*): "When a gentleman eats, he does not seek satiety."[11] Children must not harm their bodies, because even their bodies belong to their parents. For the same reason, they should refrain from becoming involved in fights.[12]

Toan reiterates that the children cannot escape retribution for their deeds. As he puts it, spitting at heaven has little effect; it just falls back on top of you.[13] This idea resonates with the Buddhist philosophy of karma, but similar notions can be found in ancient Chinese texts as well.[14] (In fact, Toan does not use Buddhist language when discussing this point.) The author also points out that those who take care of the children in lieu of their parents—grandparents, aunts and uncles, older siblings, even house clerks—deserve the same respect as parents.[15] In concluding, Toan explains that "learning" means making an effort throughout one's life not to say or do those things that one feels in one's mind to be "wrong." To ensure that his listeners would have a clear idea of the kinds of speech, for example, that would produce this inner shame, Toan offers a list: backtalk, willful talk, lying, gossip, flirting or joking between boys and girls, cruel remarks, boasting, and disgusting or immoral conversation.

The rest of *Early Lessons* is titled "Nyoshi kukyō" (Oral Instruction for Girls). The duties and roles of men and women in traditional East Asian society were clearly distinguished, but many concepts of morality pertained to both sexes. Toan stresses this point in his opening comments to girls. He remarks that those girls in the audience who understood the preceding four lessons to apply only to boys were mistaken. Boys, in turn, should listen to the lesson for girls and apply the appropriate points to themselves.

The most prominent theme in this section of the *Lessons* is that "women are separate." Girls and boys should not sit close together or place anything directly into each other's hands. Girls should not be in a place where there are no other girls, or in a dark place. The Shingaku master notes that all these things are mentioned in the *Elementary Learning;* one can infer the details of correct demeanor from these general principles.[16] Boys are like fire, Toan warns, and girls like firewood; if they get too close to each other, mistakes are bound to occur. Both Confucius and Buddha taught the separation of the sexes, for they knew how easy it is to make mistakes in this area.[17] In Toan's view, awareness of the need for separation was endowed in the original mind; even a child could discern and follow that inner voice.

The girls are also advised to obey the wishes of their parents and, later, of their husbands and parents-in-law. The Shingaku teacher duly mentions the "Three Obediences" required of women (to parents, husband, and son), adding that these, too, are detailed in the *Elementary Learning.*[18] He cautions the girls about their appearance, speech, and behavior: all must be plain and inconspicuous. Young women should concentrate on learning to write, spin, weave, wind thread, pick cotton, trim, sew, cook, boil, broil, and season food. It is best, he adds, that those of low position (commoners) not develop any skills beyond these. The girls are encouraged to speak not brilliantly, but moderately. Instead of trying to surpass others or display their talent and beauty, they should simply be gentle, diligent, and clean. They should assist in preparing offerings for the gods and buddhas, and always help their mothers. Once married, the girls should serve their husbands and parents-in-law wholeheartedly, without ever thinking of returning home. A wife must never do anything to bring shame on her husband.

In closing, Toan recommends that the girls read vernacular works such as *Essays in Idleness (Tsurezuregusa)* or the *Japanese Elementary Learning (Yamato shōgaku)* in their spare time.[19] In case they have not yet grasped the point from the preceding discussion, he reminds his wards that women are inferior by nature, a fact that they can read about in works ranging from the *Analects* to the *Sutra of Meditation on the Buddha of Eternal Life (Kanmuryōjukyō)* and *Essays in Idleness.*[20] Because of their inborn deficiency, girls must strive even harder than boys to "polish their minds."

An appendix to *Early Lessons* is also addressed to girls and women. It is titled *A Japanese Rendition of Ssu-ma Wen-kung's "Six Virtues of Women" from the "Principles of Family Behavior" (Shiba Onkō kahan fujin rikutoku wage)*. It is modeled after the eighth part of the *Principles of Family Behavior (Chia fan)*, a compilation of excerpts from the classics by the Sung scholar Ssu-ma Kuang (1019–1086). Toan's rendition is not a translation of the original work, but an entirely new essay that draws on a number of sources in addition to the original *Family Behavior*.[21] In this section, the Shingaku teacher recounts stories of exemplary women by way of inculcating six virtues: (1) submissiveness, (2) purity, (3) absence of jealousy, (4) frugality, (5) modesty, and (6) diligence.

Neither Toan's "Oral Instruction for Girls" nor his *Six Virtues of Women* is notable for any departure from standard views of the proper conduct for women during this period of Japanese history. However, it is significant that Toan designed special lessons for girls at all. Baigan had had a few female disciples, but it was Toan who developed specific programs for girls and women.[22] In the 1770s, concern for the moral education of lower-class girls and women was not yet widespread, although it became more so in the late Tokugawa period.[23] Teshima Toan's lessons for female students, although by no means innovative in content, were one of the earliest systematic efforts to teach groups of girls and women on a national scale.

The underlying premise of Toan's lessons for children was that environmental influences and the force of long habit lead to the construction of a false "self of calculation." Throughout *Early Lessons* he emphasizes the importance of understanding and practicing right conduct from a young age. He echoes Chu Hsi's comment in the "Summary Statement" ("T'i-tz'u") of the *Elementary Learning* that with the loss of elementary learning as it was known in ancient times, people lost the foundation for correct learning as adults.[24] At the end of *Early Lessons,* Toan remarks: "The aim of [the above] oral instruction of boys and girls is, in the first place, to impress upon their minds from childhood the constant principle (the path of human beings) and to teach them urgent matters that may be of assistance to them in the future after they grow up." The author explains that he developed a simplified program out of concern that the children's attention span and powers of retention were limited: "Since they are small children, it is probably difficult for them to remember and apply many points. Consequently, I am simply giving them a little bit of practical information, hoping that it may become a stepping-stone (a ladder) to enter the Elementary Learning."[25]

Toan's mention of the *Elementary Learning* in this context is not incidental. The Sung compilation for young people was one of the few texts that formed part of the official Shingaku curriculum during the late eighteenth century, and it inspired many of the themes that the Shingaku master presented to his young listeners. By Toan's time, the *Elementary Learning* had long been a cornerstone of Neo-Confucian education throughout East Asia. For ordinary Japanese people, it was, with some translation and interpretation, one of the most accessible and practical texts on child education available. Toan saw his own *Early Lessons* as an elaboration of Chu Hsi's program, an adaptation of the Neo-Confucian textual legacy to the needs of illiterate Japanese children. He hints in the above remark that *Early Lessons* was a kind of pre–*Elementary Learning*. At the end of the fourth part of the work, he reiterates that he simplified the teaching so that children would be able to remember and live up to it. He hoped to prepare the children for deeper levels of learning: "I wish with all my heart that, beginning with the *Elementary Learning*, [the children] will proceed to Japanese and Chinese writings, and that they will gradually read and listen, and advance along the path of filial piety."[26] The *Elementary Learning* was not the only text Toan drew on for his *Lessons*, as Shibata indicates in his notes to the modern edition. But it seems to have been the source of many of the ideas presented to the children, and Toan clearly envisioned it as the next step in their curriculum.

The *Elementary Learning* itself had originated in an attempt to formulate the Way of the sages in such a manner that young people could grasp its content. The "Inner Chapters," in particular, draw heavily on the *Book of Ritual* and the *Analects;* they focus on concrete prescriptions of behavior and stories of exemplary virtuous figures. Personal cultivation is presented as a tangible matter: it concerns physical appearance, specific gestures, movements, and demeanor. M. Theresa Kelleher notes that instruction in the more reflective aspect of cultivation tends to be reserved for a later stage of development, articulated in the "Outer Chapters" of the *Elementary Learning*.[27] Toan saw himself as transmitting the teaching of the Sung masters to the Japanese people; he regarded Chu Hsi's compilation as a model text for the kind of education that he wished to offer children. His talks for youngsters thus adopt a similar approach. In the *Lessons* he is predominantly concerned with prescribing specific forms of conduct; talk of meditation or the contemplative effort to find the original mind is reserved for adult audiences.

Toan first offered *Early Lessons* in the second month of 1773; one of Toan's disciples recorded the entire sequence of talks and printed it in the eighth month of the same year. The printing blocks for the text were recarved in 1778 and again in 1792; illustrated and smaller size editions were issued in 1833. The work was also included in a 1785 collection by Uekawa Kisui titled *Kōkyō dōjikun*, (*Instruction for Children on the Classic of Filial Piety*). The fifth part of the *Lessons* was reprinted in 1840 in a special Shingaku collection for women. *Early Lessons* was also

published by some Shingaku meetinghouses in the form of separate leaflets. Late Shingaku teachers routinely based their own instruction of children on Toan's text; *Old Man Dōni's Early Lessons,* recorded in 1788,
exemplifies this trend.[28] *Early Lessons* thus set the pattern for Shingaku
education of children for the rest of the Tokugawa era.

A Shingaku Primer

Another of Toan's works for children, *Shinjitsugokyō,* or *New Teaching
of Words of Truth* (1781), is a reader arranged entirely in six-character
Chinese verses.[29] The text was modeled after the well-known *Jitsugokyō,*
(Teaching of Words of Truth), a children's textbook in five-character
verse that was widely used in *terakoya* during the Edo period. The original *Words of Truth* is usually associated with a similar work, *Dōjikyō,* or
Teaching for Children; the two texts were often bound together in the
same edition.[30]

Words of Truth was popularly attributed to the great Shingon Buddhist master Kūkai (774–835), but doubts about his authorship were
already being expressed by the late seventeeth century.[31] Ishikawa estimates that *Words of Truth* originated in the Heian period (782–1181)
and was in circulation by the early Kamakura period (1182–1333).[32]
Both *Words of Truth* and its companion, *Teaching for Children,* enunci-
ate Confucian values, but they are generally Buddhist in tone, emphasizing the transience of worldly phenomena. *Teaching for Children*
addresses the reader in terms of the need to prepare for the next life; it
was probably written for young Buddhist novices or children who
resided in the temple precincts.[33] *Words of Truth* draws especially on
Confucian discourse for its ethical instruction; the author speaks of the
"gentleman" who loves wise people, in contrast to the "petty person"
who loves the fortunate. One should be filial to one's parents, who are
like heaven and earth, and render service to one's teacher and one's master, who are like the sun and the moon. The text goes on to advise peace
with one's friends, respect for one's elders, and compassion for those
who are younger.[34] In short, the Confucian morality of the Five Relations is advocated, although as part of a world-view that is fundamentally Buddhist.

In medieval Japan, when education was largely the domain of Buddhist temples, texts like *Words of Truth* and *Teaching for Children* fit the
needs of the age. Confucian values were presented as an elaboration of
one aspect of the Buddhist vision. After the beginning of the Tokugawa
era, advocates of Neo-Confucian learning gradually began to take more
intellectual initiative. This trend initially affected the education of the
upper classes; most commoners remained outside the reach of the curri-
cular materials and teaching activities of Confucian scholars. By the mid-

dle of the period, however, Neo-Confucian learning was making inroads into institutions and activities that did cater to nonsamurai—*terakoya,* moral learning schools, public lectures, and other, more informal media. At the same time, a more critical attitude toward Buddhism developed, even among those who ostensibly spoke for the less-privileged classes.[35] A late Tokugawa period merchant, Masamori Kōki (1793–1857), observed that "if one goes to the temples today, they are only teaching [children] to revere the Buddha; they don't teach good manners, much less the path of human relations." He also complained that "the *terakoya* teachers first teach books that are principally of Buddhist intent, such as the *Jitsugokyō* and *Dōjikyō,* and after that such works as *Teikin ōrai . . .* works that are not of the least use to those of the common class."[36]

In fact, despite their association with an outdated Buddhist world-view, *Words of Truth* and *Teaching for Children* did not lose their appeal in the early modern era. On the contrary, both books found a wider audience; in the eighteenth and nineteenth centuries, the cumulative number of printings ran into several tens of thousands.[37] (Of the two texts, *Words of Truth* seems to have been more widely used in *terakoya* of the time.)[38] Evidently, the books were considered useful—but mainly as a means of inculcating the Chinese characters of which they were composed. The actual content of *Teaching for Children* and *Words of Truth* became increasingly peripheral to the educational process that took place in the *terakoya.*[39] Like the medieval letters that became primers in the Tokugawa period despite their irrelevance to the new sociohistorical context, *Words of Truth* and its companion functioned chiefly as copybooks and recital texts.[40] Even at the end of the period, they were still being used to teach children how to read Chinese characters off according to Japanese syntax and pronunciation *(sodoku).*

Nevertheless, the ideas contained in these works had some influence on children in the Edo period. Dore, for one, suggests that they had considerable impact on popular thought:

> That Japan continued to be a Buddhist country into the Meiji period, not simply in the sense that funerals were conducted according to Buddhist rites, but in the sense that elements of Buddhist theology and ethics remained alive in popular attitudes to life, was probably as much due to the efforts of terakoya teachers with their *Jitsugo-kyō* and *Dōji-kyō* (not all of them priests by any means) as it was to the priests themselves and their none too frequent sermons.[41]

Precisely because of this lingering "Buddhist" influence, even as the books remained in wide use, attempts were made to revise them. The demand for textbooks that fit the ideological needs of the age more closely yet retained the mnemonically convenient style of *Words of Truth* led to a series of copybook primers patterned after the original. Ishikawa argues that these later works show a gradual shift away from the otherworldly tone of the medieval texts and a growing stress on education as a guide for navigating life in this world.[42]

The perspective of these revised versions does contrast with the Buddhist coloration of the original *Words of Truth*. However, the new social reality of the Edo period was reflected in religious traditions across the board. Buddhist responses to the new social context included modifications in teaching style; many Buddhist writer-preachers were aware of the need for a vernacular teaching relevant to the daily concerns of their constituents. But these teachers made few conspicuous attempts to develop texts or programs of lay education that took account of the special needs of children. The emerging class of Confucian scholars, in contrast, could make use of Sung compilations such as the *Elementary Learning*, which had been purposefully drawn up for the ethical instruction of literate young people. However, nonsamurai Japanese children needed a simpler, more retainable form of this Confucian moral instruction; the authors of the new primers, sensing this need, borrowed the style of the old *Words of Truth* to express the perspective of the new era.

Teshima Toan's *New Teaching of Words of Truth* was one of these attempts to adapt the style of the original work to the Neo-Confucian spirit of the Tokugawa age.[43] The original text emphasizes the benefits of book learning vis-à-vis ephemeral worldly wealth: one day's learning is "better than a thousand pieces of gold."[44] Toan introduces a different perspective in the opening lines of his work: "real learning" (*jitsugaku*) is to be valued over literary studies. "Learning" is now interpreted from the standpoint of Neo-Confucian self-cultivation:

> One does not value people because of their individual knowledge.
> One values them because they are morally upright.
> Literary learning is not the ultimate treasure;
> Real learning is considered the priceless jewel.
> Literary learning mostly generates arrogance;
> The teaching of filial piety and deference aims at selflessness.
> Rote learning is an external thing;
> The teaching of filial piety and deference is innate virtue.
> What you should learn is filial piety and deference, loyalty and trust;
> Do not envy broad erudition and great talent.[45]

Toan's repeated contrast of superficial studies and real learning does not contradict the message of the original *Words of Truth*, but highlights the internal and moral dimensions of learning. His deemphasis on literary erudition here may also be another veiled critique of "professional" learning—an attitude that (as seen in Chapter 2) underlay the Shingaku view of some Confucian scholars.

Throughout *New Words of Truth* Toan draws on classical texts to characterize his view of self-cultivation. *New Words* was designed specif-ically for young children who were learning to read Chinese characters. The author directly quotes or rephrases ancient Chinese passages in nearly every six-character line. Thus, wisdom is to know people: Shun and T'ang displayed this quality in their good judgment of human nature (*Analects* 12:22).[46] The gentleman should turn and look into himself when people do not respond to his courtesy, his love, or his attempt to govern them (*Mencius* 4A:4).[47] To fail to correct oneself after making a mistake is the real mistake (*Analects* 15:30); to engage in wrongdoing knowingly is evil, whereas to do so unknowingly is an error (cf. *Mencius* 2B:9).[48] The constant allusions to the classics include practical advice: "Do not refer to your parents as old in their presence; do not ask the elderly about their age" (*Elementary Learning* 2:5, 85).[49] The children are given detailed counsel on how to admonish their parents: first calm yourself, then lower your voice and present a cheerful countenance (*Elementary Learning* 2:22).[50] They are also reminded that a filial son does not change his father's way of doing things for three years following the father's death (*Elementary Learning* 2:26).[51]

Occasionally Toan reformulates themes that appear in the old *Words of Truth*. The earlier text warns that if one sees evil, one should give it a wide berth.[52] *New Words* cautions against associating with those who are (morally) inferior to oneself; one should keep company with the humane and the worthy in order to receive their influence.[53] The Shingaku author also expounds on characteristic Neo-Confucian con-cepts such as sincerity (Ch. *ch'eng*, J. *makoto*), a prominent theme in the *Great Learning* and the *Mean*: "If the way is not cultivated, the mind loses sincerity; sincerity is the beginning and end of everything. When people have no sincerity, they have nothing."[54] He quotes the expression "learning begins with not deceiving oneself [when alone] in a dark room" (attributed to one of the Ch'eng brothers).[55] In one passage Toan inserts his own formulation of the learning of the mind:

> To follow one's nature is the original mind;
> To violate one's nature is heresy *(itan)*.
> The original mind is in fact the mind of the Way;
> It is imperative that beginners know the original mind.
> In the learning of the mind, place priority on choosing a good teacher;
> If you do not choose a teacher, you will fall into an evil path.
> Outside of the original mind, there is no Way at all;
> When one knows the original mind, one knows the Way.[56]

Although the predominant emphasis of *New Words* is moral, occa-sionally Toan alludes to the more contemplative, mystical aspect of the learning of the mind: "The system of the mind is not concerned with words; quietly, without moving, it responds and penetrates."[57] But he is careful to point out that the teaching of the sages is not esoteric or hidden; human affairs themselves are the realm of cultivation.[58] This perspective contrasts with the old *Words of Truth,* which hints at the ephemeral nature of this world and the need to be released from the suffering associated with it.[59] The exceptional reference to Buddhism in *New Words of Truth* appears in the context of remarks about birth and death.

> Buddhas alone do not discuss death and birth;
> Are not death and birth also tremendous matters?[60]
> Therefore, "[the sage] returns to the end by inquiring into the
>   beginning.
> Thus, he knows the explanation of death and birth."[61]
> People and ghosts, this world and the next are not separate;
> Yin and yang, day and night arise from each other.[62]

The old *Words of Truth,* in contrast, lists numerous terms related to the Buddhist conception of religious cultivation:

> If one does not associate with one's friends, the Three Learnings,
> How can one travel through the forest of the Seven Requirements?
> Without riding on the boat of the Four Mentalities,
> Who can cross the ocean of Eight Sufferings?
> Although the Eightfold Correct Path is wide,
> People [who commit] the Ten Evils do not pursue it.[63]

Toward the end of his own primer, Toan counters this list by enumerating Confucian categories drawn from his favorite sources, the *Analects* and *Mencius:* "The Nine Concerns of the Gentleman" (*Analects* 16:10), "The Four Germs of Virtue" (*Mencius* 2A:6), "The Five Excellent Practices," and "The Four Wicked Practices" (*Analects* 20:2).[64] He concludes *New Words* by reiterating a point emphasized in *Early Lessons:* what one learns while young becomes the basis for one's whole life. Moreover, even among Confucians, Toan warns, there are gentlemen and "petty persons": "Do not become a petty-person Confucian!"[65]

Ishikawa believes that *New Words of Truth* was rarely used in Shingaku group meetings, training sessions, or talks on the Way; he says that it received less attention than Toan's other works from later Shingaku teachers.[66] But *New Words* was certainly used for the purpose for which Toan intended it—children's education. Several editions were issued, including one in 1782 with headnotes by Kisui.[67] Judging from the content of *New Words,* it was specifically designed for nonsamurai children. The author claims in a postscript that he did not intend the work to be distributed widely; he purportedly wrote it as a kind of supplementary textbook for the children of his own friends, most of whom were undoubtedly merchants, weavers, other artisans, and perhaps some rural dwellers. In the text itself, Toan explicitly warns against going beyond one's social position, particularly in one's aspirations for learning. His injunctions against envying the education of others may reflect the growing desirability of learning in the eyes of those who were often excluded from it. From the Shingaku viewpoint, a merchant or artisan who took pride in acquiring knowledge while neglecting the family trade risked bringing disaster on the whole family. It was only as a "retired merchant" that Toan felt he could devote himself full-time to developing his own learning. He cautions his young wards against unduly desiring things "outside" their position, a condition that he identifies with the Mencian "lost mind" (6A:8).[68] Toan's general attitude toward the existing social order was eminently conservative; he advises his young readers to accept differences in wealth, rank, and occupation as natural and appropriate.

The relatively uneducated children to whom *New Words* was addressed would have had difficulty understanding many of its classical allusions and quotations without extensive explication. The obscurity of passages such as the following seems to contradict the ostensible aim of the text as a child's primer:[69]

> *Ch'ien*, which has no form, governs by means of ease;
> *K'un*, which engages in formation, follows by means of simplicity.
> The rotation of *ch'ien* and *k'un* occurs without thought or artifice.
> The conduct of a gentleman, too, is easy and simple.[70]

However, like the book after which it was modeled, Toan's *New Words* was not necessarily designed to be understood by its readers, at least not initially. Rather, Toan simply wished to expose the youngsters to Chinese characters and terms that might be useful for a later, more serious study of the Confucian texts. As the reciting or copying exercises proceeded, the Shingaku teacher would gradually explain the meaning of such ideas as *ch'ien* and *k'un*. *New Words* was not a quick, easy way of transmitting the Shingaku teaching (as were Toan's other works for youngsters). But the author believed that by reciting the text the children would eventually gain some understanding of its content:

> In response to the request of my colleagues, I overlooked the offense of going beyond one's position and put together the sayings of the sages and worthies in six-character verses in order to make it easier for young children to read and remember. I hope [the children] will constantly recite this, so that after they grow up they will not show their respect for the *Analects, Mencius, Great Learning,* and the *Doctrine of the Mean* simply by mouthing them uselessly, but that, based on this [early training], they will develop and become mature in their understanding,

become truly clear in their minds about the principles of the virtuous nature, and embody them in their conduct.[71]

Thus, although *New Words* was intended to teach children how to read off Chinese characters, it would also familiarize them with specific ideas. Accordingly, in the text Toan deliberately concentrates on Confucian values, which he considered most important at the elementary level of education, and refrains from referring to such Buddhist themes as the transience of this world. He thereby provided the children who attended Shingaku classes with an alternative to the perspective of the widely used medieval primers. In *New Words,* as in *Early Lessons,* Toan consistently avoids the Buddhist discourse that colors many of his sermons and dialogues for adults.

Teaching Shingaku through Songs

The heart of Toan's approach to popular education is revealed in the songs *(uta)* that he wrote for children. These were not necessarily "songs" in the sense of words set to specific melodies, but verses that could be chanted rhythmically. The use of songs in Shingaku teaching did not originate with Toan. Ishida Baigan reportedly used songs from Nō plays *(yōkyoku)* as material for his evening lectures,[72] perhaps because his merchant students were familiar with the plays. However, it was Toan who first wrote and published verses for the purpose of instructing children.

Songs had become a common tool of Japanese religious educators by the mid-Edo period. Several versified works have been attributed, for example, to Rinzai Zen master Hakuin; they extol moral values, such as compassion and filial piety, as well as the virtues of Zen meditation. Hakuin's best-known work in this genre is *Zazen wasan* (Song of Zen Meditation), which is still chanted in Rinzai temples today.[73] His *Segyō uta* (Song of Almsgiving) urges people to sow seeds of charity by giving alms in this life; otherwise they may find themselves destitute in the next.[74] *Shushin obaba kohiki uta* (The Grain-Grinding Song of the Old Woman, Mind-as-Master), published in 1770, was designed to be sung to the rhythm of the grinding of rice and barley—a regular feature of daily life for many common people.[75] The song contains simple reminders of ethical principles: "One's debt to one's parents is deeper than the ocean; those who do not realize this debt are dogs and cats." But the importance of cultivating the mind is the central motif:

> If you have no mind-as-master, it is the same as a vacant house;
>   foxes and raccoons will come in and replace it.[76]
> You may look nice with your surplice and [Buddhist] robe, but
>   unless your mind-as-master is present, you're a strange creature.[77]

Such ditties were generally similar in style, regardless of the particular religious perspective from which they were written.[78] Moral exhortations are usually combined with pithy declarations of the author's faith. A *kyōka* (comic poem) master named Shiteki-ō (1718–1779), also a Rinzai monk, was active in the Kyoto and Osaka areas during the same period as Toan. Toan often quotes his poems—indeed, some of Shiteki-ō's verses sound much like Shingaku:

> Try throwing away the small mind called "I"—
> nothing will hinder you in all the Great Thousand Worlds.[79]
> Simply lowering your head is not propriety;
> [it is] lowering your heart and not being puffed up.[80]

These lines are part of a poem written in the *iroha* style, which Toan adopted for his own songs. The verses of an *iroha* song are arranged in Japanese "alphabetical" order *(i-ro-ha)*, according to the first character of each verse. *Iroha* verses were a time-honored pedagogic and mnemonic tool in traditional Japan.[81]

Toan's most famous *iroha* song is the title song of a larger collection of verses called *Jijo: Nemurizamashi* (For Boys and Girls: Waking Up from Sleep).[82] The song was first published in 1773, but as Kisui implies in the postscript to a later edition, his father had been using it as a teaching device before that time. Like *Early Lessons,* the song was printed on leaflets and distributed to the children who attended Shingaku classes. Each sheet was devoted to one verse, which was illustrated by a simple picture.[83] In his preface, Toan expresses the hope that the children will pick up the verses easily and hum or chant them while doing their daily errands ("sewing and weaving").[84] Since the song is arranged in *iroha* order with a set rhythm, this expectation was not necessarily unreasonable.

The content of *Waking Up* comprises the same combination of ethics and concern for mindfulness that characterizes Shingaku teaching in general. Many verses simply urge moral conduct (see figures 1 to 4):

> Whatever the case, do not forget to be filial toward your parents
> and faithful to your master.
> Proper behavior between men and women is a serious matter;
> evil-natured creatures are the dregs of humanity.
> If you go about saying and doing cruel things,
> they will all redound upon you.
> You may amass money out of stinginess, but
> unless you help others out of compassion, you are merely a money
> guard.

The song goes beyond listing such virtues as filial piety, chastity, kindness, and generosity, however. Nearly half of its forty-eight verses speak of the need to become free of self-centered calculation and to cultivate the mind. From the subtitle of the work *(For Boys and Girls)*, one might assume that *Waking Up* was intended exclusively for children; but parts of the song are quite profound. It assumes a somewhat more advanced understanding on the part of its readers than does *Early Lessons*. The leaflets illustrating the verses were evidently distributed not only to children, but sometimes also to adults who attended talks on the Way.[85]

Toan directly warns his wards about the perils of selfish calculation:

Figure 1.   Figure 2.

> A straight mind is warped by calculations;
>> if I don't twist it, my mind won't be warped.

The picture corresponding to this verse shows a man training a potted tree into the characteristically twisted, gnarled posture of a bonsai (fig. 5). The message is the Mencian theme of innate goodness: the mind is naturally pure and will remain so as long as one does not distort it through poor habits or bad influences. The children must learn to preserve the original condition of their minds.

Figure 3.

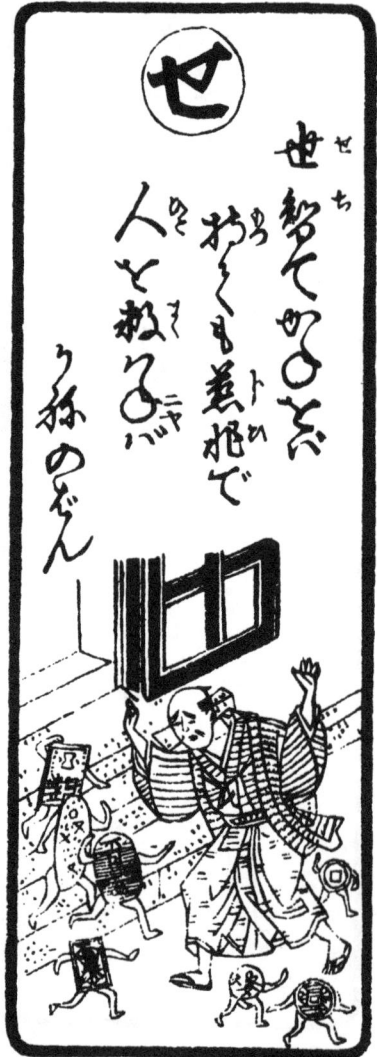

Figure 4.

As soon as you think it exists, that is calculation.
  "It exists," "it does not exist"—both are delusions.

This verse is illustrated with a picture of a woodcutter standing still in the middle of a bridge (fig. 6). He represents a person who, somewhere along the path of self-cultivation, becomes stuck on the "bridge of calculation," unable to resolve the issue of "existence and nonexistence." He is unsure whether to move forward or to go back. The point is that one must transcend dualistic thinking in order to find the original mind.[86]

Figure 5.

Figure 6.

> They come as they come, and they go as they go;
> in any case, all calculations are rubbish.

The picture shows children trying to hit some stars with a bamboo pole (fig. 7). The scene recalls a proverbial saying *(Sao dake de hoshi o utsu)* that warns against foolishly trying to "reach for the stars," or attempt the impossible. Calculations are worthless, passing phenomena; those who value such ruminations or try to hold onto them are as foolish as children who attempt to hit stars with a pole.

The mind itself is a frequent topic in the *iroha* verses. The following are three examples:

> One's mind cannot pretend that it's not at home;
> it is aware of both the good and the evil [which one commits].

It is possible to turn one's back and commit evil in a clandestine manner, but the "judge of sins" in one's mind will nevertheless evaluate all one's actions. One can pretend to be away when someone comes to the door, but one cannot pretend to be absent during one's own wrongdoing. The picture shows a man turned away from the viewer; on his back are depicted two heads, representing his evil and good selves, or the consciencelike function of the original mind (fig. 8).

> If you want to be content, know your mind;
> contentment is endowed in your mind from birth.

Here again is the Mencian emphasis on original goodness, which is the basis of happiness; the good person is a joyful person. The picture of a mother with her child highlights the point that the mind of an infant is pure and content (fig. 9). Hence, the search for happiness should begin by looking into one's own mind; in its natural state, it is at ease and content.[87]

> The mind is swayed by its surroundings;
> let's not mix with evil.

Pursuing the implications of the doctrine of natural goodness, Toan emphasizes to the children that they may become good or evil depending on their social environment. The idea that we are influenced by the company we keep is a standard Confucian motif that Toan preached repeatedly to all his audiences. The phrase "the mind is swayed by its surroundings" is taken from *Essays in Idleness*.[88] The leaflet illustration depicts only foliage (fig. 10). The leaves appear to belong to the *kaede* (Japanese maple) and the *nishiki-gi* (winged spindle tree), both of which turn red in the autumn.[89] The proverb "If you mix with vermilion, you will turn red"

(Shu ni majiwareba akaku to naru) may explain the connection between the verse and the picture: do not mix with red/leaves/evil. In short, the children should not expose themselves to undesirable influences.

Toan's trademark teaching, "knowing the original mind," is presented as a most pressing matter.

> I want to see it! I want to know it!
>> As long as I have such a resolve, my mind can be known.

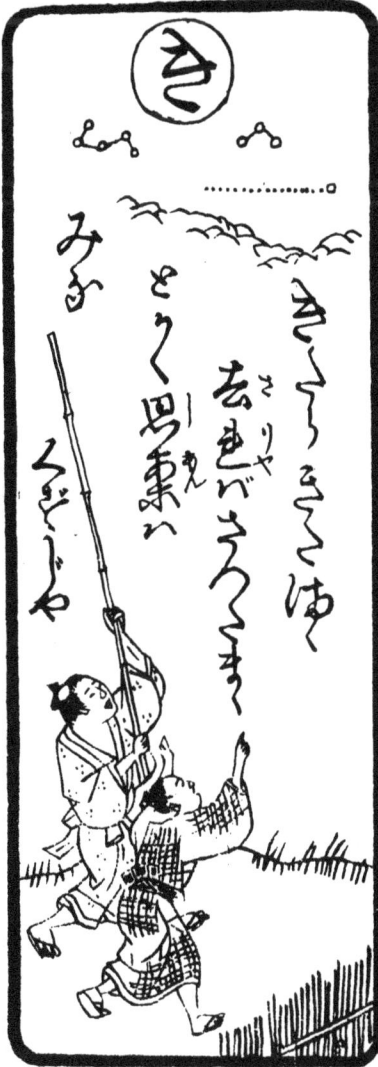 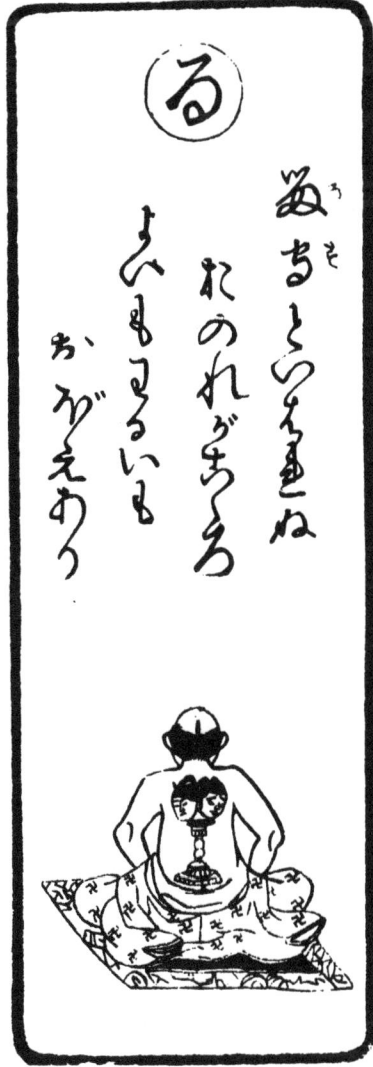

Figure 7.   Figure 8.

The verse is accompanied by a picture of a lady-in-waiting breaking off a branch (fig. 11); it may be an allusion to a passage in *Mencius* (1A:11):

> In such a thing as taking the T'ai mountain under your arm, and leaping over the North Sea with it, if you say to people—"I am not able to do it," that is a real case of not being able. In such a matter as breaking off a branch from a tree at the order of a superior, if you say to people —"I am not able to do it," that is a case of not doing it, it is not a case of not being able to do it.[90]

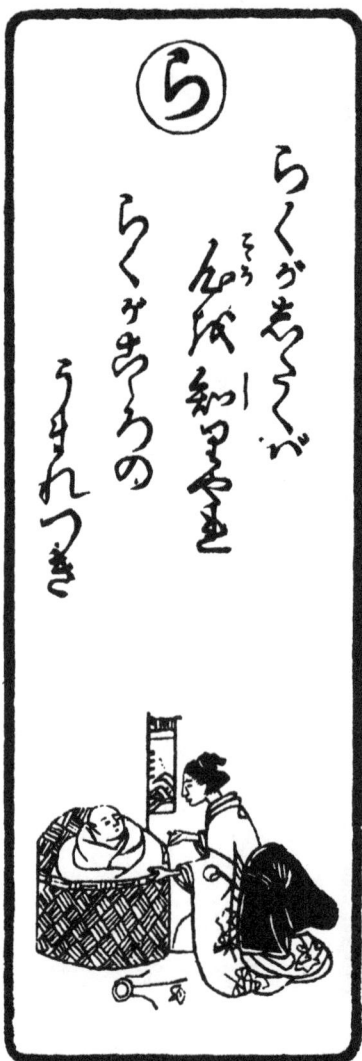

Figure 9.

Figure 10.

In other words, as long as one truly desires to find the original mind, one can. It is not an impossible feat; it is simply a matter that requires sincerity and diligent effort. However, if one does not seek the original mind during the prime of life, when one grows old (reaches the point of cultivating chrysanthemums), one will realize that one has wasted one's life:[91]

> The person who lives without knowing this knowable mind
> is indeed short-lived.

An old man is shown taking a pair of scissors from a child; he is about to trim some chrysanthemums (fig. 12).

> To lose the mind that one had found and to die in that state
> is too much to bear.

The leaflet for this verse depicts a couple quarreling: the man seems about to beat his wife (fig. 13). The cause of such poor human relations is the loss of the original mind; self-centered emotions like anger obscure the consideration for others that is an inherent principle in each one of us.

Toan does not neglect the mystical aspect of his teaching, even in this simple ditty. Several verses evoke the unfathomable dimension of the cosmos and the mind:

> The Tama [Sphere] River of Ide does not look round.
> Where does it flow? It has no end.

An astronomer is shown explaining the principles of the heavens to his pupil (fig. 14). "The Tama River of Ide" is another name for "River of Heaven" *(Ama no gawa),* the Milky Way. The verse extols the continuous revolution of the heavenly bodies and the infinity of the universe in general.

> My mind! I seek its innermost depths,
> but it is limitless.

Here the children were presented with a picture of a man gazing at an incense burner, apparently sunk deep in contemplation (fig. 15). He is probably practicing quiet sitting.[92] But one cannot discover the original mind while consciously searching for it. It emerges suddenly, in an unplanned way. The above verse stresses the infinite, boundless quality of the mind. The following line makes a similar point:

> The older things are, the more valuable;
> what about my mind, which has no beginning?

This lesson is illustrated by a picture of a seated man looking intently at a tea bowl (fig. 16). He is probably an enthusiast of the tea ceremony, an art in which the age of the instruments used is a criterion of aesthetic appreciation. Not only the bowl but the bamboo vase on the wall (which contains a flower arrangement) and the little bamboo spoon on a dish in front of the man may have been handed down through generations. Toan wishes to impress on the children that their own minds are far more valuable than any such objects. The importance of the mind is highlighted in the picture by a wall hanging of the famous Zen saying *jikishi ninshin* (directly pointing to the human mind).[93] Another verse exalts the mind further:

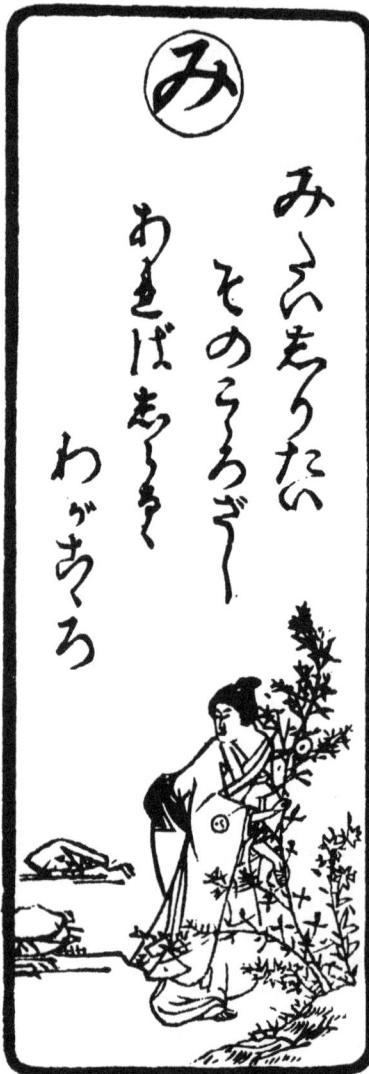

Figure 11.   Figure 12.

Indeed, the mind is a mysterious thing;
  it knows, even though it does not know.

A mother watches in amazement as her young son uses chopsticks (fig. 17). Babies are born and, before one knows it, they begin to use proper etiquette. We may not be conscious of "knowing" the rules of conduct, but we are born with an instinctive, preconscious foundation for correct behavior.

  Waking Up from Sleep was mainly intended to educate children about

Figure 13.

Figure 14.

morality and its source in the true mind, but it incidentally transmits a wealth of Japanese (and Chinese) cultural traditions. Toan and his fellow preachers were well aware that young children have difficulty absorbing abstractions divorced from a particular sociocultural context. According to modern religious educators, training in any religious tradition from the age of about six through adolescence must take account of children's need for identification with a particular society, tradition, or culture. During this period, a child's awareness of his or her own "people" should

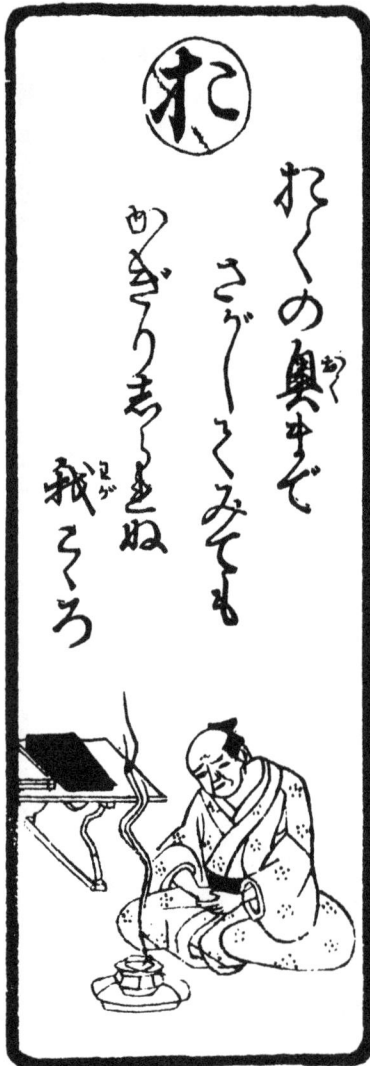

Figure 15.

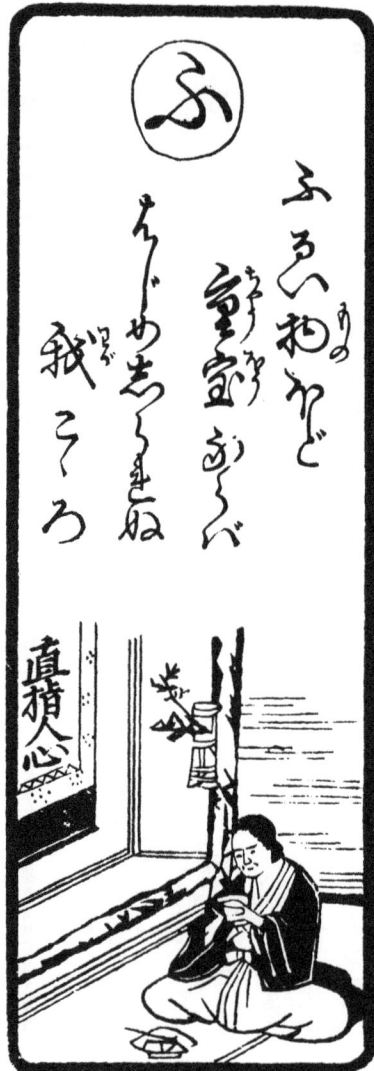

Figure 16.

be nourished through narratives and traditional practices.[94] Teshima Toan would have agreed; his lessons, verses, and leaflets informed children about such matters as the intimate link between Japan and its gods, the connection between themselves and their ancestors, the meaning of Japanese proverbs and stories, and, most eminently, the right way to behave in Japanese society. A thorough grasp of the content of the entire *Waking Up* series required mastery of considerable historical, literary, and pictorial detail. A single verse along with its illustration could have provided Toan with enough material for an entire lesson.

It is this very detail that made the song an effective teaching tool; it was an auditory and visual experience that left the children with a vivid impression of the day's message. The last three examples demonstrate the embellishing function of these background stories.

> "I want this! I want that!" Such selfish calculations are devils!
>   They torment the serene mind.

We are shown a scene from an old tale called "fox trapping" *(tsuri-gi-tsune)*, which was the theme of a Kyōgen play (fig. 18). An old fox, whose relatives had been killed by a certain trapper, takes the form of a Buddhist monk. He tries to convince the trapper to stop killing foxes, which is a violation of one of the Buddhist precepts. He has almost succeeded when, at the last minute, he spots a particularly inviting bait in one of the hunter's traps. On the leaflet it is depicted as a mouse, but more precisely, it is *nezumi no abura age*—mouse prepared with fried tofu (reportedly a favorite dish of Japanese foxes). In the fox-monk's mind, the temptation to grab the mouse conflicts with his reluctance to reveal his true identity. He is caught in a dilemma of contradictory self-centered desires or calculations *(shian)*. In the end, the fox barely escapes with his life.[95] The point of the story is that our own animal desires are the cause of our suffering; if left uncontrolled, they will torment us like devils.

> Those who try to appear clever are usually fools;
>   isn't it enough to follow common sense?

The picture that accompanies this verse shows a monk trying to pull a pot off someone's head (fig. 19); it is an allusion to a tale in *Essays in Idleness*.[96] The priests of the Buddhist temple Ninnaji had a farewell party for some young novices who were about to become priests; they all enjoyed themselves thoroughly, carousing and becoming intoxicated. One of the priests put a three-legged cauldron on his head, pushed it down past his nose, and danced around, adding to the general hilarity. But when he tried to take it off, the pot would not budge, despite all his efforts. His companions were unable to break it off from the outside.

The man's neck gradually began to swell, and his breathing became difficult. A visit to the doctor proved fruitless; the unfortunate priest's mother and friends came and wept at his bedside. Finally it was resolved that an attempt should be made at least to save his life. The pot was pulled off by force, and the monk's nose and ears were ripped off with it. A story like this would certainly have lingered in the children's memories. By telling it, Toan and other Shingaku teachers could vividly bring home the risks involved in trying to "appear clever."

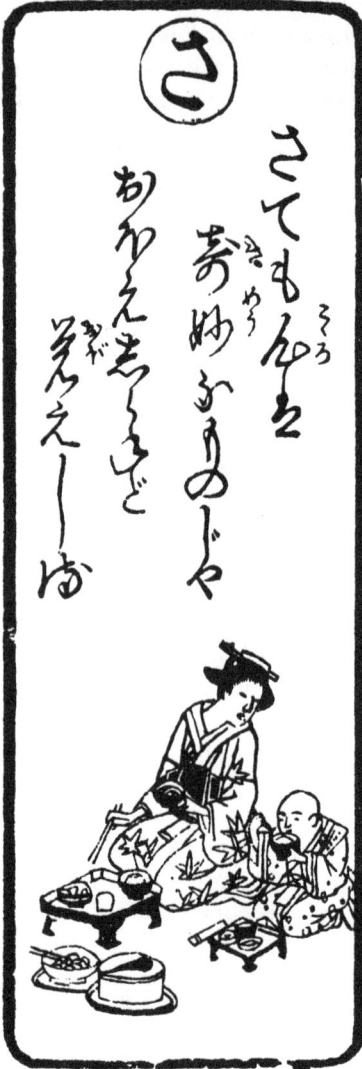

Figure 17.

Figure 18.

The final example alludes to an old tale that dates back at least to the tenth century:

> The wizard of Kume—how ludicrous!
> He looked at her false skin and was beguiled.[97]

The picture shows a man descending from the sky toward a rather buck-toothed creature who is baring her legs in a stream (fig. 20). The man is the legendary wizard of Kume, who had the power to fly through the air.

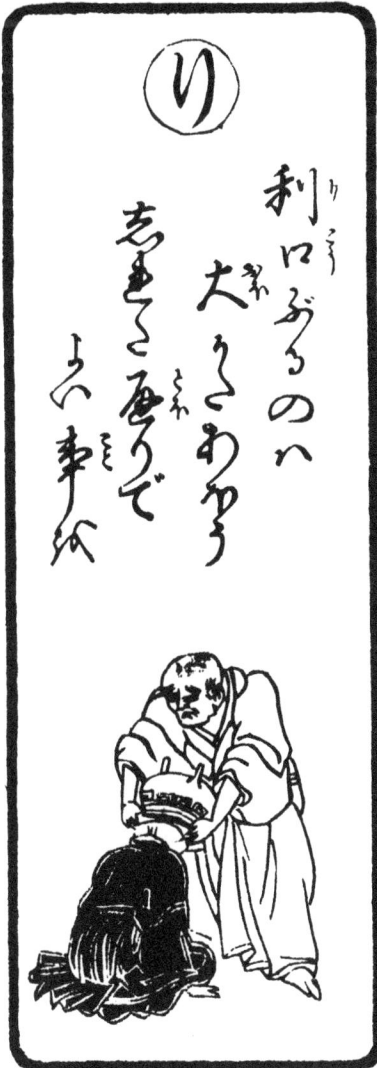

Figure 19.

Figure 20.

It is said that one day he caught sight of the beautiful white legs of a woman washing clothes in the Yoshino River, whereupon he lost his magical powers and fell back into the world of mortals. The term "false skin" *(uso no kawa)* denotes a deceptive surface with no true content behind it. For the children, the moral of the story was not to be misled by external appearances—true beauty is internal.

Waking Up from Sleep is a more engaging work than either *Early Lessons* or *New Words of Truth*. It is written in a poetic, colorful style and allows more room for the imagination than Toan's more prosaic discussions of morality. Words in the text are invariably given their native readings, so that the children could easily understand and remember them. The use of Kansai (western) dialect is prominent in the original work; a later edition aimed at the Edo area was rewritten with orthographic modifications. Because of the accessibility and appeal of the work to children and semiliterate adults, it reached a significant readership. After its first printing in 1773, *Waking Up* was republished in 1788 with a postscript by Uekawa Kisui. It was mass printed several times as single-sheet handouts *(se-in)* by various Shingaku meetinghouses, sometimes under different titles or with different pictures.[98]

The continuing popularity of the song is confirmed by its use in certain Osaka *terakoya* in the late Tokugawa period.[99] On Tanabata (Festival of the Weaver), a seasonal holiday that falls on the seventh night of the seventh lunar month, the major Osaka *terakoya* celebrated by dancing the *Ongoku odori* (Dance of Distant Lands).[100] On the evening of Tanabata, the schoolhouses were decorated with lanterns, and the little girls dressed up in identical costumes. They would tie their *obi* (belts) together, form a line, and parade through the streets, while the boys stood by on the side to ensure that the procession line was not broken. When the parade was over, the children returned to their classrooms to sing and perform the Ongoku dance. The practice predates the rise of Shingaku in the Osaka area, but after Shingaku became popular, a tune called *Ongoku iroha uta* (The *Iroha* Song of Distant Lands) was adopted by many *terakoya* as an accompaniment for the dance. Genichidō, a school founded in 1807, was particularly noted for the style of its Ongoku dance. The text of the Ongoku *iroha* song, printed on illustrated leaflets, has been preserved in Genichidō; it is none other than Toan's *Waking Up from Sleep*.[101] Toan's efforts to teach his version of the learning of the mind to children thus had impact beyond the Shingaku network itself. There is evidence that the song penetrated rural areas as well as urban centers like Osaka. Within the Shingaku community, the work continued to be used for children's classes into the early part of this century.[102]

Toan designed his educational texts for the offspring of merchants, artisans, and farmers. These boys and girls, often in demand as helpers or apprentices in their family businesses, had few opportunities to study other than irregular attendance at *terakoya*. In *Early Lessons* and *Waking Up from Sleep,* his most popular children's texts, Toan focuses on one point at a time and uses simple language; Chinese characters appear with vernacular readings on the side. Classical material is organized into concise daily lessons and illustrated through anecdotes and brief sayings as well as through pictures that were block printed and distributed on a large scale. The illustrated sheets served as visual aids that helped fix the day's lesson in the children's minds, and the prospect of receiving another picture probably motivated the youngsters to attend the next lesson.

Judging from the reprinting and continued use of Toan's texts, his techniques were effective in reaching children. Quite apart from technique, however, the practice of gathering large numbers of children and instructing them regularly in morality and etiquette is itself a notable development in the history of education in Japan. In effect, the Shingaku program for children supplemented the services offered by the *terakoya* of the time. These so-called temple schools shared no systematic approach to education, particularly moral instruction. Although the *terakoya* and the Shingaku classes catered to ordinary children of the same general age group, their curricula differed. Most *terakoya* concentrated on imparting writing and reading skills; the amount of ethical instruction offered depended on the idiosyncrasy of the individual teacher.[103] Moreover, *terakoya* teachers accepted remuneration on certain occasions, but Toan explicitly prohibited payments and gifts. His refusal to accept payment indicates at least his own perception of the difference between Shingaku lessons for children and those offered by the *terakoya*. Child education was part of the Shingaku teacher's religious mission; it was not a paid profession or job. Shingaku classes incidentally afforded less-privileged children the opportunity to practice their reading (and perhaps writing). But the program's primary aim was to provide special days each month when children could gather together and focus on principles of self-cultivation presented in terms of their cultural heritage.

Toan's system was an early attempt to impart religious and moral instruction to children of all classes in a uniform fashion throughout most of Japan. The actual impact that Shingaku had in this field is difficult to ascertain. There were close to one hundred Shingaku meetinghouses in the country by the beginning of the nineteenth century; the number nearly doubled by the Meiji Restoration. Most of these schools probably sponsored some amount of child education on a regular basis; one sign of this activity is the independent reprinting of Toan's works for children by various meetinghouses.

In content, the Shingaku contribution to child education was thoroughly inspired by Neo-Confucian traditions. Despite the considerable role played by Buddhist ideas and practices in other phases of Toan's educational program, he made few attempts to introduce such material to children. Indeed, *New Words of Truth* was probably an attempt to compensate for the inadequacies of popular Buddhist-oriented readers by providing children with a compendium of Confucian passages. *Early Lessons* was largely inspired by the standard Neo-Confucian manual for young people, the *Elementary Learning,* and was conceived as a stepping stone to the more difficult Chinese text. And in his songs for children, Teshima Toan took the popularization of the Neo-Confucian tradition one step further than Confucian scholars such as Kaibara Ekken, whose moral tracts circulated widely in the eighteenth century. The Shingaku leader identified completely with the status and ways of thinking of the common classes, especially townsfolk; he knew the language and techniques that would appeal to them most. *Waking Up from Sleep* is a skillful reformulation of the learning of the mind in popular Japanese idioms. With the publication and dissemination of this song, the peculiar Shingaku combination of moral exhortation and faith in the original mind became highly accessible to young people in Tokugawa Japan.

7

POPULARIZATION
AND REGULATION

SHINGAKU MEMBERS learned to reach and maintain the knowledge of the original mind through guidance from the master, group study, and contemplative practice. Children were grounded in the ethical premises of mind-learning by attending lessons held at the local meetinghouse, where they were taught from texts tailored to their level of understanding. But the Shingaku movement became best known for its *dōwa,* or "talks on the Way," addressed to the general public. The development of the Shingaku *dōwa* and the concomitant popularization of the movement brought new problems and renewed criticisms of Shingaku teachings. In response, Toan and his disciples instituted various regulations for the group.

The great majority of Toan's printed works are records of informal question-and-answer sessions rather than lectures. Many of these discussions *(zadan)* were probably conducted in groups smaller than those that attended public lectures, but the lectures may also have included periods in which the listeners could ask questions. The large-scale lecture or talk, in any case, is the form of teaching with which Shingaku was popularly identified. Public Shingaku sermons originated with Baigan's youthful attempts to preach the truths of Shinto in the streets of Kyoto. Later, after the founder formulated his own teaching, he practiced lecturing with similar zeal at his own residence, reportedly even when he had only one listener.[1] At first Baigan's audiences were small, but after a few years of experience he was able to draw a regular group, which sometimes numbered about thirty or forty people.[2] He began to give lectures in various places in the vicinity of Kyoto, previewing the extensive travels of later Shingaku teachers. Baigan's sessions were open to all people, regardless of class or status, and he did not charge any fees. The same policies characterized Shingaku lectures during Toan's time (although

141

participation in the guidance sessions and support meetings was restricted to full-time members).

The founder's talks were based on classical Chinese and Japanese works. He probably read out a few lines from the texts and discussed their meaning in a loose fashion, instead of giving line-by-line exegesis. Baigan had received little formal education, and at first he was criticized for giving lectures that were "nothing but *sodoku* (reading off Chinese characters)."[3] But his teaching style gradually improved; he learned to draw on popular material, including tales of filial piety and Nō songs *(yōkyoku)*, in order maintain the interest of his listeners.[4] In his *Discussion of Household Management (Seikaron)*, Baigan refers to stories of virtuous persons that had been circulated by the shogunal government in an effort to encourage moral values among the common people. While commenting on one of these tales, Baigan incidentally clarifies his view of the difference in function between popular narratives and more difficult texts: "In the past year some disciples brought a book and showed it to me. The title was *Tale of a Filial Woman of Echigo*. . . . [The story] was printed and circulated all over. Isn't that fortunate?! It was originally written in *kana* [vernacular], so I do not need to lecture on it. But I read it out when I lectured in Kyoto, Osaka, Yamato, and Kawachi."[5] Evidently, the proper material for lectures *(kōshaku* or *kōgi)* was thought to be Chinese texts, and, in fact, neither Baigan nor Toan regularly inserted vernacular tales in their talks, although both teachers used the technique from time to time.[6]

All Shingaku speakers aimed to teach moral values and principles of self-cultivation. The professional Confucian teachers of the day shared this goal but depended more on classical passages and commentary, and less on popular idioms, to achieve it. Like Baigan, later Shingaku preachers read out brief passages to their audiences, mainly to provide a starting point for an informal homily. The talk itself was formulated in terms quite different from the language of the text at hand. In its more sober form, this kind of Shingaku lecture is comparable to the Christian sermon that takes its cue from a brief Bible reading. Toan used this approach in a talk recorded under the name *Rongo kōgi* (Lecture on the *Analects*): it covers a wide range of topics and illustrative material, purportedly in order to convey the meaning of a few classical lines.[7]

The use of the expression *dōwa*, or "talk on the Way," to refer to Shingaku presentations did not emerge until after Baigan's death. The term first appears in writing in Toan's *Principles for the Assembly of Companions (Kaiyū taishi)* in 1773.[8] But "talk on the Way" and "lecture" were not clearly differentiated until several years later. Toan seems to have thought of his own presentations more as "lectures" than as "talks on the Way," but he occasionally uses the two terms interchangeably.[9] The term *dōwa* is not included in the title of any of his published works.

Uekawa Kisui also used the term "lecture" rather than "talk on the Way" to refer to his own presentations. A document attributed to Kisui, *Sansha inkan narabi ni soejō* (The Seals of the Three Meetinghouses and the Cover Letter), lists three separate teaching categories: "lectures on Confucian works," "Shingaku talks on the Way," and "discussions and support meetings." Apparently Kisui regarded lectures strictly as explications of classical Confucian passages that followed the sequence, language, and purport of the classical text.[10]

Popularization

The true *dōwa* used a plethora of analogies, metaphors, parables, popular tales, witticisms, Nō verses, and indeed any material that might effectively communicate its message. The preacher would frequently refer to Buddhist, Shinto, and Taoist as well as Confucian ideas. "Songs of the Way" *(dōka)* were also inserted; these were traditional poems or homespun verses that highlighted some aspect of the teaching. They served to capture the imaginations of listeners and to impress a point upon their memories through poetic rhythm.[11]

The transformation of the type of Shingaku lecture employed by Baigan and Toan into the distinctive *dōwa* genre took place gradually through incremental modifications in the speaking styles of several Shingaku preachers. Although the term *dōwa* and the practice of teaching large public audiences originated in Toan's time, the freestyle, storytelling talk that made Shingaku famous in the late Edo period was not characteristic of Toan's own teaching style. In his recorded talks, he often alludes to legends, tales, and popular traditions, but he rarely interrupts the exhortative flow of his discourse with stories of any length.

The key figure in the development of the *dōwa* was Nakazawa Dōni. He was the first major Shingaku teacher to use this more popular style of speaking as his principal teaching method and the first whose most important written work consists primarily of records of these talks.[12] Dōni's *Dōwa kikigaki* (Notes of Talks on the Way), published in 1794, was the earliest Shingaku work titled a *dōwa*.[13] In fact, the conventional coupling of the words *Shingaku dōwa* originated in Dōni's time. His success as a preacher is affirmed by various sources. Dōni mentions in a 1791 letter that his opening talk at Sanzensha drew five to six hundred people the first day and reached over thirteen hundred on the third day of the series, with two hundred turned away for lack of space. Another source states that in early 1794 Dōni held a seven-day, morning and evening series of talks in Tanba that drew all together 6,672 people (an average of 513 at each talk). Ishikawa concludes from his detailed research that comparable crowds came to hear Dōni on several additional occasions in Edo and other areas.[14]

There are no systematic records of attendance at all Shingaku talks during this period, but some idea of the increasing popularity of the *dōwa* may be inferred from the number of meetinghouses that were established.[15] From the time Toan founded Gorakusha in 1765 until two years after his death (a period of twenty-three years), thirty-two houses were founded. During the following fourteen years under Kisui's leadership, when Dōni was most active, as many as forty-nine new houses were established.[16] The audiences that attended talks on the Way given by later preachers were similar in size to those drawn by Dōni.

In the following comment, made in 1835, Shibata Kyūō, the former storyteller *(kōshakushi)* and Shingaku preacher par excellence, justifies his liberal *dōwa* style:

> Shingaku talks on the Way were not created for the sake of intellectuals. Our former Teacher's [Baigan's] desire was simply to inform farmers and townspeople, who are pressed by their occupations and have no free time, of the existence of the Way of the Sage. Therefore, I simplify my language a great deal, give examples, or tell humorous stories; I draw on whatever is close to the principle, whether Shinto, Buddhism, or anything at all. Please do not laugh [in the belief that] it must be a kind of joke telling. That is not my true intention; I just speak this way in order to be easily understood.[17]

Teshima Toan would not have disagreed with Kyūō's view of the essential purpose of Shingaku talks, but the earlier leader did not use such a wide variety of sources and speaking techniques as Kyūō, who was a trained raconteur. Perhaps inevitably, the greater stylistic freedom of the later preachers led to some dilution of the Shingaku message. Toan had always framed the teaching of the original mind in terms of its moral implications, but in later generations his emphasis on the nature of the mind and the discipline leading to discovery *(hatsumei)* gave way to simple moral exhortation. In fact, from the early nineteenth century, the predominant public image of Shingaku became that of preachers who gave moral homilies embellished by "humorous stories" in the style of Kyūō. Even today, scholars often characterize Shingaku after Baigan in terms of these late talks, which consist chiefly of narrative interspersed with ethical injunctions[, creating] the impression that the movement had always been a troop of morality preachers who knew how to "spin a good yarn."[18]

Many Shingaku teachers undoubtedly did "perform" in this way; they came to be regarded in the same light as the raconteurs who told battle tales or gave Shinto talks.[19] With the emergence of Shibata Kyūō and other popular preachers (such as Okuta Raijō, 1795?–1849, and Nakamura Tokusui, 1800–1856), Shingaku education was reduced almost entirely to talks on the Way. Ishikawa points out that even the word *kōshaku,* or "lecture," disappeared from use: in 1826, the categories "lectures on Confucian works" and "discussions and support meetings," used as late as 1800, were no longer listed on Shingaku teaching certificates. Kyūō's own certificate refers simply to "Shingaku talks on the Way."[20] Moreover, as the talks became more entertaining, there was a corresponding loss of emphasis on individual cultivation within the core Shingaku community. The members continued to hold support meetings, but quiet sitting reportedly declined.[21] The continuing popularity of the talks in the late Edo period was not necessarily a sign of the movement's spiritual vigor and integrity. There were reports of questionable conduct by some Shingaku preachers; other popular speakers, unconnected to the movement, sometimes gave their own "Shingaku" presentations as a way of increasing their income.[22]

Group Regulation

The growth of the Shingaku movement and the increasing popularity of its public talks prompted Toan to attempt to centralize the movement in various ways. Most of his regulatory writings are included in a collection titled *Shayaku*, or *Group Rules*. The earlier documents in this group, namely, the *Admonition* (1764), *A Summary of Guidelines for Those Who Know the Original Mind* (1772), and *The Original Mind, as Each of You Has Discovered* (1780), aim to improve Shingaku followers' understanding of the teaching and its implications for their personal behavior. Most of the later texts in the collection were sent out as circulars to all the members; from the beginning of the Tenmei period (1781), their content generally concerns the conduct and activities of itinerant preachers.[23]

The movement had expanded considerably by this time. Toan had come to feel that, without some means of control, members of the community might deviate from the spirit of Baigan's teaching. Thus, whereas the early regulations concentrate on issues of individual growth that arise out of the experience of knowing the original mind, the *Rules* of the 1780s focus on the social behavior of members and the public presentation of Shingaku. These later regulations shed light on the difficulties that Toan encountered in his efforts to maintain Shingaku standards of study and religious life. In the following discussion I will summarize the main themes of four of these documents: (1) *Guidelines for Companions Who Go to Various Regions to Give Talks on the Way* (1781), (2) *Code of Rules for Members Who Give Itinerant Lectures* (1782), (3) *Terms of Agreement for the Supervision of City and Country Members* (1784), and (4) *Special Proposals from the Director for Lectures, Discussions, and Support Meetings Held in Other Places* (1784).[24]

Toan and his successors made repeated efforts to perfect a system for certifying Shingaku teachers. In his 1781 *Guidelines*, Toan required members to prove their good standing in the movement and their qualification to represent the teaching through a number of procedures. During lecture tours, they were to carry on their persons a training certificate *(takuma fuda)* and a letter of introduction, or cover letter *(soejō)*, from Toan or another authoritative leader. These documents served to identify the traveling lecturer to members and interested parties. Evidently because of the possibility of falsification, Toan required that teachers carry both the certificate and the letter, marked with the personal seal of the leader who issued them. The training certificate was simply a slip of paper or card that contained the brief details necessary for identification of the bearer. The following is the text of a certificate conferred by a certain Okitsu Koyama upon a member named Asano Kangorō, in the area that is now Nagano prefecture:

> The sixth day of the ninth month of Kansei 10,
> *tsuchinoe uma* [1798]

[SEAL]   OKITSU KOYAMA
                                        Mizuno-uchi district, Kita-owaribe village
                                                    ASANO KANGORŌ[25]

Problems in identifying Shingaku preachers apparently continued after these instructions were issued, for the same injunctions are repeated in two 1784 circulars, the *Terms of Agreement* and the *Special Proposals*. In an addendum to the *Terms of Agreement* Toan writes: "When there are people from other places who claim to be our members, as we agreed formerly, inquire whether they carry a letter of introduction and then carefully examine the seal on it. If there is anything equivocal about it, please refuse [to acknowledge] them and promptly send word to Kyoto."[26] These deliberate precautions suggest that Shingaku faced considerable competition in the burgeoning field of preaching and storytelling during the late eighteenth century. The movement's success tempted impostors to make a living by posing as Shingaku teachers. Since most of the ideas presented in the public Shingaku talks were not exceedingly complex, unique, or esoteric, it probably was not difficult for enterprising storytellers to give *Shingaku dōwa*. This trend undoubtedly added to the growing perception of Shingaku as a morality teaching embellished by humor and anecdote. The *Group Rules* and later regulatory documents confirm that unauthorized lectures and discussions had in fact been conducted by people who were only loosely connected with Shingaku or who were immature in their grasp of the teaching. In Toan's eyes, the quality of the teaching was in danger of deteriorating; as the years passed, he expressed increasing concern about preaching conducted in areas beyond his immediate control.

Toan also asked members to report and seek approval for each of their teaching activities. In 1782 he simply requested his followers to inform their own directors whenever they gave public presentations, but in 1784 he specified that the teachers should convey this information to the directors of Meirinsha, Jishūsha, and Shūseisha, the three principal meetinghouses in Kyoto. (This rule became the basis for Uekawa Kisui's later establishment of the "Three Seals" system.) Members were also required to consult with the elders of Meirinsha before they set up meetinghouses or printed pamphlets. Particularly in his *Terms of Agreement,* Toan reveals a wariness about the public image of Shingaku and its relationship with local authorities. One item in the addendum reads: "At times of lectures and discussions, not to mention ordinarily, you should take care, in consultation with each other, that nothing appears conspicuous in any way."[27] "Conspicuous" could refer to anything in the appearance or behavior of those attending the sessions that might attract undesirable attention or raise the suspicions of the local authorities. In the *Special Proposals* issued the same year (1784), Toan expressly warns the members to heed not only the laws of the shogunate, but also the local laws: "Each region has its own regulations; you should carefully inquire about them, and if there is even the slightest problem [in regard to giving lectures], you must exercise caution without fail."[28] Similar strictures applied to the founding of meetinghouses: "You must be sure to consider seriously whether it would cause any problem with the government authorities."[29]

The struggle to maintain the quality and uniformity of an educational program on a nationwide scale would be a challenge under any circumstances, but it was particularly difficult in Japan during the early modern period, when travel and communication were still relatively limited. In his 1781 *Guidelines,* Toan exhorts his disciples to be concerned not only about how well they speak, but about how well their conduct matches their words. By 1782 he had grown so concerned about the negative impact of immature or insincere representatives of Shingaku that he prohibited public lectures and discussions entirely.

> In general, in Kyoto as well as other regions, the members themselves have become weak in polishing the innate virtue of their minds and in disciplining themselves; they have reached a point where they care only to lead other people around. Consequently, lectures and discussions have become idle talk, and in various places mistaken circumstances have arisen. We have gradually come to recognize this; therefore, from now on, it is forbidden to hold lectures and discussions for people outside the group, both in Kyoto and other regions.[30]

Shibata Minoru argues that this prohibition was prompted by a specific incident in which Shingaku standards of conduct had been violated.[31] The Ancient Learning school of Itō Jinsai had held sway in the domain of Takatsuki ever since the domain lord hired Itō Kaitei (1685–1773), Jinsai's third son, as the domain Confucian scholar. In the early 1780s, Shingaku preacher Wakizaka Gidō went to Takatsuki to teach. He spoke out against the impracticality of exegetical study of the Confucian classics (an integral part of the Ancient Learning program). This gaffe probably caused the Confucian scholars of Takatsuki to complain to the domain lord's minister. They may also have felt that Gidō was infringing on their position as official educators, or that Shingaku, which appealed overwhelmingly to the lower classes, was a threat to the public order. The affair led to an official edict in 1782 that banned "Teshima Kazaemon's" teaching throughout the domain; local officials were required to report those who placed their faith in the teaching. Needless to say, Shingaku did not make significant inroads into Takatsuki after this incident. Gidō was expelled from the Shingaku movement and remained ostracized for years (Nakazawa Dōni unofficially rehabilitated him by allowing him to teach in the Edo area). Since Toan's *Code of Rules* is dated only one month after the Takatsuki edict was issued, Shibata believes the "mistaken circumstances" to which Toan refers in his prohibition of public talks is an allusion to the Gidō incident.[32]

Toan's prohibition may well have been precipitated by the aftermath of Gidō's mistake, but the wording of the injunction indicates that the Shingaku leader felt a general need for the policy. He speaks of members' weak discipline "in Kyoto as well as other regions" and implies that the "mistaken circumstances" arose in more than one place. In another article in the same text, Toan also warns against visiting relatives or doing business in conjunction with itinerant teaching. Evidently, more than one member had adopted a casual attitude toward the mission of spreading Shingaku in the world. Toan was especially worried about the degeneration of public lectures and discussions into "idle talk"—conversations that strayed from what he considered Baigan's essential message. Nevertheless, his prohibition of public speaking in the *Code of Rules* was not absolute; he added that members who could not avoid giving presentations (perhaps in response to direct requests from local officials or prominent citizens) could acquire permission from the appropriate Shingaku directors and elder companions. Toan also continued to encourage aspiring preachers to come to Kyoto for training.

The 1782 injunction was not completely effective, for in 1784 Toan expressed his frustration about these matters even more forcefully. In *Terms of Agreement* he attributes the development of "mistaken circumstances" directly to the increase in the number of members and complains that earlier codes of conduct have not been respected. Therefore, Toan says, he is sending out a summary of the same guidelines. "Please be apprised of these items," he warns, "and observe them absolutely, so that hereafter you will make no mistakes."[33] From this time, members could teach publicly only after they received permission from the directors of the three Kyoto meetinghouses. Toan took a particularly narrow view of talks held outside of Kyoto:

> In general, it is forbidden to hold lectures, discussions, and so forth in neighboring towns and areas. Certainly, if you aspire to conduct lectures and discussions, you may endeavor to do so after coming to Kyoto ahead of time and practicing frequently, in accordance with Toan's instructions. Of course, whenever you go to other places [to teach], you should report it to Kyoto.[34]

In-house meetings did not fall under the same constraints: "If you conduct support meetings in various places in Kyoto or elsewhere that are attended only by our companions, you need not report it."[35]

Toan's anxieties about the quality of Shingaku talks thus increased significantly in his last years. In 1781 he merely asked his followers to reflect on the importance of matching their words and deeds, but in 1784, he remonstrated at length about superficial preaching: "When giving a lecture, if you concentrate only on having a great number of listeners, you will naturally lapse into idle talk. You should be concerned to teach with sincerity, without any regard for the number of listeners. Moreover, you should require the same of your organizers."[36] Retaining an audience's attention while conveying a serious religious message requires considerable preaching skill; to lighten the discourse with anecdotes, jokes, or entertaining stories is a tempting option. There were bound to be excesses on the side of "idle talk" by Shingaku teachers, who regularly faced the challenge of maintaining the interest of large numbers of uneducated people. With the further expansion of the movement after Toan's death, his cautions against superficial sermons were probably increasingly overlooked. In fact, his principal successor, Uekawa Kisui, reiterated and added to his father's regulatory codes. More than a decade after Toan's death, Kisui formalized the practice, recommended in his father's 1784 *Terms of Agreement,* of having aspiring Shingaku preachers obtain the permission of the three Kyoto meetinghouses in order to teach at large.[37] Under Kisui's system, before going to Kyoto the members were to practice teaching and receive the approval of senior members at their own meetinghouses. They could then proceed to Meirinsha, undergo further training, and finally submit their applications to all three Kyoto meetinghouses. If approved, the new preachers would each receive a document imprinted with the *Sansha inkan,* the "Seals of the Three Meetinghouses," along with a cover letter.

Once they had received the "Three Seals," lecturers no longer needed to obtain permission from Kyoto each time they wished to give a talk, as

Toan had stipulated earlier. The membership was now so large that the former system was no longer practicable. A specific letter of approval from the elders of the lecturer's own meetinghouse would suffice. After 1797, Kisui also dropped the requirement that members who discovered the original mind travel to Meirinsha to receive the Admonition; the practice had probably been a hardship for those in remote areas. Even though Kisui generally tried to increase central control over the movement's teaching activities, apparently for practical reasons, he allowed some leeway to members who lived at a distance from the headquarters. Only followers who wished to be full-fledged lecturers needed to visit Kyoto and, in theory, only at the outset of their teaching careers. Anyone who ventured to give Shingaku talks without receiving the "Three Seals," however, would be expelled from the group. The contents of the "Three Seals" document is illustrated by the following example (conferred by Kisui in 1800):

The Sanzensha Residence in Edo
Sekiguchi Hōsen

The above is without question a disciple of the late Master Ishida: you may request that he hold lectures on Confucian texts, Shingaku talks on the Way, and discussions and support meetings in your locality in accordance with your suggestions. [I certify] this as a precaution.

Son of the late Teshima Toan of Kyoto,
Uekawa Genzō
Masa'akira
[SIGNATURE]

The ninth day of the fifth month of Kansei 12, *saru* [1800]

To the Sponsors of Shingaku
in Edo and the Kantō Territories

Seals of the Three Meetinghouses of Kyoto:

Meirinsha	[SEAL]
Jishūsha	[SEAL]
Shūseisha	[SEAL]

The reverse side of such documents was sometimes inscribed with guidelines for the itinerant lecturers concerning the proper use of food, bedding, entertainment, and money, and the need for adherence to local laws.[38]

Although Kisui supervised the activities of all members, in 1798 Nakazawa Dōni issued a special code for the Sanzensha jurisdiction.[39] Much of it reiterates the Meirinsha regulations, such as the Three Seals requisite for public preaching. Dōni also stresses the importance of *dōwa* practice and of participating in study circles at the meetinghouses. He presents two additional credentials for public teaching: the *zenkō* and *zendō* seals. The *zenkō* was an assistant lecturer, a new category that may have been created because of the dearth of qualified lecturers in the Edo area. Assistant lecturers were permitted to give talks when accompanied by a full-fledged lecturer *(kōshi).*[40] The possession of the *zendō,* or "guidance," seal was the mark of a mature teacher who could give internal guidance to new members. It was a prerequisite for receiving the San-zensha cover letter, which in turn was needed in order to apply for the Three Seals in Kyoto.

Shingaku regulations thus grew in number and complexity during the 1780s and 1790s. The rules were not imposed on the members in a completely authoritarian manner. Toan makes frequent reference in his codes to "consultation with the elder companions." His decisions about the conduct of members and the qualifying procedures for teaching Shingaku were arrived at partly through a process of consensus. The closing remarks of his 1781 *Guidelines* invite some degree of response from his colleagues: "If you have an opinion, please do not hesitate to let me know of it. If, after all, you feel these methods are as they should be, I wish that you would convey them to our companions, beginning with those of your own acquaintance."[41] In fact, Toan's regulations did not function only as rules; they were company pledges that reinforced the members' commitment to the group. The *Admonition* and codes of conduct were recited regularly in group meetings. The two sections of *Principles for the Assembly of Companions* that concern the nature of support meetings were read out at the meetings every month. Toan asked that the 1782 *Code of Rules* for itinerant lecturers be recited on specific occasions twice a year.[42] Shingaku rules thus had an educational and ceremonial function, in addition to their regulatory role, in the lives of the members. Such group contracts were not unique to the Shingaku community. They were employed by other educational and social groups in early modern Japan, such as private academies and performing arts schools. Licenses, seals, and other means of identification were also not uncommon during this time.[43]

Toan's attempts to unify the movement did not stop at standardizing criteria for teaching and member identification. He also specified which books his followers should read and expound upon. Shingaku teachers had traditionally borrowed from a number of religious texts and traditions in order to convey their message; Baigan is said to have lectured on the *Analects, Mencius,* the *Doctrine of the Mean,* the *Great Learning,* the *Classic of Filial Piety,* the *Elementary Learning,* the *Book of Changes,* the *Book of Poetry, Explanation of the Diagram of the Great Ultimate, Reflections on Things at Hand, Terms on Nature and Principle Ex-*

plained,[44] *Lao-tzu, Chuang-tzu,* the *Japanese Analects,* and *Essays in Idleness.*[45] In short, he placed a heavy emphasis on Confucian and Neo-Confucian books but did not neglect the Taoist classics and several important Japanese works. In his own writings as well, Baigan displays familiarity with a wide range of sources, including some Buddhist works.

The founder's immediate disciples also routinely used diverse texts. Toan began his lecture career in 1764 with expositions of the Japanese classic *Essays in Idleness* as well as the *Doctrine of the Mean.*[46] But in 1773, when he was firmly established as head of the movement, Toan recommended that members base their studies on a more limited group of works than Baigan had used: the *Analects, Mencius,* the *Doctrine of the Mean,* the *Great Learning,* the *Elementary Learning, Reflections on Things at Hand,* and Baigan's *City and Country Dialogues* and *Frugality: Discussion of Household Management.*[47] As the movement spread and its teaching activities increased, Toan reiterated this reading list. In the 1781 *Guidelines,* he requests that discussions at support meetings focus on the same eight books.

> As for varieties of works other than these, unless they are works that I have examined, it is forbidden to read them without consultation. You had better rely on the purport of the above books when you give talks in various regions as well. In any case, talks [based on texts] that have not been carefully investigated are forbidden. Even if you have good intentions, if your understanding is poor, you will give misleading talks without realizing it.

The tone of these remarks suggests that the Shingaku leader's main concern was not to set the limits of "orthodoxy" for the members. He never mentions the dangers of "heterodox learning" *(igaku)* or "heresy" *(itan)* as opposed to "orthodox learning" *(seigaku).* Rather, Toan was aware of the uneven education of his cadre of preachers and felt it would be unwise to encourage them to study and discourse upon an unlimited number of works without guidance. Ostensibly, the restriction was not absolute but only a means of preventing poor or inaccurate teaching. Toan goes on to detail the correct procedure for dealing with books other than the eight "official" texts:

> Written works other than those established above will be investigated by me. As for any remaining books, after you bring them to Meirinsha and consult with the elder companions, if they say these books do not seem to present any difficulty, then you may read them. If the elder companions cannot come to a decision about some books, you should ask me about them. After seriously examining them, I will be able to give you an answer.[48]

It seems the members were not perfectly observant of Toan's counsel, for in 1784 he again instructed Shingaku educators to limit their reading and teaching to the eight books. At the same time, he allowed the members to peruse a wider range of texts as long as they consulted their leaders in advance.[49] The prohibition was not explicitly directed against the works of any particular school, but targeted in general books that "presented difficulty" *(kurushii)*. Toan continued to worry that members would try to read and interpret various texts on their own and, after doing so, misrepresent the teaching to the public. Such preaching would constitute "idle talk"—discourse that was not focused on the Shingaku message.

Six out of the eight recommended works were annotated or compiled by Chu Hsi. The Four Books, the *Elementary Learning,* and *Reflections on Things at Hand* constituted the first phase of book learning in the pedagogical tradition established by the Ch'eng brothers and Chu. In eighteenth-century Japan, these texts were the cornerstone of "Chinese learning" *(kangaku);* they were used as teaching material in the domain schools and private academies, which catered mostly to samurai and privileged commoners. Although the texts were written in Chinese characters, Chu Hsi's explanations of difficult terms in the Four Books and the insertion of syntactical marks and vernacular readings rendered the content accessible to determined Japanese readers. If the works were not immediately comprehensible to the unlettered, they could become so through recital and exposition by a Shingaku teacher. The books could therefore serve to inculcate even townspeople and farmers with the vocabulary of Chinese learning as well as basic Neo-Confucian teachings.

Toan's decision to restrict readings to Chu Hsi's "canon" confirms the Confucian premises of his version of the learning of the mind. From his perspective, Ishida Baigan's teaching was an inspired reformulation of Sung Neo-Confucian learning, and as Baigan's successor, Toan felt responsible to transmit this learning. He shared with many other educators of his time the faith that the Four Books, the *Elementary Learning,* and *Reflections on Things at Hand* provided a framework for learning in the broadest sense—for evaluating the issues and concerns of daily life. Despite the increasing variety of popular didactic works that were accessible during his time, Toan thus chose these compilations as the most appropriate reading for his members. But the Shingaku leader's reading list was intended to simplify the students' curriculum rather than to exclude non-Confucian or "heterodox" material from it. His own dialogues, discussions, and talks are full of allusions to works that do not appear in the official list, especially Buddhist texts. He unhesitatingly draws inspiration from the writings of Bassui, Ikkyū, Mujū, Bankei,

Munan, and Shōsan, as well as from the *Record of Lin-chi,* the *Diamond Sutra,* the *Heart Sutra,* the *Platform Sutra,* the *Blue Cliff Records* (Ch. *Pi-yen lu*), and the *Gateless Barrier* (Ch. *Wu-men kuan*). Shinto, Taoist, and other Neo-Confucian texts—even books that had long been in use within the Shingaku community (such as the *Explanation of the Diagram of the Great Ultimate* and *Terms on Nature and Principle Explained*— were also excluded from Toan's list. He justified the omission of certain Confucian works by saying: "The essential passages of the Five Classics are mostly contained in *Reflections on Things at Hand.* . . . The essential passages of the *Classic of Filial Piety* and other [books] are mostly contained in the *Elementary Learning.*"[50] For similarly practical reasons, Toan selected those Neo-Confucian works that were available in Japanese: "The Four Books, *Reflections on Things at Hand,* and the *Elementary Learning*—these three compilations are all available in *katakana* [vernacular] editions called *jimō.*"[51]

Toan evidently felt that the number and identity of books used in the reading groups, study circles, and public talks should be limited so that his followers would be able to concentrate on maintaining the experience of the original mind. It was noted earlier that Toan discouraged reading or study of any kind prior to knowing the original mind. If members became involved in comparing texts or mastering complex exegetical problems, it might hinder their progress along the Way. A limited amount of book learning was beneficial for older members and public lecturers, since it refreshed and reinforced the more intuitive understanding of the original mind that they had already experienced. But, in general, the members needed a concise, readable set of writings to which they could turn for clarification and inspiration; Toan did not want to confuse his followers or slow their spiritual quest by encouraging them to read indiscriminately. The Shingaku leader could also gain more control over the content of his preachers' talks by establishing a book list.

Modern scholars have suggested that Toan's restriction of the Shingaku study course to Neo-Confucian compilations and Baigan's books was designed to counteract criticism by Confucian purists who were uneasy about the Zen flavor of Shingaku teaching. Ishikawa argues that Toan's initial limitation of the texts in 1773 was a reaction to the charge of promoting "Zen-like" learning brought against him several years earlier in Kyoto.[52] In this view, Toan did not consider it politically wise to include Buddhist or Taoist works in the official curriculum, even though he felt free to refer to them in his own writings. But it is unlikely that the Kyoto incident alone shaped a policy that was enunciated several years later and that endured for much of the rest of Shingaku history.[53] This view also does not explain why Toan excluded Confucian as well as Taoist and Shinto texts from the curriculum. In a similar vein, it has been suggested that the restriction of Shingaku readings to standard Ch'eng-Chu compilations was a response to the shogunal government's growing preference for Chu Hsi learning in the late eighteenth century.[54] However, Toan's restriction of readings was not a political decision. He believed that the Confucian classics were a fundamental source of mind-learning and that Chu Hsi's canon was the most convenient summary of those classics. He enunciated his preference for the Sung compilations as early as 1773 and repeatedly in the early 1780s, long before the shogunal government formulated an explicit policy against heterodox teachings.[55] Toan's selection of Shingaku teaching texts certainly reflects the general intellectual trend of the time, but it was more an indication of his own faith than a response to external pressures.

Criticisms of Shingaku

Because Baigan, Toan, and their followers consistently drew inspiration from diverse religious traditions and regularly professed the equal value of the Confucian, Buddhist, and Shinto paths of self-cultivation, outside observers as well as Shingaku adepts themselves sometimes registered confusion about the actual nature and sources of the teaching. Several voices were raised in criticism of the movement as it became better known, particularly among Confucian scholars. These critics rarely failed to point out that Shingaku advocated Buddhist ideas and oversimplified the Way of the sages. Both of these charges disqualified the movement from being a bona fide school of Confucian learning.

The earliest significant reaction to Toan's activities occurred in Kyoto in the late 1760s, when the town magistrate became suspicious of Toan's practice of refusing admission fees and gifts. The Shingaku master was also charged with giving "instruction that resembled Zen learning." In defense of himself, Toan replied that this "instruction" was "[my teacher Ishida] Kanpei's contemplative practice: I teach the contemplative practice of "extending knowledge and investigating things" of the *Great Learning* to the illiterate in such a way that they will be able to understand it easily."[56] Toan thus professed to transmit a peculiar system of religious cultivation that he had learned from the founder. It probably "resembled Zen learning" because it involved some form of sitting meditation or koan-style interviews between Toan and his disciples, or perhaps a combination of both. Toan's system, "extending knowledge and investigating things," denoted specific contemplative exercises intended to prepare the Shingaku adept for discovery of the original mind.

Similar suspicions and criticisms of Shingaku were articulated more clearly in the late 1780s and early 1790s, as the movement spread further. Nakai Chikuzan was particularly vehement about the Zen element in Shingaku:

The followers of the Ishida school . . . advance Buddhist ideas under the name of Confucianism, and gather people without any connection. . . . They use Zen learning as a hidden device to make all people engage in the path of enlightenment, and they teach that one can grasp the Way without even a speck of education. This is something that greatly harms people's minds. . . . In due order this [school], too, should preferably be suppressed.[57]

Chikuzan presented this view to Matsudaira Sadanobu in 1789, but apparently it had little effect on the government's general policy toward the movement. However, the Kansei prohibition of heterodox learning, which Sadanobu sanctioned in the following year, did affect the official atttitude toward Shingaku in at least one instance. After the edict was issued, the shogunal school Shōheikō did not permit affiliates of "heterodox" schools to sit for final examinations. Nakazawa Dōni's disciple Suzuki Ryūsuke was excluded from the examinations because the school administrators concluded that Sekimon Shingaku did not meet the criteria of true Chu Hsi learning (Shushigaku). Even though Nakazawa Dōni professed Chu Hsi learning, the heads of the college determined: "He is uneducated, and thus has a facile way of teaching. He cannot serve as an instructor for the various samurai."[58] Dōni's lack of education, rather than the heterodox overtones of his teaching, is cited as the main reason for the decision against Ryūsuke. But it is unlikely that Dōni's Buddhist predilections escaped the notice of the doyens of the school.[59]

The attitude of Confucian scholars and intellectuals toward the Shingaku movement continued to be ambivalent at best. Ban Kōkei (1733–1806), a National Learning scholar who was well versed in both Buddhist and Confucian studies, summed up scholars' doubts and confusion about the movement at the end of the eighteenth century:

When one reads [Toan's] writings, the purport follows Harima Zen master Bankei's teaching of the unborn Buddha-mind; therefore, it may be disparaged as "Zen Confucianism." But it may also be based on Wang Yang-ming's theory of "innate knowledge of the good and innate ability."[60] . . . [Toan's] disciples are utterly illiterate; they constantly give popular talks and are very much in circulation. Because of this, those who are lettered despise it greatly; yet from the beginning [Toan's disciples] never claimed to educate scholars.[61]

Kōkei pinpoints the reasons why Shingaku had little prestige in the Confucian intellectual world: it was influenced by Buddhism and it was addressed to the masses. These two charges were linked together as often as not, for Buddhist preaching had long been associated with gatherings of commoners and "vulgar" popularizing methods. Shingaku was perceived as similar to Buddhism not only in the content of its teaching, but in its educational approach.

As time passed, the real demand for Shingaku educational services counterbalanced these charges. The Bakufu appreciated the Shingaku preachers for its own reasons. Sadanobu, for example, employed Dōni and his disciples to shore up popular ethical instruction in shogunal territories.[62] The preachers' simple, engaging manner of presenting the Way was an effective means of reaching the less educated. Although such figures as Satō Issai (1772–1859) and Sakuma Shōzan (1811–1864) repeated the standard criticisms of the movement later in the period, they now admitted that a teaching tailored to the needs of commoners might indeed serve some beneficial purpose. Issai, who became a teacher at Shōheikō in 1841, commented: "There is a sort of thing called Shingaku in the world, and it is not without some small benefit to women and persons of low status. However, it is essentially in the category of 'village virtue.'[63] If men of rank study it, they will sink into the conventional ways of the world and lose the spirit of rightness."[64] Sakuma Shōzan similarly admitted that Shingaku talks on the Way could be helpful to people in their daily lives, but he insisted that the teaching was not true Confucianism. Like Chikuzan, he felt Shingaku was especially pernicious because it presented Buddhist ideas under Confucian guise.[65]

Shingaku was not necessarily well regarded in Buddhist circles either. In one of his talks, Nakazawa Dōni recounts the story of a disciple who was ridiculed and snubbed by his Zen associates after he joined the Shingaku movement and experienced his original mind.[66] In a 1782 work called *The Whipping Rod of the Original-Mind Devil (Honshin oni ga utsu tsue)*, a Buddhist writer criticized the facility with which Shingaku members found their original minds. Kamizawa Takken, the author of *Okinagusa* (Pasqueflowers), also ridiculed the shallow nature of "Teshima enlightenment" *(Teshima satori)*.[67]

Sekimon Shingaku would never be fully accepted by or integrated into the Confucian or Buddhist establishments of the Tokugawa period. Depending on the critic's perspective, it was seen either as a Zen-like rendition of the Way of the sages or a Confucianized form of Zen. In reality, it was a distinctive religious community with its own criteria for selecting ideas and practices from these and other systems. However, in Tokugawa Japan, moral and religious knowledge was usually transmitted by official educators or religious professionals. Lectures on the Confucian Way were the task of *jusha* (Confucian scholars); Zen education, too, even in the form of popular sermons for the laity, was normally supervised by monks, not by unlettered, unaffiliated lay people. Shingaku represented an implicit challenge to a social order in which the construction and communication of knowledge was, in theory, restricted to certain educated groups.

Toan professed to be simply a retired merchant devoted to the Way; he refused to present himself as a learned teacher of any kind. He did not claim to be an instructor of Zen, even though he acknowledged the similarity and even the identity of his teaching with some types of Zen. When questioned by his followers about difficult Zen sayings, Toan invariably denied any expertise. He responded to a question about the *Record of Lin-chi* by confessing, "I am basically unlettered in Chinese; I am extremely poor in Zen learning."[68] He was even more reluctant to present himself as a teacher of Shinto. When queried about native texts, he would defer to the erudition of Shinto instructors or priests. "I don't know the meaning of Shinto books because I haven't studied them," he would say. "You should go ask at that school."[69] On one such occasion he was quite vehement: "Do you think I am a retired man or a Shintoist? As you can see, I am a retired man. You should go ask at that school about this matter of the 'Age of the Gods.'[70] It's a mystery; I don't know."[71]

Toan's modest insistence on being an "amateur" was partly rhetorical. In fact, he was familiar with the contents of many Buddhist and Shinto works, for he refers to them in his writings. But Toan tended to disapprove of "professional" intellectuals—especially Confucian scholars who appeared to emphasize book learning over moral cultivation. The Shingaku leader was not alone in wishing to distance himself from "shallow" textual learning; the late Kokugaku popularizer Hirata Atsutane (1776–1843) similarly disclaimed scholarly status, openly attacking professional educators of all kinds.[72] Toan, however, was committed to restoring the ancient Way of Confucius and Mencius; in his discourses he occasionally refers to Shingaku as "our Confucian way" (*waga ju no michi*).[73] He felt impelled to formulate the essence of this "Way" and enliven it for ordinary people—a task that Confucian scholars, because of their very erudition, were incapable of performing. Toan and his followers saw themselves as transmitters of the Confucian Way, but they were not (and implicitly refused to be) Confucian scholars.

The social identity of Shingaku teachers was therefore ambiguous. To the public, Shingaku teachers appeared to be Confucian scholars, or perhaps professional storytellers without the customary Buddhist garb. Yet, unlike either of these, they relayed their message through a network of schools all over the country and accepted no fees. There was no clear precedent in eighteenth-century Japan for organized religious teachers who were unaffiliated with a Buddhist or Shinto community or a Confucian school. Shingaku drew heavily on these established traditions, but the group itself was a new social and religious phenomenon. Thus, as Shingaku developed into a large-scale movement, its teachers struggled to establish their intellectual and social identity. The popularization of the "talks on the Way" and the further expansion of the movement led to deviations from standards of conduct that had been easier to maintain when the group was smaller. Conflicts with local authorities, problems in controlling preachers, and a perceived deterioration in the quality of Baigan's teaching all prompted Toan and his successors to define the movement through a variety of centralizing efforts: codes of conduct, teaching qualifications, identification procedures, and an official curriculum. By the beginning of the nineteenth century, Shingaku had become an organized religious institution of near national dimensions.

CONCLUSION

How DID THE quest of the original mind come to attract ordinary people in Tokugawa Japan? I have attempted to elucidate this question by identifying the simplifying and syncretizing strategies that informed the Shingaku program. Teshima Toan contributed to the larger Ch'eng-Chu "learning of the mind" primarily by adapting it to the needs of Japanese people who had little access to formal education. Following his teacher Baigan's example, he reformulated the ideas of the Sung masters into a simple, concise theme—knowing the original mind. On the practical level, he and his followers favored pedagogical methods that did not require full literacy, most notably public lectures. The success of Shingaku preaching owed much to the rhetorical legacy of Buddhist preachers and storytellers who used idiomatic language and engaging metaphors to convey their teachings to large gatherings. Baigan's followers took advantage of this stylistic heritage to render the learning of the mind more palatable to common people than were Neo-Confucian scholastic presentations. Shingaku teachers also benefited from the proliferation of vernacular didactic works in eighteenth-century Japan. They routinely enlivened their sermons with material drawn from both Confucian tracts and Buddhist discourses.

Shingaku adapted Neo-Confucian mind-learning not only by conveying its basic tenets through Buddhist-like preaching, but also by synthesizing these tenets with Zen ideas and practices. Although Neo-Confucian thinkers had often decried the influence of Zen, through Sekimon Shingaku it assisted in the popular transmission of Ch'eng-Chu ideas. The resonance between the two systems dated back to the Sung, when Neo-Confucian preoccupation with self-cultivation was first stimulated by Ch'an.[1] In Japan there was already a long history of interaction between Confucian, Buddhist, and Shinto traditions prior to the Tokugawa period. With the onset of the new era, Neo-Confucian learning became the prevalent philosophy of the educated class, and as Tokugawa culture developed, people of all classes were increasingly exposed to this learning through informal channels. Meanwhile, Zen was also circulating in newly simplified forms, both oral and written. Baigan, Toan, and their followers created a popular synthesis of these two traditions.

Toan was familiar both with older vernacular Buddhist works, such as those of Mujū and Ikkyū, and with the recorded talks of Tokugawa Zen popularizers. Bankei, Munan, Takuan, Shōsan, and others provided the Shingaku leader and his followers with both intellectual and stylistic inspiration. These Zen masters presented their teachings in an uncomplicated, practical manner that was highly accessible to less-educated people. Toan was inspired by the commonality between this popular Zen and the Sung learning of the mind. The Zen preachers' own use of Confucian terminology undoubtedly encouraged his identification of the two teachings. Thus, in his talks and writings, the Shingaku leader equates the Mencian "original mind" with the "unborn Buddha-mind," "no self," "no body" and "no eye." His "no calculation" echoes Confucian warnings against cunning, anxiety, and overzealousness but, at the same time, strikingly resembles Zen master Takuan's usage. Similarly, Toan used "investigation of things," a step in the *Great Learning,* to designate a peculiar method of training students in the selfless nature of human experience—a method that resembled Zen praxis more than the studious process envisioned by Chu Hsi.

Toan's reinterpretations of Confucian terms and forays into Zen discourse do not occur as isolated instances in his works; they are numerous and consistent enough to suggest his acceptance of key Mahayana Buddhist teachings, such as that of emptiness. The notion of emptiness is a corollary of the Buddhist teaching of "no self." It signifies that phenomena have no abiding selves, essences, or identities; they are simply a series of constantly changing, interdependent conditions and thus are transient and illusory. When Toan uses "no self" in his writings, however, he does not necessarily mean that the self is "empty" in the sense that it has no permanent essence. His cosmological framework appears to be substantialist: he generally assumes that the world, as a whole and in its parts, is an enduring substance. Reality is composed of things that have form (the human body, the earth) and things that are formless (the mind, heaven). Both visible and invisible things are composed of vital energy *(ki),* which is permanent and substantial. Given these premises, one might surmise that Toan does not intend words like "empty" or "no self" in the Mahayana sense. He does not deny the lasting existence of any essence or self, but merely advocates the ethical transcendence of the human self. Toan's "no self" may simply be a metaphor for the Neo-Confucian idea of harmony with all things—"having no mind of one's own."

Moreover, particularly in his *Admonition* and other regulatory writings, Toan stresses the intrinsic connection between knowing the original mind and conducting a moral life. He implies that the original mind is itself the Way: it contains the principles of the Five Relations. In daily life, calculations may obscure these principles, but as long as one is mindful, the innate values will emerge, enabling one to make correct moral decisions. This identification of the original mind with unchanging moral principles does not accord with a strict Mahayana interpretation of "no self." If there is no permanent essence in the world, in the final analysis even the Confucian ethical system of the Five Relations belongs to the realm of empty, conditioned phenomena. Many Mahayana Buddhist philosophers would argue that such virtues as loyalty and filial piety are not absolute values in themselves; they are provisional concepts or aids in the process of spiritual growth that leads to the truth of emptiness. In this view, these conventional virtues ultimately should be enacted from the deeper perspective of wisdom and compassion based on emptiness.

It is unlikely that Toan concerned himself with these ramifications of the Buddhist idea of no self. Yet the Shingaku teacher's no self sometimes connotes more than the orthodox Neo-Confucian view of selflessness, as is particularly evident in his "Guidance" talks, reserved for committed members. Here Toan strives to show his followers that the mind that generates calculations is an illusory, artificial construct and that the processes of sensation and cognition are not directed by any internal agent. The mind is simply the reality of the moment ("the fan"). This approach goes beyond Ch'eng Hao's vision of forming "one body with heaven and earth and all things." Toan identifies the idea that the mind is constituted by whatever comes into its purview with the Neo-Confucian idea of "responding to things as they come." But he overlooks the original assumption behind the Neo-Confucian phrase—that an individual self exists and in some way directs the act of "responding." According to Toan's presentation, one does not respond to the fan: one *is* the fan.

The classical "method of the mind" mentioned in Chu Hsi's preface to the *Doctrine of the Mean* is based on a distinction between the "mind of the Way" and the "human mind." In the Ch'eng-Chu tradition, the human aspect of the mind is fallible, but it is not an illusion or a temporary construct. The human mind is believed to possess an enduring identity of its own; it is a living force that must be acknowledged and disciplined. But in his "Guidance" talks, Toan suggests that the self from which calculations seem to arise has no lasting reality. Here the Shingaku master's concept of no self seems closer to the Mahayana Buddhist position than one might infer from his cosmological and ethical statements.

He goes beyond the Neo-Confucian view of moral self-transcendence but does not seem to acknowledge the possible implications of no self in the Mahayana tradition.

Logical inconsistencies were of little concern to Toan. The Japanese Zen masters to whom he turned for inspiration did not dwell, in their popular talks, on the philosophical complexities of emptiness. Toan took the words of these masters at face value; he understood Zen at a level where it indeed showed affinities with Ch'eng-Chu discourse. To the Shingaku leader, Bankei's "unborn Buddha-mind" and Chu Hsi's "unobstructed clear virtue" appeared to be the same: a pure, spontaneous awareness, imparted to all human beings at birth, that could evaluate and respond properly to all the situations of daily life. For Toan's purposes, the rest was of little importance.

Shingaku addressed people's needs in Tokugawa Japan not only by adapting Buddhist rhetorical skills and marshaling currrent Zen discourse to help popularize the Neo-Confucian learning of the mind. It also exploited the pedagogical strengths of both traditions, using each in distinct ways to create a comprehensive training program. The Shingaku identification of Neo-Confucian and Zen learning may be seen as a philosophical equation inspired by faith in the universality of the true mind. But it was also a practical synthesis, designed to implement a particular educational strategy.

Teshima Toan's commitment to Neo-Confucian educational premises is conspicuous in two aspects of his teaching activities: his reading list for members and his instruction of children. In an effort to simplify and unify the study process, the Shingaku leader required members to base their study and teaching on the Four Books, *Reflections on Things at Hand, Elementary Learning,* and Ishida Baigan's writings. Although Toan was not attempting to define Shingaku in terms of "orthodox" sources, he did assume the superiority of the widely used Neo-Confucian compilations. He believed the learning process should be rooted in the ancient Confucian tradition, and despite the great variety of vernacular didactic books in circulation, Chu Hsi's editions of the Chinese classics remained the most authoritative and concise expression of that tradition. The same perspective is revealed in Toan's teaching program for children. Like Chu Hsi, he wished to instill fundamental notions of morality and etiquette in young people before introducing the less tangible aspects of self-cultivation. Once the children learned moral values, they would have the correct foundation for understanding the nature of the original mind. Talk of "no self" or "no body" and the use of enigmatic "koans" and contemplative practices were reserved for later phases of Shingaku study. The Buddhist writings and sayings that Toan used in adult pedagogical contexts could not themselves provide a graduated system of moral education. In his regular lessons for children, Toan turned instead to the Confucian classics, particularly as summarized in the *Elementary Learning,* for practical rules of conduct. The same concern for imbuing children with Confucian morality is reflected in his transformation of the Buddhist-oriented primer *Words of Truth (Jitsugokyō)* into a Confucian reader.

The Shingaku master believed that the education of the whole person involved different materials and methods at different stages of development. After the young people had mastered the more concrete rules and rituals, they would be able to benefit more fully from the abstract-sounding ideas and mystical practices that Toan introduced to adult audiences. Older Shingaku students were encouraged to spend time in self-scrutiny and contemplation, reinforced by exchanges with their master and peers. The heavy emphasis on ethics and etiquette in children's education eventually gave way to an approach that fostered deeper intellectual reflection and pointed beyond it to the nondiscursive realm of the original mind. The adult member would enter a period in which the ideas imbibed unquestioningly during childhood and adolescence might no longer seem absolute or effective, at least not in the simple sense in which they were first understood. This period was critical for the Shingaku adept. Doubts about basic concepts and values that the member had always assumed led to a struggle and a search for deeper meaning, ideally resulting in the discovery of the original mind. Like Hakuin and other Zen masters, Teshima Toan emphasized the essential role of doubt in the path to enlightenment. Shingaku teachers' use of popular koans or "problems" was designed to help their students develop this inner struggle. The search propelled members to reexperience the truth of the conventional moral axioms with which they had long been familiar; ultimately, they reaffirmed the same values from the "enlightened" perspective of the original mind.[2]

The influence of Zen, accordingly, is most prominent in Shingaku practices associated with the event of knowing the true mind. Indeed, the centrality of the discovery experience in Shingaku religious life parallels that of enlightenment in Zen. Much like the Zen seal of approval, the Shingaku Admonition certified the authenticity of the discovery and was required for public teaching. The pivotal role played by the experience of the mind in Shingaku clearly sets it off from the orthodox Neo-Confucian tradition, which neither required nor institutionalized an enlightenment event. The same reliance on Zen praxis characterized Shingaku contemplation, which was thought to nurture the experience of the original mind. Toan and his close disciples diverged significantly in their practice of quiet sitting from the scholarly tradition enunciated by the Chu Hsi school. Toan warned that the initial search for the original mind could be hampered by book learning or intellectual activity, whereas Chu Hsi's followers regarded quiet sitting as a preparation for such activity. Ariyama Gentō's advocacy of regulated group sitting similarly contradicts Chu Hsi's position against regimentation of the practice. Gentō employed the Neo-Confucian rhetoric of mind cultivation, but he turned to Sōtō regulatory texts, rather than Ch'eng-Chu works, for practical guidelines on meditation.

Most Neo-Confucian texts failed to prescribe methods for finding the true mind that were feasible for the ordinary Tokugawa citizen. Although the Ch'eng-Chu "method of the mind" involved "such disciplines as self-watchfulness, caution, and apprehension, [and] holding to reverence,"[3] tangible aids for maintaining these internal attitudes were generally left to the discretion of the individual Confucian scholar. Quiet sitting and keeping a journal of one's daily progress were two visible approaches to inner cultivation, but they were not prescriptive features of the Neo-Confucian learning of the mind. Scholars generally reinforced their determination to perfect themselves by studying the classics. But in Tokugawa Japan, only the educated elite could adopt this approach to learning. Most Shingaku followers spent their days buying and selling, weaving or practicing other crafts, and farming. Teshima Toan could not simply urge these busy people to "watch over themselves" or to "hold to reverence." To pursue the original mind successfully, townspeople and villagers required a life of faith more like that of a lay Zen adept than that of a Confucian scholar, including frequent interaction with a master, regular peer support, shared rituals, techniques for meditation, concise "problems" to solve, certification of enlightenment, and even a fan to contemplate. Shingaku relied chiefly on Confucian ideas for the ethical segments of its teaching program, but when it came to the search for and experience of the original mind, its teachers used Zen models.

Baigan's followers created a workable religious system, then, not only by simplifying Neo-Confucian discourse and conflating it with popular Zen, but by selectively arranging Confucian and Zen pedagogies within a developmental framework. Furthermore, in the late eighteenth century the movement enjoyed an energy, uniformity, and autonomy that compared favorably with the established religious traditions from which it drew. Buddhist preachers of particular sects shared a common religious outlook, but they did not generate special texts or systematic programs for teaching morality to children on a large scale. Even the relatively few temple priests who taught children (especially in the rural areas) relied mostly on copybooks and outdated readers like *Words of Truth*.[4] Confucian scholars, for their part, were steeped in texts and concepts regarding the ethical education of both children and adults; but their teaching reached mostly samurai and a few privileged commoners. As a whole,

Confucian scholars did not make the effort to convey their learning to large numbers of common people; those who did were often limited in influence to the domains in which they served. Shingaku, in contrast, was a relatively autonomous group; not dominated by institutional ties with any particular region or established school, its representatives were free to carry the teaching all over Japan. They combined the advantages of several educational legacies—the popularizing skills of Buddhist preachers, the moral discourses of Neo-Confucians, and the spiritual praxes of Zen masters—and infused this synthesis with the "missionary" energy characteristic of new religious groups.

Even after taking account of the ways in which Shingaku rendered itself appealing to common people in the Edo period, we must still ask why this movement, given its simplifying, synthesizing nature, spread in late eighteenth-century Japan. Moral and religious ideas proliferated in Tokugawa society by means of various informal media. In the face of this cultural expansion, townspeople like Toan and Dōni (and, earlier, Baigan) felt impelled to marshal their time and resources in order to grasp these ideas, synthesize them into a practicable system, and share them with others. Other religious communities (Pure Land Buddhist preachers, the agrarian Hōtoku movement, Shinto popularizers, and others) also disseminated moral knowledge among the populace. But Shingaku was distinctive for its sustained, systematic efforts to translate the Neo-Confucian discourse of the educated elite into terms that could be understood by all. What the movement offered townspeople and rural dwellers, however, was not only a popularized version of the respected textual tradition of the time. Essentially, Shingaku spread in the late eighteenth century because it gave people a way of conceptualizing themselves and their relation to the increasingly complex world in which they lived—complete with an organized spiritual discipline that could be pursued in the context of everyday life.

The key to Shingaku's appeal was precisely this sensitivity to the "context of everyday life"—an awareness that was relatively undeveloped in the established ideological and religious systems. Shingaku followers accordingly eschewed not only the impractical, scholarly elements of the Neo-Confucian program; they also implicitly rejected the lifestyle traditionally required of dedicated Zen Buddhists. The philosophy of the original mind involved a lifetime commitment to fulfilling the Way of the sages, that is, the ethics of the Five Relations, and to working hard in one's "allotted" occupation. Relinquishing family life in favor of a monastic existence (the common course for serious Zen adepts at this time) was not considered particularly conducive to knowing the original mind or to fulfilling its dictates. Full participation in the web of human relationships, with all the concomitant responsibilities, was believed to be the best exercise of the innate understanding. Moreover, a house-holder committed to Shingaku could attain discovery of the original mind within a few years of study; Zen enlightenment ordinarily required many years of arduous spiritual effort. Shingaku held out a goal that seemed comparable to Zen *satori,* but the path it advocated was more suited to the needs of busy lay people. Accordingly, some individuals were drawn to Shingaku as a substitute for lay Zen.[5]

Nakazawa Dōni, in particular, pursued much of his religious quest within a Nichiren and Zen Buddhist context before he encountered Shingaku. His central religious experience, the discovery of the meaning of "Wondrous Dharma," was regarded in the Shingaku community as equivalent to knowing the original mind, even though Dōni reached his experience under the guidance of Rinzai masters. But if Dōni was deeply versed in Zen, why did he choose to become a Shingaku preacher? His dialogues and talks on the Way do not indicate any loss of faith in the Buddhist world-view, although he habitually identifies Buddhist notions with Confucian and Shinto ideas. Perhaps he regarded Shingaku as a kind of *upaya,* or expedient means; by teaching it he could help people improve their moral understanding and thereby take the first step on the path to enlightenment. It is unlikely, however, that Dōni's motives were so complex. He had spent most of his life in the weaving trade and was not learned in Chinese. He was probably poorly acquainted with the original sources of both the Buddhist and the Confucian traditions. He may have undergone rigorous koan training under the guidance of his Rinzai masters, but he displays greatest familiarity with popular Bud-dhist discourse. Dōni's understanding of Zen may not have been much more intricate than that of his teacher Toan, who evidently absorbed it in the simplified way that preachers like Bankei taught it. For Dōni, "seeing into one's nature," grasping the "Wondrous Dharma," and "knowing the original mind" were identical both in theory and in his own experience. Like Toan, he was not concerned with possible conflicts between the original premises of these ideas.

Dōni's affiliation with Shingaku was informed by practical as well as spiritual considerations. He probably found more opportunity for reli-gious activism in Shingaku than in Rinzai circles. Despite the increasing popularization of Zen, lay believers in the early modern period remained in a fundamentally passive position vis-à-vis the clergy. Lay people could attend occasional public sermons, or perhaps meditation sessions, led by monks; Zen practitioners seem to have been less active in lay societies than members of other Buddhist sects. Monastic training was virtually a prerequisite for transmitting Zen to others. Dōni's family responsibilities and lack of education did not necessarily preclude his teaching Zen on a limited scale, if his enlightenment were indeed approved by bona fide

Zen masters. But his religious life as a lay adept was undoubtedly enhanced by joining Shingaku and becoming a lecturer. In the latter capacity he could establish meetinghouses and lead others to "enlightenment" all over the country, while remaining immersed in "everyday life."

Shingaku thus offered people a system for ordering their spiritual and social existence that was more workable than either Zen monasticism or Neo-Confucian scholarship. Toan and his followers were not unique in this regard; especially in the late Tokugawa period, numerous popularizers emphasized the practical, "everyday" nature of learning.[6] In fact, Shingaku illustrates a general trend toward the "laicization" of religious and moral education in Tokugawa society. In the late eighteenth century, this trend was accompanied by a tension between common people's growing involvement in the creation and transmission of moral knowledge and the conservative social implications of that knowledge. Shingaku was a form of learning constructed by ordinary people in an attempt to interpret the world in which they lived. In this sense, the movement reflects the increasing intellectual and religious autonomy of some sectors of the Tokugawa population. Shingaku efforts to teach non-samurai children exemplify the "progressive" dimension of the group. Teshima Toan instituted ethical instruction for youngsters of all social classes in the 1770s, long before the need for such a program became widely acknowledged in the nineteenth century. His establishment of special sessions for girls on a countrywide scale was a pioneering effort in itself. The scale and uniformity of Shingaku lessons is particularly significant: whether in rural areas or in urban centers, children who attended these classes received the same basic instruction in ethics and self-cultivation. In this regard, Shingaku may be seen as an early harbinger of modern universal education. Toan and his followers were teaching Japanese children of all classes and both sexes on a nationwide scale almost a century before the Restoration.

In the impetus that it gave to education, Shingaku fulfilled its Mencian premise that all people, regardless of social status, are equally endowed with the potential for moral perfection—the original mind. The group's activities brought out and reinforced people's sense that they could develop and transmit their own systems of knowledge.[7] Indeed, some Confucian ideologues, apprehensive of the increasing number of cultural forms that circulated in the late eighteenth and early nineteenth centuries, felt that Shingaku's "unofficial" religious activity might lead to further erosion of ethical and civil ideals. Such critics perceived Shingaku teachers as vulgar popularizers, akin to Buddhist preachers; from their viewpoint, the new teaching represented a potential threat to the social order in which the transmission of values was traditionally restricted to specific professional groups. By the late eighteenth century, the growing pool of ideas available to people of the lower classes had created an implicit disjunction between the society envisioned by the Tokugawa rulers and the actual social experience of most citizens. The economic and cultural autonomy of nonsamurai groups no longer cohered with the official exclusion of these estates from wider spheres of knowledge. H. D. Harootunian has suggested that

> the explosion of new forms of knowledge in late Tokugawa Japan was increasingly difficult to assimilate to the categories of the existing political system. What occurred in the late eighteenth century was the recognition, first in the cities but soon exported to the countryside, that the opposition of ruler-ruled and external-internal had exhausted its productivity and was incapable of constructing a vision of the political that could accommodate the complexity and plurality of the social urban environment.[8]

According to the traditional "external-internal" paradigm, intellectual, or "internal," learning was the domain of the ruling samurai, whereas merchants, artisans, and peasants were destined to concentrate on their respective physical, or "external," tasks. Knowledge necessary for fulfilling these tasks as well as a modicum of instruction in the civil premises of the existing social system were viewed by many intellectuals as the proper extent of education for the mass of commoners. Yet in the late eighteenth century, Shingaku members and other "ordinary people" were both producing and avidly consuming their own forms of learning.

Nevertheless, the potential threat represented by Shingaku's autonomous religious activity never materialized. The actual content of the teaching was not conducive to social or intellectual "autonomy"; Shingaku shared the shogunal premise that nonsamurai should fulfill their allotted roles in the society by producing services and goods rather than ideas or culture. Indeed, once the government noticed the conservative civil and ethical implications of the Shingaku teaching, it enlisted Toan's eloquent followers to help indoctrinate people in loyalty, filial piety, frugality, and diligence.

The new religions that emerged during the first half of the nineteenth century provide an instructive comparison. Older, established forms of religion, serviced primarily by Buddhist and Shinto clergy, lacked the power to inspire many people in late Tokugawa Japan. In the troubled economic and social conditions of the times, new forms of faith appeared, ranging from mass pilgrimages and local cult revivals to the more systematic offerings of the new religions. These groups advocated communal solidarity, succor of the poor, and the importance of daily life as a context for ultimate fulfillment. Many were led by a charismatic founder who claimed special access to divine inspiration, often manifested through healing powers.[9] Harootunian notes that the new religions appealed especially to lower-class people who sought to create "autonomous communities." Their search for new communities and systems of ideas through which they could articulate their social and spiritual identity implied a criticism of the existing social order.[10] Members of the new religions deviated from the hierarchical social structures of the time by espousing egalitarian principles within their organizations.

This stance reflected a number of ongoing developments from earlier in the period. One was the popularization of lay societies *(kō)*, which allowed believers more autonomy in relation to clerical establishments. Another was the spread of Neo-Confucian ideas of self-improvement. In the late period, even the lower ranks of society were acquainted with the fundamental Neo-Confucian idea that individual cultivation is the foundation for social well-being. Helen Hardacre has suggested that this emphasis on cultivation of the self was a formative influence on the world-view of the new religions.[11] The Neo-Confucian program encouraged a degree of spiritual self-reliance, since it did not require the intervention of clerical mediators or ritual experts. In fact, lay activism was a characteristic feature of the popular new groups.

In the late eighteenth century, just before the new religions appeared, Shingaku members also placed a high value on community. They followed an explicit code of behavior and reinforced their solidarity with each other through shared ritual events and study. Their countrywide network of meetinghouses supplied "inner spaces" in which the "companions" could enjoy fellowship and mutual encouragement. Moreover, the Shingaku movement evinced egalitarian tendencies not unlike those of the later groups. True to its Neo-Confucian sources, Shingaku taught that personal cultivation was the cornerstone of social harmony; like the new religions (and other forms of modern spirituality that had roots in the Bakumatsu period), the movement made no distinctions between lay and clergy.[12] Although Shingaku was benignly guided by a hierarchy of leaders, decisions were often reached through a process of consultation among senior members. Most eminently, Shingaku shared the practical emphasis of the later groups; its teachers skillfully fashioned ideas and methods to suit the quotidian needs of their constitutents.

However, despite the seeds of communalism, egalitarianism, and autonomy in Shingaku, its members did not develop these incipient tendencies into a corollary critique of the existing sociopolitical order, as did followers of some new religions. To be sure, Toan's teaching of the original mind, universally endowed in all individuals, implied a "dangerously optimistic belief in the essential goodness of human nature,"[13] but it confined that optimism to discourse on religious and moral potential, failing to apply it in any discernible manner to the political order of the time.

Shingaku did not aim to create a radical socioreligious alternative, but merely to render the spiritual and social order more harmonious and fulfilling. Shingaku masters thus never identified themselves with deities whose religious authority somehow transcended the political order, nor did they become channels for the healing powers of such deities.[14] In fact, Shingaku did not aim to improve people's material circumstances in any immediate, tangible manner.[15] Unlike some of the new communities, Sekimon Shingaku did not purport to represent the interests of the penurious. Although its popular audiences undoubtedly included impoverished people, its most active members were townspeople and farmers who had sufficient resources and energy to maintain local Shingaku activities.

The fate of Shingaku in the early years of modern Japan brings into relief its transitional nature as a body of ideas that contained both conservative and forward-looking elements. After the Meiji Restoration, the organization itself virtually disappeared; only a handful of the most important meetinghouses survived into the modern period. The breakdown of the Shingaku network was the result of several circumstances. An oft-cited explanation is Shingaku's close association with the shogunate. This relationship dated back to the Kansei era (1789–1800), when Matsudaira Sadanobu hired Dōni and his disciples to give talks in areas controlled by the Bakufu. During the first half of the nineteenth century, the shogunal authorities repeatedly and explicitly sanctioned Shingaku sermons; when the regime finally lost power, Shingaku was also discredited. A more fundamental reason for the group's sudden decline was the dramatic change in the socioeducational needs of the Japanese people. Shingaku preachers had provided all classes of Tokugawa citizens, including women and children, with access to moral learning based on the classical Confucian curriculum used in samurai schools. The establishment of public, universal education in the Meiji period, with its greater emphasis on inculcating practical skills, obviated the demand for itinerant moral preachers. Another factor that contributed to Shingaku's deterioration was the new policy of *shinbutsu bunri* (separation of *kami* and buddhas). The promotion of a "pure" Shinto ideology and the accompanying anti-Buddhist sentiment that manifested itself in the early Meiji were inimicable to the syncretic nature of Shingaku, whose teachers had long combined native beliefs with Buddhist, Confucian, and Taoist ideas.

A less noted reason for Shingaku's decline was the internal degeneration and fragmentation of the movement itself, which began decades before the Restoration. The rate at which new meetinghouses appeared decreased significantly after the Bunsei era (1818–1830). Shingaku's growth during its "golden age" in the late eighteenth century had been sustained by a well-developed system of religious training. The experience of knowing the original mind, required of all preaching members, was formally certified by Shingaku masters. The popular talks that led to the movement's expansion were thus originally inspired by each preacher's personal religious experience. The talks were designed to be the public facet of a comprehensive program of religious education, but as the demand for large-scale preaching increased, some members lost sight of the more introspective dimensions of the learning of the mind. Shibata Kyūō and other late preachers concentrated almost entirely on moral exhortation rendered entertaining through storytelling. Regular members of the group still attended study meetings and lectures, but they seem to have neglected contemplative practices. Even though the public demand for "talks on the Way" continued, the religious community experienced a loss of vitality.

The collapse of the Shingaku organization at the time of the Restoration was therefore related to a number of developments, both external and internal to the movement itself. But these forces did not eradicate the legacy of Shingaku. On a tangible level, its educational infrastructure and teaching methods proved useful to early Meiji educators. The close relations between Shingaku and other educational institutions that developed in the late Edo period carried over into the new era.[16] In a number of domains, Shingaku teachers had given regular public talks; some had assisted in establishing official schools for commoners. Not infrequently, the members had spoken in local *terakoya*.[17] Shingaku teachers continued to play a role in early Meiji schools. Talks on the Way were a regular part of the curriculum in Kyoto's new elementary school system *(bangumi shōgakkō)*; they were held six times a month in most of the sixty-four schools until 1873. Moreover, several Shingaku meetinghouses themselves became elementary schools, especially in Kyoto and Osaka.[18]

In a more lasting manner, Shingaku assisted in the formation of ethical attitudes that are still powerful forces in Japanese society today. In this sense, Robert Bellah's selection of Baigan and his group as paradigmatic of the role of religion in spreading values in Tokugawa Japan was quite appropriate. However, as Bellah himself cautioned, Shingaku was not simply an ethical teaching. Particularly after Baigan's death, it blossomed into a comprehensive spiritual discipline that could be successfully pursued in the context of everyday life. By synthesizing Neo-Confucian self-cultivation with popular Zen, Baigan's followers created a practicable system of faith that prefigured the lay-oriented religious movements of the modern era.

NOTES

Introduction

1. "Mind," *shin* or *kokoro* in Japanese, should be understood as the human psyche in its broadest sense, encompassing the functions of emotion and volition as well as intellect. In this study, the capitalized "Shingaku" refers only to the religious teaching and community founded by Ishida Baigan and developed by Teshima Toan.

2. Treatments of Baigan are discussed below. The later phases of Shingaku history have been covered in a general manner by several Japanese scholars; the most detailed treatment is Ishikawa Ken's *Sekimon Shingaku shi no kenkyū*, which focuses on Shingaku's institutional development. Shibata Minoru's *Shingaku* is a concise account of the history of the movement and its ideas. I have been guided by the works of these two scholars throughout my research; in subsequent footnotes "Ishikawa" and "Shibata" refer to them unless otherwise indicated. To my knowledge, the only Western study of the development of Shingaku under Teshima Toan is Jennifer Robertson's "Rooting the Pine: Shingaku Methods of Organization," a survey of Shingaku institutions and activities. Robertson's essay is not sensitive to the religious dimension of Shingaku.

3. These two expressions derive from a passage in the *Book of History* attributed to the sage king Yü: "The human mind is insecure, the mind of the Way is barely perceptible. Have utmost refinement and singleness of mind. Hold fast the Mean!" Translation adapted from Wm. Theodore de Bary, *Neo-Confucian Orthodoxy and the Learning of the Mind-and-Heart*, 73.

4. See his *Neo-Confucian Orthodoxy* and its sequel, *The Message of the Mind in Neo-Confucianism*.

5. The term appears in this sense in the titles of Neo-Confucian works that circulated in early Tokugawa Japan, such as the Ming compilation *Chu-tzu hsin-hsüeh lu* (Record of Master Chu's Learning of the Mind).

6. *Jigo shū* 5:27b–28b, in *Ekken zenshū* 2:278–279. Kumogawa Kōki's *Shingaku ben* (1685) also emphasizes that the true learning of the mind is that of Chu Hsi, not that of Wang (Ishikawa, *Sekimon*, 30).

7. See Yamashita Ryūji, "Nakae Tōju's Religious Thought and Its Relation to 'Jitsugaku.' "

8. Banzan did not call his own teaching "learning of the mind." (*Shūgi washo*, 14–15, 213. I am indebted for these references to Ian James McMullen of the Oriental Institute of Oxford University, England.) The popular Zen preacher Suzuki Shōsan (1579–1655) made some remarks about *shingaku* in 1652 that may indicate that this term was already associated with the school of Tōju and/or Banzan:

> "When people listen a little to *shingaku,* they all suddenly become *shingaku* followers. No matter how much people listen to my talks, not even one of them truly hears [what I am saying]. It's a strange thing. Well, maybe it's because *shingaku* is concerned with action, so it can be practiced just as it is, whereas my system is an ascetic discipline that is concerned with the mind, so it is not easy for anyone to become good at it." At the time someone said,
>
> "*Shingaku* criticizes the Buddhist Dharma, so it is the wrong path." When our teacher [Shōsan] heard this, he said,
>
> "That is not so. *Shingaku* is the blossoming of the Buddhist Dharma. Its popularity is a good sign that the Buddhist Dharma is rising up." (*Roan-kyō*, in *Suzuki Shōsan dōjin zenshū*, 171)

One of Wang Yang-ming's important doctrines was the unity of knowledge and action, which led to deemphasis of the quietistic tendencies of Neo-Confucianism and greater affirmation of spontaneous action. Moreover, Wang's thought was perceived to be more open to the influence of Buddhism than the orthodox Ch'eng-Chu tradition. Shōsan's view of *shingaku* as a form of learning that stressed action rather than introspection and that was somehow related to Buddhism even while critical of it may reflect the popular perception of the Ō Yōmei (Wang Yang-ming) school. Cf. Herman Ooms, *Tokugawa Ideology: Early Constructs, 1570–1680,* 136. Shōsan's remarks could not possibly have referred to Sekimon Shingaku at this early date.

9. Toan may have used Ming compilations or Japanese editions of Ch'eng-Chu writings, but these would be difficult to identify since they are composed mostly of earlier material. There is no exact list of the books that Toan read, except for the Shingaku curriculum itself (see Chapter 7). However, on pages 175–176 of *Teshima Toan zenshū* (hereafter, TTZ), editor Shibata Minoru includes a book dealer's catalogue of works that was appended to Toan's essay *Waga tsue* (My Walking Stick). The essay was first published in 1775 and was reissued posthumously in 1789 with a new postface. Shibata does not clarify whether the list appeared with the first publication, the second, or both. The part of the catalogue entitled "Principal Books Used by Master Teshima" includes many Neo-Confucian and several Taoist and Shinto books. Buddhist works are relegated to another category, "Recorded Sayings That May Be of Assistance in [the Study of] Shingaku." "Principal Books" lists some Ming works, including the aforementioned *Record of Master Chu's Learning of the Mind (Chu-tzu hsin-hsüeh lu* or *Hui-an Chu hsien-sheng hsin-hsüeh lu),* a 1534 work by Wang Ming. The printing blocks for this work were redone in Japan in 1663 and it was reprinted sev-

eral times. Also included in the list is *Hsin-ching fu-chu* (The Heart Classic, Supplemented and Annotated), a 1492 edition of Chen Te-hsiu's *Hsin-ching* (Heart Classic), by Ch'eng Min-cheng (1445–1499+), which had influenced Yi T'oegye and Tokugawa Neo-Confucians. See de Bary, *Neo-Confucian Orthodoxy,* 176–177, regarding these works and their place in the history of mind-learning. As for Japanese editions of Ch'eng-Chu discourses on the mind, one of the works in the book dealer's catalogue is *Shushi seiza setsu* (Master Chu's Theory of Quiet Sitting), a compilation of the Kimon school of Yamazaki Ansai.

10. The Sung masters themselves apparently did not use the term *hsin-hsüeh* (de Bary, *Message of the Mind,* 27).

11. *Shingaku gorinsho* is often associated with two other anonymous works of this period, *Kana shōri* (The Principles of Human Nature, in the Vernacular) and *Honsaroku* (The Record of the Lord of Sado). Both Hayashi Razan and Fujiwara Seika have been proposed as the author of these texts. For studies of this literature, see Imanaka Kanshi, *Kinsei Nihon seiji shisō no seiritsu: Seikagaku to Razangaku;* Ishige Tadashi, "*Shingaku gorinsho* no seiritsu jijō to sono shisōteki tokushitsu: *Kana shōri, Honsaroku* rikai no zentei to shite"; and Yamamoto Shinkō, "*Shingaku gorinsho*" no kisoteki kenkyū, which includes several versions of the text. The standard modern edition of *Shingaku gorinsho* is in NST 28:257–267. Ooms offers an analysis of these works in *Tokugawa Ideology,* 86–93.

12. Translation adapted from de Bary, *Neo-Confucian Orthodoxy,* 73.

13. Yamamoto, "*Shingaku gorinsho,*" 120.

14. The latter was illustrated by a certain Hishigawa Shisen in 1675. In his 1667 *Shingaku ron* (Discussion of Mind-Learning), Tokigawa Josui attributes *Shingaku gorinsho* to Kumazawa Banzan (who denied authorship, however). See Ishikawa's discussion in *Sekimon,* 23–33, and Shibata Minoru, "Sekimon Shingaku ni tsuite," 452–455.

15. Ooms refers here to *Shingaku gorinsho* and related writings (*Tokugawa Ideology,* 83).

16. The title of this work appears in a catalogue of ca. 1667 (Shibata, *Shingaku,* 7); according to *Kokusho sōmokuroku,* it was published in 1650. For a brief discussion of earlier Chinese Buddhist uses of *hsin-hsüeh,* see Araki Kengo, "Confucianism and Buddhism in the Late Ming," 39–40.

17. *Hotoke no za,* "seat of the Buddha," is also the name of a type of bee nettle. *Shingaku tenron* has a 1751 postface; it is reproduced in *Taishō shinshū daizōkyō* (hereafter T), 82:656–684.

18. See Yamamoto's study of later versions of *Shingaku gorinsho* in "*Shingaku gorinsho*" no kisoteki kenkyū.

19. Most of the secondary Japanese scholarship on Shingaku cited in this book includes some attempt to identify its philosophical and religious influences. The two most recent and accurate treatments of this issue in the West are, regarding Neo-Confucian influence on Ishida Baigan, Wm. T. de Bary's remarks in "Neo-Confucian Cultivation and the Seventeenth-Century Enlightenment," 148–153; and regarding Buddhist influence on Baigan and his followers, Paul B. Watt, "The Buddhist Element in Shingaku, 'The Learning of the Heart.' "

20. See, for example, Tetsuo Najita, *Visions of Virtue in Tokugawa Japan:*

The Kaitokudō Merchant Academy of Osaka, 96; Minamoto Ryōen, "Interaction Between Confucianism and Buddhism in the Tokugawa Period."

21. For a concise summary of its past usage in the study of religion, see André Droogers, "Syncretism: The Problem of Definition, the Definition of the Problem," 9–13; for arguments against the term's meaningfulness, see Robert Baird, *Category Formation and the History of Religion,* 142–152. Judith Berling attempts to refute Baird and proposes her own definition of "syncretism" in *The Syncretic Religion of Lin Chao-en,* 1–13.

22. Baird, *Category Formation,* 151.

23. Maruyama, *Studies in the Intellectual History of Tokugawa Japan,* 142.

24. I distinguish here between the process in which different ideas and practices are blended and the result of that interaction. The syncretic process is fluid: concepts, practices, and rituals are being considered, adopted, and reinterpreted. In this inchoate phase, there may well be a measure of "incoherence," for ideas have been identified with each other, but their differences may not yet be resolved or even noted. The end result of the process, however, is not necessarily "syncretism" in Baird's sense. As Edward T. Ch'ien points out, it may be a "synthesis" in which the various elements are thoroughly integrated. See his *Chiao Hung and the Restructuring of Neo-Confucianism in the Late Ming,* 2.

25. Several Japanese studies are listed in the Bibliography; see especially Shibata Minoru's *Shingaku* and *Baigan to sono monryū,* Iwauchi Seiichi's *Kyōikuka toshite no Ishida Baigan,* and Ishikawa Ken's *Sekimon Shingaku shi no kenkyū.* Paolo Beonio-Brocchieri's book *Religiosità e ideologia alle origini del Giappone moderno* is an extensive overview of Baigan's life, sociohistorical context, works, and teaching; it includes a content analysis and a translation of an important section of Baigan's major work, *Tohi mondō* (City and Country Dialogues). A rather poor English rendition of this Italian translation appears in *Serie Orientale Roma* under the title "*Seirimondō:* Dialogue on Human Nature and Natural Order." An important late Shingaku figure, Kamada Ryūō, is the topic of Ingrid Schuster's *Kamada Ryūkō* [sic] *und seine Stellung in der Shingaku;* and a much older German study of Shingaku is Horst Hammitzsch's "Shingaku: Eine Bewegung der Volksaufklärung in der Tokugawazeit."

26. *Tokugawa Religion: The Values of Pre-Industrial Japan,* reprinted in paperback in 1985 under the title *Tokugawa Religion: The Cultural Roots of Modern Japan* with a new introduction by the author.

27. For Weber's theory, see especially *The Protestant Ethic and the Spirit of Capitalism* and "The Protestant Sects and the Spirit of Capitalism."

28. *Tokugawa Religion,* 131.

29. Ibid., 196.

30. The official structure of Tokugawa society, derived from the traditional Chinese view of four social classes, included samurai, peasants, artisans, and merchants, in descending order of status. The profit that merchants made from transactions was considered immoral, because it was not produced by the labor of their own hands. In the face of this ideology, Ishida Baigan proclaimed that all four classes performed valuable functions in society and that the merchant's profit was comparable to the stipend that samurai received from their lords.

Baigan was not alone in his affirmation of the value of the merchant way; Bellah cites Miura Baien (1723–1789), Motoori Norinaga (1730–1801), and Kaiho Seiryō (1755–1817) as other examples of this trend (*Tokugawa Religion,* 160–161). An earlier example is Nishikawa Joken (1648–1724), discussed by Najita in *Visions of Virtue,* 48–56.

31. This expression was originally used by Miyamoto Mataji in "Sekimon Shingaku to shōnin ishiki," 29.

32. Examples of this type of critique of Bellah are Sakai Takahito, "Sekimon Shingaku no igi to genkai: sono tsūzoku dōtoku e no tenraku no keiki ni tsuite"; Ogasahara Makoto, " 'Nihon kindaika' ron no saikentō—Sekimon Shingaku ni mirareru gendai shisō to sono genkai"; and Tsuda Hideo, *Kinsei minshū kyōiku undō no tenkai,* 15. See also Minamoto Ryōen's critical discussion of Shingaku's role in the development of Japan's economic ethic, in *Kinsei shōki jitsugaku shisō no kenkyū,* 43–50. Still others have disputed the validity of Bellah's concept of central or core values; for a brief summary, see Helen Hardacre, *Kurozumikyō and the New Religions of Japan,* 42–43.

33. Bellah, *Tokugawa Religion,* 158, 174.

34. The ethic of loyalty, centered on the emperor, led to highly "irrational" consequences in later Japanese history. Maruyama therefore doubted whether the function of such particularistic moral values was indeed analogous to the role of the universalistic Protestant ethic in the rise of the modern West. He felt Bellah's view of the contribution of religion to modernization was too optimistic, for its effects might be thought to include "the tragedy of '45." "Berā no *Tokugawa jidai no shūkyō* (1957)," 116.

35. The key problem is the definition of "modernization" itself; for a discussion of the various factors involved in characterizing Japanese modernization, see John W. Hall, "Changing Conceptions of the Modernization of Japan."

36. Bellah responds to and accepts Maruyama's key criticism in "Reflections on the Protestant Ethic Analogy in Asia," Chap. 3 of his book *Beyond Belief,* esp. pp. 56–57; and more recently in his "Introduction to the Paperback Edition," *Tokugawa Religion,* xi–xxi. He now feels that the book's greatest failing is the theory of modernization itself (ibid., xviii).

37. Major Japanese collections of historical documents concerning education invariably include Shingaku writings. Examples are *Ishida Baigan, Teshima Toan,* vol. 4 of *Sekai kyōiku hōten: Nihon kyōiku hen;* and *Shingaku hen,* vol. 4 of *Nihon kyōiku bunko* (hereafter NKB). Ronald Dore and Herbert Passin discuss Shingaku briefly in their surveys of Tokugawa education; see, respectively, *Education in Tokugawa Japan,* 236–238, and *Society and Education in Japan,* 40–41.

38. *Tokugawa Religion,* 165.

39. Here I follow Wilfred C. Smith's view of religion as "faith" that is articulated through various "cumulative traditions" (although I do not dispense with the term "religion" itself, as he advocates) and Paul Tillich's definition of faith as "a total and centered act of the personal self, the act of unconditional, infinite and ultimate concern." See Smith's seminal *The Meaning and End of Religion* and Tillich's *The Dynamics of Faith,* 8.

1: Popular Learning in Tokugawa Japan

1. Shibata (following Ishikawa's research), *Shingaku,* 102.

2. With limited sources it is not possible to specify the precise social status or occupation of the people who were exposed to the teaching. The audiences of public Shingaku lectures undoubtedly included a greater percentage of impoverished, uneducated commoners than did the smaller groups of committed members who regularly frequented the Shingaku schools. The most active members were generally townspeople or wealthy villagers.

3. Information about the Hayashi school (Shōheikō) is drawn from Ishikawa Ken, *Kinsei no gakkō,* ,31–33, 58; Tsuda Hideo, *Kinsei minshū,* 7; Umihara Tōru, *Gakkō,* 46–47; and Dore, *Education,* 224.

4. Passin, *Society and Education,* 19–20. For remarks on the domain schools, see Ishikawa Ken, *Nihon shomin kyōiku shi,* 81–139; and Dore, *Education,* 222–224. A more recent analysis of domain school admission of common people is Chapter 2 of Umihara Tōru's *Kinsei no gakkō to kyōiku,* 52–82.

5. Ishikawa, *Shomin,* 134; Dore, *Education,* 220–222.

6. Dore, *Education,* 226.

7. The categories of local school, domain school, private academy *(shijuku),* and "temple school" *(terakoya)* are somewhat artificial; in reality the nature and function of these schools overlapped. Ishikawa divides local schools into two types, small domain schools intended for children of retainers employed in rural areas and schools for commoners *(Shomin,* 139–140).

8. Dore, *Education,* 227–228; Ishikawa, *Shomin,* 140–141. According to the limited historical sources available, most schools for commoners that developed in association with a popular lecture system appeared only after the beginning of the Kansei era—some years after the death of Teshima Toan.

9. Ishikawa, *Sekimon,* 330. Ishikawa regards Heishū as a pioneer of the moral instruction school *(Shomin,* 140).

10. Tsuda Hideo discusses Gansuidō in his book *Kinsei minshū kyōiku undō no tenkai.* For a recent study of Kaitokudō in English, see Najita, *Visions of Virtue.*

11. An early private academy that admitted commoners in large numbers was Kogidō, founded in 1680 by Itō Jinsai. The later schools of Motoori Norinaga (1730–1801) and Hirose Tansō (1782–1856) also stand out in this regard.

12. The meaning of the term *terakoya* has been debated. Several words were used in the Edo period to refer to the school, but after the middle of the period they coalesced into *terakoya* 寺子屋. 寺小屋 is a mistaken rendition that gave rise to the idea that the *terakoya* was a "temple hut" rather than a "room where temple children" studied. The term "temple children" had come to refer simply to the children of local families, that is, families included in the "parish" of the particular temple. For *terakoya* in the Edo period, see Umihara's summary in *Gakkō,* 92–93, and his more detailed analysis in *Kinsei no gakkō,* 293–353, which draws on a wide variety of primary and recent secondary sources. Tone Keizaburō gives a detailed analysis of *terakoya* in Bushū (especially the area that is today's Saitama prefecture) in *Terakoya to shomin kyōiku no jisshōteki*

kenkyū. Older treatments in English are contained in Passin, *Society and Education,* 27–37, and Dore, *Education,* 252–290.

13. Umihara, *Gakkō,* 92. Buddhist priests tended to play a larger role in rural *terakoya;* see the charts in Tone, *Terakoya,* 271–272, for the social origins of teachers in the Saitama area schools.

14. The era is named after the prominent political figure of the time Tanuma Okitsugu (1719–1788), senior councillor to shogun Ieharu.

15. Ishikawa, *Sekimon,* 226–230. For an informative study of popular protests during the 1780s, see Anne Walthall, *Social Protest and Popular Culture in Eighteenth-Century Japan.*

16. Ooms, *Charismatic Bureaucrat: A Political Biography of Matsudaira Sadanobu, 1758–1829,* 138. For sociopolitical conditions and educational policy in the last decades of the eighteenth century, see Ishikawa, *Sekimon,* 226–240, 312–333.

17. Sadanobu's attempt to revive the spirit of shogun Yoshimune's Kyōhō (1716–1735) reforms distinctly affected the educational environment of the time. Efforts were made to standardize samurai training at the shogunal and domain schools. The new policies included the 1790 "Ban on Heterodoxy," which proclaimed Chu Hsi's interpretation of the Confucian tradition to be the official teaching of the shogunal schools. See Robert L. Backus, "The Kansei Prohibition of Heterodoxy and Its Effects on Education." The edict itself is translated in Ryusaku Tsunoda, Wm. Theodore de Bary, and Donald Keene, comps., *Sources of Japanese Tradition* 1:493–494.

18. This was not simply moral idealism, but a deliberate effort to increase the agrarian population. Yamashita Takeshi discusses Sadanobu's efforts to revive educational policies for commoners in his book *Edo jidai shomin seisaku no kenkyū,* 54ff. For a study of Sadanobu in English, see Ooms, *Charismatic Bureaucrat.*

19. Ishikawa, *Sekimon,* 326.

20. For example, the rate of new *terakoya* jumped in the Tenmei years to an average of twelve per year, compared to three per year in the 1760s and 1770s. The proliferation increased during the following Kansei and Kyōwa (1801–1803) periods. These statistics are based on the limited records available. Ishikawa believes the numbers were probably greater (*Sekimon,* 234–235). See his charts (ibid., 236) or Umihara, *Gakkō,* 93. Umihara discusses the growing demand for *terakoya* education among townspeople (*Kinsei no gakkō,* 301). There were corresponding increases in the number of other types of private schools, including the Shingaku schools themselves.

21. This set of moral exhortations was also distributed to *terakoya* as part of Yoshimune's reform program in the early eighteenth century. Written by Muro Kyūsō in 1722, it is an exposition of the early Ch'ing moral tract *Liu yü yen-i* (The Extended Meaning of the Six Precepts), based on Ming T'ai-tsu's "Six Precepts" of 1397.

22. George Sansom, *A History of Japan, 1615–1867,* 102–103, translates a 1658 example. The *gonin-gumi* were groups of five households who were mutually responsible for each other and whose leaders acted in a number of official

capacities. *Wakamonogumi,* organized groups of male youths, also played an educational role in Tokugawa villages.

23. Yokoyama Toshio, " 'Han kokka' e no michi," cited by Richard Rubinger in his own summary of restrictions on travel and their growing ineffectiveness (*Private Academies of Tokugawa Japan,* 16–23, citation on p. 20).

24. The traveling led to the popularization of vernacular guidebooks. During the seventeenth century there was a parallel increase in popular travel and in the number of common people who were literate. Lawrence Bresler, "The Origins of Popular Travel and Travel Literature in Japan," 183.

25. Both *kōshaku* and *kōdan* originally denoted a presentation in which passages or terms from a text, usually a literary classic or a religious scripture, were explained or embellished. In the Buddhist community there was a distinction between the traditional sermon, which explicated the meaning of an idea or passage from scripture, and the informal or "performed" sermon, which required some artistic skill; *kyōten kōshaku,* or simply *kōshaku,* usually meant a detailed exposition of Buddhist scripture. Confucian scholars, for their part, regarded *kōshaku* strictly as an expository talk that stayed close to the text, whereas *kōdan* involved the freedom to entertain the audience by means of engaging digressions (Enkō Shinji, "Kōdan," 2:512; Sekiyama Kazuo, *Sekkyō no rekishiteki kenkyū,* 251). By the Meiji Restoration the two words had become virtually interchangeable.

26. Enkō, "Kōdan," 512; Yokoyama Tatsuzō, *Nihon kinsei kyōikushi,* 345; for the educational role of Shinto shrines during the Edo period, see Kishimoto Yoshio, *Kinsei Shintō kyōiku shi,* 202.

27. Examples of the early theorists are Hayashi Razan (1583–1657), Watarai Nobuyoshi (1615–1690), Yoshikawa Koretaru (1616–1694), and Yamazaki Ansai. See Peter Nosco, *Remembering Paradise: Nativism and Nostalgia in Eighteenth-Century Japan,* 43–44, and also his "Masuho Zankō (1655–1742): A Shinto Popularizer between Nativism and National Learning," 177–178. Regarding Zankō, see Taira Shigemichi, "Kinsei no Shintō shisō," 556–558; and Nosco, "Zankō."

28. "Zankō," 181.

29. *Ishida Baigan zenshū* (hereafter IBZ), ed. Shibata Minoru, 2:621, translated in Bellah, *Tokugawa Religion,* 220. Some modern scholars have even attempted to establish a direct connection between Baigan and Zankō, but we may only speculate that Baigan heard of Zankō's ideas and was inspired by his activism. See, for example, Shibata Minoru, "Ishida Baigan to Masuho Zankō." Kishimoto goes so far as to consider Shinto the basis of Shingaku thought (*Kinsei Shintō,* 273–286). Zankō's popular style did influence other non-Shinto storytellers such as Shidōken (1683–1765) and even the writer Hiraga Gennai (1728–1779). Nakano Mitsutoshi, "Masuho Zankō no hito to shisō," 413.

30. For details on Bunkō and other storytellers, see Enkō Shinji, "Kōshakushi," 490. Bunkō supposedly gave a talk in 1757 called "Shingaku hyōri banashi" (A Two-sided Shingaku Talk), in which he poked fun at Shingaku preachers. Since Sekimon Shingaku had not expanded significantly beyond the Kyoto area in 1757, however, it is hard to imagine that Bunkō was satirizing it at

this time in Edo. Perhaps the Ō Yōmei school was intended. *Konsaisu jinmei jiten: Nihon hen,* 900; Yokoyama Tatsuzō, *Nihon kinsei kyōiku shi,* 346.

31. See his book *Sekkyō no rekishiteki kenkyū.*

32. Regarding the *otogishū,* see ibid., 244–245. Sekiyama underscores the overlooked contributions of several Pure Land figures to early modern preaching.

33. According to Watanabe Kunio, he defrocked at the age of sixty-one (*Shintō shisō to sono kenkyūshatachi,* 183). Nosco follows Nakano in the position that Zankō was only forty-three at the time ("Zankō," 178).

34. See Sekiyama, *Sekkyō,* 244; for remarks on the Buddhist connections of these storytellers, see ibid., 252.

35. Tsuda, *Kinsei minshū kyōiku,* 6.

36. For the above comments on lecturing in the Hayashi and Kimon schools, see Yokoyama Tatsuzō, *Nihon kinsei kyōiku shi,* 132–133, 140–141. Yokoyama gives an excerpt of one of Naokata's talks on the *Analects* on pp. 136–139.

37. Ibid., 133.

38. From the preface to *Yakubun sentei,* translated in Dore, *Education,* 141; see also Passin, *Society and Education,* 190–194.

39. For the Confucian scholar's educational roles in Tokugawa Japan (tutoring and school teaching), see John W. Hall, "The Confucian Teacher in Tokugawa Japan," 281–285.

40. One memorandum from the late Edo suggests that farmers in the Mito domain regarded these lectures as abstruse and unrelated to their practical needs (Dore, *Education,* 241).

41. He returned to Nagoya to study under Nakanishi Tan'en. Heishū and Tan'en are usually classified as representatives of the "eclectic" Neo-Confucian trend *(setchūgaku)* that developed in the second half of the Edo period; for details about Heishū see Nakamura Yukihiko, "Kaidai 1," 518–523; and Michiko Aoki and Margaret Dardess, "The Popularization of Samurai Values: A Sermon by Hosoi Heishū."

42. Aoki and Dardess, "Popularization," 395.

43. See Hosoi Heishū, *Heishū zenshū* (ed. Takase Daijirō), 915–949; Aoki and Dardess translate the sermon in "Popularization", 400–413.

44. Cited in Takase Daijirō, *Hosoi Heishū,* 1107. This remark may apply only to Heishū's popular talks; he probably reverted to a more formal style when teaching domain lords or domain school students.

45. In Aoki and Dardess' translation, *honshin* (original mind) and *jisshin/jitsu no kokoro* (true mind) are rendered as *makoto* (Aoki and Dardess, "Popularization," 406, 413; cf. Hosoi Heishū, *Heishū zenshū,* 932, 948, respectively).

46. Regarding the development of printing and vernacular works, see Richard Lane, "The Beginnings of the Modern Japanese Novel: *Kana-zōshi,* 1600–1682"; and Karasawa Tomitarō, "Nihon kyōiku shi tsūron," 99–100.

47. Lane, "Beginnings," 651–652.

48. In the narrow sense of the term used by modern scholars, *kanazōshi* refers to vernacular short stories that developed out of medieval tale genres and led up to the more realistic *ukiyozōshi* of the Genroku period. I use the term in its broader sense to refer to the entire range of prose books, written in *kana* or *kana*

mixed with a few well-known Chinese characters, that aimed to edify as well as entertain.

49. Yamashita, *Edo jidai,* 369.

50. *Iroha* songs, as well as *Jitsugokyō* and *Dōjikyō,* two well-known children's textbooks that were often illustrated, are discussed in Chapter 6.

51. Yamashita, *Edo jidai,* 376; the examples of illustrated books he gives are mostly from late in the Edo period.

52. *Kakun* were codes of conduct transmitted from one generation to the next within samurai families. The genre was gradually popularized; codes from the Muromachi period later became public reading material. See Carl Steenstrup, "The Imagawa Letter: A Muromachi Warrior's Code of Conduct Which Became a Tokugawa Schoolbook"; and Mark Ramseyer, "Thrift and Diligence: House Codes of Tokugawa Merchant Families." Teshima Toan's mentor Saitō Zenmon drew up a code for his offspring that is probably representative of the merchant *kakun* of his time; it is reproduced and discussed in Takenaka Yasukazu, "Saitō Zenmon no kahō."

53. Both of these works are contained in *Kinsei chōnin shisō,* ed. Nakamura Yukihiko, *Nihon shisō taikei* (hereafter NST), 59:85–174 and 175–233, respectively. Najita discusses their content in *Visions of Virtue,* 48–56 and 20–21, respectively.

54. Baigan's work is contained in NST 42:9–32, and Toan's, in TTZ, 1–18 and 197–208, respectively.

55. TTZ, 176. The story about the loyalty and righteousness of Hachisuke of Sunshū, *Sunshū chūgi Hachisuke den,* is very likely Tomioka Ichoku's *Notes on the Conduct of Hachisuke of Sunshū (Sunshū Hachisuke gyōjō kikigaki,* 1770); Fuse Shōō compiled *Notes on the Conduct of [the Filial Son] Nishioka Gihei (Nishioka [kōshi] Gihei gyōjō kikigaki,* 1770), and Kamata Issō wrote *The Story of the Filial Daughter Moyo [of Wadamura] in Washū (Washū [Wadamura] kōjo Moyo no den,* n.d.).

56. The last title appears not in the section on loyalty and filial piety books, but in the list of books that Toan purportedly used (TTZ, 175–176). According to *Konsaisu jinmei jiten,* the name of the author is pronounced Fujii Raisai and his dates are 1626–1706 (p. 952); Ueno Yōzō gives his dates as 1618–1709 ("Fujii Ransai"). Perhaps because his books reflect unambiguous moral values and are relatively free of difficult passages or scholarly commentary, they remained useful to later generations of educators. According to the editions extant today, *Stories of Filial Children of Our Country* was reprinted in 1685, 1686, and 1687; and *Record of Good Deeds in Japan,* in 1713 and 1774. Ransai also wrote *Fujin yashinai-gusa* (Cultivation for Ladies, 1689) and a revised edition of *Essays in Idleness (Tsurezuregusa tekigi),* purified of passages that he evidently believed were morally misleading.

57. The work has a preface dated 1658 and was published in 1738; it is reproduced in cursive script in Yamazaki Ansai, *Zoku Yamazaki Ansai zenshū* 3:157–205; a printed version is contained in NKB 9:25–95.

58. This was a 1655 Japanese rendition of Liu Hsiang's *Stories of Chaste Women (Lieh-nü chuan,* first century B.C.E.), attributed to Kitamura Kigin (1624–1705).

59. Toan's epilogue to *Early Lessons (Zenkun)*, for example, is inspired by a Chinese tract for women; see Chapter 6.

60. There were various publications under these titles, not only didactic works, but also copybooks and "sentimental stories" *(ninjōbon)*. For examples of the didactic type, see NKB 9. *Analects for Women* is attributed to Kaibara Ekken. Other examples of this genre include *Tales of Famous Women (Meijo monogatari*, 1670), and the aforementioned *Cultivation for Ladies* by Ransai.

61. As a single work, *Onna daigaku* in block-print form dates only from 1790. The oldest extant block print of *Onna daigaku* is part of *Onna daigaku takara bako* (The Treasure Chest of Great Learning for Women), a compilation printed in 1716. The *Treasure Chest* was in demand throughout the eighteenth and early nineteenth centuries. By 1874 it had gone through eleven block editions, not to mention numerous revised editions that added illustrations and other edifying items. Even after the Meiji Restoration, *Treasure Chest* was set in movable type and used until the end of World War II in secondary education for girls. Ishikawa Matsutarō, *"Onna daigaku."*

62. Furukawa Tetsushi, *Nihon dōtoku kyōiku shi*, 158. A look at the dates of extant editions reveals that five of Ekken's popular works went through at least three to five printings each by the end of the Tokugawa period. For a recent study of Ekken, see Mary Evelyn Tucker's *Moral and Spiritual Cultivation in Japanese Neo-Confucianism: The Life and Thought of Kaibara Ekken (1630–1714)*, which includes a translation of one of Ekken's popular moral discourses, *Precepts for Daily Life in Japan (Yamato zokkun)*. His disciple Takeda Shun'an (Sadanao) was also a popularizer; he wrote two of the "tales of virtue" listed in the Shingaku book dealer's catalogue: *The Story of Shōsuke, a Filial Son of [the Land of] Chikuzen (Chikuzen [no kuni] kōshi Shōsuke den*, 1729), and *Stories of [Filial Children,] Good People of [the Land of] Chikuzen (Chikuzen [no kuni kōshi] ryōmin den*, 1741–1742).

63. The source is *Tōsei heta dangi*, (Clumsy Sermons for Today's World); see Furukawa, *Nihon dōtoku kyōiku shi*, 191.

64. Shibata Minoru, *Baigan to sono monryū*, 100.

65. Furukawa, *Nihon dōtoku kyōiku*, 191.

66. Ibid., 173.

67. Sekiyama, *Sekkyō*, 307. The *dangibon*, a type of sermon book that combines humor with a didactic aim, was popular from about the 1750s to the 1780s; Sekiyama seems to believe that the spread of Sekimon Shingaku was one factor in the development of this genre, but he does not give any evidence in support of his view (ibid., 254).

68. Whereas the sermon proper *(seppō* or *sekkyō)* is oral, *hōgo* usually indicates a written form. However, the *hōgo* may be a record of a particular sermon. For remarks on vernacular Dharma talks, see Miyasaka Yūshō, "Kaisetsu," 4–6; and Inoue Yoshimi, *Nihon kyōiku shisō shi no kenkyū*, 185, 193–194.

69. Chōmei's and Musō's dates are 1153–1216 and 1275–1351, respectively. All the above works appear in the Shingaku book dealer's list (TTZ, 176). Bassui's teachings underwent a revival in the early Tokugawa period (Peter Haskel, "Bankei and His World," 454, n. 42). *Enzan wadei gassui shū*, published in 1386, records Bassui's responses to questions from clergy and laity. It is con-

tained in Bassui Tokushō, *Bassui*, 151–412. For a translation, see Arthur Braverman's *Mud and Water: A Collection of Talks*.

70. For example, Nanmei, the author of the eighteenth-century sermon book *Sand and Pebbles Continued (Zoku shasekishū)*, was a True Pure Land monk. Robert Morrell, *Sand and Pebbles (Shasekishū): The Tales of Mujū Ichien, a Voice for Pluralism in Kamakura Buddhism*, 66.

71. Sekiyama, *Sekkyō*, 188–192.

72. In *Rongo kōgi*, ostensibly a lecture on the *Analects*, Toan draws on *Shasekishū* twice (TTZ, 461–462 and 481–482).

73. Mujū's inclusivism reflects the Tendai universalism that dominated Buddhism in his time. See Morrell, *Sand and Pebbles*, 6–7. Toan may also have appreciated the section of *Sand and Pebbles* in which Mujū evaluates Buddhist preachers and sermons; the Shingaku leader similarly cautioned his own followers against superficial or wrongly motivated talks. See ibid., 182–194, for translated excerpts, and TTZ, 586, 588, and 592, for Toan's strictures. According to Sekiyama, Mujū was a great preacher himself, and his works *Sand and Pebbles* and *Casual Digressions (Zōtanshū)* were originally written as material for his sermons (*Sekkyō*, 160–179). Morrell argues that Mujū's relations with his parishioners gradually deteriorated, however (*Sand and Pebbles*, 50–51).

74. For a translation and study of Ikkyū's Chinese poetry, see Sonja Arntzen's *Ikkyū and the Crazy Cloud Anthology: A Zen Poet of Medieval Japan*.

75. Sanford, *Zen-man Ikkyū*, ix–xi.

76. Sanford gives a synopsis of "Ikkyū's" work (*Zen-man*, 198), but he overlooks the distinction between the original *Mizu kagami* and "*Mizu kagami* me nashi gusa*," a later, anonymous commentary on the former work. I have translated Toan's own version in " 'No Eye: A Word to the Wise': Teshima Toan's Commentary on Ikkyū's *Mizu Kagami*," in *The Eastern Buddhist*, n.s., 24, no. 2 (Autumn 1991): 106–122.

77. *Amida hadaka monogatari* is listed along with the other Buddhist works in the Shingaku book list (TTZ, 176). Many of Ikkyū's Japanese poems *(waka)* are contained in the Tokugawa corpus of legendary tales *Ikkyū banashi*, so their attribution is suspect. Sanford seems to feel that the *waka* from the prose works are more likely to have been written by Ikkyū himself (*Zen-man*, 120). Cf. Arntzen, (*Ikkyū*, 180, n. 37). *Me nashi yōjin shō* contains many of the Japanese poems attributed to Ikkyū.

78. *Zen-man*, 247.

79. Sanford follows Robertson, "Rooting the Pine," 321–322, who cites the talks of Shibata Kyūō, the former storyteller who became active in Shingaku near the end of the Edo period. The transformation of the Shingaku lecture after Toan is discussed in Chapter 7.

80. Suzuki Daisetsu, *Zen shisō shi kenkyū 1: Bankei Zen*, 234–235; this remark is part of Suzuki's argument for Bankei's unique position in the history of Japanese Zen.

81. Haskel, "Bankei and His World," 101–103.

82. Ibid., 112.

83. For example, *Fudōchi shinmyōroku*, *Tōkai yawa*, and *Ketsujōshū*, all of which are contained in volume 5 of *Takuan oshō zenshū*.

84. For this aspect of Takuan, see Minamoto Ryōen, *Jitsugaku,* 282–314.

85. He was also acquainted with the works of Chen Te-hsiu, including the annotated version of Chen's *Heart Classic* that influenced the development of the learning of the mind in Korea and Japan.

86. Munan had studied as a layman under Gudō for as many as twenty years. He gradually gathered his own disciples, one of whom, Shōju Etan, became Hakuin's teacher. For information on Munan, see Tōrei Enji, "The Biography of Shidō Munan Zenji," translated by Kobori Sōhaku and Norman Waddell. Munan's *Sokushinki* is translated by the same translators; *Jishōki* is translated by Priscilla Pedersen. For the Japanese texts, I have consulted *Munan kana hōgo.*

87. Priscilla Pedersen, "Shidō Munan in Zen Tradition," 22.

88. *Munan kana hōgo,* 361–399, passim.

89. Royall Tyler has translated *Mōanjō* and *Banmin tokuyō* in *Selected Writings of Suzuki Shōsan,* 31–74. For the following discussion of Shōsan I have also drawn on the introduction to *Selected Writings* (pp. 1–8) and Tyler's remarks in "The Tokugawa Peace and Popular Religion: Suzuki Shōsan, Kakugyō Tōbutsu, and Jikigyō Miroku," esp. 93–101.

90. Tyler, *Selected Writings,* 166. Shōsan claimed to be the first to advocate this perspective, but it is not foreign to Mahayana Buddhism and had been expressed in Japan previously. However, Shōsan was more simplistic and radical in his emphasis on the identity of the religious and secular realms. One of Shōsan's contemporaries, Takuan, made a similar but slightly more precise statement: "When the law of the Buddha is fulfilled, it is the same as the law of the world. When the law of the world is fulfilled, it is the same as the law of Buddha. The Way is simply daily life" (*Ketsujōshū,* in *Takuan oshō zenshū* 5:7–8).

91. Tyler, "Popular Religion," 98.

92. Tyler concludes that Shōsan's teaching was only marginally Buddhist in content: "one possible dead end in the evolution of Buddhist thought" ("Popular Religion," 101).

93. Ooms discusses Shōsan's role as ideological disseminator in *Tokugawa Ideology,* 122–143.

94. An example of Toan's reference to Shōsan is in TTZ, 772–773.

95. I return to this theme in Chapter 3. One scholar has argued, rather implausibly, for the possibility of a direct link between Shōsan and Ishida Baigan, perhaps through Baigan's teacher Oguri Ryōun (Inoue, *Nihon kyōiku shisō,* 200–206).

96. I have based most of my remarks about Bankei's life and teaching style on comments in Peter Haskel, *Bankei Zen: Translations from the Record of Bankei,* xvii–xxxvi; Norman Waddell, *The Unborn: The Life and Teaching of Zen Master Bankei, 1622–1693,* 3–33.

97. Haskel, "Bankei and His World," 139–140, 162.

98. According to Waddell, at Bankei's death in 1693, over 400 priests and monks and 270 nuns were his personal disciples, and more than 5,000 men and women had received the lay precepts from him (*Unborn,* 23). Haskel reports that Bankei accepted 50,000 disciples during his lifetime, of whom about 400 became enlightened under him ("Bankei and His World," 212).

99. A collection of his talks was first published in 1758. Bankei's works are

collected in *Bankei zenji zenshū,* ed. Akao Ryūji. I have also used *Bankei zenji goroku,* ed. Suzuki Daisetsu.

100. Toan himself acknowledges this debt in one of his talks (NST 42:123).

101. Toan's contemporary, Rinzai master Hakuin Ekaku, is the most important Zen figure for understanding the religious life of Nakazawa Dōni and his followers in Edo. Hakuin Zen has been the dominant influence on the Edo (Tokyo) school of Shingaku from the late Tokugawa period.

2: Teshima Toan and the Shingaku Community

1. TTZ, 595–605. Except where indicated otherwise, the following details regarding Toan are drawn from this source.

2. See Shibata Minoru, *Baigan to sono monryū,* 93–109.

3. Toan's childhood name was Sōkichirō, his personal names were Takafusa and Makoto, and his common names were Gen'uemon and Kazaemon. He took the literary names Tōkaku and Toan later in life; Ōgen was his honorary name.

4. Cf. IBZ 2:626–627, trans. in Bellah, *Tokugawa Religion,* 204–205.

5. TTZ, 600; Kannon is Kanzeon-bosatsu (Avalokiteśvara), the popular bodhisattva of compassion who attends at the side of Amida Buddha. Kiyomizu temple is in Kyoto, as is the shrine (Kitano) where Toan's father paid reverence to the Sumiyoshi gods. The Hase temple is in Nara. I have not identified the Buddhist priest Jimon.

6. She is buried next to Toan in the Toribeyama cemetery in Kyoto.

7. In descending order of age, they were Komori Baifu, Saitō Zenmon, Kimura Shigemitsu, Kurosugi Masatane, Sugiura Shisai, Jion-ni Kenka, Tomioka Ichoku, and Kanbe Kishū. Teshima Toan was the youngest at age twenty-seven (Ishikawa, *Sekimon,* 213). In addition to Zenmon and Toan, Shisai, Shigemitsu, Jion-ni, and Ichoku became active teachers.

8. Ishikawa, *Sekimon,* 214.

9. The agreement was written up under the title *Renchū shimeshi-awase (Associates' Agreement)* (ibid., 216–217).

10. Ibid., 223.

11. IBZ 2:633, translated in Bellah, *Tokugawa Religion,* 209–210 (I have made orthographical changes).

12. *Saitō sensei gyōjō,* quoted in Iwauchi Seiichi, *Kyōikuka toshite no Ishida Baigan,* 226, and in Izuyama Zentarō (Kakudō), "Shingaku to Zen," 53.

13. Following Ishikawa Ken, based on his readings in *The Writings of Zenmon (Zenmon bunsho) (Sekimon,* 85–86).

14. Takenaka Yasukazu, "Saitō Zenmon no kahō," 2; Ishikawa, *Sekimon,* 219.

15. TTZ, 597–598.

16. TTZ, 598, 600.

17. TTZ, 603.

18. TTZ, 598.

19. TTZ, 599.

20. TTZ, 597. Cf. Baigan's manner of dressing (IBZ 2:626, translated in Bellah, *Tokugawa Religion,* 204). The matter of correct dress echoes *Analects* 10:6.

21. Toan finished compiling it in 1763.

22. To commemorate the event, Toan wrote a short essay called *Chaku kin'i no kai* (An Explanation of Why I Wear *Kin'i*), printed as one-page leaflets; it is contained in TTZ, 512–513.

23. NKB 4:760–763 contains an undated version of this work entitled *Teshima Wa'an sensei jiseki;* it was probably compiled in the early nineteenth century. Except where indicated otherwise, the following information is based on this account.

24. The boy received the personal name Ken; his childhood name was Jirō-kichi, and his common names were Gen'uemon and, later, Ka'uemon. Haryō and Wa'an were literary names; Shika was an honorary name.

25. A candle or oil-based wick in a paper-covered lantern.

26. Until then it had presumably been Uekawa Gen'uemon.

27. NKB 4:762.

28. My source for the following, except where noted, is a copy of an anonymous, unpublished, unpaginated manuscript entitled "Summary of the Memoir of Master Uekawa Kisui" ("Uekawa Kisui sensei jiseki ryaku") lent to me by Shibata Minoru from the Meirinsha collection; the manuscript is undated but seems to have been compiled in the mid-nineteenth century.

29. He was originally called Yoshinori; his common name was Genzō. Later he received the personal name Seiyō (Masa'akira) and the honorary name Shiyō. Tōkai and Kisui were two of his literary names. Other names he used were Bunji and Sōbei (see Matsuda Hakken, "Uekawa Kisui: Shingakusha retsuden 5," part 1, 56). *Shingaku* 190–195.

30. Shibata, "Sekimon Shingaku ni tsuite," NST 42:487. Kisui's parentage is not known with certainty. By Toan's time, there had been a series of adoptions between the Shiga, Uekawa, Tominaga, and Teshima families. According to one view, the Shiga family was the main house *(honke)* of the Uekawa. Kisui is called a "child of the main Uekawa house," but he was considered a Shiga until his adoption, when he became responsible for a side branch of the Uekawa family; thus, his name changed from Shiga Yoshinori to Uekawa Masa'akira.

31. *Analects* 12:20; "Uekawa Kisui jiseki," n.p.

32. For a reproduction of the chart, see NST 42:202–203.

33. See, for example, Shibata, *Monryū,* 160, and also his "Sekimon Shingaku ni tsuite," 488–489.

34. Shibata, *Shingaku,* 90.

35. NST 42:204–205.

36. He added such material to at least eighteen Shingaku works (Ishikawa, *Sekimon,* 339).

37. See comments by Ishikawa Ken in Nakazawa Dōni, *Dōni-ō dōwa,* ed. Ishikawa Ken, 332.

38. Shibata, *Shingaku,* 91–94.

39. Ishikawa, *Sekimon,* 339.

40. The followers of Dōni undoubtedly compiled a biography of their master after he passed away, but it is no longer extant. After the turn of the eighteenth century, Dōni's headquarters, Sanzensha, suffered a number of fires; the original manuscript was probably lost during this period. Several secondhand accounts of Dōni's life have been preserved; they may be based on recollections of the original

or simply on anecdotes that were handed down by word of mouth. My principal source for Dōni's life, the undated *Summary of the Memoir of Master Dōni (Dōni sensei jiseki ryaku)*, is one of these second-generation compilations; it was probably completed in the middle of the nineteenth century. It is contained on pp. 15–23 of a booklet entitled *The Memoirs of Master Teshima Toan and Master Nakazawa Dōni (Teshima Toan sensei, Nakazawa Dōni sensei on-jiseki)*, issued by Sanzensha in Tokyo in 1939. Another secondhand version of Dōni's biography immediately follows in the same booklet. A note appended to Yamada Keisai's 1938 preface to the booklet states that the first version is taken from a manuscript in the collection of a certain Akatani Jurō of Tsuruoka, whereas the second is one of several manuscripts in the Sanzensha collection. The latter, Sanzensha, manuscript seems to have been compiled during the Meiji period, sometime after 1879, under the auspices of such Shingaku leaders as Takahashi Kōun, Naganuma Tangetsu, and Kawajiri Hōkin. The editor of the Tsuruoka manuscript is unknown, but the account is apparently older than the Sanzensha version. There are a number of slight discrepancies between the two texts, including some explicit insertions in the Sanzensha version by its Meiji editors. Information on Dōni's life is also drawn from the preface to the fifth part of *Dōni-ō dōwa*, ed. Ishikawa, 144–146; Ishikawa Ken's timeline in the same edition of the *Dōwa*, 329–338; and Shibata, "Sekimon Shingaku ni tsuite," 482–484. Dōni's alternate names are listed under "Nakazawa Dōni" in the Glossary.

41. Nichiren (1222–1282) taught his followers that they could be saved by reciting the Daimoku, i.e., the name of the Lotus Sutra: "Reverence to the Lotus Sutra of the Wondrous Dharma" *(Namu myōhō renge kyō)*.

42. Kishibojin is a Buddhist deity who is believed to help sick children.

43. *Toan, Dōni on-jiseki*, 18.

44. The *Memoir* refers to his practice at this time interchangeably as both Zen meditation *(zazen)* and quiet sitting *(seiza)*.

45. *Sokushin konjiki no Mida nari.* I have not yet identified the source of this saying.

46. There is some question about the year in which this occurred. Shingaku sources indicate the year as 1765 or 1766, but Tōrei's biographer Taikan Bunshu (1766–1842) says the sermon series at Tōji-in took place in 1768–1769. See Nishimura Eshin, ed., *Tōrei oshō nenpu*, 208–211. I am indebted to Michel Mohr for pointing out this discrepancy to me.

47. *Shohō jissō.* This phrase expresses the Mahayana Buddhist idea that all things in the universe are the form of true reality.

48. *Toan, Dōni on-jiseki*, 18–19. The closing expression, *itten shikai kai ki myōhō*, might be inspired by Nichiren. See, for example, the concluding passage of his *Hokke shuyōsho* (Grasping the Essence of the *Lotus*), T 84:280c.

49. *Toan, Dōni on-jiseki*, 20.

50. *Nakazawa Dōni sensei shonyū banashi*, 21.

51. For a discussion of "foolish talk and dazzling rhetoric," see Margaret Childs, "Kyōgen-kigo: Love Stories as Buddhist Sermons."

52. *Kyōge betsuden furyū monji*, a famous early Zen saying that is traditionally attributed to Bodhidharma.

53. *Huai-nan tzu*, Tao-ying hsün section, cited in Shibata, NST 42:208n.

54. *Analects* 1:6.

55. I.e., Confucius, Buddha, and Lao-tzu.

56. *Analects* 12:1.

57. NST 42:208–209.

58. See Ishikawa's comment in Nakazawa, *Dōwa,* ed. Ishikawa, 333. This incident is discussed further in Chapter 7.

59. Some sources give the date of the founding of Sanzensha as 1783 rather than 1781.

60. "Sekimon Shingaku ni tsuite," 484.

61. NST 42:195–196.

62. I.e., relations between parent and child, lord and retainer, husband and wife, elder and younger, and between friends.

63. The above is based on Ishikawa Ken's timeline, in Nakazawa, *Dōwa,* 334–336.

64. Shibata, *Shingaku,* 78.

65. I have not verified the accuracy of Shibata's allegation that infanticide actually decreased in these areas. He mentions by name only Utsunomiya in Shimono and does not cite any sources. "Sekimon Shingaku ni tsuite," 486.

66. These works are collected in Nakazawa, *Dōwa.*

67. They are mostly stored in Tokyo, in the collections associated with Sanzensha.

68. Ishikawa, *Sekimon,* 247.

69. *Analects* 2:14.

70. *Analects* 13:23.

71. *Analects* 15:21.

72. NST 42:191 (lower margin).

73. *Shisho shūchū* [Ch. *Ssu-shu chi-chu*] 1, in *Shushigaku taikei* (hereafter SGT) 7:57.

74. SGT 7:248.

75. NST 42:191–192 (upper margin).

76. NST 42:192–193 (lower margin).

77. TTZ, 589.

78. TTZ, 590. These repeated requests for harmony in the group may also have been a response to tensions among the members.

79. TTZ, 589.

80. Bellah identifies the "integrative" function of adherence to shared values within a group as one of the characteristic features of Tokugawa Japanese social structures (*Tokugawa Religion,* esp. 30–31).

81. I follow Shiraishi Masakuni's account, though his sources are not clear ("Shingaku kyōka no hōhō," 32–42).

82. TTZ, 598.

83. Najita, *Visions of Virtue,* 77.

84. Ibid., 77–78.

85. See Thomas Hong-chi Lee, "Chu Hsi, Academies and the Tradition of Private *Chiang-hsüeh.*"

86. There were twenty-two active meetinghouses by the end of 1785, the year before Toan's death (Ishikawa, *Sekimon,* 276).

87. Ibid., 269.

88. Bellah, *Tokugawa Religion,* 167, following Shiraishi ("Shingaku kyōka," 6–7), who does not specify his sources.

89. The pictures are reproduced in Ishikawa, *Sekimon,* 270–271; they were published in a document entitled *Shokoku shagō* (The Names of the Meeting-houses in Various Regions).

90. The historian of education Umihara Tōru includes Shingaku houses in his survey of Japanese educational institutions (*Gakkō,* 68–69).

91. TTZ, 593.

92. TTZ, 586–587, 593.

93. TTZ, 588, 591, 592.

94. Shiraishi, "Shingaku kyōka," 9.

95. In some cases, domain officials or samurai provided assistance, but most of the urban meetinghouses were funded by private individuals. In the rural villages, well-known Shingaku preachers occasionally enlisted the cooperation of a powerful person in the village. But according to Shibata, there is no evidence of samurai-level or government involvement in the establishment of meetinghouses in farm villages (*Shingaku,* 103–104).

96. *Kotowari,* in TTZ, 594; this may be the notice mentioned in Toan's *Memoir* (*Teshima Toan sensei jiseki,* TTZ, 598).

97. Quoted in Ishikawa, *Sekimon,* 246.

98. TTZ, 663.

99. According to the traditional Confucian view, one's body appertains to one's parents and therefore should not be damaged in any way, even after death.

100. TTZ, 664.

101. TTZ, 663.

102. For pertinent remarks by Baigan, see, for example, *Tohi mondō,* in *Kinsei shisōka bunshū,* ed. Kodaka Toshirō, in *Nihon koten bungaku taikei* (hereafter NKBT) 97:396.

3: Teshima Toan's Teaching

1. Toan's teaching became known as Shingaku, "learning of the mind (heart)," by 1779 at the latest (Ishikawa, *Sekimon,* 34).

2. Elsewhere Baigan does distinguish the two terms more strictly according to the Neo-Confucian theory of correspondence between the polarities of *ri-ki* (Ch. *li-ch'i,* principle–vital energy) and *sei-jō* (Ch. *hsing-ching,* nature-emotions) (Shibata, *Shingaku,* 36).

3. In *Chōsō shinwa* (New Talks from Chōsō), Toan says: "If we say only 'mind,' there is both a good mind and an evil mind, but if we add the word 'original' and say 'original mind,' since this is the mind that manifests itself in accordance with our fundamental nature, it is always the good mind, and it is not at all different from 'nature' " (TTZ, 248). In *Chishin bengi,* he remarks: "Knowing the original mind is the same as knowing the nature. Nature is difficult to teach as principle. Therefore I simply teach 'knowing the original mind' " (NST 42:131).

4. IBZ 1:5.

5. The full comment reads: "Clear virtue is what Heaven imparts to human beings; it is empty, mysterious, and unobscured *(hsü ling pu mei)*. Moreover, it

encompasses all principles and responds to all things" (SGT 7:351). Wing-tsit Chan translates *hsü* (J. *kyo*), originally a Taoist term, as "vacuous" in order to distinguish it from *k'ung (kū),* the Buddhist term for "empty" (*A Sourcebook in Chinese Philosophy,* 142, 788). In Toan's discourses I translate *kyo* as "empty" or "emptiness" in order to bring out the ambiguity of the term (i.e., it does not mean nothing is there), to which Toan himself refers. I translate *rei* as "mysterious" because the ability of the empty/clear original mind to deal with all things is beyond comprehension; thus, *reimyō* is occasionally given the reading *fushigi ni akiraka.*

6. "Seventeenth-Century Enlightenment," 185–186.

7. Even in its strict Mahayana Buddhist sense, "emptiness" means that things do not exist independently of each other and that nothing has an identity or essence of its own. Therefore, *kū,* like *kyo,* does not mean that nothing is there or that phenomenal reality does not exist.

8. NST 42:138.

9. *Religious Experience,* 127–129.

10. NST 42:118.

11. NST 42:138.

12. de Bary, "Seventeenth-Century Enlightenment," 151, 165.

13. In other words, it is not an interdependence based on the Mahayana ontology of dependent origination. Cf. Chang Tsai (1020–1077), whose doctrine of the oneness of humanity and all things, expressed in the *Western Inscription (Hsiming),* is based on a metaphysics of *ch'i* (vital energy or material force) (Chan, *Sourcebook,* 497–498, 501–504). "Mystical" here refers to the experience of reality without the mediation of subject-object structures of thought, i.e., the religious experience of transcendence of the self.

14. The last phrase is from *Lin-chi lu (The Record of Lin-chi),* in T 47:500a. For the probable locus classicus, see section 6 of *Chuang-tzu: Basic Writings,* trans. Burton Watson, 73. Toan's text is in TTZ, 340–341.

15. "Right thought" consists of thoughts of selfless renunciation and love extended to all beings; in Mahayana Buddhism it is based on the awareness of the empty nature of the dharma elements that constitute all phenomena.

16. NST 42:123.

17. Pedersen, "Shidō Munan," 26.

18. NST 42:136.

19. TTZ, 522.

20. TTZ, 772–773.

21. TTZ, 285.

22. "*Mizu kagami* [chū] me nashi gusa" (1675 block-print ed., repr. in 1805, Kyoto), 8a. The author of this commentary is unknown.

23. *Shusei setsu,* in *Chōsen no Shushigaku, Nihon no Shushigaku 1,* SGT 12:284.

24. Takuan Sōhō, *Takuan,* ed. Ishikawa Hakugen, 199–200. For this and the following passages, I have consulted the translations by William S. Wilson in *The Unfettered Mind: Writings of the Zen Master to the Sword Master.*

25. *Takuan,* 217–218.

26. Ibid., 218.

27. Ibid., 221.

28. TTZ, 292–293.

29. TTZ, 423, 455–456.

30. NST 42:221, 228, 330.

31. TTZ, 427; Nakazawa, *Dōni-ō dōwa,* ed. Ishikawa, 119.

32. NST 42:121.

33. *Tohi mondō,* in NKBT 97:445–446. The *shi* of *shiryo,* like the *shi* of *shian,* is interchangeably represented by two characters, 思 and 私.

34. NST 42:121. Toan also uses the expressions "good calculation" and "bad calculation," implying that calculation itself is not evil (NST 42:122). Kinami Takuichi comments that *shian* can be seen as the beginning of "evil" in that it leads to the dualistic confrontation between good and evil impulses ("Bankei rikai no ippōto: Toan no Shingaku kara," 81).

35. TTZ, 392.

36. NST 42:122.

37. Wing-tsit Chan, trans., *Reflections on Things at Hand,* 128. *Chin-ssu lu* was compiled by Chu Hsi and Lü Tsu-ch'ien (1137–1181) in 1175–1178. All quotations from *Chin-ssu lu* follow Chan's translation; here the word Chan renders as "anxiously" is *chi p'o* (J. *kyūhaku*) (Chu and Lü, *Kinshiroku* [Ch. *Chin-ssu lu*], 245 [no. 14]).

38. TTZ, 392–393.

39. NST 42:122–123.

40. TTZ, 344–345. I have not yet identified the source of this anecdote.

41. "Cunning" is Chan's translation of *chih* (J. *chi*) (*Reflections,* 40; Chu and Lü, *Kinshiroku,* 67 [no. 4]).

42. *A History of Chinese Philosophy* 2:449.

43. TTZ, 330.

44. *Kono omoi no okoru sono saki o magekagamuru.*

45. TTZ, 331.

46. NST 42:138.

47. TTZ, 249. Takuan had used similar language to speak of the original mind and its distortion: "The original mind, like water, does not rest in one place. The deluded mind is like ice; one cannot wash one's hands or head with ice. . . . If the mind hardens in one place and fixes itself on one thing, it is like when ice hardens and cannot be used freely" (*Takuan,* 220–221).

48. Cf. *Mencius* 4B:12.

49. TTZ, 249.

50. IBZ 2:623, trans. in Bellah, *Tokugawa Religion,* 201–202.

51. TTZ, 251.

52. By dualistic conceptualization I mean thought that proceeds according to subject-object categories. *Fushō* derives from the Buddhist idea of *fushō fumetsu,* according to which there is a reality beyond the impermanency of birth and death, that is, "unborn and undying."

53. Translated in Haskel, *Bankei Zen,* 95. Bankei himself occasionally speaks of the unborn in terms of the "original mind."

54. For Bankei's own account of his quest for "clear virtue," see *Bankei zenji zenshū,* 13.

55. *Sangai yui isshin;* this phrase derives from a line in the *Avataṁsaka Sutra*

(J. *Kegon kyō*), cited in T 10:288c: "The Three Worlds are only one mind," i.e., all things are the manifestation of the mind.

56. *Ichinen fushō* refers to the enlightened state, or Buddha-nature, which is free of deluded thoughts.

57. TTZ, 403–404.

58. For example, "The unborn Buddha-mind that is received at birth from one's parents is mysteriously clear" (*Bankei zenji goroku*, 16). Haskel renders this phrase "marvelously illuminating" (*Bankei Zen*, 29, 35, 86).

59. TTZ, 43; see also TTZ, 405. For an example of the original expression, see *Bankei zenji goroku*, 34.

60. That is, in accordance with *pratītya samutpāda*, dependent origination.

61. For this use of the term "substantialist," see Abe Masao, "Substance, Process and Emptiness," 4–5.

62. NST 42:123.

63. Kinami, "Bankei," 83.

4: Knowing the Original Mind

1. TTZ, 588 and 592.

2. TTZ, 425.

3. The version in *Teshima Toan zenshū* is undated; it was probably compiled during or immediately after Toan's lifetime. The opening passage of one talk deals with the proper procedure for meeting new *shūgyōnin*, or trainees, and stipulates that members must have permission (certified by a sealed document) in order to give their own guidance talks. TTZ, 426.

4. The "talks for beginners" are contained in three works: (1) the first three talks of *Essentials of Good Guidance*, collectively entitled *Oral Address for Shingaku Beginners* (*Shingaku shonyū no mono ni kuju no ji*) (TTZ, 417–434); (2) *Master Teshima's Oral Instruction* (*Talks for Beginners*) (*Teshima sensei kuju banashi* [*shonyū banashi*]), dated 1779 (TTZ, 445–456); and (3) *Master Nakazawa Dōni's Talks for Beginners* (*Nakazawa Dōni sensei shonyū banashi*).

5. See Rodney Taylor, "Acquiring a Point of View: Confucian Dimensions of Self-Reflection," 148–152.

6. TTZ, 323.

7. NST 42:134.

8. TTZ, 340–341.

9. TTZ, 323. Toan is referring to a line he just quoted, ostensibly a comment by "Master Ch'eng," i.e., one of the Ch'eng brothers: *Kojin michi o mireba bunmei nari. Yue ni sono kotoba kaku no gotoshi.* (The ancients saw the Way clearly; therefore they spoke like this.) I have not yet located the source of this passage.

10. TTZ, 417–418. The following summary is based primarily on *Oral Address for Shingaku Beginners* in *Essentials of Good Guidance*. *Master Teshima's Oral Instruction* (*Talks for Beginners*) includes many of the same themes.

11. Translated in Philip B. Yampolsky, *The Zen Master Hakuin*, 144. See Isshū Miura and Ruth Fuller Sasaki, *Zen Dust: The History of the Koan and Koan Study in Rinzai* (*Lin-Chi*) *Zen*, 247, regarding the expression "ball of doubt."

12. TTZ, 426.

13. TTZ, 422.

14. TTZ, 419–420.

15. TTZ, 420.

16. For a psychologist's discussion of "experiential education," see Abraham Maslow, *Religions, Values and Peak Experiences*, 89.

17. TTZ, 424. The poem appears in Munan, *Munan kana hōgo*, 339.

18. TTZ, 425. The mind or heart was popularly associated with the abdomen.

19. TTZ, 427–428.

20. TTZ, 428.

21. From *Sokkō roku kaien fusetsu*, in which Hakuin discusses preparation for the experience of seeing into one's nature (trans. in Miura and Sasaki, *Zen Dust*, 42). The question of whether the mind is inside or outside the body reappears in another compilation attributed to Toan, "Seeing and Hearing: Forty-eight Cases" ("Kenmon shijū hassoku"), case no. 27 (discussed in Chapter 5).

22. TTZ, 446–447

23. TTZ, 429–430.

24. TTZ, 430–431.

25. For the source of these terms, see Chapter 3, especially note 5.

26. The passage is attributed to Ch'eng Hao. Cf. Chan's translation, "broad and extremely impartial" (*Reflections*, 40). Toan uses a different character, "open" 廓然 , in place of the original "broad" 擴然 (TTZ, 431; cf. Chu and Lü, *Kinshiroku*, 66 [no. 4]).

27. TTZ, 433.

28. TTZ, 434.

29. See Chan, *Sourcebook*, 84–94, for a translation and discussion of the *Great Learning;* see also Daniel K. Gardner, *Chu Hsi and the Ta-hsüeh.*

30. As Chu Hsi says, "If we wish to extend our knowledge to the utmost, we must investigate the principles of all things we come into contact with, for the intelligent mind of man is certainly formed to know, and there is not a single thing in which its principles do not inhere" (trans. in Chan, *Sourcebook*, 89).

31. Chan, *Sourcebook*, 611.

32. Chan, *Reflections*, 91–92.

33. This account of Wang's views is based on his remarks in "Inquiry on the *Great Learning*," translated by Wing-tsit Chan in *Instructions for Practical Living and Other Neo-Confucian Writings by Wang Yang-ming*, 278–279.

34. Wang, *Instructions*, 279.

35. Chan, *Sourcebook*, 682–683.

36. See Chan's comments in Wang, *Instructions*, xxxiii.

37. Not even the Shingaku book dealer's list (TTZ, 175) includes any important work of the Wang Yang-ming school, although it does list *Chu-tzu yü-lu* (The Recorded Sayings of Master Chu), presumably compiled by Chou Ju-t'eng (1547–1629) of the T'ai-chou school.

38. For this passage and the rest of the exchange, see *Ishida sensei goroku*, in IBZ 1:530–531.

39. TTZ, 309–310.

40. TTZ, 430.

41. Furthermore, Wang Yang-ming, unlike Toan, was critical of Buddhist

notions, particularly the Zen doctrine of the mind. For a summary of Wang's relationship with Buddhism, see Wing-tsit Chan, "How Buddhistic Is Wang Yang-ming?"

42. TTZ, 434.

43. TTZ, 433.

44. TTZ, 434.

45. Nakazawa, *Dōni shonyū banashi,* 48.

46. Dōni quotes the *Avataṁsaka Sutra,* the *Diamond Sutra,* and the *Lotus Sutra* and the *Dainichi Sutra,* on pp. 17, 20, and 39, respectively, of *Dōni shonyū banashi;* Toan's talks for beginners contain quotations from the *Diamond* and *Heart* sutras; see TTZ, 430 and 452, respectively. In one passage, Dōni quotes Wang Yang-ming, a phenomenon that I have not encountered in Toan's works (*Dōni shonyū banashi,* 13–14). The source is Wang's *Denshūroku* [Ch. *Ch'uan-hsi lu*], 487, translated by Chan in Wang, *Instructions,* 223.

47. *Dōni shonyū banashi,* 51. These famous Zen sayings are traditionally attributed to Bodhidharma. For details on their origin and meaning, see Miura and Sasaki, *Zen Dust,* 229–230.

48. TTZ, 456.

49. Nakazawa, *Dōni shonyū banashi,* 51–52.

50. TTZ, 434.

51. Shibata Minoru agrees that "discovery" may be an appropriate English equivalent of *hatsumei* on these grounds (personal communication, March 23, 1987). Bankei also taught that the unborn Buddha-mind with which one is endowed at birth gradually becomes obscured by self-indulgence *(mibiiki),* delusions, and bad habits.

52. Nakazawa, *Dōni shonyū banashi,* 51–52.

53. *Mokugyo,* a Buddhist ritual instrument carved in the approximate shape of a fish, which is rhythmically struck during sutra recitation.

54. Nakazawa, *Dōni shonyū banashi,* 52.

55. Quoted in Ishikawa Ken, "Shingaku shū shonyū banashi hen 1: Kaisetsu," 10–11, from an unpublished text entitled "Sugiura sensei kuju banashi" (Master Sugiura's Talks). The author is probably Sugiura Sōchū (1723–1809), who studied under Baigan, Saitō Zenmon, and Tomioka Ichoku.

56. TTZ, 439.

57. Koans are stories or questions used by Zen masters to convey the essence of their teaching and help bring on the state of enlightenment in their disciples. Because they did not consider enlightenment to be fully communicable through words or logical analysis, the ancient Zen masters asked questions, often phrased in simple terms and inspired by the immediate situation, which forced their students to transcend dualistic modes of thought and grasp the truth experientially. Later Zen teachers adopted these ancient "cases," such as the *Mu* koan, and used them to train their own disciples. It is said that when Chao-chou was asked, "Does a dog have Buddha-nature?" he replied, "Mu!" This is the first koan in the Sung collection *Mumonkan* (Ch. *Wu-men kuan,* "The Gateless Barrier") (T 48:292c–293a). For more detailed treatments of the history and significance of the koan, see Miura and Sasaki, as well as Akizuki Ryōmin, *Zen nyūmon: kōan sanjū-san soku.*

58. Akizuki Ryōmin, *Hakuin zenji,* 141–142.

59. William James calls it the "passive" quality of mysticism; in theistic traditions it manifests as the view that the experience derives from a higher power (*The Varieties of Religious Experience*, 293–294).

60. For details, see IBZ 2:623, trans. in Bellah, *Tokugawa Religion*, 201–202.

61. For this account of Toan's discovery, see TTZ, 601. Another account of the same experience appears in *Toan sensei goroku*, in TTZ, 660–661. In the latter version Zenmon hits a table instead of Toan's face and, perhaps more significantly, Baigan gives the following response to Toan's report of his insight:

> Now there is nothing else for you yourself to do but to nourish the nature that you have known. This time you have become separate from the one that until now has served as your "I"; but the "one thing" *(ichimotsu)* that believes "I have known the nature" has been created in you. This, in fact, is the illness known as "viewing" *(ken)*. The nature is something that is unknowing. You must quickly remove this illness.

After this response, the account continues, Toan spent years striving to rid himself of his tendency to conscious "viewing," which gradually became weaker.

62. NKB 4:761.

63. Kusunoki Masashige (1294–1336), the lord of Kawachi, fought on the side of Emperor Go-Daigo during the period of the Northern and Southern Dynasties. I have not been able to trace this allusion; Masashige's interest in Zen is probably fictional. See Uemura Seiji, *Kusunoki Masashige*, 198–200.

64. I.e., preserving his mind of innate goodness and nourishing his nature (*Mencius* 7A:1). This account is contained in the aforementioned anonymous manuscript "Uekawa Kisui sensei jiseki ryaku," n.p.

65. The latter version has its locus classicus in the *Book of Changes* (*Ekikyō* 2:430, trans. James Legge, in *Yi King*, 422 [no. 3]).

66. Nakazawa Dōni's experience is described in Chapter 2; although it took place in a Buddhist context, his enlightenment displays the same features.

67. In Dōni's case we are not told whether the Zen qualifications that he allegedly possessed exempted him from this requirement in Shingaku; he had already received the approval of Zen master Reigen.

68. TTZ, 434.

69. TTZ, 583.

70. The 1784 *Terms of Agreement* stipulates that the Admonition is to be conferred at Meirinsha in Kyoto (TTZ, 590). Members traveled there from all over Japan to complete their religious training and to receive it (see Ishikawa, *Sekimon*, 242–243).

71. The connection between discovering the original mind and full qualification as a member of Shingaku is confirmed by methods of record keeping. Although some meetinghouses did keep records of people who attended general educational activities, this effort was sporadic. The extant documents that list the names of people who received the Admonition are more systematic sources of the names and provenances of Shingaku members. According to Toan's *Memoir*, his *Lineage of the Disciples of Master Ishida (Ishida sensei monjin fu)* records the names of followers who knew the "innate nature." I was unable to gain access to this document, reportedly held in the Meirinsha collection in Kyoto.

72. Translated in Miura and Sasaki, *Zen Dust*, 41.

73. Waddell, *Unborn*, 45.

74. For the following discussion of Neo-Confucian enlightenment, see de Bary, "Seventeenth-Century Enlightenment," esp. 173–184.

75. Sung master Ch'eng I said: "One must investigate one item today and another item tomorrow. When one has accumulated much knowledge, he will naturally achieve thorough understanding like a sudden release" (translated in Chan, *Reflections*, 92).

76. For testimonies of Neo-Confucian enlightenment experiences in the Ming period, see, for example, Kao Pan-lung's graphic account, translated by Rodney Taylor in "Acquiring a Point of View," 158; or Jen Yu-wen, "Ch'en Hsien-chang's Philosophy of the Natural," 57. Wm. T. de Bary gives accounts of the experiences of Ch'en Hsien-chang (1428–1500) and Wang Ken (1483?–1540) ("Individualism and Humanitarianism in Late Ming Thought, 158).

77. "Seventeenth-Century Enlightenment," 151. Although full consideration of Baigan's thought and its sources cannot be attempted here, it bears mention that Baigan's exchange with his teacher after his first insight into the nature has a subtle Zen flavor that is not fully conveyed by Bellah's English translation (*Tokugawa Religion*, 201). When Ryōun asked Baigan whether his meditation had "ripened," Baigan replied, "It is like this! Like this!" *(nyoze nyoze)*, and "motioned in the air with his pipe" (see IBZ 2:623). It was not Ryōun but Baigan who motioned with his pipe—he used this physical gesture to indicate what he had experienced. Moreover, Baigan answered his teacher's query with a standard Zen phrase, *nyoze*. The evidence for Ryōun's Zen (possibly Ōbaku) connections is summarized in Izuyama Kakudō, "Zen to Shingaku," 242–243.

78. Toan's *Memoir* was compiled by his disciples nearly two decades after his death. All "sacred biographies" contain some mythical elements, and certain details of Toan's "enlightenment" may not have found their way into the *Memoir* account; but it is unlikely that the central theme of the experience was substantially altered.

79. A possible exception is Wang Ken, who transmitted his teaching only to those who were ready for it; see de Bary, "Individualism," esp. 174–175.

80. For example, the Sung Ch'an master Ta-hui Tsung-kao (1089–1163) is said to have had eighteen great enlightenments and countless small ones (Akizuki, *Hakuin zenji*, 164).

81. After the successful penetration of the *hosshin* koan in the attainment of *kenshō*, one faces the challenges of the *kikan, gonsen, nantō,* and *goi* koans (Akizuki, *Hakuin zenji*, 138–185; Miura and Sasaki, *Zen Dust*, 46–72). According to Akizuki, Hakuin rejected Bankei's "unborn Zen" because it focused on a one-time insight and did not provide for postenlightenment training. This is not necessarily an accurate view of Bankei, however; cf. his remarks translated in Waddell, *Unborn*, 134–135.

82. Ishida Baigan himself did not marry, not because of his Buddhist inclinations, but because he simply felt that "if I were encumbered with a wife, I fear I would lose the Way" (IBZ 2:638, translated in Bellah, *Tokugawa Religion*, 214). He also did not agree with the prohibition of eating meat, which is one of the five precepts for Buddhist laity (IBZ 1:53). See also Paul B. Watt, "The Buddhist Element in Shingaku," 11.

83. Buddhist critics of Shingaku are mentioned in Chapter 7.

84. TTZ, 417. Baigan's immediate disciples, at first slow to believe in their own potential, thus advanced quickly once they began to have faith (IBZ 2:633, translated in Bellah, *Tokugawa Religion,* 209–210).

85. *Mu ichi motsu;* this expression is traditionally (but incorrectly) attributed to the Sixth Patriarch of Ch'an, Hui-neng: "From the first not a thing is" (Ch. *pen-lai wu-i-wu*). See Philip Yampolsky, Introduction, in *The Platform Sutra of the Sixth Patriarch,* 94.

86. TTZ, 435.

87. TTZ, 435–436.

88. Translated in Chan, *Reflections,* 19. Toan alludes to this saying in TTZ, 436, for example.

89. TTZ, 436; cf. R. H. Blyth's translation in *Zen and Zen Classics* 5:177.

90. TTZ, 436.

91. TTZ, 436. *Mochi* are made by pounding cooked rice.

92. See, for example, *Bankei zenji goroku,* 13–14. According to Buddhist tradition, hungry ghosts, beasts, and fighting demons *(aśuras)* represent three of the "Six Ways" or levels of existence in which one remains until one is free of the illusory cycle of birth and death.

93. TTZ, 437.

94. TTZ, 437.

95. TTZ, 584. The prefatory remarks to Toan's *Principles for the Assembly of Companions (Kaiyū taishi)* also emphasize the need for daily effort following realization of the "germ" of the original mind (NST 42:186).

96. TTZ, 584.

97. TTZ, 584–585; see also NST 42:135–136 for a similar caution against neglecting conventional devotions.

98. "Transcendent" here refers not simply to independence from the material universe but to participation in a universal principle underlying both the spiritual and material dimensions of reality.

99. TTZ, 584.

100. Translation adapted from Chan, *Reflections,* 44; cf. *Yi King,* trans. Legge, 420.

101. Toan defines reverence and rightness in Buddhist terms as well (NST 42:123–124).

102. Translated in Chan, *Reflections,* 139, 142.

103. Satō Naokata, for example, argues for an intrinsic connection between reverence and quiet sitting (SGT 12:294).

104. TTZ, 441.

105. *Kaiyū taishi,* in NST 42:186. "Daily renewal" derives from a passage in the *Book of Changes:* "Daily renewal means 'flourishing virtue' " (*Ekikyō* 2:321; cf. *Yi King,* trans. Legge, 356 [no. 28]).

106. NST 42:186.

107. See, for example, IBZ 1:113; Baigan's approach is discussed by Imai Jun in "Ishida Baigan no 'katachi' to 'kokoro' no mondai," 163–178.

108. TTZ, 252.

109. TTZ, 454–455.

110. Translated in Chan, *Reflections,* 44.

111. TTZ, 438; cf. TTZ, 250–251.

112. TTZ, 438.

113. NST 42:134–135.

114. NST 42:137.

115. TTZ, 590.

116. TTZ, 585.

117. TTZ, 585–586.

118. NST 42:126.

119. Translation adapted from Chan, *Reflections*, 44.

120. TTZ, 441.

121. TTZ, 441.

122. TTZ, 439.

5: Methods of Cultivation

1. NST 42:189.

2. Tanabe Ryūzō, "Seiza to kaiho," 36–37. The meetings may have been open to serious beginners as well.

3. TTZ, 590.

4. According to Toan, " 'Getting it for oneself' simply means that people who study the Way should grasp it in themselves thoroughly; and based on that understanding they should embody it in their persons and refrain from violating their original minds" (NST 42:195 [upper margin]). De Bary discusses the idea of "getting it for oneself" (J. *jitoku*, Ch. *tzu-te*) in *The Liberal Tradition in China*, esp. 60–61. The concept of "being watchful over oneself when alone" (J. *shindoku*) (NST 42:189), i.e., maintaining the same moral standards that one would in public, derives from passages in the *Great Learning*, commentary, chap. 6, and the *Doctrine of the Mean*, chap. 1.

5. NST 42:190–191.

6. NST 42:192.

7. The above account of the study circle and reading group is based on Shiraishi's description in "Shingaku kyōka," 42–43; as he does not identify his sources, I assume he draws on relatively late, perhaps nineteenth-century, accounts or even on his own observation of Shingaku in the prewar period. There are no detailed descriptions of this kind in the late eighteenth-century Shingaku works that I have read.

8. NST 42:189; Shiraishi gives a wider range of texts ("Shingaku kyōka," 43).

9. Translated in Joseph J. Spae, *Itō Jinsai: A Philosopher, Educator and Sinologist of the Tokugawa Period*, 158–159.

10. Ibid., 172.

11. I have translated *kaidoku* as "reading group" for Shingaku, but Sorai's *kaidoku* seems closer to the Shingaku study circle *(rinkō)*. Sorai's method was developed further by other teachers and was a regular practice in "merit-oriented" private schools by the nineteenth century (Rubinger, *Private Academies*, 53).

12. IBZ 2:625, translated in Bellah, *Tokugawa Religion*, 203; Tanabe quotes some answers written by Baigan's disciples ("Seiza to kaiho," 38).

13. The three activities were not necessarily rigidly distinguished. As in Jinsai's

school, the Shingaku group leader's question was often related to the foregoing discussion of classical passages.

14. As mentioned in Chapter 2, Wa'an reportedly used Baigan's and Toan's recorded answers to train himself; Tanabe cites such answers from a text compiled in 1828–1829 ("Seiza to kaiho," 48).

15. TTZ, 796, no. 218.

16. TTZ, 803, no. 239; "the single path of ascendance," *kōjō no ichiro*, indicates the ultimate realm of enlightenment or the path by which one attains it. Reading 向上 for 高上.

17. TTZ, 819–820; nos. 281–287.

18. TTZ, 779–780, no. 168.

19. TTZ, 807, no. 248. This translation is tentative. *Shosa*, which I have translated as "deeds," is also a Buddhist term that can mean reading scriptures and reciting the *nenbutsu*.

20. This is a late Tokugawa period compilation by Hirano Kitsu-ō (purportedly modeled after the 1307 text *Zenrin ruiju* [Ch. *Ch'an-lin lei-chü*], "Zen Koans, Classified," published in Japan in 1362). It is included in the Sanzensha manuscript "Nakazawa Dōni-ō ni kansuru bunken" (Documents Concerning Old Man Dōni), a compilation completed by the Shingaku leader Yamada Keisai sometime between 1945 and 1955. The latter also contains "Shingaku shūyōshō" (Shingaku Selections), an Edo period manuscript of unknown authorship; and "Dōwa kibun" (Notes from Talks on the Way), a collection of Shingaku works edited by Dōni's disciple Owada Heibei. In some parts of the "Documents," several Shingaku masters' answers to the same *sakumon* are transmitted together. For example,

> Question: What is the function of an *andō* lamp?
> Master Dōni replied: Bright.
> Mr. Mozuto replied: Fire.
> Master [Fuse] Shō-ō replied: I was relieved *(andō itashimashita)*.
> You should answer differently from the answers of the three masters above.
>
>   ("Nakazawa Dōni-ō ni kansuru bunken," n.p.)

21. "Sekimon sakumon ruiju," n.p. Jizō is the Japanese name of the Bodhisattva Kṣitigarbha; he is revered as a protector of deceased children.

22. The above *sakumon* are taken from "Master Dōni's Problems (The Three Hundred Cases)" ("Dōni sensei sakumon [sanbyaku soku]"), contained in "Shingaku shūyōshō," n.p.

23. "Nakazawa Dōni-ō ni kansuru bunken," n.p. One *to* is approximately five U.S. gallons.

24. In addition, "Hyaku shu," (The Hundred Verses), perhaps inspired by the hundred-koan collection *Hekiganroku* (Ch. *Pi-yen lu*, "Blue Cliff Record"), was attributed to Dōni by the prewar Shingaku leader Hayano Hakuin, though Ishikawa questions the attribution (*Sekimon*, 150). Dōni's "Sanbyaku soku" (Three Hundred Cases) may be modeled after the 1235 koan collection by Dōgen (1200–1253), also called *Sanbyaku soku*. For the annotated 1767 version of Dōgen's work, see Eihei Dōgen, *Nenpyō sanbyaku soku*.

25. Shibata Minoru did not include them in *Teshima Toan zenshū* because there is no certain evidence of Toan's authorship and because he believes the enigmatic style of the questions is unlike that of Toan's other writings (personal conversation, 1986). However, Toan's authorship is not disputed by such Shingaku scholars as Ishikawa (*Sekimon*, 150) and Izuyama ("Zen to Shingaku," 250). A handwritten copy of the vernacular "Forty-eight Cases" was kindly prepared for me by Koyama Shikei, the current leader of Sanzensha, along with a copy of the Chinese version. The *sakumon* are still used in Sanzensha today; the answers are not circulated.

26. Translated in Miura and Sasaki, *Zen Dust,* 44.

27. Yoel Hoffman, trans., *The Sound of One Hand: 281 Zen Koans with Answers,* 48, no. 52.

28. This saying appears in *Zenrin kushū,* originally published in 1688, and is translated in Miura and Sasaki, *Zen Dust,* 115, no. 185. See Chapter 3, note 14, above, for the Chinese sources.

29. It is contained in the eleventh-century biographical Ch'an compilation *Ching-te ch'uan-teng lu* (The Ching-te [Era] Record of the Transmission of the Lamp); see T 51:430b.

30. The last *sakumon* (with slightly different wording) appears in "Dōni sensei sakumon," where Dōni replies by reciting the *nenbutsu* ("Nakazawa Dōni-ō ni kansuru bunken," n.p.). This *sakumon* is comparable to the koan "If you're a Zen monk, try and say it with your mouth closed" (see Hoffman, *Sound,* 68, no. 73; see also TTZ, 762, no. 123).

31. Translated in Miura and Sasaki, *Zen Dust,* 233. The same idea informs a famous verse by Fu Ta-shih: "Empty-handed, yet holding a hoe; walking, yet riding a buffalo" (ibid., 49; see also Hoffman, *Sound,* 31, no. 32).

32. Chou's dates are 1017–1073; for his teaching, see Chan, *Sourcebook,* 463. The "successors" of the Ch'eng brothers are Yang Shih (1053–1135), Hsieh Liang-tso (1050–1103), Li T'ung (1093–1163), and Lo Tsung-yen (1072–1135).

33. For the following discussion of Chu Hsi's views on quiet sitting, I have relied on Okada Takehiko, *Zazen to seiza,* especially 115–126, and on Rodney Taylor, "Chu Hsi and Quiet-Sitting: Advocacy or Ambivalence?"

34. See Taylor, "Quiet-Sitting," 18–19. This passage is quoted by Ariyama Gentō in "Seizagi," discussed below. Chu also mentions the practice of looking at one's nose (but not quiet sitting per se) in his discussion of breath control, *T'iao-hsi chen* (Taylor, "Quiet-Sitting," 21–22).

35. Ibid., 27.

36. Ibid., 23.

37. Naokata edited and wrote a preface for *Seiza shūsetsu* (Collected Explanations of Quiet Sitting), a compilation of Chu Hsi's remarks on quiet sitting by Naokata's disciple Yanagawa Gōgi. The preface is contained in SGT 12:280–281, 439. Gōgi's original compilation, which includes ninety-seven entries, is called *Shushi seiza setsu;* Naokata reduced the entries to thirty and added four more of his own selection. The two works were completed in 1714 and 1717, respectively. For details, see Yamazaki Michio, "Satō Naokata no seiza setsu." Naokata's vernacular works about quiet sitting are *Shusei setsu* (The Theory of Regarding Quietude as Fundamental) and *Seiza setsu hikki* (Notes on the Expla-

nation of Quiet Sitting), recorded by his disciple Atobe Yoshiaki (1659–1729). They are contained in SGT 12:282–310. The following discussion is based mainly on these two works.

38. In fact, Naokata uses several military metaphors in these works. For example, if one fails to concentrate on "the quiet place," one cannot win in swordplay; one must move straight forward out of that inner quietude, without hesitating (SGT 12:283). Cf. Takuan's similar analogy, discussed in Chapter 3.

39. SGT 12:286; the distinction between *mihatsu* and *ihatsu* (Ch. *wei-fai, i-fa*) is based on a passage in the *Doctrine of the Mean,* chapter 1: "Before the feelings of pleasure, anger, sorrow, and joy are aroused, it is called equilibrium (*chung,* centrality, mean). When these feelings are aroused and each and all attain due measure and degree, it is called harmony" (translated in Chan, *Sourcebook,* 98).

40. SGT 12:294.

41. A late Tokugawa Neo-Confucian who was influenced by the Kimon school describes the immediacy of this "unmanifest" level of experience: "When one does quiet sitting and one's mind is at ease, one's eyes see colors just as they are, one's ears hear sounds just as they are, one's nose smells scents just as they are, and one's hands and feet move naturally in accordance with their created function: one's self has nothing to do with it" (Kusumoto Tanzan [1828–1883], *Gakushūroku,* quoted in Okada, *Zazen,* 155).

42. SGT 12:301.

43. SGT 12:295.

44. SGT 12:289.

45. SGT 12:308.

46. SGT 12:285–287.

47. SGT 12:302. Naokata was an outstanding lecturer; perhaps quiet sitting enhanced his own educational powers!

48. SGT 12:284.

49. SGT 12:291.

50. SGT 12:303.

51. SGT 12:293.

52. SGT 12:296.

53. The *Memoir* references are translated in Bellah, *Tokugawa Religion,* 201–202, 210. See also Ishikawa, *Sekimon,* 148.

54. In *Tokugawa Religion* (for example, p. 210) Bellah translates *kufū* as "meditation," which is a common Buddhist sense of the term, particularly in relation to working on a Zen koan. In Ch'eng-Chu Neo-Confucianism, *kufū* (Ch. *kung-fu*) refers to the effort to improve onself during active as well as contemplative periods. The Shingaku usage seems to lie somewhere in between these two emphases; it includes the sense of effort or working but refers most often to a contemplative type of exertion that takes place during quiet sitting or while struggling with a problem posed by the master. Consequently, I have translated *kufū* as "(contemplative) effort," "practice," or "discipline."

55. See Ishikawa, *Sekimon,* 150–151.

56. Wa'an's enthusiasm for the practice is confirmed by his conversation with Ariyama Gentō, reported in the latter's preface to "Seizagi" (Rules for Quiet Sitting).

57. The practice of quiet sitting and its conflation with Zen sitting in Shingaku is also evinced by Kamada Ryūō's *Seizasetsu* (Theory of Quiet Sitting). I have been unable to see this early nineteenth-century work (according to the head of today's Sanzensha, Koyama Shikei, it may now be lost), but Izuyama says it contains acknowledged excerpts from Dōgen's *Fukan zazengi* ("Shingaku to Zen," 82). See also Tanabe, "Seiza to kaiho," 25, and Ishikawa, *Sekimon,* 151–152.

58. TTZ, 259.

59. SGT 12:284.

60. A block-print edition of "Seizagi" is held in the Kyoto University library.

61. Ch'eng I is omitted even though Chu Hsi ultimately followed his perspective on quiet sitting more closely than that of his brother.

62. Yanagida Seizan, "Kaisetsu," 224–227.

63. Excerpts from it date even earlier. According to Yanagida, when Ch'ang-lu Tsung-tse first compiled the *Ch'an-yüan ch'ing-kuei* in 1103, it did not yet include this *Tso-ch'an i,* although he is often presumed to be the author of it (ibid., 227–233). The 1202 text is reprinted with commentary in *Shinjinmei Shō-dōka, Jūgyūzu, Zazengi,* 147–164.

64. There is little evidence that Po-chang ever wrote the the so-called *Po-chang ch'ing-kuei.* See Martin Collcutt, *Five Mountains: The Rinzai Zen Monastic Institution in Medieval Japan,* 136–138, and Carl Bielefeldt, *Dōgen's Manuals of Zen Meditation,* 58–59, esp. n. 12.

65. Dōgen was responsible for a number of *zazengi* texts; in the following discussion I refer to the so-called *rufu,* or "popular," version of *Fukan zazengi* (Universally Recommended Principles of Sitting Meditation), which Bielefeldt dates sometime between 1242 and 1246. It was reprinted several times during the Edo period. There is also a *Fukan zazengi* holograph by Dōgen, dated 1233; the *Shōbōgenzō zazengi,* usually dated 1243, is essentially a Japanese version of the central part of the popular text, which deals with practical aspects of meditation. For details on the chronology and relations between these (and other) texts by Dōgen and for comparative translations of them and Tsung-tse's *Tso-ch'an i,* see chapters 1 and 2 and pp. 174–187, respectively, of Bielefeldt's *Dōgen's Manuals.* See also Norman Waddell and Masao Abe, "Dōgen's *Fukanzazengi* and *Shōbō-genzō zazengi.*" The Chinese text of *Fukan zazengi* is reproduced in T 82:1a–1b (no. 2580).

66. Yanagida, "Kaisetsu," 230.

67. "Seizagi," 4a. See Chu Hsi, *Kaian sensei Shu Bunkō bunshū,* 5:3571 [51:29a].

68. The preface is dated 1739, the notes 1738. I have based my remarks here on the text and commentary of *Kūin Menzan oshō kinhinki,* which is reprinted in *Sōtōshū zensho.*

69. Gentō's reliance on Sōtō texts in his "Rules" is unacknowledged. It was conventional to use material from other sources without identifying it, and except for the lines from Chu Hsi, none of the sources of the text are identified.

70. A late exception to this tradition may be the quiet sitting of Kusumoto Tanzan, who received the influence of Ming figures like Kao Pan-lung as well as that of the Kimon school. He set up a schedule that included doing quiet sitting three times a day for a period of time measured by the burning of one incense

stick and required that his students also engage in the practice (Okada, *Zazen,* 142–145). It is not clear to me whether this was a group activity.

6: Shingaku for Children

1. This arrangement is depicted in NST 42:160–161.

2. Ibid.

3. There are brief notes at the beginning and the end of each lesson in the original text that indicate that they were printed as *se-in* and eventually bound together.

4. Noted by Shibata Minoru in *Sekimon shingaku,* NST 42:162n. See *Hsiao hsüeh* 1 ("Li-chiao"): 2, reproduced and annotated in Chu, *Shōgaku,* ed. Uno Seiichi, 18. The original passage is from the *Book of Ritual,* translated by James Legge in *The Li Ki* 1:478.

5. Chu, *Hsiao hsüeh* 2 ("Ming-lun"): 5; Chu, *Shōgaku,* 44; trans. *Li Ki* 1:68.

6. NST 42:164n.; Chu, *Hsiao hsüeh* 1:3; Chu, *Shōgaku,* 24; trans. *Li Ki* 1:69–70.

7. Cf. the *Elementary Learning:* "Pride should not be allowed to grow" (Chu, *Hsiao hsüeh* 3 ["Ching-shen"]: 2; Chu, *Shōgaku,* 140; trans. *Li Ki* 1:62). The second theme also appears in the *Elementary Learning:* "At the age of seven, boys and girls did not occupy the same mat nor eat together" (Chu, *Hsiao hsüeh* 1:2; Chu, *Shōgaku,* 18; trans. *Li Ki* 1:478.

8. Chu, *Hsiao hsüeh* 2:90; Chu, *Shōgaku,* 121; drawn from *Mencius* 4B:30, translated by James Legge, in *The Works of Mencius,* 337.

9. NST 42:167.

10. Chu, *Hsiao hsüeh* 3:2; Chu, *Shōgaku,* 140; trans. *Li Ki* 1:62.

11. NST 42:169n.; Chu, *Hsiao hsüeh* 3:11; Chu, *Shōgaku,* 148.

12. NST 42:170n. The Confucian axiom that one's body belongs to one's parents is expressed in the *Classic of Filial Piety,* chap. 1; see *The Hsiao Ching,* trans. Mary L. Makra, 2–3.

13. According to Shibata, this popular saying is an allusion to the *Forty-two-Chapter Sutra* (J. *Shijūnishōkyō*). Toan quotes from *Mencius* (4A:8) to reinforce the point.

14. For example, in the *Book of Changes:* "The family that accumulates goodness is sure to have superabundant happiness, and the family that accumulates evil is sure to have superabundant misery" (translated by Legge in *Yi King,* 419).

15. The *Elementary Learning* also discusses the proper attitude to have toward elders (Chu, *Hsiao hsüeh* 2:61; Chu, *Shōgaku,* 108; trans. by Legge in *Li Ki* 1:68).

16. See Chu, *Hsiao hsüeh* 2:65; Chu, *Shōgaku,* 100; trans. *Li Ki* 1:454–455.

17. Here, as above, Toan presumably refers to the lay Buddhist precept against adultery.

18. Chu, *Hsiao hsüeh* 2:66, originally a passage from the early Han work *Ta-tai li,* "pen-ming" section; Chu, *Shōgaku,* 102, 104n. Related passages from the *Elementary Learning* are 2:1 and 2:11, regarding obedience of the woman to her parents and parents-in-law. See Chu, *Shōgaku,* 36, 49; trans. by Legge in *Li Ki* 1:450–451, 455–456, respectively.

19. The latter could be any one of a number of works of this title, including Yamazaki Ansai's version, published in 1660. A certain Tsujiwara Genpu (or

Kikken) wrote a *Yamato shōgaku*, published in 1659, which was also loosely based on Chu Hsi's compilation. Kaibara Ekken's disciple Takeda Shun'an wrote a work of the same name (n.d.), but it was not published until 1837 (see Uno's remarks in Chu, *Shōgaku*, 4).

20. The full passage from *Kanmuryōjukyō* is cited by Shibata, in NST 42:176n.; also see *Analects* 17:25 and Yoshida Kenkō, *Tsurezuregusa*, ed. Kidō Saizō, 124 (no. 107), translated by Donald Keene, *Essays in Idleness: The Tsurezuregusa of Kenkō*, 90.

21. Shibata, *Sekimon shingaku*, NST 42:178n.

22. Another text that Toan wrote for his female followers is *Onna myōga kai* (An Explanation of Spiritual Protection for Women, 1776). By the 1780s and 1790s, classes for women were a regular feature of Shingaku education. See Ishikawa, *Sekimon*, 166.

23. Until the end of the period, domain institutions generally excluded girls and women; they had more access to private schools, especially urban *terakoya*. According to Umihara Tōru, these larger *terakoya* tended to instruct girls as a separate group, often using a female instructor, and some used texts designed especially for girls. However, in contrast to Shingaku, the texts were mostly *ōraimono* (copybooks), and the instruction focused on writing skills. In *Kinsei no gakkō to kyōiku*, Umihara gives a detailed analysis of girls' education in this period (pp. 316, 247–292).

24. Chu, *Shōgaku*, 12.

25. NST 42:177.

26. NST 42:171.

27. "A Content Analysis of the *Hsiao-hsüeh*," 12–13, 30; see also the revised published version, titled "Back to Basics: Chu Hsi's *Elementary Learning (Hsiao-hsüeh)*." In his *Japanese Elementary Learning*, which follows the basic framework of the Sung work more closely than *Early Lessons*, Yamazaki Ansai also stresses practical points, using anecdotal material from Japanese traditions as well as the original text (NKB 9:25–95).

28. *Dōni-ō zenkun*, in Nakazawa, *Dōni-ō dōwa*, 313–325. The above bibliographical details are drawn from Shibata Minoru's comments in TTZ, 3.

29. A photographic reproduction of the text, purportedly in Toan's own hand with Japanese side-readings and punctuation added, is contained in TTZ, 267–279; a modern printed edition appears in NKB 9:3–8.

30. *Jitsugokyō* is printed in NKB 9:1–2. There is a quaint translation of *Dōjikyō*, "A Translation of the 'Dou-zhi keu'—'Teaching for the Young,'" by B. Chamberlain in *Transactions of the Asiatic Society of Japan*. I have not seen his translation of the former text, *"Jitsu-go-Kiyō."* For a general discussion of *terakoya* texts, including these two works, see Dore, *Education*, 275–290.

31. Ishikawa Ken, *"Jitsugokyō, Dōjikyō ni tsuite no kenkyū*," 54.

32. *Dōjikyō*, popularly attributed either to the T'ang poet Po Chü-i (772–846) or to Anzen (a disciple of the Tendai monk Ennin; 794–864), may have been written somewhat later, perhaps in late Kamakura (Ishikawa, *"Jitsugokyō,"* 55–57).

33. Ibid., 62–63. Ishikawa also discusses the stylistic differences between the two texts on pp. 60, 65.

34. *Jitsugokyō*, 1.

35. For example, Nakai Chikuzan of Kaitokudō or the head teacher of Gansuidō, Tsuchihashi Tomonao (1685–1730); see Najita, *Visions,* 178, and Tsuda, *Kinsei minshū kyōiku,* 9–10, respectively.

36. Quoted by Furukawa Tetsushi, *Nihon dōtoku kyōiku,* 181–182. The second passage comes from *Keizai mondō hiroku* (A Secret Record of Dialogues about the Economy). *Teikin ōrai* was a popular letter-writing copybook that also originated in medieval times.

37. This number is exclusive of editions that were printed in combination with other works, particularly *ōraimono* (Ishikawa, "*Jitsugokyō,*" 66–70). For a detailed chart of the various editions of *Jitsugokyō* and its spin-offs, see Ishikawa, *Waga kuni ni okeru jidōkan no hattatsu,* 353–373.

38. Furukawa, *Nihon dōtoku kyōiku,* 179.

39. Ishikawa, "*Jitsugokyō,*" 70. Furukawa also doubts whether *terakoya* pupils absorbed much Buddhist faith from these two texts during the Edo period (*Nihon dōtoku kyōiku,* 181).

40. An example of an epistle that became a copybook is the Imagawa letter, written in the late fourteenth or early fifteenth century; it was republished at least 220 times during the Edo period (Steenstrup, "Imagawa Letter," 296).

41. Dore, *Education,* 281.

42. For example, the 1680 work *Meigokyōjishō* (Selections from Brilliant Words for Children) draws heavily on contemporary primers and practically oriented children's works but is written in the same style as *Words of Truth* (Ishikawa, "*Jitsugokyō,*" 74–75). Other works included in Ishikawa's analysis are *Shiyōshō* (Record of Essentials), an early Kamakura text, and *Kyōjisho* (A Book for Teaching Children), a late Kamakura text that was not published until 1658.

43. Ishikawa includes it in his survey ("*Jitsugokyō,*" 76).

44. *Jitsugokyō,* 1.

45. TTZ, 267a–267b.

46. TTZ, 270b–270c; the original passage reads: "[In commenting on Confucius' words about wisdom, Tzu-hsia said:] When Shun possessed the Empire, he raised Kao Yao from the multitude and by so doing put those who were not humane at a great distance. When T'ang possessed the Empire, he raised Yi Yin from the multitude and by so doing put those who were not humane at a great distance" (translation adapted from Confucius, *The Analects,* trans. D. C. Lau, 117). Kao Yao was Emperor Shun's minister of laws and punishments; Yi Yin helped Emperor T'ang found the reign of Yin.

47. TTZ, 272d.

48. The original passage reads: "If [the Duke of Chou] caused this knowingly, then he was not humane; if he caused it without knowing, then he was unwise" (TTZ, 268a).

49. Chu, *Shōgaku,* 44 and 115, respectively; TTZ, 247b.

50. Chu, *Shōgaku,* 59.

51. Ibid., 61; TTZ, 276b.

52. *Jitsugokyō,* 2.

53. TTZ, 267d, 274b.

54. TTZ, 271d.

55. In Chinese, *Hsüeh shih pu ch'i an-shih* (TTZ, 274c). The attribution is in

the seventeenth-century work *Cheng-tzu t'ung* compiled by Chang Tzu-lieh (fl. 1627); the saying is not in Ch'eng Hao and Ch'eng I, *Nitei zensho* (Ch. *Erh-Ch'eng ch'üan-shu*). Toan again warns against self-deception in TTZ, 273b.

56. TTZ, 269b–269c.

57. TTZ, 268c–268d. The "system" or "method" of the mind, *hsin-fa* in Chinese, is a term used in Ch'eng-Chu texts to denote the cultivation of the mind; Chu Hsi uses it in the opening lines of his commentary on the *Mean*, in which he paraphrases comments by the Ch'eng brothers (*Shisho shūchū*, in SGT 8:15). The term is discussed in detail by de Bary in *Neo-Confucian Orthodoxy*, 128–130, and *Message of the Mind*, 32–35. Toan's use of the expression here is exceptional; it may be a quotation. The second clause derives from a passage in the *Book of Changes*, "Hsi-tz'u chuan" (*Ekikyō* 2:352). "It" seems to refer in the original context to the process of transformation. In Legge's translation the full passsage reads: "In (all these operations forming) the Yi [Changes], there is no thought and no action. It is still and without movement; but, when acted on, it penetrates forthwith to all phenomena and events under the sky" (*Yi King*, 370 [no. 62]).

58. TTZ, 269b.

59. *Jitsugokyō*, 1.

60. *Hotoke hitori shishō o dan sezu;* / *shishō mo mata ōinarazuya.* The meaning of these lines is obscure; *hotoke*, or *"buddha,"* is also a popular term for dead persons.

61. *Changes*, "Hsi-tz'u chuan" (*Ekikyō* 2:316); trans. by Legge in *Yi King*, 353 (no. 21): "(The sage) . . . knows the causes of darkness [the next world] . . . and light [this world]. He traces things to their beginning, and follows them to their end;—thus he knows what can be said about death and [birth]."

62. TTZ, 268d–269a.

63. *Jitsugokyō*, 1. The Three Learnings are the precepts, meditation, and wisdom; the Seven Requirements for reaching enlightenment (reading *shichikaku* for *shichigaku*) are selecting the (correct) dharma, effort, joy, agreeableness, nonattachment, concentration, and tranquility. The Four Mentalities are essentially compassion and almsgiving (*jihi kisha*); the Eight Sufferings are birth, age, illness, death, separation (from those one loves), encounter (with those one hates), nonattainment (of what one desires), and suffering associated with the senses. The Eightfold Path is right views, right resolve, right speech, right conduct, right livelihood, right effort, right mindfulness, and right concentration; the Ten Evils are killing, stealing, sexual immorality, lying, greed, anger, wrong views, deluded speech, fanciful talk, and slander.

64. TTZ, 275c–275d, 277a, 277c–278a; the passages are in *The Analects*, trans. Lau, 140–141, 82–83, 159, and 160, respectively.

65. TTZ, 278a.

66. *Sekimon*, 48.

67. The latter was entitled *Rigaku shinryō* (A Ferry for the Study of Principle); see Shibata, "Kaisetsu," in TTZ, 6. See also Ishikawa's chart in *Waga kuni ni okeru jidōkan no hattatsu*, 370–371.

68. TTZ, 267d.

69. This point could also be made about Chu Hsi's *Elementary Learning*, even

though Chu Hsi was concerned that the compilation not include material that would be too difficult for beginners; see Kelleher, "Back to Basics," 222–223.

70. TTZ, 270d. *Ch'ien* and *k'un* are the first two hexagrams in the *Book of Changes*. They are usually associated with heaven and earth, or male and female principles. The above passage is probably an allusion to the *Changes*, "Hsi-tz'u chuan" (*Ekikyō* 2:307), translated by Legge in *Yi King*, 349 (nos. 6–7): "It is by the ease with which it proceeds that [Ch'ien] directs (as it does), and by its unhesitating response that [K'un] exhibits such ability. (He who attains to this) ease (of Heaven) will be easily understood, and (he who attains to this) freedom from laborious effort (of the Earth) will be easily followed." In the second line of the allusion Toan substitutes *ts'ung* (follows) for *neng* (exhibits such ability).

71. TTZ, 278c–278d; the postscript is dated the twelfth month of 1781.

72. Iwauchi, *Kyōikuka*, 115.

73. Translated in Miura and Sasaki, *Zen Dust*, 251–253.

74. Hakuin, in Naoki Kimihiko, ed., *Hakuin zenji minshū no kyōka to shoga no shashin shū*, 47.

75. Yampolsky briefly comments on the latter work (*Hakuin*, 231); the song is printed in *Hakuin oshō zenshū* 6:231–238, and in Akizuki, *Hakuin zenji*, 214–223.

76. Quoted in Akizuki, *Hakuin zenji*, 215.

77. Quoted in ibid., 217.

78. Another eighteenth-century example is Motoori Norinaga's *Tamaboko hyakushu* (One Hundred Verses of the Jeweled Halberd) published in 1787 (Shibata, *Monryū*, 110).

79. Shiteki-ō Nyounsha (Tetsudō) was also known as Yamada Shin'uemon. Excerpted from "Iroha uta," in Katō Tetsudō, *Nihon ijin shinkō jitsuden*, 540; originally published in block print in 1777, in "Nyoun Shiteki-ō kana seppō, furoku iroha uta." The last phrase, a Buddhist term *(daisen sekai,* or *sanzen daisen sekai),* indicates the entire universe.

80. Shiteki-ō, in *Nihon ijin,* Katō, 543.

81. For example, in the Sengoku period (1477–1573), *iroha uta* were used to rouse up the spirits of Satsuma domain warriors; see Hayashi Yoshihiko, *Satsuma han no kyōiku to zaisei narabini gunbi*, 185.

82. See NST 42:144–145. The collection was compiled by a disciple, Nakashima Hokyō, and includes another of Toan's *iroha* songs, written in 1771, plus three other versified tracts, some of which may not have been authored by Toan. According to Shibata, these other works were not as widely disseminated as the first song (*Monryū,* 117).

83. Shibata implies that the pictures were later additions, not necessarily Toan's own creations—though they certainly did not violate his intentions (*Monryū,* 111). The pictures reproduced here are excerpted from a 1917 Meirinsha block-print edition of "Jijo: Nemurizamashi," kindly given to me by Shibata.

84. NST 42:144.

85. Shibata also implies that this was the case (*Monryū,* 118).

86. Here I follow a commentary on the text, *Nemurizamashi no ryaku kai,* by Shibata Kendō. Evidently because of the quantity of cultural detail needed to

understand the connection between the song and the pictures, by late Meiji times it became necessary to record the background stories or lessons. Kendō's commentary was printed as a booklet by Meirinsha in 1911.

87. Shibata Kendō, *Nemurizamashi*, 7a.

88. Yoshida, *Tsurezuregusa*, 78 (no. 58), trans. Keene, 52.

89. Shibata Kendō believes the latter are spring blossoms (*Ryaku kai*, 10a–10b).

90. Translated by Legge, in *The Works of Mencius*, 142–143; here I follow Shibata Kendō, *Ryaku kai*, 11b. Both Dobson and Lau interpret *che-chih* (J. *setsushi*) as either cracking or massaging an elder's joints rather than breaking off a branch (*Mencius*, trans. W. A. C. H. Dobson, 11; trans D. C. Lau, 56). Toan follows Chu Hsi's (and Legge's) interpretation: to break off a branch at the order of a superior means "something that is not difficult. . . . It is only up to oneself" (SGT 8:91).

91. Shibata Kendō suggests this as a tentative interpretation of verse 12 (*Ryaku kai*, 12a).

92. Shibata Kendō titles this "A picture of [a person] engaging in the contemplative practice of quiet sitting *(seiza kufū)*" (ibid., 8b).

93. The verse itself, about the "mind that has no beginning," also has Zen connotations; cf. the Zen saying about one's "original aspect" *(honrai no menmoku)* and the comparable Shingaku *sakumon* discussed in Chapter 5.

94. See, for example, Gabriel Moran, *Religious Education Development: Images for the Future*, 148–150, 200. Moran discusses primarily Western religious education, but I believe his remarks are applicable in a general sense to the East Asian context as well.

95. "Tsuri-gitsune," in NKBT 43:457.

96. Yoshida, *Tsurezuregusa*, 72; trans. Keene, 46–47 (no. 53).

97. This anecdote is also mentioned in *Tsurezuregusa*, 28, trans. Keene, 8–9 (no. 8). The wise man of Kume was the founder of Kumedera, a temple in Yamato.

98. Shibata, "Kaisetsu," in TTZ, 2, comments facing 49; see also *Monryū*, 118. Robertson reports that Shingaku writers borrowed mass-produced pictures called Ōtsu-e to illustrate their works ("Rooting the Pine," 327–328).

99. The following account is drawn from Ototake Iwazō, *Nihon shomin kyōiku shi* 2:460–461.

100. *Ongoku* originally meant territories far from Kyoto; in the Edo period it was used to refer to territories under direct shogunal control, which included Osaka.

101. Ototake seems unaware of Toan's authorship.

102. Shibata, *Monryū*, 118; "Kaisetsu," in TTZ, 2.

103. At best, the approach taken to moral learning in the "temple schools" is exemplified by works like the 1695 *Sasayama Baian terako seikai no shikimoku* (Terakoya Precepts). Like Toan's *Early Lessons*, the precepts deal with etiquette and proper conduct for children, but they focus mainly on behavior at the writing school itself. Compared to Toan's *Lessons*, there is less attention to the underlying rationale for moral behavior (The "Terakoya Precepts" are translated by Dore in *Education*, 323–326).

7: Popularization and Regulation

1. IBZ 2:625; translated in Bellah, *Tokugawa Religion,* 203.

2. Ishikawa, *Sekimon,* 165.

3. NST 42:12.

4. Iwauchi, *Kyōikuka,* 115–119; Ishikawa, *Sekimon,* 159.

5. NST 42:12–13.

6. As noted in Chapter 1, Shingaku teachers not only referred to stories of filial piety in their lectures, but also wrote them.

7. Namely, *Analects* 1:1, 4, 5, 7, and 8. Toan's allusions range from Mujū Ichien's *Shasekishū, Bonmōkyō* (Brahma-Net Sutra) and the sayings of Zen master Baiten to the works of Chu Hsi and the Ch'eng brothers.

8. Ishikawa, *Sekimon,* 190.

9. "Talks on the Way" is used throughout the 1781 *Shohō e dōwa ni on-ide no hōyūchū on-kokoro-e no daitai* (Guidelines for Companions Who Go to Various Regions to Give Talks on the Way), whereas "lectures" is used in the similar document of the following year *Shachū junkō kokoro-e sadamegaki* (Code of Rules for Members Who Give Itinerant Lectures).

10. Ishikawa, *Sekimon,* 163; cf. Mashita Saburō's typology of talks on the Way in "Shingaku dōwa no gengoteki seikaku."

11. For the above general description of *dōwa,* I have consulted Shibata Kendō, "Dōwa no honshitsu to sono kōzō," 3–6, and Shiraishi Masakuni, *Sekimon Shingaku no kenkyū,* 42–43.

12. *Shōō dōwa* (Shōō's Talks on the Way) was compiled after the death of Fuse Shōō (1784). It is not really a record of his talks on the Way, but rather a compilation of his writings and answers to questions; see Ishikawa's discussion in *Sekimon,* 86–87.

13. Its subsequent edition, *Dōni-ō dōwa,* was published in three parts, in 1795, 1796, and 1800.

14. *Sekimon,* 169.

15. Talks were not always held in the meetinghouses themselves, however, especially if seating was insufficient.

16. The establishment of meetinghouses continued apace during the early decades of the nineteenth century. By about 1830 there were 160 new meetinghouses throughout Japan (Shibata, *Shingaku,* 99–101). Shibata cautions that the exact history of the meetinghouses is difficult to trace because, although many thrived under the leadership of their respective housemasters or lecturers, they tended to decline when these leaders passed away. In addition, after the Restoration only the main meetinghouses in Kyoto, Tokyo, and Osaka survived; records for the others are scarce.

17. Excerpted from *Kyūō dōwa* (Kyūō's Talks on the Way), 235–236.

18. For example, Robertson ("Rooting the Pine," 321–322); Robertson translates *dōwa* as "parable."

19. Miyamoto Mataji, *Chōnin shakai no gakugei to Kaitokudō,* 30.

20. Ishikawa, *Sekimon,* 163–164. By "certificate" here I mean the "Seals of the Three Meetinghouses," discussed below.

21. Regarding the neglect of quiet sitting, see ibid., 152–153.

22. Ibid., 170. Baba Bunkō, mentioned in Chapter 1, prefigured this pattern of imitating Shingaku.

23. The logistics of teaching arrangements also receive attention: Toan asks teachers to consult each other with regard to organizing lectures at the meetinghouses, requests female elders to teach Shingaku to women, and gives advice regarding the building of meetinghouses.

24. The reproduction in TTZ, 592–593, of this last document is undated, but Ishikawa says it was completed in the seventh month of 1784 (*Sekimon*, 242).

25. *Nagano-ken kyōiku shi* 7:693, no. 268. It is likely that members also carried the *Admonition* with them as further proof of their qualifications.

26. TTZ, 591.

27. TTZ, 591.

28. TTZ, 592.

29. TTZ, 593.

30. TTZ, 588.

31. For the following account, see *Monryū*, 119–132. Takatsuki domain was in Settsu—today's northern Osaka district and eastern Hyōgo prefecture.

32. *Monryū*, 126.

33. TTZ, 589–590.

34. TTZ, 591.

35. TTZ, 590.

36. TTZ, 592.

37. For the following, see Ishikawa's reprint and discussion of Kisui's 1797 code of conduct, *Sadamegaki*, in *Sekimon*, 334–337.

38. Ishikawa reproduces both the recto of the 1800 Three Seals document and the verso of a later one, 1830s or early 1840s (*Sekimon*, 336).

39. *Tōsho shachū mōshi-awase sadamegaki* (Code of Rules for the Members of this Area). The following account is based on Ishikawa, *Sekimon*, 341–345.

40. Another rank, the *chūkō*, was developed later; these "intermediate lecturers" could give talks unaccompanied as long as they had permission from their leaders (Ishikawa, *Sekimon*, 354–355, including n. 14).

41. TTZ, 588.

42. TTZ, 590.

43. Shibata, *Shingaku*, 75–76.

44. *Hsing-li tzu-i*, by the Neo-Confucian scholar Ch'en Ch'un (1159–1223). It has been translated by Wing-tsit Chan under the title *Neo-Confucian Terms Explained (The "Pei-hsi tzu-i") by Ch'en Ch'un, 1159–1223.*

45. IBZ 2:625, translated in Bellah, *Tokugawa Religion*, 203.

46. TTZ, 603.

47. *Kaiyū taishi*, 189.

48. TTZ, 587.

49. TTZ, 592.

50. NST 42:189.

51. *Jimō* literally means "instructing the ignorant" or "instructing children"; Shibata identifies the editor of these *katakana* works as Nakamura Tekisai

(1629–1702), a prolific Confucian scholar who was himself the son of a dry goods merchant (NST 42:189).

52. *Sekimon*, 248–249. Cf. Shibata's general remarks in *Monryū*, 129–130. The incident is discussed further below.

53. It is worth noting that the Kyoto magistrate's action also had no impact on Toan's policy of refusing admission fees (see Chapter 2).

54. This interpretation is related to the speculation, mentioned in Chapter 2, that Kisui's depiction of Shingaku as an orthodox Ch'eng-Chu transmission in his lineage chart was a reverberation of the 1790 shogunal edict against heterodox learning. See Shibata, *Monryū*, 160.

55. The Kansei edict of 1790, in any case, was directed primarily at shogunal educational institutions and their officials; it did not actually restrict transmission of "heterodox" ideas in general.

56. From *Sanzensha nenpu* (Sanzensha Annals), compiled by Kawajiri Hōkin in 1898; quoted in Ishikawa, *Sekimon*, 246. Other sources clarify that the magistrate in office at the time was Ishikawa Masatake; his tenure ran from 1766 to 1769.

57. *Sōbō kigen*, "Shukke no koto," in *Nakai Chikuzan to Sōbō kigen*, 272–273.

58. *Shōheigaku tomegaki* (Notices of the Shōhei School), section on "Examination of Learning," nineteenth day of the second month of 1794, reprinted in Ishikawa, *Sekimon*, 1353.

59. The three heads who advised that Ryūsuke be excluded were Bitō Jishū (1745–1813), Okada Kansen (1740–1816), and Shibano Ritsuzan (1736–1807); all three were instrumental in the campaign against heterodox learning.

60. In Chinese, *liang-chih liang-neng;* these terms derive from *Mencius* 7A:15: "What people can do without learning is innate ability. What they know without reflecting is innate knowledge of the good." Wang Yang-ming emphasized the "innate knowledge of the good" as the primary source of moral knowledge.

61. "Teshima Toan," in *Kinsei kijin den*, 168–170.

62. Ishikawa discusses the relation between Sadanobu and Shingaku in detail (*Sekimon*, 1107–1108).

63. The term *kyōgen* (Ch. *hsiang-yüan*) derives from *Analects* 17:13 and *Mencius* 7B:37. It implies the efforts of a "petty person" or country boor who gains the approbation of others through external conformity with morality.

64. Cited in Ishikawa, *Sekimon*, 1351.

65. See Ishikawa, *Kinsei no gakkō*, 97; also Passin, *Society and Education*, 41.

66. *Dōni-ō dōwa*, ed. Ishikawa, 116–117.

67. Ishikawa Ken, "Shingaku shū shonyū banashi hen: Kaisetsu," 12. At the same time, Takken testifies to the popularity of Shingaku in *Okinagusa*, 584–585.

68. TTZ, 710.

69. TTZ, 395.

70. The "Age of the Gods" ("Kami no yō") is the first chapter of the ancient Japanese work *Nihongi* (Chronicles of Japan).

71. TTZ, 786. By saying "it's a mystery *(shinpi),*" Toan implies that the meaning of the chapter is a secret teaching that can be conveyed only by representatives of the Shinto faith.

72. See H. D. Harootunian, *Things Seen and Unseen: Discourse and Ideology in Tokugawa Nativism,* 193. I am indebted to Harry Harootunian for bringing the parallel between Atsutane's and Toan's views of professional scholarship to my attention.

73. TTZ, 339. On another occasion, in response to the question of whether Zen and Confucianism are the same, Toan says that Bankei Zen is the same as *kochi no oshie* (our teaching), i.e., Confucianism (NST 42:123). Ishida Baigan had also referred to his teaching as "Confucian" (*Tohi mondō,* 376).

Conclusion

1. For remarks on the nature of Buddhist influence on Sung Neo-Confucianism, see de Bary, "Seventeenth-Century Enlightenment" 161–162. In the late Ming, many Neo-Confucians—especially in the T'ai-chou school—drew direct inspiration from Ch'an. Studies of Ming Neo-Confucians influenced by Buddhism are contained in de Bary, ed., *Self and Society in Ming Thought* and idem, *The Unfolding of Neo-Confucianism.* Araki Kengo's essay "Confucianism and Buddhism in the Late Ming" provides a good outline of the positions of some of these thinkers and their relations with the Ch'eng-Chu, Wang Yang-ming, and Buddhist schools of self-cultivation. His book *Mindai shisō kenkyū* contains more detailed studies. Lin Chao-en also drew heavily on Buddhist meditative techniques to supplement his Confucian theoretical framework (Berling, *Syncretic Religion,* esp. 71).

2. I have been assisted in my general thinking about this process by Gabriel Moran's *Religious Education Development* and James W. Fowler's *Stages of Faith: The Psychology of Human Development and the Quest for Meaning.*

3. De Bary, *Message of the Mind,* 33–34.

4. Saitō Akitoshi cites only the work of *terakoya* teachers in his discussion of the Buddhist contribution to nonsamurai children's education (*Nihon Bukkyō kyōiku shi kenkyū,* 326–383).

5. Dōni was the first prominent Shingaku follower said to have had previous Zen training. But the trend of Shingaku associates practicing Zen may be traced as far back as Baigan's teacher Oguri Ryōun, who is thought to have been an Ōbaku practitioner. Late in the Tokugawa period, many Rinzai practitioners studied and taught Shingaku in the Edo branch of the movement, centered on Sanzensha.

6. See, for example, Harootunian's discussion of Hirata Atsune and the exaltation of "ordinary" people's learning (*Things Seen and Unseen,* 189–195).

7. Kawamura Taiichi has suggested, for example, that Shingaku activities in Chōshū domain late in the period helped people develop awareness of the need for education and showed them that they could arrange for it themselves. The practice of supporting Shingaku circuit lectures was part of a trend toward autonomous education in the villages, spearheaded by wealthy merchants and peasant leaders, that extended into Meiji times. Kawamura believes that the presentation

of Shingaku talks on the Way contributed to the development of a socioeconomic basis for modern education in Chōshū domain ("Chōshū-han ni okeru Shingaku dōwa no kyōiku shiteki igi," 38–42).

8. "Late Tokugawa Culture and Thought," 171.

9. For a summary of the characteristics of new religions of this time, see ibid., 215–222.

10. The desire to change the conditions of the time sometimes resulted in a dramatic call for "world renewal," or *yonaoshi*. But many followers of new religions saw themselves as providing "relief in a context of scarcity and unrelieved hardship, rather than as challenging the established world of politics and public authority" (ibid., 217).

11. *Kurozumikyō and the New Religions of Japan*, chap. 1, esp. 10–18.

12. The increased attention to lay concerns was manifested in established as well as new religious groups. Some late Tokugawa–early Meiji Rinzai masters moved toward a "Confucianized Zen" that was more open to the domestic context. It is worth noting that Imakita Kōsen, who opened Zen practice to lay people at Engaku-ji, was well grounded in Neo-Confucian learning; one of his lay Dharma successors, Kawajiri Hōkin, was the director of Shingaku's Sanzensha in the Meiji period.

13. Harootunian, "Late Tokugawa Culture," 222.

14. In contrast, the founder of Kurozumi-kyō, Kurozumi Munetada (1780–1850), was a healer. Kurozumi, who himself seems to have been influenced by Shingaku, identifed strongly with Amaterasu and her salvific powers. See Hardacre, *Kurozumikyō*, 45–46, 53–55; and Harootunian, "Late Tokugawa Culture," 222–225.

15. Many Shingaku members, beginning with Baigan himself, did involve themselves in particular efforts to relieve poverty or hardship, but these efforts were not a vital or conspicuous feature of the Shingaku program as a whole. Regarding Toan's attitude, Ban Kōkei avers in his *Kinsei kijin den* that "it is well known that when the price of rice rose in recent years [the 1770s and 1780s], many of the people who gave alms to the poor were from [Teshima Toan's] school." See Takahashi Shunjō, "Shingakusha no shakai jigyō," 27–28.

16. Richard Rubinger's essay "Education: From One Room to One System" provides a larger context for understanding the changes and continuities that characterized education in the Bakumatsu to early Meiji years.

17. Regarding Chōshū domain's sponsorship of Shingaku talks, for example, see Umihara Tōru, *Meiji isshin to kyōiku*, 41–46; and Kawamura Taiichi, "Chōshū-han ni okeru Shingaku," 37–42. The Matsuyama domain meetinghouse functioned as the local school for over sixty years (Kageyama Noboru, *Ehime-ken no kyōiku shi*, 211–215). Some Osaka *terakoya* sponsored regular Shingaku talks; in Genichidō, girls were required to recite Toan's *Early Lessons*. The Osaka authorities, who repeatedly lauded the "Teshima school of Shingaku" in decrees issued in the 1840s, apparently considered it a worthy supplement to the *terakoya* program (Ototake, *Nihon shomin kyōiku shi*, 2:458–460, 468–469). The most systematic treatment of the relations between Shingaku and government-sponsored schools is contained in Ishikawa, *Sekimon*, 1093–1367.

18. See Umihara, *Gakkō*, 116–119; and Shibata, *Shingaku*, 170–172. Endō

Masatsugu (1836–1900), a founding father of one of these schools—Nisshō Elementary School—was the offspring of a marriage between Uekawa Kisui's daughter and a descendant of Saitō Zenmon. Masatsugu was well acquainted with Shingaku and met regularly with other descendants of Baigan's disciples to study the "Way" (*Nisshō hyakunen shi*, 156–157). I am grateful to Yokoyama Toshio for bringing to my attention the role of the Endō family in Shingaku.

GLOSSARY

This list includes most personal names, terms, and titles that are cited in the text and notes and that do not appear in the Bibliography. Names of places and institutions other than Shingaku meetinghouses are omitted.

Akatani Jurō 赤谷重郎
Akindo yawasō 商人夜話草
Amida 阿彌陀
*Amida hadaka
    monogatari* 阿彌陀裸物語
andō, andon 行灯
Anzen 安然
aruji 主
Asano Kangorō 浅野勘五郎
Atobe Yoshiaki 跡部良顕

Baba Bunkō 馬場文耕
Baiten Mumyō 梅天無明
Baiten zenji hōgo 梅天禅師法語
bakuhan 幕藩
bangumi shōgakkō 番組小学校
Banmin tokuyō 万民德用
Bitō Jishū 尾藤二洲
Bokumon 木門
Bonmōkyō 梵網経
bonpu 凡夫
bunbetsu 分別

Ch'ang-lu Tsung-tse 長蘆宗賾
Chang Tsai 張載
Chang Tzu-lieh 張自烈
Ch'an-yüan ch'ing-kuei 禅苑清規

Chao-chou 趙州
che-chih, J. setsushi 折枝
Ch'en Ch'un 陳淳
Ch'eng Min-cheng 程敏政
Cheng-tzu t'ung 正字通
Ch'en Hsien-chang 陳獻章
Chen Te-hsiu 真德秀
chi, Ch. chih 智
Chia fan 家範
chiang-hsüeh 講学
chichi kakubutsu 致知格物
ch'ien 乾
chih liang-chih 致良知
*Chikuzen [no kuni kōshi] ryōmin
    den* 筑前の國孝子良民傳
Chikuzen [no kuni] kōshi Shōsuke den
    筑前の國孝子正助傳
ching, J. kei 敬
Ching-te ch'uan-teng lu 景德伝燈錄
chi-p'o, J. kyūhaku 急迫
ch'iung-li, J. kyūri 窮理
chōnin 町人
Chōnin bukuro 町人囊
Chōnin kōken roku 町人考見錄
Chou Ju-teng 周汝登
Chou Tun-i 周敦頤
chu-ching 主靜

217

chūkō　中講
chung　中
Chu-tzu hsin-hsüeh lu　朱子心學錄
Chu-tzu yü-lu　朱子語錄

Daimoku　題目
dangibon　談義本
dansho　斷書
Dōjikyō　童子教
dōka　道歌
dōwa　道話
Dōwa kikigaki　道話聞書

Endō Masatsugu　遠藤全受
Enni Ben'en　円爾弁円
Ennin　円仁
Enzan wadei gassui [shū]
　盬山和泥合水集

Fudōchi shinmyōroku　不動智神妙錄
Fujii Ransai　藤井懶斎
Fujin yashinai-gusa　婦人養草
Fujiwara Seika　藤原惺窩
fukatoku　不可得
Fukushima　福島
fumai, Ch. pu mei　不昧
Fuse Shōō　布施松翁
fushō　不生
fushō fumetsu　不生不滅
fushō no busshin　不生の仏心
Fu Ta-shih　傅大士

gakumon　學問
Gakushūroku　學習錄
geryō　仮量
gōgaku　郷学
goi　五位
gonin-gumi　五人組
gonsen　言詮
Gorakusha　五楽舎
goroku　語錄
Gudō Tōshoku　愚堂東寔

hakarai　計らい
hankō　藩校
hatsumei　發明

Hayano Hakuin　早野柏蔭
Hayashi Razan　林羅山
Heike monogatari　平家物語
Hiraga Gennai　平賀源内
Hirata Atsutane　平田篤胤
Hirose Tansō　広瀬淡窓
hōgo　法語
hojinshi　輔仁司
Hōjō Gen'yō　北條玄養
Hōjōki　方丈記
Honchō kōshiden　本朝孝子傳
honrai no menmoku　本来の面目
Honsaroku　本佐錄
honshin　本心
honshin hatsumei (honshin o hatsumei
　suru)　本心發明（本心を發明
　する）
honshin o shiru　本心を知る
Honshin oni ga utsu tsue
　本心鬼が捶杖
hōshin hotsugo　放心発悟
Hosshin shū　発心集
hossu　払子
Hotoke hitori shishō o dan sezu;
　shishō mo mata ōinarazuya
　佛獨不談死生死生不亦大乎
Hōtoku　報德
hotsugo　發悟
hōyū　朋友
Hsieh Liang-tso　謝良佐
Hsi-ming　西銘
Hsin-ching　心經
Hsin-ching fu-chu　心經附註
hsin-fa, J. shinpō　心法
Hsing-li tzu-i　性理字義
Hsüeh shih pu ch'i an-shih
　学始不欺暗室
hsü-ling pu mei　虚靈不昧
Hui-an Chu hsin-hsüeh lu
　晦庵朱心學錄

i　意
i, J. gi　義
ichimotsu　一物
ichinen fushō　一念不生
igaku　異学
ihatsu, Ch. i-fa　以發

ihatsu no ba 以發の場
Ikkyū Sōjun 一休宗純
Imakita Kōsen 今北洪川
inka 印可
iroha いろは
Ishida sensei monjin fu
　　石田先生門人譜
Ishikawa Masatake 石河政武
ishiki 意識
itan 異端
Itō Jinsai 伊藤仁斎
Itō Kaitei 伊藤介亭
itten shikai kai ki myōhō
　　一天四海皆歸妙法

jen, J. jin 仁
jibutsu 事物
jihi kisha 慈悲喜捨
jikei 持敬
jikishi ninshin 直指人心
jimō 示蒙
Jimon 慈門
jinshin kyūri 尽心窮理
Jion-ni Kenka 慈音尼兼葭
jiseki 事蹟
jishō 自性
Jishōki 自性記
"Jishūroku" 時習録
Jishūsha 時習舎
jisshin, jitsu no kokoro 實心
jitoku, Ch. tzu-te 自得
jitsugaku 實學
jitsuroku 實録
jitsuwa 實話
Jizō 地蔵
jō, Ch. ching 情
jusha 儒者

kai 會
kaidoku 會読
kaiho 會輔
Kaiho Seiryō 海保青陵
kaihojō 會輔場
kaiyūshi 會友司
kakun 家訓
Kamada Issō 鎌田一窓

Kamada Ryūō 鎌田柳泓
"Kami no yō" 神の代
Kamo no Chōmei 鴨長明
kana hōgo 假名法語
Kana retsujo den 假名烈女傳
Kana shōri 假名性理
kanazōshi 假名草子
Kanbe Kishū 神戸亀州
kangaku 漢学
Kanmuryōjukyō 観無量寿経
Kannon 観音
kanpo 緩歩
Kanzeon-bosatsu 観世音菩薩
Kao Pan-lung 高攀龍
katachi ni yoru kokoro 形による心
Kawajiri Hōkin 川尻宝岑
Kegon-kyō 華嚴経
Keizai mondō hiroku 経済問答秘録
ken 見
kenshō 見性
kenyaku 倹約
kessei 結制
Ketsujōshū 結繩集
ki, 'Ch. ch'i 氣
kikan 機関
Kimon 崎門
Kimura Shigemitsu 木村重光
kinhin 經行
kin'i 巾衣
Kinoshita Jun'an 木下順庵
Kishibojin, Kishimojin 鬼子母神
Kitamura Kigin 北村季吟
kō, Ch. chiang 講
kochi no oshie こちの教
kōdan 講談
kōdanshi 講談師
kōgi 講義
Kojin michi o mireba bunmei nari.
　　Yue ni sono kotoba kaku no
　　gotoshi. 古人見道分明。
　　故其言如此。
kōjō no ichirō 向上の一路
kokoro 心
kokorozashi o tatsu, Ch. li-chih 立志
kokugaku 國学
Kōkyō dōjikun 孝經童子訓
Komori Baifu 小森賣布

kono omoi no okoru sono saki o
    magekagamuru　此思ひの發る其
    さきを典屈る
kōsha　講舎
kōshaku　講釋
kōshakushi　講釋師
kōshi　講師
kōshiden　孝子傳
Kōshinsha　盍簪舍
ko-wu, J. kakubutsu　格物
Koyama Shikei　小山止敬
kū, Ch. k'ung　空
kufū, Ch. kung-fu　工夫
Kumazawa Banzan　熊沢蕃山
Kumogawa Kōki　雲川弘毅
k'un　坤
Kurosugi Masatane　黒杉政胤
Kurozumi Munetada　黒住宗忠
kurushii　苦しい
Kusumoto Tanzan　楠本端山
Kusunoki Masashige　楠木正成
kyōge betsuden furyū
    monji　教外別伝不立文字
Kyōgen　狂言
kyōgen, Ch. hsiang-yüan　郷原
Kyōjisho　教兒書
Kyōkeisha　恭敬舍
Kyōkun zatsu nagamochi　教訓雜長持
kyōkunsho　教訓書
kyorei, Ch. hsü-ling　虛靈
kyosei　虛靜
kyōten kōshaku　経典講釋
kyōyusho　教諭所
kyūri jinsei　窮理盡性

liang-chih liang-neng　良知良能
Li T'ung, Yen-p'ing　李侗　延平
Lieh-nü chuan　烈女傳
Lin Chao-en　林兆恩
Lin-chi lu　臨濟錄
Liu Hsiang　劉向
Liu-yü yen-i　六諭衍義
Lo Tsung-yen　羅從彦

makoto　誠
Masuho Zankō　増穂残口
Matsudaira Sadanobu　松平定信

Meigokyōjishō　明語教兒抄
Meijo monogaturi　名女物語
Meirinsha　明倫舍
Meiseisha　明誠舍
me nashi　目なし
mibiiki　身贔屓
mihatsu, Ch. wei-fa　未發
ming-te, J. meitoku　明德
Mitsui Takafusa　三井高房
Miura Baien　三浦梅園
Mizu kagami　水鏡
Mōanjō　盲安杖
mokugyo　木魚
Motoori Norinaga　木居宣長
mu, Ch. wu　無
mu ichi motsu　無一物
Muchū mondō　夢中問答
muga, ware nashi　無我
Mujū Ichien　無住一円
mukō e wa yukazu ni　向ふへは行
    かずに
munen　無念
Muneyasu　宗禋
Muro Kyūsō　室鳩巣
mushin, Ch. wu hsin　無心
mushin, mi nashi　無身
Musō Soseki　夢窓疎石
myōhō　妙法

Naganuma Tangetsu　長沼潭月
Nakae Tōju　中江藤樹
Nakamura Tekisai　中村惕斎
Nakamura Tokusui　中村德水
Nakanishi Tan'en　中西淡淵
Nakashima Hokyō　中島保教
Nakazawa Dōni, Yoshimichi,
    中澤道二　義道
    Kameyakyūbei, 亀屋久兵衛
    Teitokuin Hōgen Nisshin
    貞徳院法玄日信
Nanmei　南溟
Namu myōhō renge kyō
    南無妙法蓮華経
nenbutsu　念仏
neng　能
ninjōbon　人情本
Ninomiya Sontoku　二宮尊德

Nishikawa Joken 西川如見
Nishioka [kōshi] Gihei gyōjō
　kikigaki 西岡孝子儀兵衛行状聞書
nisshin no kufū 日新の工夫
nyoze 如是

Oguri Ryōun 小栗了雲
Ogyū Sorai 荻生徂来
Okada Kansen 岡田寒泉
Okitsu Koyama 興津湖山
Okuta Raijō 奥田頼杖
omoi 思い
omoi-ire 思い入れ
Ongoku iroha uta,
　　odori 遠国いろは歌　踊り
onibi 鬼火
Onna chūyō 女中庸
Onna daigaku 女大学
Onna daigaku takara bako
　女大学宝箱
Onna rongo 女論語
Onna shōgaku 女小学
ōraimono 往来物
Ōshima Urin 大島有隣
otogishū 御伽衆
Ōtsu-e 大津絵
Owada Heibei 大和田平兵衛

pen-lai wu i-wu 本来無一物
Pi-yen lu, J. *Hekiganroku* 碧巌録
Po-chang ch'ing-kuei 百丈清規
Po-chang Huai-hai 百丈懐海
Po Chü-i 白居易

Reigen Etō 霊源慧桃
reimyō, fushigi ni akiraka 霊明
Renchū shimeshi-awase 連中示合
ri, Ch. li 理
Rigaku shinryō 理學津梁
Rikuyu engi tai i 六諭衍義大意
rinkō 輪講
Roankyō 驢鞍橋
rōyū 老友

Sadamegaki 定書
Saigyō 西行
Saitō sensei gyōjō 斎藤先生行状

Saitō Zenmon (Masakado), Hokuzan
　斎藤全門　北山
Sakuma Shōzan 佐久間象山
sakumon, Ch. ts'e-wen 策問
Sangai yui isshin 三界唯一心
Sansha inkan narabi ni soejō
　三舎印鑑並添状
Sanzen daisen sekai 三千大千世界
Sanzensha 参前舎
Sanzensha nenpu 参前舎年譜
Sao dake de hoshi o utsu
　竿竹で星を打つ
satori 悟
Segyō uta 施行歌
sei, Ch. hsing 性
seigaku 正學
Seijō Genshi 星定元志
sei o shiru 性を知る
se-in 施印
seiza, Ch. ching-tso 靜坐
seiza [no] kufū 靜坐工夫
Seizasetsu 靜坐説
Sekimon Shingaku 石門心學
sekkyō 説教
seppō 説法
setchūgaku 折衷學
Shasekishū 沙石集
shashu 舎主
shian, Ch. ssu-an 思案
shian bunbetsu 思案分別
shian nashi 思案なし
Shibano Ritsuzan 柴野栗山
shichi 私知
shichikaku 七覚
Shidōken 志道軒
Shiga Mohyōe Morinobu
　志賀茂兵衛盛言
shijuku 私塾
Shijūnishōkyō 四十二章経
shin, kokoro, Ch. hsin 心
shin, mi 身
shinbutsu bunri 神佛分離
shindoku 慎独
shingaku, Ch. hsin-hsüeh 心學
Shingaku ben 心學辨
Shingaku danjo kagami 心學男女鏡
Shingaku dōka 心學道歌

Shingaku hotoke no za 心學仏の座
"Shingaku hyōri banashi"
　　心學表裏話
Shingaku jikkai no zu 心學十戒の図
Shingaku kyōkunsho 心學教訓書
Shingaku mondō 心學問答
Shingaku ron 心學論
shinpi 神秘
shiryo 思慮
Shiyōshō 至要鈔
Shōbōgenzō zazengi 正法眼蔵坐禅儀
Shōheigaku tomegaki 昌平學留書
shohō jissō 緒法実相
shōjiki 正直
shōjin 小人
Shōju Etan 正受慧湛
Shokoku shagō 諸國舍號
shōnen 正念
shosa 所作
shūgyō 修行
shūgyōnin 修行人
Shūhō Myōchō 宗峰妙超
Shu ni majiwareba akaku to naru
　　朱に交われば赤くとなる
Shushin obaba kohiki uta
　　主心お婆婆粉引歌
Shushi seiza setsu 朱子静坐説
Shushigaku 朱子学
sodoku 素読
Sokkō roku kaien fusetsu
　　息耕録開筵普説
Sokushinki 即心記
Sokushin konjiki no Mida nari
　　即身金色の彌陀也
Ssu-ma Kuang, Wen-kung 司馬光
　　温公
Sugiura sensei kuju banashi
　　杉浦先生口授話
Sugiura Shisai 杉浦止齋
Sugiura Sōchū 杉浦宗仲
sūgu, Ch. tsou-yü 驟虞
Sunshū chūgi Hachisuke den, gyōjō
　　kikigaki 駿州忠義八助傳行状
　　聞書
Suzuki Ryūsuke 鈴木隆助

Ta-hui Tsung-kao 大慧宗果
T'ai-chi t'u-shuo 太極図説
Taiheiki 太平記
Taikan Bunshu 大観文珠
taisaku 對策
Takahashi Kōun 高橋好雪
Takeda Shun'an, Sadanao 竹田春庵
　　定直
Takigawa Josui 瀧川如水
takuma fuda 琢磨札
takumi 巧み
Tamaboko hyakushu 玉鉾百首
tamashii 魂
Tanuma Okitsugu 田沼意次
Tao-che Ch'ao-yüan, J. Dōsha
　　Chōgen 道者超元
Ta-tai li 大戴礼
Teikin ōrai 庭訓往来
tenaraisho 手習所
terakoya 寺子屋
Teshima Muneyoshi, Gaigaku
　　手島宗義　益岳
Teshima satori 手島悟
Teshima Toan, Tōkaku, Takafusa,
　　手島堵庵　東郭　喬房
　　Shin, Ōgen, Sōkichirō, 信　応元
　　宗吉郎
　　Gen'uemon, Kazaemon 源右衛門
　　嘉左衛門
Teshima Wa'an, Ken, Haryō
　　手島和庵　建　巴陵
　　Shika, Jirōkichi, 子和　治郎吉
　　Gen'uemon, Ka'uemon 源右衛門
　　嘉右衛門
T'iao hsi-chen 調息箴
"T'i-tz'u" 題辭
Tōkai yawa 東海夜話
Tokiwagi 常盤木
tokō 都講
tokuyō 德用
Tomioka Ichoku 富岡以直
Tōrei Enji 東嶺圓慈
Tōsei heta dangi 当世下手談義
Tōsho shachū mōshi-awase
　　sadamegaki 当所社中申合定書

Tsuchihashi Tomonao 土橋友直
tsuji dangi 辻談義
ts'ung 従
Tsurezuregusa tekigi 徒然草摘義

Uekawa Kisui, Seiyō (Masa'akira),
　上河洪水 正揚
　Genzō, Shiyō, Tōkai, 愿蔵　子鷹
　東海
　Yoshinori, Bunji, Sōbei 義言　文次
　荘兵衛
ukkari hotsugo うつかり發悟

waga ju no michi 我儒の道
wakamono-gumi 若者組
Wakizaka Gidō 脇阪義堂
Wang Chi 王畿
Wang Ken 王艮
Wang Ming 王冀
Warongo 和論語
Washū [Wadamura] kōjo Moyo no
　den 和州和田村孝女茂代の傳
Watarai Nobuyoshi 度会延佳
Wu-men kuan, J. Mumonkan 無門関

yakubun sentei 譯文筌蹄
Yamada Keisai 山田敬齋

Yamato izenroku 大和為善錄
Yamato zokkun 大和俗訓
Yanagawa Gōgi 柳川岡義
Yang Shih 楊時
Yi T'oegye 李退溪
yōkyoku 謡曲
yonaoshi 世直
Yoshikawa Koretaru 吉川惟足
yukata 浴衣

zadan 坐談
zatsuwa 雑話
zazen, Ch. tso-ch'an 坐禅
zazengi, Ch. tso-ch'an i 坐禅儀
Zazen wasan 坐禅和讃
zen 善
zendō 善導
zenkō 前講
zenkun 前訓
Zenmon bunsho 全門文書
Zenrin kushū 禅林句集
Zenrin ruiju, Ch. Ch'an-lin lei-
　chü 禅林類聚
Zoku shasekishū 続沙石集
Zōtanshū 雑談集

BIBLIOGRAPHY

Works in Japanese and Chinese

The place of publication for the works listed here is Tokyo unless otherwise indicated.

Collections Cited by Abbreviation

IBZ   *Ishida Baigan zenshū* 石田梅岩全集 (The Complete Works of Ishida Baigan). Ed. Shibata Minoru 柴田実. 2 vols. 1956. Reprint. Osaka: Seibundō, 1972.

NKB   *Nihon kyōiku bunko* 日本教育文庫 (Library of Japanese Education). 12 vols. Dōbunkan, 1910–1911.

        9: *Kyōkasho hen* 教科書篇 (Textbook Section). 1911.

        4: *Shingaku hen* 心學篇 (Shingaku Section). 1910.

NKBD   *Nihon koten bungaku daijiten* 日本古典文学大事典 (Encyclopedia of Classical Japanese Literature). 6 vols. Iwanami shoten, 1983–1985.

NKBT   *Nihon koten bungaku taikei* 日本古典文学大系 (Great Collection of Classical Japanese Literature). 100 vols. Iwanami shoten, 1957–1968.

        42–43: *Kyōgen shū* 狂言集 (Collected Kyōgen Plays). Ed. Koyama Hiroshi 小山弘志. 2 vols. 1960–1961.

        83: *Kana hōgo shū* 假名法語集 (Collected Vernacular Buddhist Sermons). Ed. Miyasaka Yūshō 宮坂宥勝. 1964.

        97: *Kinsei shisōka bunshū* 近世思想家文集 (Collected Writings of Early Modern Thinkers). Ed. Ienaga Saburō 家永三郎 et al.

NST   *Nihon shisō taikei* 日本思想大系 (Great Collection of Japanese Thought). 67 vols. Iwanami shoten, 1970–1982.

        28: *Fujiwara Seika, Hayashi Razan* 藤原惺窩・林羅山. Ed. Ishida Ichirō and Kanaya Osamu 石田一郎・金谷治. 1975.

30: *Kumazawa Banzan* 熊沢蕃山. Ed. Gotō Yōichi and
Tomoeda Ryūtarō 後藤陽一・友枝龍太郎. 1971.

39: *Kinsei Shintō ron: zenki kokugaku* 近世神道論. 前期国学
(Early Modern Shinto Theory: Early National Learning). Ed.
Taira Shigemichi and Abe Akio 平重道. 阿部秋生. 1972.

42: *Sekimon Shingaku* 石門心学 (The Ishida School of Mind
Learning). Ed. Shibata Minoru 柴田実. 1971.

47: *Kinsei kōki juka shū* 近世後期儒家集 (Confucian Writings
from the Late Part of the Early Modern Period). Ed. Nakamura Yukihiko and Okada Takehiko 中村幸彦. 岡田武彦.
1972.

59: *Kinsei chōnin shisō* 近世町人思想 (The Thought of Townspeople in the Early Modern Period). Ed. Nakamura Yukihiko
中村幸彦. 1975.

60: *Kinsei shikidōron* 近世色道論 (Theories of Romantic Love
in the Early Modern Period). Ed. Noma Kōshin 野間光辰.
1976.

SGT   Shushigaku taikei 朱子学大系 (Great Collection of Chu Hsi Learning). 15 vols. Meitoku shuppansha, 1974–.

7–8: *Shisho shūchū* [Ch. *Ssu-shu chi-chu*] 四書集注 (Commentaries on the Four Books). Ed. Suzuki Yoshijirō 鈴木由次郎.
2 vols. 1974.

12: *Chōsen no Shushigaku, Nihon no Shushigaku 1*
朝鮮の朱子学. 日本の朱子学 1 (Korean Chu Hsi Learning,
Japanese Chu Hsi Learning 1). Ed. Abe Yoshio 阿部吉雄.
1977.

T   *Taishō shinshū daizōkyō* 大正新修大蔵経 (The Taishō Re-edition of
the Great Treasury of Buddhist Scriptures). 85 vols. Taishō issaikyō
kankōkai, 1924–1934.

TTZ   *Teshima Toan zenshū* 手島堵庵全集 (The Complete Works of
Teshima Toan). Ed. Shibata Minoru 柴田実. 1931. Reprint. Osaka:
Seibundō, 1973.

UNPUBLISHED MANUSCRIPTS AND BLOCK-PRINT EDITIONS

Ariyama Gentō 有山玄統. "Seizagi" 靜坐儀 (Rules for Quiet Sitting). Preface,
1785. Block print. Kyoto University Library, Kyoto.

"Kenmon shijū hassoku" 見聞四十八則 (Seeing and Hearing: Forty-Eight
Cases). Attributed to Teshima Toan 手島堵庵. N.d., n.p. Sanzensha collection, Tokyo.

"*Mizu kagami* [chū] me nashi gusa" 水鏡注目なし草 (A Commentary on the
Water Mirror: No Eye). 1805 reprint of 1675 block-print edition. Hanazono University Library, Kyoto.

Nakazawa Dōni 中澤道二. "Dōni sensei sakumon (sanbyaku soku)" 道二先生
策問(三百則) (Master Dōni's "Problems" [The One Hundred Cases]).
Contained in "Shingaku shūyōshō."

———. "Nakazawa Dōni-ō ni kansuru bunken" 中澤道二翁に関する文献

(Documents Concerning Old Man Nakazawa Dōni). Ed. Yamada Keisai 山田敬齋. 3 pts. 1945–1955(?). N.p. Sanzensha collection, Tokyo.

"Dōwa kibun" 道話記聞 (Notes from Talks on the Way). Ed. Owada Heibei 大和田平兵衛. 1813. Sanzensha collection, Tokyo.

"Sekimon sakumon ruiju" 石門策問類聚 (Questions of the Ishida School, Classified). Comp. Hirano Kitsu-ō 平野橘翁. Late Edo period. Sanzensha collection, Tokyo.

"Shingaku shūyōshō" 心学集要鈔 (Shingaku Selections). Edo period. Meiseisha collection, Osaka.

Shiteki-ō Nyounsha (Tetsudō) 紫笛翁如雲舍（拙堂）. "Nyoun Shiteki-ō kana seppō, furoku iroha uta" 如雲紫笛翁假名説法付錄いろは歌 (The Vernacular Sermons of Old Man Nyoun Shiteki, Including his Iroha Song). 1777 block print. Tamazawa University, Tokyo.

Teshima Toan 手島堵庵. "Jijo: Nemurizamashi" 兒女ねむりざまし (For Boys and Girls: Waking Up from Sleep). Block-print reproduction, 1917. Meirinsha collection, Kyoto.

Uekawa Kisui 上河淇水. 1789 postface to "Seizagi" by Ariyama Gentō. 8b. Kyoto University Library, Kyoto.

"Uekawa Kisui sensei jiseki ryaku" 上河淇水先生事蹟略 (A Summary of the Memoir of Master Uekawa Kisui). N.d., n. p. Meirinsha collection, Kyoto.

Published Primary Sources

Bankei Yōtaku 盤珪永琢. *Bankei zenji zenshū* 盤珪禅師全集 (The Complete Works of Zen Master Bankei). Ed. Akao Ryūji 赤尾龍治. Daizō shuppan, 1976.

———. *Bankei zenji goroku* 盤珪禅師語録 (The Recorded Sayings of Zen Master Bankei). Ed. Suzuki Daisetsu 鈴木大拙. Iwanami shoten, 1941.

Ban Kōkei 伴蒿蹊. *Kinsei kijin den* 近世畸人伝 (Biographies of Unusual People in the Early Modern Period). Ed. Munemasa Isō 宗政五十緒. Tōyō bunko 202. Heibonsha, 1972.

Bassui Tokushō 抜隊得勝. *Bassui* 抜隊. Ed. Furuta Shōkin 古田紹欽. Nihon no Zen goroku 11. Kodansha, 1975.

Ch'eng Hao and Ch'eng I 程顥. 程頤. *Nitei zensho* [Ch. *Erh-Ch'eng ch'üan-shu*] 二程全書 (The Complete Works of the Two Ch'engs). Ed. Araki Kengo 荒木見悟. 2 vols. Kyoto: Chūbun shuppansha, 1979.

Chu Hsi 朱熹. *Kaian sensei Shu Bunkō bunshū* [Ch. *Hui-an hsien-sheng Chu Wen-kung wen-chi*] 晦庵先生朱文公文集 (The Collected Works of Master Hui-an Chu Wen-kung). Ed. Okada Takehiko 岡田武彦. Kinsei kanseki sōkan 15. Kyoto: Chūbun shuppansha, 1972.

———. *Shisho shūchū*. See SGT 7–8.

———. *Shōgaku* [Ch. *Hsiao hsüeh*] 小学 (The Elementary Learning). Ed. Uno Seiichi 宇野精一. Shinshaku kanbun taikei 3. Meiji shoin, 1965.

Chu Hsi and Lü Tsu-ch'ien 朱熹. 呂祖謙, comps. *Kinshiroku* [Ch. *Chin-ssu lu*] 近思録 (Reflections on Things at Hand). Ed. Ichikawa Yasuji 市川安司. Shinshaku kanbun taikei 37. Meiji shoin, 1975.

Eihei Dōgen 永平道元. *Dōgen zenji zenshū* 道元禅師全集. (The Complete

Works of Zen Master Dōgen). Ed. Ōkubo Dōshū 大久保道舟. 2 vols. 1944. Reprint. Chikuma shobō, 1969–1970.

———. *Fukan zazengi* 普勧坐禅儀 (Universally Recommended Rules for Zen Meditation). T 82:1a–1b. Also contained in *Dōgen zenji zenshū* 2:6.

———. *Nenpyō sanbyaku soku* 拈評三百則 (The Three Hundred Cases, Critically Explained). *Dōgen zenji zenshū* 1:571–613.

Ekikyō [Ch. *I ching*] 易経 (The Book of Changes). Ed. Suzuki Yūjirō 鈴木由次郎. Zenshaku kanbun taikei 9–10. 2 vols. Shūeisha, 1974.

Fuse Shōō 布施松翁. *Shōō dōwa* 松翁道話 (Shōō's Talks on the Way). Iwanami shoten, 1936.

Hakuin Ekaku 白隱慧鶴. *Hakuin oshō zenshū* 白隱和尚全集 (The Complete Works of the Reverend Hakuin). 8 vols. Ryūginsha, 1934–1935.

Hosoi Heishū 細井平洲. *Heishū zenshū* 平洲全集 (The Complete Works of Heishū). Ed. Takase Daijirō 高瀬代次郎. Ryūbunkan, 1921.

Ikkyū banashi 一休話 (Tales of Ikkyū). Yūhōdō bunko 22. Yūhōdō, 1927.

Ishida Baigan 石田梅岩. *Kenyaku: Seikaron* 倹約斎家論 (Frugality: Discussion of Household Management). NST 42:9–32.

———. *Tohi mondō* 都鄙問答 (City and Country Dialogues). NKBT 97:349–516.

Ishida Baigan, Teshima Toan 石田梅岩・手島堵庵. Vol. 4 of *Sekai kyōiku hōten: Nihon kyōiku hen* 世界教育宝典日本教育篇 (Treasury of World Education: Japanese Education). 8 vols. Tamagawa daigaku shuppanbu, 1965–1968.

Ishida sensei jiseki 石田先生事蹟 (The Memoir of Master Ishida). IBZ 2:621–640.

Jitsugokyō 實語教 (Teaching of the Words of Truth). NKB 9:1–2.

Kaibara Ekken 貝原益軒. *Ekken zenshū* 益軒全集 (The Complete Works of Ekken). 8 vols. Ekken zenshū kankōbu, 1910–1911.

Kamizawa Takken 神沢貞幹. *Okinagusa* 翁草 (Pasqueflowers). In *Nihon zuihitsu taisei, dai san ki* 日本随筆大成第三期 (Great Compendium of Japanese Miscellanies, Third Series), vol. 13. Nihon zuihitsu taisei kankōkai, 1929–1931.

Kumazawa Banzan 熊沢蕃山. *Shūgi washo* 集義和書 (Collected Writings on Morality, in Japanese). NST 30:7–356.

Menzan Zuihō 面山瑞方. *Kūin Menzan oshō kinhinki* 空印面山和尚經行軌 (The Reverend Kūin Menzan's Rules for Walking Zen). In *Sōtōshū zensho* 曹洞宗全書 (Complete Writings of the Sōtō Sect), *Chūkai* 註解 (Commentaries and Expositions), 623–637. Sōtōshū zensho kankōkai, 1929–1930.

Muin Dōhi 無隱道費. *Shingaku tenron* 心學典論 (Classical Discussion of the Learning of the Mind). T 82:656–684.

Nakai Chikuzan 中井竹山. *Nakai Chikuzan to "Sōbō kigen"* 中井竹山と「草茅危言」(Nakai Chikuzan and His "Unsparing Counsel"). Ed. Inagaki Kunisaburō 稲垣國三郎. Taishō yōkō, 1943.

Nakazawa Dōni 中澤道二. *Dōni-ō dōwa* 道二翁道話 (Old Man Dōni's Talks on the Way). Ed. Ishikawa Ken 石川謙. Iwanami bunko 1234–1235. Iwanami shoten, 1935.

————. *Dōni-ō dōwa* 道二翁道話. Ed. Shibata Minoru 柴田実. Selections. NST 42:207–232.

————. *Nakazawa Dōni sensei shonyū banashi* 中沢道二先生初入咄 (Master Nakazawa Dōni's Talks for Beginners). Ed. Ishikawa Ken 石川謙. *Kokoro* 心 (Mind), 26 [5.5] (Jan. 1958): 4–52.

Nichiren 日蓮. *Gosho zenshū* 御書全集 (Complete Works [of Nichiren]). 2 vols. Sōka gakkai, 1952.

————. *Hokke shuyōsho* 法華取要抄 (Grasping the Essentials of the *Lotus*). T 84:278–280.

Satō Naokata 佐藤直方. Preface to *Seiza shūsetsu* 靜坐集説 (Discourses on Quiet Sitting). Comp. Yanagawa Gōgi 柳川剛義. SGT 12:280–281.

————. *Seiza setsu hikki* 靜坐説筆記 (Notes on the Theory of Quiet Sitting). SGT 12:287–310.

————. *Shusei setsu* 主靜説 (The Theory of Regarding Quietude as Fundamental). SGT 12:282–287.

Shibata Kyūō 柴田鳩翁. *Kyūō dōwa* 鳩翁道話 (Kyūō's Talks on the Way). NST 42:233–292.

Shidō Munan 至道無難. *Munan kana hōgo* 無難假名法語 (Munan's Vernacular Dharma Talks). In *Zenmon hōgo shū* 禅門法語集 (Collected Dharma Talks of the Zen School), ed. Yamada Kōdō 山田孝道, 1:323–399. Kōyūkan, 1921.

Shingaku gorinsho 心学五倫書 (The Learning of the Mind and the Five Moral Relations). NST 28:257–267.

Shinjinmei, Shōdōka, Jūgyūzu, Zazengi 信心銘. 証道歌. 十牛図. 坐禅儀 (Inscription of the Mind of Faith, Song of the Path to Enlightenment, The Ten Ox-Herding Pictures, and Rules for Zen Meditation). Ed. Kajitani Sōnin, Yanagida Seizan, and Tsujimura Kōichi 梶谷宗忍. 柳田聖山. 辻村公一. Vol. 16 of *Zen no goroku* 神の語録 (Recorded Zen Sayings). Chikuma shobō, 1974.

Suzuki Shōsan 鈴木正三. *Suzuki Shōsan dōjin zenshū* 鈴木正三道人全集 (The Complete Works of Suzuki Shōsan, Man of the Way). Ed. Suzuki Tesshin 鈴木鉄心. Sankibō busshorin, 1962.

Takuan Sōhō 沢庵宗彭. *Takuan* 沢庵. Ed. Ichikawa Hakugen 市川白弦. Nihon no Zen goroku 13. Kodansha, 1978.

————. *Takuan oshō zenshū* 沢庵和尚全集 (The Complete Works of the Reverend Takuan). 6 vols. Kōgeisha, 1928–1930.

Teshima Toan 手島堵庵. His writings can be found in TTZ, NST, and NKB. The following are cited in the text and notes:

————. *Chaku kin'i no kai* 着巾衣解 (Explanation of Why I Wear *Kin'i*). TTZ, 512–513.

————. *Chishin bengi* 知心辨疑 (Clearing Up Doubts about Knowing the Mind). TTZ, 31–46; NST 42:129–141.

————. *Chōnin: Shindai hashiradate* 町人身體はしら立 (For Townsfolk: Building the Foundation of One's Fortune). TTZ, 1–18.

————. *Chōnin shindai naoshi* 町人身體なをし (Maintaining One's Fortune as a Townsperson). TTZ, 197–208.

———. *Chōsō shinwa* 朝倉新話 (New Talks from Chōsō). TTZ, 243–264.

———. *Dansho* 斷書 (Admonition). TTZ, 583.

———. *Hatsumei no hito e no kuju* 發明の人への口授 (Oral Instruction for People Who Have Discovered [the Original Mind]). TTZ, 440–441.

———. *Hatsumei sokuji no kuju* 發明即時の口授 (Oral Instruction Immediately after Discovery). TTZ, 435–439.

———. *Honshin o shiru mono wa mamorubeki no tairyaku* 知本心者可守之大略 (A Summary of Guidelines for Those Who Know the Original Mind). TTZ, 584.

———. *Igaku gyokusō* 為學玉箒 (The Jeweled Broom of Learning). TTZ, 299–358.

———. *Isho kōgi* 遺書講義 (Lecture on the Writings Left Behind [by Master Baigan]). TTZ, 181–186.

———. *Jijo: Nemurizamashi* 兒女ねむりざまし (For Boys and Girls: Waking Up from Sleep). NST 42:144–147; TTZ, 47–68.

———. *Kaihojō on-itonami nasaritaki mune o on-mōshi-ide nasari-sorō kata e mōshi-ire-sorō jōjō* 會輔場御營被成度旨御申出被成候方へ申入候條條 (Instructions for Persons Who Wish to Set Up Meetinghouses). TTZ, 593.

———. *Kaiyū taishi* 會友大旨 (Principles for the Assembly of Companions). NST 42:185–200; TTZ, 95–116.

———. *Kotowari* 斷り (Notice). TTZ, 594.

———. *Me nashi yōjin shō* 目なし用心抄 (No Eye: A Word to the Wise). TTZ, 281–298.

———. *Mōanjō jo* 盲安杖序 (Preface to *A Safe Staff for the Blind*). TTZ, 522; NKBT 83:241.

———. *Onna myōga kai* 女冥加解 (An Explanation of Spiritual Protection for Women). TTZ, 187–196.

———. *Ono ono honshin wa on-hatsumei no tōri* 各本心は御發明の通 (The Original Mind, as Each of You Has Discovered). TTZ,,585–586.

———. *Rongo kōgi* 論語講義 (Lecture on the *Analects*). TTZ, 457–482.

———. *Shachū junkō kokoro-e sadamegaki* 社中巡講心得定書 (Code of Rules for Members Who Give Itinerant Lectures). TTZ, 588–589.

———. *Shayaku* 社約 (Group Rules). TTZ, 583–594.

———. *Shian nashi no setsu* 私案なしの説 (An Explanation of No Calculation). TTZ, 401–416.

———. *Shiba Onkō kahan fujin rikutoku wage* 司馬温公家範婦人六德和解 (A Japanese Rendition of Ssu-ma Wen-kung's "Six Virtues of Women" from the *Principles of Family Behavior*). NST 42:178–182; TTZ, 88–92.

———. *Shingaku shonyū no mono ni kuju no ji* 心学初入の者に口授の辞 (Oral Address for Shingaku Beginners). TTZ, 417–434.

———. *Shinjitsugokyō* 新實語教 (New Teaching of the Words of Truth). TTZ, 265–280; NKB 9:3–8.

———. *Shohō e dōwa ni on-ide no hōyūchū on-kokoro-e no daitai* 諸方へ道話に御出の朋友中御心得の大體 (Guidelines for Companions Who Go to Various Regions to Give Talks on the Way). TTZ, 586–588.

———. *Teshima sensei ikō tōmon shū* (*Toan sensei goroku*) 手島先生遺稿答

問集（堵庵先生語錄）(Manuscript of Collected Dialogues Left Behind by Master Teshima [Master Toan's Recorded Sayings]). TTZ, 615–861.

———. *Teshima sensei kuju banashi (shonyū banashi)* 手島先生口授話（初入ばなし）(Master Teshima's Oral Instruction [Talks for Beginners]). TTZ, 443–456.

———. *Tohi shachū torishimari mōshi-awase no jōmoku* 都鄙社中取締申合之條目 (Terms of Agreement for the Supervision of City and Country Members). TTZ, 589–591.

———. *Waga tsue* 我津衛 (My Walking Stick). TTZ, 117–180.

———. *Yoso e kōshaku narabi ni zadan kaiho nado ni on-ide no setsu betsu shite tokō yori mōshi-ire sorō jōjō* 他所へ講釋並座談會輔等に御出之節別而都講より申入候條條 (Special Proposals from the Director for Lectures, Discussions, and Group Meetings Held in Other Places). TTZ, 592–593.

———. *Zadan zuihitsu* 坐談隨筆 (Notes of a Conversation). NST 42:117–127; TTZ, 19–30.

———. *Zendō shuchi* 善導須知 (The Essentials of Good Guidance). TTZ, 415–442.

———. *Zenkun* 前訓 (Early Lessons). NST 42:159–183; TTZ, 69–94.

Teshima Toan sensei jiseki 手島堵庵先生事蹟 (The Memoir of Master Teshima Toan). TTZ, 597–605.

Teshima Toan sensei, Nakazawa Dōni sensei on-jiseki 手島堵庵先生・中沢道二先生御事蹟 (The Memoirs of Master Teshima Toan and Master Nakazawa Dōni). Sanzensha, 1939.

Teshima Wa'an sensei jiseki 手島和庵先生事蹟 (The Memoir of Master Teshima Wa'an). NKB 4:760–763.

"Tsuri-gitsune" 釣きつね (Fox trapping). NKBT 43:453–460.

Uekawa Kisui 上河淇水. *Shingaku shōden no zu* 心学承伝之図 (Diagram of the Transmission of the Learning of the Mind). NST 42:202–203.

Wang Yang-ming (Shou-jen) 王陽明（守仁）. *Denshūroku* [Ch. *Ch'uan-hsi lu*] 伝習錄 (Instructions for Practical Living). Ed. Kondō Yasunobu 近藤康信. Shinshaku kanbun taikei 13. Meiji shoin, 1961.

Yamazaki Ansai 山崎闇斎. *Yamato shōgaku* 大和小學 (The Japanese Elementary Learning). In Yamazaki Ansai, *Zoku Yamazaki Ansai zenshū* 續山崎闇斎全集 (The Complete Works of Yamazaki Ansai, Continued), 3:157–205. Matsumoto shoten, 1937. Also contained in NKB 9:25–95.

Yoshida Kenkō 吉田兼好. *Tsurezuregusa* 徒然草 (Essays in Idleness). Ed. Kidō Saizō 木藤才蔵. Shinchōsha, 1977.

SECONDARY SOURCES

Akizuki Ryōmin 秋月龍珉. *Hakuin zenji* 白隠禅師 (Zen Master Hakuin). Kodansha, 1985.

———. *Zen nyūmon: kōan sanjū-san soku* 禅入門公案三十三則 (Introduction to Zen: Thirty-three Koans). Chōbunsha, 1976.

Araki Kengo 荒木見悟. *Mindai shisō kenkyū* 明代思想研究 (Studies in Ming Thought). Sōbunsha, 1972.

Enkō Shinji 延広真治. "Kōdan" 講談 (Lectures). NKBD 2:512–513.

———. "Kōshakushi" 講釈師 (Storytellers). NKBD 2:489–490.

Furukawa Tetsushi 古川哲史. Nihon dōtoku kyōiku shi 日本道徳教育史 (The History of Japanese Moral Education). Kadokawa shoten, 1962.

Hayashi Yoshihiko 林吉彦. Satsuma han no kyōiku to zaisei narabi ni gunbi 薩摩藩の教育と財政並軍備 (Education, Finance, and Armaments in Satsuma Domain). Kagoshima: Kagoshima shiyakusho, 1939.

Imai Jun 今井淳. "Ishida Baigan no 'katachi' to 'kokoro' no mondai" 石田梅岩の「形」と「心」の問題(The Problem of "Form" and "Mind" in Ishida Baigan). In Ishida Baigan no shisō—"kokoro" to "kenyaku" no tetsugaku 石田梅岩の思想—「心」と「倹約」の哲学 (The Thought of Ishida Baigan—the Philosophy of "Mind" and "Frugality"), ed. Furuta Shōkin and Imai Jun 古田紹欽・今井淳, 163–178. Perikan-sha, 1979.

Imanaka Kanshi 今中寛司. Kinsei Nihon seiji shisō no seiritsu: Seikagaku to Razangaku 近世日本政治思想の成立惺窩学と羅山学 (The Establishment of Early Modern Japanese Political Thought: The Learning of Seika and the Learning of Razen). Sōbunsha, 1972.

Inoue Yoshimi 井上義巳. Nihon kyōiku shisō shi no kenkyū 日本教育思想史の研究 (Studies in the History of Japanese Educational Thought). Keisō shobō, 1978.

Ishige Tadashi 石毛忠. "Shingaku gorinsho no seiritsu jijō to sono shisōteki tokushitsu: Kana shōri, Honsaroku rikai no zentei to shite" 「心学五倫書」の成立事情とその思想的特質—「仮名性理」「本佐録」理解の前提として (The Creation of The Learning of the Mind and the Five Moral Relations and Its Intellectual Characteristics: Premises for Understanding Human Nature and Principles, in the Vernacular and Record of the Lord of Sado). NST 28:490–504.

Ishikawa Ken 石川謙. "Jitsugokyō, Dōjikyō ni tsuite no kenkyū" 實語教. 童子教についての研究 (Research Concerning Teaching of Words of Truth and Teaching for Children). Shisō 思想 (Thought), 189 (Feb. 1938): 53–79.

———. Kinsei no gakkō 近世の学校 (Early Modern Schools). Kōryūsha, 1957.

———. Nihon shomin kyōiku shi 日本庶民教育史 (The History of Popular Education in Japan). Tamagawa daigaku shuppanbu, 1972.

———. Sekimon Shingaku shi no kenkyū 石門心学史の研究 (Research in the History of Sekimon Shingaku). Iwanami shoten, 1966.

———. "Shingaku shū shonyū banashi hen: Kaisetsu" 心学集初入㗖篇解説 (Collected Shingaku Talks for Beginners: Commentary). Kokoro 心 (Mind), 24 [5.3] (Sept. 1957):3–29.

———. Waga kuni ni okeru jidōkan no hattatsu わが国における児童観の発達 (The Development of Ideas about Children in Our Country). Seishisha, 1976.

Ishikawa Matsutarō 石川松太郎. "Onna daigaku" 女大学 (The Great Learning for Women). NKBD 1:537.

Iwauchi Seiichi 岩内誠一. Kyōikuka toshite no Ishida Baigan 教育家としての石田梅岩 (Ishida Baigan as an Educator). Ritsumeikan, 1934.

Izuyama Zentarō (Kakudō) 偈豆山善太郎 (格堂). "Shingaku to Zen" 心學と禪 (Shingaku and Zen). In *Shingaku*, vol. 5 (noncontinuous pagination).

———. "Zen to Shingaku" 禅と心学 (Zen and Shingaku). In *Zen to bunka* 禅と文化 (Zen and Culture), 239–255. Vol. 5 of *Kōza Zen* 講座禅 (Zen Lectures). Ed. Nishitani Keiji 西谷啓治. Chikuma shobō, 1968.

Kageyama Noboru 影山昇. *Ehime-ken no kyōiku shi* 愛媛県の教育史 (The History of Education in Ehime Prefecture). Kibunkaku shuppan, 1983.

Karasawa Tomitarō 唐沢富太郎. "Nihon kyōiku shi tsūron" 日本教育史通論 (An Outline of the History of Japanese Education). In *Nihon kyōiku shi* 日本教育史 (The History of Japanese Education), ed. Tōkyō kyōiku daigaku kyōikugaku kenkyūshitsu 東京教育大学教育学研究室 (Tokyo Education University Education Seminar). Kaneko shobō, 1951.

Katō Tetsudō 加藤咄堂. *Nihon ijin shinkō jitsuden* 日本偉人信仰実伝 (True Accounts of the Faith of Great Japanese People). 2 vols. Daitō shuppan, 1937.

Kawamura Taiichi 河村太市. "Chōshū han ni okeru Shingaku dōwa no kyōiku-shiteki igi" 長州藩における心学道話の教育史的意義 (The Significance for the History of Education of Shingaku Talks on the Way in Chōshū Domain). *Yamaguchi-ken chihō shi kenkyū* 山口県地方史研究 (Studies in the Regional History of Yamaguchi Prefecture), 4 (Nov. 1960): 37–42.

Kinami Takuichi 木南卓一. "Bankei rikai no ippōto: Toan no Shingaku kara" 盤珪理解の一方途―堵庵の心学から (One Way to Understand Bankei: From the Perspective of Toan's Shingaku). *Zen bunka* 禅文化 (Zen Culture), 10–11 (Apr. 1958): 75–86.

Kishimoto Yoshio 岸本芳雄. *Kinsei Shintō kyōiku shi* 近世神道教育史 (The History of Shinto Education in the Early Modern Period). 1962. Reprint. Aikawa shobō, 1975.

Kokusho sōmokuroku 國書総目録 (A Comprehensive Catalogue of Japanese Books). 9 vols. Iwanami shoten, 1963–1976.

Konsaisu jinmei jiten: Nihon hen コンサイス人名辞典日本篇 (Concise Dictionary of People's Names: Japan). Ed. Ueda Masaaki 上田正昭 et al. Sanseidō, 1976.

Maruyama Masao 丸山眞男. "Berā no *Tokugawa jidai no shūkyō* (1957)" ベラーの「徳川時代の宗教」(一九五七年)(Bellah's *Tokugawa Religion* [1957]). *Kokka gakkai zasshi* 国家学会雑誌 (Magazine of the National Learned Society), 72.4 (Apr. 1958): 95–116.

Mashita Saburō 真下三郎. "Shingaku dōwa no gengoteki seikaku" 心學道話の言語的性格 (The Linguistic Character of Shingaku Talks on the Way). In *Shingaku* 1 (noncontinuous pagination).

Matsuda Hakken 松田柏軒. "Uekawa Kisui: Shingakusha retsuden 5" 上河淇水心学者列伝. 五 (Lives of Shingaku Teachers 5: Uekawa Kisui). 2 pts. *Sekimon Shingaku* 190–195 (8 May 1942): 56–59 and (8 Nov. 1942): 19–25.

Minamoto Ryōen 源了円. *Kinsei shoki jitsugaku shisō no kenkyū* 近世初期実学思想の研究 (Studies in Practical Learning Ideas of the First Part of the Early Modern Period). Sōbunsha, 1980.

Miyamoto Mataji 宮本又次. *Chōnin shakai no gakugei to Kaitokudō* 町人社会の学芸と懐徳堂 (The Literary Culture of Townspeople and Kaitokudō). Bunken shuppan, 1982.

———. "Sekimon Shingaku to shōnin ishiki" 石門心学と商人意識 (Sekimon Shingaku and Merchant Consciousness). In *Shingaku* 2 (noncontinuous pagination).

Miyasaka Yūshō 宮坂宥勝. "Kaisetsu" 解説 (Commentary). NKBT 83:3–44.

Nagano-ken kyōiku shi 長野県教育史 (The History of Education in Nagano Prefecture). Nagano: Nagano-ken kyōiku shi kankōkai, 1972.

Nakamura Hajime 中村元. *Bukkyōgo daijiten* 佛教語大辞典 (Dictionary of Buddhist Terms). 1981. Reprint. Tōkyō shokan, 1985.

Nakamura Yukihiko 中村幸彦. "Kaidai 1" 解題 1 (Explanatory Notes 1). NST 47:518–538.

Nakano Mitsutoshi 中野三敏. "Masuho Zankō no hito to shisō" 増穂残口の人と思想 (Masuho Zankō: The Man and His Thought). NST 60:401–411.

Naoki Kimihiko 直木公彦, ed. *Hakuin zenji minshū no kyōka to shoga no shashin shū* 白隠禅師民衆の教化と書画の写真集 (Zen Master Hakuin's Popular Moral Teaching, and Reproductions of His Calligraphy and Paintings). Ryūginsha, 1957.

Nishimura Eshin 西村惠信, ed. *Tōrei oshō nenpu* 東嶺和尚年譜 (Chronology of the Life of the Reverend Tōrei). Vol. 8 of *Kinsei Zensō den* 近世禅僧伝 (Biographies of Early Modern Zen Monks). Kyoto: Shibunkaku, 1981.

Nisshō hyakunen shi 日彰百年誌 (Nisshō: A Record of the Last Hundred Years). Kyoto: Keirakusha, 1971.

Ogasahara Makoto 小笠原真. "'Nihon kindaika' ron no saikentō—Sekimon Shingaku ni mirareru gendai shisō to sono genkai" 「日本近代化」論の再検討—石門心学に見られる近代思想とその限界 (A Reconsideration of the "Japanese Modernization" Debate—Modern Thinking in Sekimon Shingaku and Its Limits). *Ōtani gakuhō* 大谷学報 (Ōtani Gazette) 50.2 (1970):1–25.

Okada Takehiko 岡田武彦. *Zazen to seiza* 坐禅と静坐 (Zen Meditation and Quiet Sitting). Daigaku kyōikusha, 1977.

Ototake Iwazō 乙竹岩造. *Nihon shomin kyōiku shi* 日本庶民教育史 (A History of Popular Education in Japan). 3 vols. Mekuro shoten, 1929.

Sakai Takahito 逆井孝仁. "Sekimon Shingaku no igi to genkai: sono tsūzoku dōtoku e no tenraku no keiki ni tsuite" 石門心学の意義と限界—その通俗道徳への転落の契機について (The Significance and Limitations of Sekimon Shingaku: The Inherent Conditions of Its Degeneration into Common Morality). *Rikkyō keizaigaku kenkyū* 立教経済学研究 (Research of the Rikkyō Faculty of Economics) 18.4 (Feb. 1965): 221–249.

Saitō Akitoshi 斉藤昭俊. *Nihon Bukkyō kyōiku shi kenkyū* 日本仏教教育史研究 (Studies in the History of Japanese Buddhist Education). Kokusho kankōkai, 1978.

Sekiyama Kazuo 関山和夫. *Sekkyō no rekishiteki kenkyū* 説教の歴史的研究 (Historical Research on Sermons). Kyoto: Hōzōkan, 1973.

Shibata Kendō 柴田謙堂. "Dōwa no honshitsu to sono kōzō" 道話の本質

とその構造 (The Essence and Structure of the Talk on the Way). In *Shingaku* 2 (noncontinuous pagination).

———. *Nemurizamashi no ryaku kai* ねむりざまし畧解 (A Brief Commentary on *Waking Up from Sleep*). Kyoto: Meirinsha, 1911.

Shibata Minoru 柴田実. *Baigan to sono monryū* 梅岩とその門流 (Baigan and His Disciples). Kyoto: Minerubua shobō, 1977.

———. "Ishida Baigan to Masuho Zankō" 石田梅岩と増穂残口 (Ishida Baigan and Masuho Zankō). In *Ishida Baigan no shisō: Kokoro to kenyaku no tetsugaku* 石田梅岩の思想「心」と「倹約」の哲学 (The Thought of Ishida Baigan: The Philosophy of "Mind" and "Frugality"), ed. Furuta Shōkin and Imai Jun 古田紹欽・今井淳, 193–201. Perikan-sha, 1979.

———. "Kaisetsu" 解説 (Commentary). TTZ, 1–11.

———. "Sekimon Shingaku ni tsuite" 石門心学について (Concerning Sekimon Shingaku). NST 42:449–516.

———. *Shingaku* 心学. Nihon rekishi shinsho pt. 3, no. 35. Jibundō, 1967.

Shingaku 心學. 7 vols. Yūzankaku, 1941–1942.

Shiraishi Masakuni 白石正邦. *Sekimon Shingaku no kenkyū* 石門心学の研究 (Research on Sekimon Shingaku). Seibidō shoten, 1920.

———. "Shingaku kyōka no hōhō" 心學教化の方法 (Shingaku's Educational Methods). In *Shingaku* 4 (noncontinuous pagination).

Suzuki Daisetsu 鈴木大拙. *Zen shisō shi kenkyū 1: Bankei Zen* 禅思想史研究(一)盤珪禅 (Studies in the History of Zen Thought 1: Bankei Zen). Iwanami shoten, 1943.

Taira Shigemichi 平重道. "Kinsei no Shintō shisō" 近世の神道思想 (Early Modern Shinto Thought). NST 39:507–558.

Takahashi Shunjō 高橋俊乗. "Shingakusha no shakai jigyō" 心学者の社会事業 (Shingaku Members' Social Work). In *Shingaku* 4 (noncontinuous pagination).

Takase Daijirō 高瀬代次郎. *Hosoi Heishū* 細井平洲. Ryūbunkan, 1919.

Takenaka Yasukazu 竹中靖一. "Saitō Zenmon no kahō" 斎藤全門の家法 (Saitō Zenmon's House Rules). *Setsuen* 説苑 (Theories), 4.3 (Mar. 1956). Offprint.

Tanabe Ryūzō 田辺留蔵. "Seiza to kaiho" 静坐と會輔 (Quiet Sitting and Support Meetings). In *Shingaku* 2 (noncontinuous pagination).

Tone Keizaburō 利根啓三郎. *Terakoya to shomin kyōiku no jisshōteki kenkyū* 寺子屋と庶民教育の実証的研究 (Empirical Research on Temple Schools and Popular Education). Yūzankaku, 1981.

Tsuda Hideo 津田秀夫. *Kinsei minshū kyōiku undō no tenkai* 近世民衆教育運動の展開 (The Evolution of the Movement for Popular Education during the Early Modern Period). Ochanomizu shobō, 1978.

Uemura Seichi 植村清一. *Kusunoki Masashige* 楠木正成. Shibundō, 1962.

Ueno Yōzō 上野洋三. "Fujii Ransai" 藤井瀬斎. NKBD 5:251.

Umihara Tōru 海原徹. *Gakkō* 学校 (Schools). Nihon shi shōhyakka 15. Kondō shuppansha, 1979.

———. *Kinsei no gakkō to kyōiku* 近世の学校と教育 (Schools and Education in the Early Modern Period). Kyoto: Shibunkaku, 1988.

———. *Meiji isshin to kyōiku* 明治維新と教育 (The Meiji Restoration and Education). Minerubua shobō, 1972.

Watanabe Kunio 渡辺国雄. *Shintō shisō to sono kenkyūshatachi* 神道思想とその研究者たち (Shinto Thought and Its Scholars). Kinseisha, 1954.

Yamamoto Shinkō 山本真功. *"Shingaku gorinsho" no kisoteki kenkyū* 「心学五倫書」の基礎的研究 (Fundamental Research on *The Learning of the Mind and the Five Moral Relations*). Gakushūin daigaku, 1985.

Yamashita Takeshi 山下武. *Edo jidai shomin seisaku no kenkyū* 江戸時代庶民政策の研究 (A Study of Policies Toward Common People in the Edo Period). Kōkura shobō, 1969.

Yamazaki Michio 山崎道夫. "Satō Naokata no seiza setsu" 佐藤直方の静坐説 (Satō Naokata's Theory of Quiet Sitting). *Shibun* 斯文 (This Learning), 25 (1959): 21–43.

Yanagida Seizan 柳田聖山. "Kaisetsu" 解説 (Commentary). *Shinjinmei, Shōdō-ka, Jūgyūzu, Zazengi*, 181–240.

Yokoyama Tatsuzō 横山達三. *Nihon kinsei kyōiku shi* 日本近世教育史 (The History of Education in Early Modern Japan). Dōbunkan, 1904.

Yokoyama Toshio 横山俊夫. "'Han kokka' e no michi" 「藩国家」への道 (Toward the "Domain State"). In *Kasei bunka no kenkyū* 化政文化の研究 (Studies in the Culture of the Bunka and Bunsei Eras), ed. Hayashiya Tatsusaburō 林屋竜三郎, 81–130. Iwanami shoten, 1976.

Works in Western Languages

Translations are listed under the name of the original author unless the translator's comments have been cited.

Abe Masao. "Substance, Process and Emptiness." *Japanese Religions* 11, nos. 2–3 (Sept. 1980): 4–34.

Aoki, Michiko Y., and Margaret B. Dardess, trans. "The Popularization of Samurai Values: A Sermon by Hosoi Heishū." *Monumenta Nipponica* 31, no. 4 (Winter 1976): 393–413.

Araki Kengo. "Confucianism and Buddhism in the Late Ming." In *The Unfolding of Neo-Confucianism,* ed. William Theodore de Bary et al., 39–66. New York: Columbia University Press, 1970.

Arntzen, Sonja, trans. *Ikkyū and the Crazy Cloud Anthology: A Zen Poet of Medieval Japan.* Tokyo: University of Tokyo Press, 1986.

Backus, Robert L. "The Kansei Prohibition of Heterodoxy and Its Effects on Education." *Harvard Journal of Asiatic Studies* 39, no. 1 (1979): 55–106.

Baird, Robert D. *Category Formation and the History of Religion.* The Hague: Mouton, 1971.

Bassui Tokushō. *Mud and Water: A Collection of Talks.* Trans. Arthur Braverman. San Francisco: North Point Press, 1989.

Bellah, Robert N. "Reflections on the Protestant Ethic Analogy in Asia." Chapter 3 of his *Beyond Belief.* New York: Harper and Row, 1976.

———. *Tokugawa Religion: The Values of Pre-Industrial Japan.* 1957. Reprinted under the title *Tokugawa Religion: The Cultural Roots of Modern Japan*. New York: Free Press, 1985.

Beonio-Brocchieri, Paolo. *Religiosità e ideologia alle origini del Giappone moderno*. Milan: Istituto per gli Studi di Politica Internazionale, 1965.

Berling, Judith. *The Syncretic Religion of Lin Chao-en*. New York: Columbia University Press, 1980.

Blyth, R. H. *Zen and Zen Classics*. 5 vols. Tokyo: Hokuseido, 1962.

Bresler, Lawrence. "The Origins of Popular Travel and Travel Literature in Japan." Ph.D. dissertation, Columbia University, 1975.

Chamberlain, Basil Hall. "A Translation of the 'Dou-zhi keu'—'Teaching for the Young.'" *Transactions of the Asiatic Society of Japan*. 9:223–248. Yokohama: R. Meiklejohn and Co., 1881.

Chan, Wing-tsit. "How Buddhistic Is Wang Yang-ming?" *Philosophy East and West* 12, no. 3 (Oct. 1962): 203–215.

———. *A Sourcebook in Chinese Philosophy*. Princeton: Princeton University Press, 1963.

———, trans. *Reflections on Things at Hand*. Comp. Chu Hsi and Lü Tsuch'ien. New York: Columbia University Press, 1967.

Ch'en Ch'un. *Neo-Confucian Terms Explained (The "Pei-hsi tzu-i") by Ch'en Ch'un, 1159–1223*. Trans. Wing-tsit Chan. New York: Columbia University Press, 1986.

Ch'ien, Edward T. *Chiao Hung and the Restructuring of Neo-Confucianism in the Late Ming*. New York: Columbia University Press, 1986.

Childs, Margaret. "Kyōgen-kigo: Love Stories as Buddhist Sermons." *Japanese Journal of Religious Studies* 12, no. 1 (March 1985): 91–104.

Chuang-tzu: Basic Writings. Trans. Burton Watson. New York: Columbia University Press, 1964.

Collcutt, Martin. *Five Mountains: The Rinzai Zen Monastic Institution in Medieval Japan*. Cambridge: Harvard University Press, 1981.

Confucius. *The Analects*. Trans. D. C. Lau. New York: Penguin Books, 1979.

———. *The Analects of Confucius*. Trans. Arthur Waley. New York: Random House, 1938.

de Bary, William Theodore. "Individualism and Humanitarianism in Late Ming Thought." In *Self and Society in Ming Thought*, ed. Wm. Theodore de Bary, 145–247. New York: Columbia University Press, 1970.

———. *The Liberal Tradition in China*. New York: Columbia University Press, 1983.

———. *The Message of the Mind in Neo-Confucianism*. New York: Columbia University Press, 1989.

———. "Neo-Confucian Cultivation and the Seventeenth-Century Enlightenment." In *The Unfolding of Neo-Confucianism*, ed. Wm. Theodore de Bary et al., 141–216. New York: Columbia University Press, 1970.

———. *Neo-Confucian Orthodoxy and the Learning of the Mind-and-Heart*. New York: Columbia University Press, 1981.

Dore, Ronald. *Education in Tokugawa Japan*. 1965. Reprint. London: Athlone Press, 1984.

Droogers, André. "Syncretism: The Problem of Definition, the Definition of the Problem." In *Dialogue and Syncretism: An Interdisciplinary Approach,* ed. Jerald Gort et al., 7–25. Grand Rapids, Michigan: Wm. B. Eerdmans, 1989.

Fowler, James. *Stages of Faith: The Psychology of Human Development and the Quest for Meaning.* San Francisco: Harper and Row, 1981.

Fung Yu-lan. *A History of Chinese Philosophy.* 2 vols. Princeton: Princeton University Press, 1953.

Gardner, Daniel K. *Chu Hsi and the Ta-hsüeh.* Cambridge: Harvard University Press, 1986.

Hall, John W. "Changing Conceptions of the Modernization of Japan." In *Changing Japanese Attitudes Toward Modernization,* ed. Marius B. Jansen, 7–41. Princeton: Princeton University Press, 1965.

———. "The Confucian Teacher in Tokugawa Japan." In *Confucianism in Action.* ed. David Nivison and Arthur Wright, 268–301. Stanford: Stanford University Press, 1959.

Hammitzsch, Horst. "Shingaku: Eine Bewegung der Volksaufklärung in der Tokugawazeit." *Monumenta Nipponica* 4, no. 1 (1941): 1–32.

Hardacre, Helen. *Kurozumikyō and the New Religions of Japan.* Princeton: Princeton University Press, 1986.

Harootunian, H. D. "Late Tokugawa Culture and Thought." In *The Cambridge History of Japan,* vol. 5, *The Nineteenth Century,* ed. Marius B. Jansen, 168–258. Cambridge: Cambridge University Press, 1989.

———. *Things Seen and Unseen: Discourse and Ideology in Tokugawa Nativism.* Chicago: University of Chicago Press, 1988.

Haskel, Peter. "Bankei and His World." Ph.D. dissertation, Columbia University, 1988.

———, trans. *Bankei Zen: Translations from the Record of Bankei.* New York: Grove Press, 1984.

Hoffman, Yoel, trans. *The Sound of One Hand: 281 Zen Koans with Answers.* New York: Basic Books, 1975.

The Hsiao Ching. Trans. Mary L. Makra. New York: St. John's University Press, 1961.

Ishida Baigan. "*Seirimondō:* Dialogue on Human Nature and Natural Order." Trans. Paolo Beonio-Brocchieri. In *Serie Orientale Roma,* 36:51–112. Rome: Istituto per gli Studi del Medio ed Estremo Oriente, 1967.

James, William. *The Varieties of Religious Experience.* First published 1902. New York: Mentor, 1958.

Jen Yu-wen. "Ch'en Hsien-chang's Philosophy of the Natural." In *Self and Society in Ming Thought,* ed. Wm. Theodore de Bary, 53–92. New York: Columbia University Press, 1970.

"*Jitsu-go-Kiyō.*" Trans. Basil Hall Chamberlain. *Cornhill Magazine,* 15 Aug. 1876.

Kelleher, M. Theresa. "Back to Basics: Chu Hsi's *Elementary Learning (Hsiaohsüeh).*" In *Neo-Confucian Education: The Formative Stage,* ed. Wm. Theodore de Bary and John W. Chaffee, 219–251. Berkeley: University of California Press, 1989.

————. "A Content Analysis of the Hsiao-hsüeh." Paper presented to the Columbia University Neo-Confucian Seminar, New York City, 1 March 1985.

Lane, Richard. "The Beginnings of the Modern Japanese Novel: *Kana-zōshi, 1600–1682.*" *Harvard Journal of Asiatic Studies* 20, nos. 3–4 (Dec. 1957): 644–701.

Lee, Thomas Hong-chi. "Chu Hsi, Academies and the Tradition of Private *Chiang-hsüeh.*" *Han-hsüeh yen-chiu (Chinese Studies)* 2, no. 1 (June 1983): 301–329.

The Li Ki. Trans. James Legge. 2 vols. The Sacred Books of the East, 27–28. 1885. Reprint. Delhi: Motilal Banarsidass, 1986.

Maruyama, Masao. *Studies in the Intellectual History of Tokugawa Japan.* Trans. Mikiso Hane. Tokyo: Princeton University Press and University of Tokyo Press, 1974.

Maslow, Abraham. *Religions, Values and Peak Experiences.* 1970. Reprint. New York: Penguin Books, 1976.

Mencius. *Mencius.* Trans. W. A. C. H. Dobson. London: University of Toronto Press and Oxford University Press, 1963.

Mencius. *Mencius.* Trans. D. C. Lau. New York: Penguin Books, 1970.

Mencius. *The Works of Mencius.* Trans. James Legge. 1895. Reprint. New York: Dover Publications, 1970.

Minamoto Ryōen. "Interaction Between Confucianism and Buddhism in the Tokugawa Period." *Tōhoku daigaku Nihon bunka kenkyūjo kenkyū hōkoku* 20 (March 1984). Offprint.

Miura Isshū and Ruth Fuller Sasaki. *Zen Dust: The History of the Koan and Koan Study in Rinzai (Lin-Chi) Zen.* Kyoto: First Zen Institute of America in Japan, 1966.

Moran, Gabriel. *Religious Education Development: Images for the Future.* Minneapolis: Winston Press, 1983.

Morrell, Robert E., trans. *Sand and Pebbles (Shasekishū): The Tales of Mujū Ichien, a Voice for Pluralism in Kamakura Buddhism.* Albany: State University of New York Press, 1985.

Munan. *Jishō-ki.* Trans. Kusumita Priscilla Pedersen. *Eastern Buddhist*, n.s., 8, no. 1 (May 1975): 96–132.

————. *Sokushin-ki.* Trans. Kobori Sōhaku and Norman Waddell. *Eastern Buddhist*, n.s., 3, no. 2 (Oct. 1970): 89–117; 4, no. 1 (May 1971): 116–123, and no. 2 (Oct. 1971): 119–127.

Najita, Tetsuo. *Visions of Virtue in Tokugawa Japan: The Kaitokudō Merchant Academy of Osaka.* Chicago: University of Chicago Press, 1987.

Nosco, Peter, ed. *Confucianism and Tokugawa Culture.* Princeton: Princeton University Press, 1984.

————. "Masuho Zankō (1655–1742): A Shinto Popularizer between Nativism and National Learning." In Nosco, ed., *Confucianism and Tokugawa Culture,* 166–187.

————. *Remembering Paradise: Nativism and Nostalgia in Eighteenth-Century Japan.* Cambridge, Mass.: Council on East Asian Studies, Harvard University, 1990.

Ooms, Herman. *Charismatic Bureaucrat: A Political Biography of Matsudaira Sadanobu, 1758–1829.* Chicago: University of Chicago Press, 1975.

————. *Tokugawa Ideology: Early Constructs, 1570–1680.* Princeton: Princeton University Press, 1985.

Passin, Herbert. *Society and Education in Japan.* 1965. Reprint. Tokyo: Kodansha International, 1982.

Pedersen, Priscilla. "Shidō Munan in Zen Tradition." M.A. thesis, Columbia University, 1972.

Proudfoot, Wayne. *Religious Experience.* Berkeley: University of California Press, 1985.

Ramseyer, Mark. "Thrift and Diligence: House Codes of Tokugawa Merchant Families." *Monumenta Nipponica* 34, no. 2 (Summer 1979): 209–230.

Robertson, Jennifer. "Rooting the Pine: Shingaku Methods of Organization." *Monumenta Nipponica* 34, no. 3 (Autumn 1979): 311–332.

Rubinger, Richard. "Education: From One Room to One System." In *Japan in Transition from Tokugawa to Meiji,* ed. Marius B. Jansen and Gilbert Rozman, 195–230. Princeton: Princeton University Press, 1986.

————. *Private Academies of Tokugawa Japan.* Princeton: Princeton University Press, 1982.

Sanford, James. *Zen-man Ikkyū.* Ann Arbor, Mich.: Scholars Press, 1981.

Sansom, George. *A History of Japan, 1615–1867.* Stanford: Stanford University Press, 1963.

Sawada, Janine A. " 'No Eye: A Word to the Wise': Teshima Toan's Commentary on Ikkyū's *Mizu Kagami.*" The Eastern Buddhist, n.s., 24, no. 2 (Autumn 1991): 98–122.

Schuster, Ingrid. *Kamada Ryūkō* [sic] *und seine Stellung in der Shingaku.* Wiesbaden: Harrassowitz, 1967.

Smith, Wilfred Cantwell. *The Meaning and End of Religion.* New York: Mentor Books, 1964.

Spae, Joseph J. *Itō Jinsai: A Philosopher, Educator and Sinologist of the Tokugawa Period.* 1948. Reprint. New York: Paragon Book Reprint Corporation, 1967.

Steenstrup, Carl. "The Imagawa Letter: A Muromachi Warrior's Code of Conduct Which Became a Tokugawa Schoolbook." *Monumenta Nipponica* 28, no. 2 (Autumn 1973): 295–316.

Takuan Sōhō. *The Unfettered Mind: Writings of the Zen Master to the Sword Master.* Trans. William S. Wilson. Tokyo: Kodansha International, 1986.

Taylor, Rodney. "Acquiring a Point of View: Confucian Dimensions of Self-Reflection." *Monumenta Serica* 34 (1979–1980): 145–170.

————. "Chu Hsi and Quiet-Sitting: Advocacy or Ambivalence?" Paper presented to the Columbia University Neo-Confucian Seminar, New York City, 4 March 1988.

Tillich, Paul. *The Dynamics of Faith.* New York: Harper and Row, 1957.

Tōrei Enji. "The Biography of Shidō Munan Zenji." Trans. Kobori Sōhaku and Norman Waddell. *Eastern Buddhist,* n.s., 3, no. 1 (June 1970): 122–138.

Tsunoda, Ryusaku, Wm. Theodore de Bary, and Donald Keene, comps. *Sources of Japanese Tradition.* 2 vols. New York: Columbia University Press, 1958.

Tucker, Mary Evelyn. *Moral and Spiritual Cultivation in Japanese Neo-Confucianism: The Life and Thought of Kaibara Ekken (1630–1714).* Albany: State University of New York Press, 1989.

Tyler, Royall, trans. *Selected Writings of Suzuki Shōsan.* Cornell University East Asia Papers, no. 13. Ithaca, New York: China-Japan Program, Cornell University, 1977.

———. "The Tokugawa Peace and Popular Religion: Suzuki Shōsan, Kakugyō Tōbutsu, and Jikigyō Miroku." In Nosco, ed., *Confucianism and Tokugawa Culture,* 92–119.

Waddell, Norman, trans. *The Unborn: The Life and Teaching of Zen Master Bankei, 1622–1693.* San Francisco: North Point Press, 1984.

Waddell, Norman, and Masao Abe, trans. "Dōgen's *Fukanzazengi* and *Shōbōgenzō zazengi.*" *The Eastern Buddhist,* n.s., 6, no. 2 (Oct. 1973): 115–128.

Walthall, Anne. *Social Protest and Popular Culture in Eighteenth-Century Japan.* Tucson: University of Arizona Press, 1986.

Wang Yang-ming. *Instructions for Practical Living and Other Neo-Confucian Writings by Wang Yang-ming.* Trans. Wing-tsit Chan. New York: Columbia University Press, 1963.

Watt, Paul B. "The Buddhist Element in Shingaku, 'The Learning of the Heart.' " Manuscript prepared for *Encyclopedia of World Spirituality.* New York: Crossroad Press, forthcoming.

———. "Jiun Sonja (1718–1804): A Response to Confucianism within the Context of Buddhist Reform." In Nosco, ed., *Confucianism and Tokugawa Culture,* 188–214.

Weber, Max. *The Protestant Ethic and the Spirit of Capitalism.* Trans. Talcott Parsons. London: Allen and Unwin, 1930.

———. "The Protestant Sects and the Spirit of Capitalism." In *From Max Weber: Essays in Sociology,* trans. H. H. Gerth and C. Wright Mills, 302–322. New York: Oxford University Press, 1946.

Yamashita Ryūji. "Nakae Tōju's Religious Thought and Its Relation to 'Jitsugaku.' " In *Principle and Practicality,* ed. Wm. Theodore de Bary and Irene Bloom, 307–335. New York: Columbia University Press, 1979.

Yampolsky, Philip, trans. *The Platform Sutra of the Sixth Patriarch.* New York: Columbia University Press, 1967.

———. *The Zen Master Hakuin.* New York: Columbia University Press, 1971.

The Yi King. Trans. James Legge. The Sacred Books of the East, 16. 1882. Reprint. Delhi: Motilal Banarsidass, 1966.

Yoshida Kenkō. *Essays in Idleness: The Tsurezuregusa of Kenkō.* Trans. Donald Keene. New York: Columbia University Press, 1967.

INDEX

ABOUT THE AUTHOR

Janine Anderson Sawada received her Ph.D. from Columbia University in 1990. Her research for *Confucian Values and Popular Zen* was funded in part by the Japan Foundation and the Whiting Foundation. Professor Sawada is currently on the faculty of the Department of Religious Studies at Grinnell College.